Song on My Lips

Jazz Greats were My Mentors

Song on My Lips

Jazz Greats were My Mentors

Stephen T. Botek M.D.

Granville Island Publishing

Library and Archives Canada Cataloguing in Publication

Botek, Stephen T., 1929 –

Song on my lips : jazz greats were my mentors / Stephen T. Botek. — 1st ed.

1. Clarinetists — United States — Biography. 2. Jazz musicians — United States — Biography. 3. Jazz — History and criticism. I. Title.

ML419.B748A3 2008 788.6'2092 C2008-903243-8

Editor Kyle Hawke • Musician Biographies Kyle Hawke • Cover and Text Designer Kate Moore • Researcher Victoria Gibson • Proofreader Neall Calvert • Fact Checker Cody Adam • Indexer bookmark: editing & indexing • Cover image Mark Perrault • Cover Concept Kyle Hawke

---

First edition

Granville Island Publishing
212-1656 Duranleau
Vancouver, BC
V6H 3S4
1-877-688-0320
www.GranvilleIslandPublishing.com

ISBN 978-1-894694-68-1 (bound)
ISBN 978-1-894694-56-8 (pbk.)

Printed in Hong Kong

Dedication

I dedicate this book to mentors.

Mentors come in every size and shape and can be found everywhere — musicians, academics, professional colleagues, high-school classmates, band buddies, and of course family: parents, siblings, and friendly aunts and uncles. These generous, unselfish, and caring individuals take us under their wing and by being patient, unjudgmental, and long-suffering, guide and shape our future.

I salute them and in all humility, from the bottom of my heart, thank those countless many who helped me become self-actualized.

In addition, I must offer my respect to those wonderful buddies warmly remembered in this book who have, to my regret, passed away:

Alex L. Shigo
Barney Mallon
Art Rubart
Alyce Bokrosh
William Dupree
Wilfred and Gerald Beal
John Hill
George Sabol
Kenneth Zmuda

May their souls rest in peace.

Stephen T. Botek

Photo Credits

The personal photos in four of the sections come from the Botek family collection.

Photos in the musician section — Tommy Dorsey, Charlie Shavers, Charlie Parker, Red Rodney, Dizzy Gillespie, Buddy DeFranco, Benny Goodman, Gene Krupa, Goodman and Krupa, Leonard Feather, Phil Woods and Gene Quill, Maynard Ferguson and Glenn Miller — are printed with the permission of *Down Beat* magazine.

The three Buddy DeFranco photos come from the DeFranco family collection courtesy of the publisher of his book, Malcolm S. Harris of Parkside Publications

The Glenn Gould photo is courtesy of the Canadian Broadcasting Corporation.

While a major effort was made to identify all photographers, in a few cases we did not succeed. Please contact us if you can help with any omissions or errors."

Acknowledgments

No one who writes a book ever does it completely alone. I received invaluable help (the story of my life!) from individuals too numerous to mention. A few must receive special thanks:

My wife, Ruth A. Botek, for her patience, tolerance, and typing. Buddy DeFranco, who since 1946 has remained a faithful friend, guru, and impeccable guide. My sisters, Jo, Betty, and Ginny Botek, for reading and for finding family photos and other useful memorabilia. Charles and Cecelia Tucker, for their help with photos and proofreading; their hundred-percent encouragement was faultless. Reuben and Mildred Heller, for supplying not only childhood band photographs, but also years of cherished friendship.

Jo Blackmore and her family and friends. A better publisher couldn't be found! Lucky for me to be marooned on an island (Granville Island) with her and her staff. Kyle Hawke, editor extraordinaire, who patiently tolerated and corrected my mistakes. Victoria Gibson, computer expert, lover of jazz, and untiring organizer. Thanks for believing in me!

Phil Woods, for sharing information about Gene Quill from his book *A Life in E-Flat*. Frank Alkyer of *Down Beat* magazine and Adam Michlin for their time and efforts in gathering photographs. Malcolm S. Harris of Parkside Publications for providing photographs of Buddy DeFranco that were originally published in *A Life in the Golden Age of Jazz: A Biography of Buddy DeFranco.*

Contents

by Buddy DeFranco

Steve Botek's *Song on My Lips* offers an entirely different perspective. Instead of the hero worship or romanticism usually offered up when discussing American jazz and big band music, Steve presents his own story without setting himself as part of an elite fraternity. He remembers what jazz meant and that its accessibility was meant for all. In doing so, he invites readers to recognize that jazz, like much else in life, is within their grasp if they only make the decision and follow through with dedication.

Steve was indeed a talented young musician, but he himself will be the first to tell you that this wasn't some magical gift conferred on him. He put in the time, the effort, and most of all, the passion to make his dreams into reality. He listened not only to the music but the life around him, discovering what lay behind the instruments — taking the time to understand the colorful people who populated the field.

Sharing this understanding is a natural move for Steve, who would never have managed the opportunities and experiences he did were it not for his unwillingness to hold back or be held back, to give in to the expectations of society. Much is credited to the movements of the 1960s, but they were a continuation of what had gone before. Jazz was not simply music — it was a way of living, a conversation among equals that threatened entrenched ideas of race, gender, religion, sexuality, wealth, and propriety. The change that America experienced in the '60s and beyond, even to the present day, gestated in the goodwill of musicians and was born kicking, screaming, and wailing on the stages of small clubs, in tiny studios, and in the hearts of anyone willing to listen.

As a performer of that era, I whizzed through life relying on instinct as well as study. Steve's take on things included another component — detailed analysis of the often complicated people in the sometimes complicated world of music. His skill in breaking down a difficult piece of music so that he could absorb it extended to breaking down the complexities of the human spirit, which were let loose through many a horn, pounded out on many a drum, and sung to many a willing ear. His later career as a psychiatrist was a natural extension of this ability. In music, it allowed him to jump past expectations and assumptions and reach to the core of commonality with the many great musicians he met and played alongside, understanding them intuitively in the time it would take most people just to introduce themselves.

This book details Steve's journey where he lets music lead him back to himself. His skills are honed through perseverance and force of will, then finally turned on himself to lead him to the life he wanted. Like any young man exploring new perspectives he could have gotten lost in the trappings, but Steve heard what was essential through the music and played his own song.

I invite you to read this book and hear the music.

Chapter 1 Blame It On My Youth

Sitting smack-dab in the heart of Pennsylvania coal-mining country, Lansford offered two futures for its children: mining and music. Mining was a given, with mines encircling the town and employing most of its residents. Music was a pipe dream, but one given possibility by the shadows of the town's best-known sons.

Tommy and Jimmy Dorsey hailed from Lansford, Tommy Sr having been a music teacher in town. Residents were more likely to play an instrument than not — hardly unusual for the day, but the focus on playing was certainly more than you could expect in any community of similar size.

For most, music was a way to pass the time, to say what society and proper manners prevented otherwise, and to express oneself. For a select few of us, it seemed that it could be a way out.

In 1935, I was 5 with two older sisters — a younger sister and brother were to come later. Betty was seven years older than me and played violin. Josephine ('Jo' to the family) was almost five years my senior and played accordion. They performed together as The Botek Duo, dressed in European costumes my father would find. They were featured on local radio shows, in talent shows, at church picnics, etc. In town, a musician of any note was a local celebrity, and both were duly celebrated.

Lansford, situated 110 miles due west of New York City and 95 miles north of Philadelphia, had 10,000 residents, and was less than a mile square. Large, rolling hills surrounded the town, in sharp contrast to the pits dug to extract coal from underneath us. About twenty churches served the populace, as did a few department stores. One of these, Bright's, was a miners' store where the locals could buy on credit and have the amount deducted from their next paycheck in the tradition of the old company store.

My first band was a ragtag marching band of twenty-two kindergarten kids. Even kindergarten was not seen as too early to begin immersion in music. Attendance was non-compulsory and I was one of few Catholic kids to attend the classes held in the Lansford public high school. The building was a large, friendly cube, more artistic in design than anything else in town. Classes held near the main door kept us from mixing with the high-school students. Our classroom even had its own built-in bathroom with what is now a fairly standard commercial toilet, something I had never seen before. Unsure how it worked, I had to be instructed by my teacher how to flush it, and then comforted by her when the loud flush and the movement scared me enough that I ran out wild-eyed. That might seem unusual by today's standards, but no more so than a kindergarten marching band.

Most immigrant parents (practically *all* Catholics) preferred only parochial schooling. As a Slovak child, I would be expected not to participate, but my mother had spent a few of her formative years in California and Montana, and compared to the locals was a West Coast progressive. She wanted me to have all the preparation possible and made all the arrangements without a thought as to what the people in the next pew might think about this Catholic family that sent their kids to public school.

Our teacher, Mrs. Woods, was a beauty: motherly, married, and full of smiles. A short, blonde woman, she was slightly on the plump side, which only accentuated her maternal image. All of us immediately warmed to her. About thirty-five, she was the same age as our mothers. One afternoon she gathered the twenty-two of us together and formed a band. I was handed a full-size tambourine while the boy next to me — tall, handsome, and 100-percent sure of himself — began working a plastic flute. This was Charles, my age practically to the day, a future musician, football player, sports announcer, class officer, and master make-out artist.

Standing next to him was a friendly-looking, short-statured brunette with large brown smiling eyes.

"This is Faye," he said to me. "Faye Balliet."

And without another word, he turned to face her and gently placed his hands on both her shoulders and passionately kissed her.

Wow! I thought. *And smack on her lips. That sure is different than kissing my mother or one of my sisters.*

My mother picked me up from kindergarten that day. It was only two-and-a-half blocks home, but there was one main street I would have to cross, and she wanted to be sure I knew how to do so properly. Charles flew out of the school as we reached the car, running and jumping past other kids. He waved to me as he reached the sidewalk, then quickly headed off home.

"Who's that?" she asked me.

"That's Charles," I told her. "I don't know his last name."

"He's a handsome little devil," she mused. "Looks a bit like Freddie Bartholomew. That photogenic little rascal is easily a poster boy."

At the time, children were often referred to by the family name — adults would have referred to me as 'the Botek boy'. So when my mother called Charles "a poster boy", I heard it as "a Poster boy", naturally assuming Poster was his last name. As children were to be seen and not heard, I went quite some time without questioning or even discussing this assumption. Sometime later that year I found out Charles' actual name, but I still remember him as 'Poster-boy Charles'.

Kindergarten had to end sometime, and I was quite proud as the day approached. It was a significant year which stands out in my memory as my sister Agnes, who we would come to call 'Ginny', was born. I'd learned much in school, but I'd also learned from my mother how to socialize with the rich kids and navigate their regal airs, which made crossing the highway safely by myself seem easy by comparison. My dad taught me who the town drunks were and how to avoid them, as well as those town residents who talked to themselves.

I wasn't too concerned about them, though. My nemesis was the town's assortment of police dogs (German shepherds) and bull dogs. I was halfway home one beautiful April day when my eyes boggled as I saw what was coming my way: Prince, the neighborhood police dog, unescorted and looking mean as ever. I had seen him catch, shake, and chew up stray cats that happened to cross his path. We had had a couple of cats of our own at one point, but my father decided to end their lives the day they scratched up my arms. He locked them into a large tin can and dosed them with chloroform gas.

I tried to calm Prince down by repeating his name with as much authority as I could command, but he kept coming at me. I imagined Dad avenging me by trying to gas him. Prince jumped onto me, his claws ripping a huge gash into my only pair of school pants. He opened his mouth and seemed headed for a bite of my pelvis. I lurched backwards and avoided his bite — or so I thought. Unknown to me at the time, the tip of one of his large fangs had sunk itself gently into my groin. I had to defend myself — tit for tat — and I kicked out hard. My right foot slammed into his privates. Prince backed away and, yelping in pain, fled down the street in a loping run.

It was only on my way home, the adrenaline surge gone, that I realized I had been bitten. Initially I decided not to tell anyone, but the instant my mother saw me, she knew. Beyond the gash in my pants, I was breaking the old rule that boys don't cry. I'd been bitten a few times before, and she could do the math. The pain in my groin had been increasing and I told her the whole story, nervously pointing to my crotch to indicate where I'd been bitten.

Her apron flew off and she hurried me hand-in-hand eight blocks to the doctor's office. "It's Wednesday," she noted. "Dr. Tomchick has afternoon hours today."

The waiting room was empty — not even a nurse or receptionist, just empty chairs lining the four walls of the front room of this home office. A door opened and a tall, attractive woman in a white uniform entered.

"Hello, Mrs. Botek. And how are you, Stephen?"

I was taken aback, wondering how this strange woman knew my name. I was also surprised to see a woman doctor, something far ahead of the times. It wasn't that she was a doctor that was surprising to me even though, as my mother later told me, "Women in the medical profession are as rare as hen's teeth." Here was a woman practicing medicine and I didn't know about her.

Dr. Tomchick asked what had happened and my mother told her, while I just looked sheepish. When she asked to take a look, I hesitated.

"It's okay," my mother told me. "This is Dr. Tomchick."

So, off came the pants and underwear, and the doctor moved in to examine me. I looked away, embarrassed.

"Aw, the little S.O.B. just nicked you," she said, leaving me to wonder what the term meant. "Some mercurochrome, a booster shot of tetanus, and you'll be fit as a fiddle."

After I received a quick dab and a needle prick, my mother paid the $5 office fee, plus $2 for the injection.

Strolling home, Mother stopped at the pharmacy operated by Margaret Lill, the county's only woman pharmacist. I didn't realize it at the time, but my mother was probably making an active effort to support these pioneers. She ordered two large double-dip chocolate cones and then told Mrs. Lill that we had just come from Dr. Tomchick's office and that she really knew her stuff. After that, she never mentioned the incident again.

I never asked how Dr. Tomchick knew me. After all, these were still the days when kids were to be seen and not heard. Past that, it wasn't that unusual — there were countless adults who had met me when I was too young to remember. I never saw Dr. Tomchick again, either. Still, I finally got the answer to my unasked question. In 1991 my brother Francis presented me with a box of papers he had discovered when preparing to sell our family estate. One particular document hit me like a freight train — my name was printed there in large gold letters. It was my birth certificate, something I had never seen before. Beside my date of birth and place of birth, there was the name of the doctor who delivered me: Dr. Susan Tomchick.

Eventually I entered the first grade of St. Michael's Catholic school. No matronly Mrs. Woods here — short, stern-faced, and strict Sister Mathodia, stick a-swingin', ruled the roost. This being 1936, things were starting to heat up in old Deutschland and most of the parochial-school nuns were recent immigrants.

Both my older sisters had attended first grade under Sister Mathodia and so she knew the Boteks. As our name started with 'B', alphabetical seating put all of us in the front row, eye-to-eye with the sister. My sisters had been good students and I knew I couldn't match them academically. To compensate I played it cool, developing an angelic front to win the nun over. It worked, saving me from many a beating, her stick moving on to the next unfortunate. It never won me any warmth, though, and I still had to fend off accusations of this or that — smoking, for one. But in the end, it was a nun who forced me to learn to lie.

I quickly forgot about smooth Poster-boy Charles and his obliging friend Faye. As first-generation Slovaks, we were made to believe we were living on the wrong side of the tracks, and non-Catholic kids really seemed hard to get to know. "Snobs," my older sister Betty would have said, "with their noses in the air." Our elders preached, "Stick with your own kind, play in your own neighborhood, keep a low profile, and for God's sake, don't get in any trouble — stay away from sin!"

Aw! But fate has its way. There was music in the air. And needless to say, music transcends all boundaries. My all-too-often dictatorial dad threw his hat into the ring as well. "You're six now. Time to pick an instrument to play. You should follow your older sisters and play something to accompany their violin and accordion. We'll have a trio in the house."

His voice was warm and friendly, which caught me off-guard. If he had been his usual self, I never would have chosen the instrument he played — the clarinet. Normally, Dad would *order* me to do this or that, never ask. That he actually let me choose was a surprise. Jo's accordion seemed too heavy and unwieldy (consider my size at the time!) and the sounds I had managed to make on Betty's violin were no incentive. I thought the clarinet would be a good choice for simple reasons — it would be easy to carry, for one, and playing it didn't seem like a lot of work. It was quite popular at the time, with more kids studying clarinet than any other band instrument. I may have heard Benny Goodman or Artie Shaw and liked the sound, but any other reasons didn't stand out. I didn't choose it because Dad played it, but as he was being nice, I didn't see any reason to avoid it. Given what I know now, I would have started with piano before moving on to clarinet, then saxophone and trumpet, and worked on voice the whole way through.

* * *

The year I turned ten was hectic. The two being connected, we moved both our house and family-owned grocery store through which we provided most of Lansford with their groceries and fresh meats. The new location was larger, providing more room for a family that had expanded with the birth of my brother Francis that year. As well, Dad could carry more items in the store to satisfy the expanding tastes of Lansford's citizens. We still had to compete with the A&P and at least five other mom-and-pops, but they didn't offer the personal service or the homemade specialties Dad did.

Thanks to good music teachers — my dad always believed in hiring the best — by age 10 I had a history of being sought after to perform publicly. My super-fast, flawless rendition of Rimsky-Korsakov's "Flight of the Bumblebee" had become my signature piece. I had been introduced to it by John Pry, a private teacher Dad had hired to compensate for the lack of a music program in our parochial school. A machinist for the railroad by day, Pry taught privately in his home. Rumor had it he had studied 'in the city' (I never asked which one, but in Lansford the phrase could apply to either New York City or Philadelphia) with Henri Selmer, an instrument maker whose name was the mark of a superior clarinet and whose instruments still are at the top of the field today. Unusual for the time, Pry didn't restrict himself to the classics, ragtime, and Dixieland, and even taught me some Woody Herman solos.

Those 50¢ lessons led to more. Pry would take me along to his Thursday sessions with the Mantzville Band. Impressed with my facility, he found gigs where I could solo, advertised my young talents, and had me accepted into an independent, non-profit adult concert band. Of course, all the playing was for the sake of playing, with little money changing hands — there were two or three occasions where I maybe made $5. All the men in the band (there were no women) were older — the next-youngest about sixteen, the rest in their twenties, thirties, and forties. I stuck out like a sore thumb visually, but musically I held my own. We practiced once a week; rehearsals were held in the upstairs loft of an old country barn. The leader, John Burns, played excellent trumpet and led the band while leaning on a large crutch, as he had lost a leg in some sort of accident. Knowing my place, I never inquired.

Here I learned to *really* sight-read — to play a piece never seen before almost perfectly.

Mr. Pry had a daughter, Lorraine, about age fifteen, who had lost her mother a few years earlier — again, I didn't ask the details. She attended one particular concert, an evening affair held on a small Pennsylvania farm with a makeshift outdoor stage and a large booth that served hot food and cold beer. It being a country picnic, the scent of cows and crops pervaded the air. Even my dad attended with one of his male workers, possibly a fan of music, but I wondered, was Dad there for the booze or to hear his twelve-year-old son play his solo?

Nevertheless, the long, featured solo went well. At intermission the band immediately headed to the bar to take advantage of our only pay for the gig — free food and drink. They drank beer after beer, as I tried to match their pace with sodas. Others at the bar pulled me aside to shower me with praise. Surprise of surprises, even my dad congratulated me — a rare experience even at that age. He was proud, even bragging to his drinking buddies that *this* was his son, and I was unsure how to deal with it, but other matters took precedence. I left him at the bar as Lorraine invited me to meet her girlfriend Mary.

We moved to her father's car, parked in a field and well-hidden from view. The girls had told me they had something to show me. We sat three abreast in the front seat when Lorraine said, "You did such a great job playing, Mary thought she'd like to give you a kiss. A *French* kiss."

"What's that?" I asked.

Well, the rest is history. Poster-boy Charles did it in kindergarten, I waited until that day. Life afterwards, as the second half of the concert proved, was more passionate than ever.

Rumors fly in a small town — the local newspaper wrote about "the young Benny Goodman, Botek," and the town was abuzz. Practically the next day, a representative came to St. Michael's seventh-grade class to invite me, although not enrolled in the public school system, to become a full member of the public high school band. This was an honor, and I was scared. I didn't know any of the high school kids and the band had almost one hundred members. It seemed like it might be a chore rather than an honor. Still, I could sight-read like a demon by that time, and with my newfound experience with a girl, had a new confidence. That confidence was becoming necessary.

After all, there was the war.

The war was making home-front soldiers of us all. Pennsylvania was known for its high number of military enlistees, and everyone felt a personal connection to the war in Europe. Supplies became scarce, with many items impossible to find. Lucky Strike cigarettes changed their longtime green package to a white one with ads proclaiming, "Lucky Strike Green has gone to war!" The presumption was that the government needed the green dye for some reason. Copper pennies were taken out of production, with dull white ones replacing them. No new cars were produced, and gasoline was rationed strictly — you even had to be careful to maintain your tires, as rubber had gone to war alongside Lucky Strike Green. Everything was saved and recycled: tin cans, tinfoil, cardboard boxes, newspapers, old clothes and rags, any iron or steel, rope and string, and even bacon drippings and waste fat, which my dad would diligently save from his butcher's block and sell to the government at a nominal price.

I was twelve when the U.S. joined the war in 1941. As kids, we would go and 'pick some silver' or search through gutters and garbage cans for tinfoil — usually found in discarded cigarette packs. The 'silver' would need to be soaked to remove the white paper backing and then would be sold to a ragman for $2 a pound, but we could get more if we delivered it ourselves to a county center or city. It was only thirty years after the war that I found out what the 'silver' was for. My wife Ruth's cousin had been a bombardier in the Royal Canadian Air Force and had flown countless bombing missions in World War II. Hampers of the tinfoil, cut into strips, were emptied from the bomb bay to confound enemy radar before the bombs were dropped.

Families had ration books with small stamps for fresh meat and canned items, to be surrendered on purchase. When making deliveries, we were warned to bring back any goods where the customer didn't have ration stamps, whether or not they had the money. The family grocery store offered some relief. We didn't abuse the privilege, but with a grocery store came extra scraps and cuts of meat. As well, civilian cars were issued large 'A' decals to place in their rear windows; as a commercial establishment, we were given a 'C' decal and could drive on days when the 'A' cars were not allowed on the road. Having use of the truck meant I could get to music lessons on time, could accept dance jobs, could take 'silver' where I could get the most money for it, and could go to the railroad station to travel out of town.

The greatest relief though was music, and we thrilled to the latest jazz. The music was the sound of freedom, partly because it emanated from a free country and partly because it spoke of the hopes and dreams of poor blacks. Jazz became the soundtrack for both a country at war and a people rising from oppression.

While I was still in seventh grade, I fell quite ill. I have a vivid recollection of looking at my then-new Mickey Mouse wristwatch and watching the time pass, having nothing else to do but wish I was elsewhere. The diagnosis was the skin disease impetigo, which I only found out when I overheard my mother talking outside my room to the doctor. At first I heard her wrong and thought I was doomed with 'infantile paralysis'. Immediately my Catholic upbringing sprang into action, with mortal and venial sins dancing through my head as I went over how I was guilty enough to deserve such a fate. A minute later she repeated herself and there was relief.

The doctor prescribed Kenelog cream, which my mother set to rubbing all over my body. As she did, she chided me for my part in the war effort.

"It's that tinfoil!" she would howl at me. "Stop picking that dirty stuff! Even your sisters are ill now! For God's sake, let Uncle Sam pick his own filthy junk, war or no war!"

This wasn't my first childhood illness, and I knew the routine. When I was better, my mother would write me a note to take to school: "Please excuse Stephen as he was ill." There would be no date and no details, so each time I'd take a day to play hooky and run around in the nearby woods before bothering to return to the school.

That's exactly what I planned after my bout with impetigo. I started out walking that Friday morning through the patch of forest I used as a shortcut to school but, once out of sight, I charged deep into the woods. I climbed a tall tree from where I could see all the other kids filing into school. I was about twenty-five feet up and could see the main highway that ran through the town, as well as the one that ran a mile above, up on Summit Hill.

I wedged myself securely and comfortably between two strong branches. Then out came the cigar I was anxious to try, as well as the latest *Batman* comic. I had made an agreement with my classmate, George Sabol. He had lent me the comic and was going to play hooky and join me that afternoon. If he failed to join me, the comic became mine. I read the comic and fell away from the world, peaceful as a mourning dove high above the world of men. All of a sudden I became aware of how quiet it was — *too* quiet.

Something told me to look down — my guardian angel, perhaps. My heart almost stopped. Standing there, almost directly below me was a tall man, about twenty-one years old, wearing a leather jacket and cap, the kind with aviator goggles attached like a World War I flyer would have worn. He just stood there, scanning the highway about thirty-five feet in front of him. *Oh, God*, I thought, *it's the truant officer! Dad will kill me!*

I quietly stuffed the half-smoked cigar into a hole in the tree trunk, then rolled the comic up tight and wedged it tightly between two branches. I stood up slowly and carefully, hugging the tree trunk as tightly as I could, hoping to seem like part of the tree. I didn't make a sound, just watched in fear. The man never looked up, just moved his head to follow the occasional car rolling down the hill. I started to think I was in the clear. Not only did he not seem to think about looking up, he wasn't acting like a truant officer.

It was just as I was starting to breathe a sigh of relief when it happened. He opened his fly, took out his penis, and began to masturbate. *Oh, shit!* I thought. *Please don't do that with me here*. I thought he would kill me if he saw me. My silent plea didn't help in the least. He kept on jerking off with one hand while he pulled his goggles down over his face. Then, penis still in hand, he slowly began walking towards the highway. Coming down the road in the distance was a woman, and when I saw her, it all became clear to me. I once overheard my dad telling a friend that the neighbors' maid was almost raped as she walked down the Summit Hill road.

This was the guy, the one the police were looking for. He was working himself into an erotic frenzy for the sake of attacking this poor unsuspecting woman. Now, I was *sure* he would kill me! Luckily, just as the woman came close, a car came cruising down the hill. He withdrew, sinking back out of sight into the bushes. She passed by safely.

The car had gone, the woman was safely past us, but he was still there, hidden somewhere in the brush. I couldn't see him, I had no idea how close to my tree he might be, but I knew one thing: I had to get out of there! I slowly climbed down, trying to keep on the side opposite where I'd last seen him and trying to keep as quiet as possible. The twenty-five feet down now seemed like a hundred. My knees started to shake, wobbling almost uncontrollably, making the descent harder and harder as I went. When I was still about ten feet from the ground, panicking with my heart thumping like a bass drum in my chest, I decided to just jump. I hit the ground squarely and went immediately into a run through the woods, down the highway, over a guard rail, and down into a deep coal bank, running along the pit for about a half-mile until I was finally sure I was alone and safe.

That afternoon, George kept his promise and joined me in the woods. I only told him I'd lost his comic book. I didn't tell anyone what I had seen — not even the police, despite that I could have perfectly described this pervert. Playing hooky was a serious matter and I was as sure that Dad would have killed me for it as I was that the pervert might have killed me for squealing.

The weekend passed uneventfully, but Monday morning when we were back at school, the nun found out from George's sister that he hadn't been sick Friday afternoon. She forced a confession out of him — both the secular kind and the sacrament — then announced his punishment: ten swats on his behind with her bamboo switch.

"Nothing doing!" shouted George, and he hid from her at the back of the class.

George was the biggest football player in our class, and he had moves. She gave chase and he ducked, dodged, and deked. The rest of the class was stifling laughter, lest the switch fly their way, but I was feeling bad for having dragged George into this situation *and* having lost his comic. Finally, with George standing at the ready at the back of the class in case she made another attempt, the nun gave up. He stood there through the entire class, and then ran to make his way out when the bell rang.

It was the same circus the next day. And the next.

She waited. Only after five days did he finally surrender. The sister had him bend over a small wooden stepladder then beat him ten times with her switch, being careful to hit both ass cheeks. I sat just five feet away, watching the dust fly up from his old brown corduroy pants as she wailed away and he moaned and groaned. I was feeling for him through it all, but I was also wondering: would he squeal on me?

He didn't, of course. All kids stuck together — nobody snitched or squealed. Still, when we talked later, George made sure I knew I owed him.

"And Steve, when you get me that issue of *Batman*," he grinned, "you're getting me the new *Superman*, too."

* * *

Peter was 13 years old and a member of our street gang, which was a far cry from what we know as street gangs today. He had a pre-war Elgin 26-inch white-walled balloon-tire bicycle. I immediately wanted one when I saw it, and my mother set to finding me one. Sears and Roebuck had sold out of them but, searching through the mail-order catalogs and spending hours on the phone, she managed to secure the last one Montgomery Ward had. With the war on, everything was in high demand and short supply and this was a triumph.

This was not only a bike, this was my 'in' with the gang. Unlike today's street gangs, this one seemed to consist of cycling around for a while, then stopping to talk and smoke — without getting off our bikes, of course. We would complain about Hitler and the war, Peter often talking about castrating that 'brazen little bastard paper-hanger'. A common complaint was about the cigarettes we got. With the war on, the good brands were being sent to our G.I.s overseas, which we didn't begrudge them, but we were left with new off-brands, Wings and Fatimas, and stale Old Golds and Kools. According to Peter, these smelled worse than Mildred from school, known for never taking a bath and stinking once a month from 'the curse'.

Dick Jonas, at the ripe old age of 14, was another member of the gang. He was the center of attention when he returned to us after having his tonsils and adenoids taken out. He had to spend time stuck in bed and his parents wouldn't let us come in to see him. We would call to his window from outside. Once, while we were there, the neighbor called out of his window to Dick's dad, "How's your Dick, Mr. Jonas?"

Dick grinned at his window, but his throat was still too sore to yell. His father could speak fine, but hadn't heard the neighbor and called over for him to repeat himself, wondering why the group of us were grinning. Even louder, the neighbor yelled out, "I said, 'How's your Dick, Mr. Jonas?'"

This time, the message was received loud and clear. Dick's dad simply smiled and gave a thumbs-up out the window before retreating inside. The group of us, still beaming, threw in a V-for-victory sign.

Dick, in his hoarse whisper, reminded us of how the group of us had gone up to Peter's house when he was sick and, as his father spoke little English, asked him, "Mr. Jennetti, how's your Peter?"

In his thick Italian accent, he replied with a glowing smile, "Ah, my Peter! He's A-OK. My Peter, no problems. *Molto bene. Grazie!*"

Peter had been around the corner, laughing so hard he almost swallowed his cigarette.

I looked up to these guys. They were all at least a year older than I was, and they seemed to know more than me about everything — about girls, about sex, about penises and pubic hair, and about puberty. Pretty much everything I was going through, they'd been through before. That included surgery. When Dick was well enough to go out, he told us the story over a cigarette. Like a fisherman, the story got bigger with each telling.

"I had a spinal," he grimaced in recounting. "See, if you're over twelve, they won't give you ether, you have to get the needle."

At this point, he would take a slow drag on his cigarette, then demonstrate the length of the needle with his fingers — one of the details that kept growing.

"The needle enters your spine," he would continue in a conspiratorial tone. "It goes up from below, and then, once it's way up into your back, it opens on all sides like an umbrella. Shit, I couldn't see a thing, but I heard the nurse call it an 'umbrella needle'.

"You go to sleep quick. Then, when you wake up, you're bleeding from the mouth so, immediately, they have you suck on ice. Then, they fill you with ice cream. Just ask for it and they give it to you — vanilla, chocolate, strawberry, and even a *new* flavor they don't usually give to kids — *coffee.*"

"See," he would continue with an expert air, "coffee stimulates you, excites you, and older folks know how horny we kids are. Hell, those long bus rides for the school band always give me the biggest hard-on, and I'm not surrounded by nurses then!"

Despite all the conversation and explanations, none of us ever found out what adenoids were.

I was two months away from finishing at school and moving on to high school when our family doctor said he was troubled by *my* tonsils and adenoids. He scheduled me for surgery at our local hospital, Coaldale State, since renamed Miners Memorial Hospital not just in honor of the many miners who died in the area but also owing to its history, having been built by the local anthracite miners. The beds there would be filled at most times by these selfsame poor, hardworking coal diggers — suffering and all too often dying from mine explosions, black lung disease, chronic asthma, infected fingers and eyes, and last but not least, cirrhosis of the liver. The last was due to the prevalence of alcoholism which also brought cancers, hypertension, diabetes, and osteoarthritis.

The spinal haunted me, but I was going to be brave. With the war on, there was no shortage of inspiration for bravery. And an all-ice-cream diet didn't hurt. Still, I was getting more anxious about the needle by the day. My mother knew, just like she seemed to know everything, but she said nothing about it.

It was a warm April day when my mother and I went down to the hospital. I would have to stay overnight so Mother insisted I bathe and put on clean underwear — times were different and these were things that usually happened on a weekly basis. I quietly agreed — my thoughts were focused on that crazy umbrella needle. I was thirteen and there would be no way around it.

The receptionist asked, "What's his full name?"

My mother told her and she dutifully wrote it down. My hands were sweating.

The receptionist asked, "What's your address and phone number?"

My mother told her and she dutifully wrote it down. My knees were beginning to shake.

The receptionist asked, "How old is he?"

My heart sank. My lip began to tremble.

Without batting an eye, my mother told her, "He's twelve."

I felt a wave of relief crest over me. *Oh, thank you, Mother, you did it again. You surprised me in the best possible way, and I love you for it.* She bent down and gave me a warm kiss farewell, saying she would pick me up tomorrow. Then fixing me in her gaze, she smiled, "Don't be scared."

There were no further instructions, no further delays. They took me to the O.R., where a doctor was bent over a table sharpening his knives. A nurse was shaking a small can of something that looked like bug spray. I was sent into the corner to undress, put my clothes in a bag, and put on a surgical gown. I thought I was complying, but the nurse barked out, "Underwear, too. And don't fuss with the back — I'll tie you up."

Once she did, she quickly ordered me onto the table and began to tightly strap me down. The doctor was preoccupied doing whatever it was that he was doing. He never spoke a word and I never saw his face. The nurse tested my straps, ignoring my assurances that they were tight. She pulled out a large wad of cotton and soaked it with the fluid in the can before pressing it hard over my nose.

It was at this point that I remembered hearing about the similarity between ether and chloroform. Chloroform I knew as my father's method of getting rid of cats. The nurse's voice intoned, " . . . breathe . . . breathe . . ." as I kicked and fought. I quickly reminded myself that it was better than the needle. As she pressed down, my mind bounced between those horrible war movies about the troops in WW I being gassed and the cats, but I was falling asleep.

The next thing I remember was waking up in a strange bed with a sweet but unfamiliar voice repeating my name, " . . . Stephen . . . Stephen . . . Stephen . . . wake up, Stephen . . ."

I heard her and figured she was my nurse but I couldn't stay awake and managed nothing more than a moan. She asked, "Stephen, how old are you? Stephen . . ."

I started to tell her I was thirteen, but caught myself just in time.

"Twelve."

She seemed satisfied and I fell back into a deep sleep. My rest was short-lived, however. Suddenly I was awake again. Someone was reaching up under my nightgown, a hand heading for my privates. I was tired enough that I didn't really mind. The hand undid my gown. It was my nurse. She was still there and again, that sweet voice broke the silence.

"I'm going to take your temperature," she explained.

"Down there," I said, unable to muster any surprise in my voice.

"Yes," she replied, matter-of-factly.

She greased up the thermometer, inserted it gently, and ordered me not to move. *Oh, God!* I thought. *You think I'd dare move with a piece of glass up me?* I was petrified it would break. It seemed like an eternity before she pulled it out.

"Oh, you're doing fine, Stephen," she told me. "Now, are you hungry?"

She gave me ice chips to suck on and offered me three flavors of ice cream. I ordered them all and she even joined me, though she stuck to the strawberry.

It wasn't long before my mother arrived to pick me up. She treated me like a king, and even Dad was super nice. My throat was slow to heal. I had been ordered to stay indoors and rest for a week, but after four days the warm April weather got to me. I convinced my mom to let me join my friends, who were running and playing outside.

That ended quickly. I wasn't out long before I found myself spitting up blood. I went back in to Mother, who took me back to the doctor, who sent me back to bed, again for a week. Ten days passed before all the bleeding had stopped. By this time I was sick to death of ice cream and begging for something else. Not even coffee flavor or that brand-new one, pistachio, was tolerable.

Much of this time was spent looking over wistfully at my clarinet. I had left it for about two weeks. My teacher had told me I'd be a bit rusty, but practicing my Klose exercises would solve the problem. When I was sure that I'd spent enough time waiting to heal, I wet the reed, tightened the ligature, placed the horn in my mouth, and began to blow.

God! What happened to this horn? I thought as I heard the sounds that were coming out. *Did the wood rot? Did the holes expand from the heat in the house?* A quick inspection showed that the horn was the same as I had left it. It turned out that my air passage had expanded — I had no tonsils or adenoids (whatever they were). My throat was more open now. As well, the inside lining of it was now ragged and needed more time to heal.

I kept blowing, obtaining only a *poof, poof* sound.

I went to my dad. "Pop, after the operation, I can't play the clarinet!" I frantically explained. "Maybe now I'll never play again!"

Dad, smiling, calmly told me to wait a couple of weeks. The weeks passed with visions of chloroformed cats and mustard-gas attacks. No one could give me any real assurances, and I got more and more panicked. Three weeks later, however, I blew my clarinet and though playing it felt 'off', I hit a note that sounded right.

And then another.

Nikolai Rimsky-Korsakov

Born in Tikhvin, Russia in 1844, Nikolai Rimsky-Korsakov took to music at an early age. His aristocratic family, however, saw music as inappropriate for their social standing and pushed him to study at the School for Mathematical and Navigational Sciences in St. Petersburg. While at school, he took piano lessons and attended concerts, sparking a devotion to symphonic music. He joined the Imperial Russian Navy, following his elder brother who, responsible for Nikolai's welfare, then decided to cancel his lessons. He maintained informal musical associations when he was not at sea, and was soon encouraged to compose.

Korsakov began composing in 1861 while still in the Russian Navy, producing one of the earliest Russian symphonies. Later he would work with four other Russian composers in a group that became well-known as 'The Five' in the English-speaking world, though in their native tongue they were known as 'The Mighty Handful'. It was only *after* achieving global fame that he even started attending a conservatory.

Soon Korsakov would be named Professor of Practical Composition and Instrumentation at the St. Petersburg Conservatory. At the school, his students included Sergei Prokofiev and Igor Stravinsky, as well as other noted composers and performers. He remained in the Navy even as a professor and, in 1873, was named the first Inspector of Music Bands of the Navy.

Korsakov later became a conductor and performed internationally, though mostly in Russia. In 1886 he inaugurated a series of symphonic concerts spotlighting Russian compositions, for which he shared conducting duties until he was diagnosed with neurasthenia, a stress-related nervous disorder, in 1892. Feeling a creative block he withdrew, expecting to give up composing entirely, until the following year which brought the death of Tchaikovsky and a number of new opportunities in its wake.

Korsakov's political views led to his dismissal from his professorial position when he stood in support of 100 students expelled for taking part in the 1917 February Revolution. He was reinstated after other faculty members resigned and over 300 students walked out in protest.

Interestingly, Korsakov suffered from synaesthesia, a condition where sensory input is often 'translated' by the wrong sense. As such, he associated a color with each major key. Perhaps this helps explain his ability to capture a vivid visual image in music, one that has resonated with musicians and audiences for over a century.

Korsakov died in 1908, survived by his wife, Nadezhda, and their seven children. His grave is in his hometown of Tikhvin, 125 miles east of St. Petersburg.

"Flight of the Bumblebee"

Nikolai Rimsky-Korsakov wrote "Flight of the Bumblebee" as an interlude for his 1900 opera *The Tale of Tsar Saltan*. An orchestral piece that closes the first tableau of the third act, it was easily turned into a concert piece by leaving out the vocal line from the opera. Transformed from a prince, a bumblebee flying in the scene is the source of the common name of the piece, which was not used in the original.

The original score called for different instruments to work together, considered a challenge for solo musicians because of the fast-paced frenzy of chromatic sixteenth notes. The speed required to move from note to note is such that soloists who can manage "Flight of the Bumblebee" often use it to demonstrate their virtuosity. While it is often played on violin as originally written (with the solo player taking on the parts written for voice), many other instruments have been used to perform it.

Perhaps the most familiar of these is Billy May's 1966 arrangement as performed by Al Hirt on trumpet, renamed "Green Hornet" and used as the theme song of the T.V. series of the same name, which introduced Bruce Lee — the preceding radio series had used a rendition much closer to the original. Hirt's recording was also used on the soundtrack of the movie *Kill Bill.* May changed the piece enough that he was granted copyright for his version even though Korsakov's original was the obvious parent version.

Other notable renditions include a version on kazoo performed by Barry Manilow with full orchestral backing. Spike Jones' first album included an arrangement for trombone, with the performers laughing audibly at the results of this valiant attempt. Yehudi Menuhin was known for his violin performances of the piece, which he often used to entertain Allied troops during World War II. Sergei Rachmaninoff wrote an arrangement for piano, one of the earliest transcriptions for a solo instrument. Even heavy metal and techno versions exist of this beloved piece.

Chapter 2 My Buddy

My oldest sister, Betty, chose to finish her final year of high school at Germantown High School in Philadelphia, with the goal of studying violin and music in general at the nearby Hahn School of Music. Jo, my other older sister, had become an extremely gifted accordionist by age sixteen, and worked regularly with professional players who taught her well. I was playing comfortably enough but I had not yet found a personal master teacher who could give me the confidence in my own ability to really shine. As such, I was a bit reticent about making the leap to the public school band. Not only would I be younger than the high school students, I was not one of the rich Anglo-Saxon kids and I didn't think I would fit in. Then there was the band itself — the very one which Thomas Dorsey Sr had led for nine years, and whose standards were still expected to reflect his tenure.

Any fears I had were short-lived. One autumn Monday night I had my first encounter with my new band, as well as with John Lauer, the school superintendent. It was Mr. Lauer himself who wanted me for the band, having either noticed my musical talent or having had it brought to his attention. He took it on himself to quell my apprehensions, then introduced me to the band, along with a few other new young members from other local parochial parishes. When he mentioned my school, assuming he would have no idea where St. Michael's was, I blurted out, "Oh, that's the red building on top of the hill!"

Everyone laughed, and Mr. Lauer, to save face for me, returned, "You're right — I often do confuse those parochial schools that sit up there on the hill!"

After the introduction, someone tapped me on the shoulder. It was Poster-boy Charles — as handsome as ever, smooth as silk, and trying his best to put me at ease.

"You sit here," he said, pointing out a seat. "I sit there, and *she* sits next to her brother Bobby, the first clarinetist."

She? I wondered, but a look over was answer enough. Faye Balliet, the girl from kindergarten, walked over, clarinet in hand, and sat down.

"We met before," she said by way of introduction. "But I can't remember where."

Any fool could have seen Faye was quite mature for her age with her tight-fitting yellow sweater, full sensuous lips, etc. I'm sure I blushed but did not remember either — at least, I pretended not to.

Her brother Bobby was three years older, standing five-foot-ten and wearing glasses. He was the leader of the clarinet section — all twenty of us. With a professorial attitude, he would watch over us, never actually demonstrating anything, but ready to turf anyone who couldn't keep up. I was moved next to him after the bandleader discovered I played *almost* as well as he did.

Faye was always fair and friendly. When I joined, she played fourth-chair clarinet, but that didn't last. She was also seriously studying the piano and as time progressed her clarinet playing plateaued but her piano playing skyrocketed. Eventually she became the band's piano accompanist, and later she would become invaluable to me in my soloist days.

Poster-boy Charles could never shed his regal demeanor. His looks, charm, and ambition kept him an engineer of events and connections, making them happen on a whim. And as we sat next to each other at the bi-weekly band practice, we made much small talk, lots of which was peppered with innuendo about sex — he was much freer on the subject than anyone else. Still, I never could really get into his head.

For Bobby's part, his distance was likely grounded in the fact that he felt protective of his younger sister, something he would communicate with nothing more than tone of voice when introducing her: "This is *my sister*." "Hands off" wasn't spoken, but it was understood. Bobby was always Mister Business, the concert master. He formed a clique with Faye and Charles that no one else could enter. I never hung out with them socially and was never allowed *in*. To them, I was simply a fine up-and-coming clarinet player and nothing else, so I was invisible to them outside the confines of the band. Consequently I never bonded with Faye until after Bobby graduated two years later in 1945. Then I became first clarinetist and I was *in*.

The role made me the equivalent to the concert master for the orchestra, taking over from Bobby. Poster-boy Charles and Faye saw to it that I was elected president. Faye became my accompanist, but *not* my girlfriend — I always preferred blondes anyway. Still, Faye was super. Her piano playing was outstanding. And although she got nicknamed 'Sweater Girl', I know she honestly loved music more than showing off her well-endowed bosom. Not that she had any qualms about doing the latter.

Another Charles — Charlie Tucker — entered the Lansford High School Senior Band at the same time as me. Like me, he was Slovak, his family name having been changed from Tokar. He was a short, blond, clean-cut guy with a full mouth of beautiful white teeth that just sort of welcomed you when he smiled. He played drums so, as was the norm in a hundred-piece band, we never sat close to each other. However, when we played parades, the drummers marched directly in front of the clarinets. One day, with the parade stopped, we began to talk and that conversation began a friendship that lasts to this day. We talked about everything — life, girls, people, money, crime, but the focus eventually settled on the one interest we shared the most: our love for jazz.

Jazz, a psychiatrist once told me, was my first love. He was right. Charlie similarly felt a deep, sincere love for the music. This shared devotion, once it became evident, cemented us together like superglue, bonded us like blood brothers. We began to look after each other. Over the years, we constantly shared anything to do with jazz: records, books, magazines, and concerts. What big bands we didn't see in Pennsylvania, we would see in New York City in later days.

Charlie and I would both not only end up taking lessons in New York but also have the chance to immerse ourselves in its jazz scene. There, either on and around 52nd Street or in the Broadway theatre matinées, we would see Claude Thornhill, Buddy Rich (playing an entire show one-armed as his other one was broken!), Duke Ellington, Art Tatum, Tal Farlow, Red Norvo, J.J. Johnson & Kai Winding, Stan Getz, Dizzy Gillespie, Bird, Bud Powell, Fats Navarro, Miles Davis, John Coltrane, and more. Being a drummer, Charlie naturally focused on other drummers but he always knew and paid close attention to all the good horn men. Illinois Jacquet so mesmerized Charlie playing his signature song "Flying Home" at the Seventh Avenue Metropole Café, he was speechless for a good five minutes. That was all yet to come, though, and I was still unsure of how to find my master teacher.

Jo had been granted a scholarship to study music. She was using it to finance weekly train trips to New York City. There she studied with Joe Biviano, a disciple of accordion great Pietro Diero. She was also fortunate enough to take a few lessons with the outstanding blind jazz pianist Lenny Tristano. Still in their teens, both my sisters had found their master teacher, and I learned from their example, knowing I had to find mine.

My sister Jo, though a fan of jazz stylings, was playing her accordion with a small band. The bandleader, Mickey, was of Hungarian and Slovak descent with Gypsy leanings. Whatever ethnic group the band played for, he would supply appropriate music — polkas, czardas, mazurkas, waltzes, jigs, marches, horas, tarantellas, tangos, foxtrots, jazz. Anything was on the menu: if you paid, he played. They would collect money in the *f*-holes of Mickey's upright bass, to be distributed after the show. For one particular wedding,

Mickey had borrowed a bass from another band as his was in for repairs. The end of that night saw only a small trickle of money and the band found that there was a trapdoor on the back of the bass, and somebody had been helping themselves to the booty. The band went without, as blame was impossible to apportion. Looking back, I think the thief was Mickey himself, though I could never prove it.

Such antics and the wild changes in style of music didn't keep me from joining the band in the spring of 1946. With the war finally over, celebration was the order of the day and the band was in fairly high demand. While my heart lay with jazz, I knew I had a lot still to learn from any type of music and paying gigs were more than an enticement, so I didn't think twice when asked to join. Jo and I had a natural sibling rivalry at home — she used to side with my father and snitch on me regularly — but when we played together, we were the best of friends.

Jazz was still enjoyed on my own time and in tandem with Charlie Tucker. We would discuss the players, the songs, the stylings — all at length, and practice the music ourselves. We regularly attended dances at the Lakewood Ballroom close to town to hear the latest bands and music. It was with religious fervor that Charlie called me to say that Tommy Dorsey's band would be playing the ballroom in a few weeks. Lakewood was the *in* place to be on Thursday nights, and sooner or later every big-name band played there. This however was something *extra* special — Tommy Dorsey was coming home.

Lakewood, being mere miles from the place of his birth, had meaning to Tommy. A large, plain wooden box, it sat high atop a hill looking over the coal pits. In fact, the ground below it had been mined out by the previous generation, including Tommy's father. The elder Dorsey had toiled in the mines until he was offered a job as director of all public school bands — an offer that our church chose my father to present, as he was an amateur musician, a respected businessman, and was one of the few with a car to make the trip. As much as the Dorsey boys enjoyed the big time, they didn't forget their roots.

Rickety steps left you feeling unsure as you made your way up to the door, but once inside, the structure felt solid as a rock, even when filled to capacity — legally 1,500, but on very busy nights it seemed like 2,500. The interior was about the size of a football field, with no carpeting and no decorations, just a big empty shell with high rafters.

Dances at the ballroom would start around 8:30 p.m. and last until midnight. There was a regular rhythm to them — bands would play for about an hour, take a twenty-five minute intermission, then repeat the process. There would be nights when the crowd would be so excited, so appreciative, that they wouldn't stop applauding. Often this would get the band members pumped up and they would play through midnight for another half-hour or so, until even the crowd's enthusiasm could no longer keep them standing.

As a regular, I heard stories about the shows I hadn't seen. One involved Tommy Dorsey's group years earlier, a quartet that night, which quit at the stroke of midnight. Taskmaster that he was, he packed up and rushed the band out through the pleading crowd to a gig in nearby Lansford. That was the annual Firemen's Ball where he, Boomie Richman, Ziggy Elman, and Buddy Rich jammed with the Lansford orchestra well into the morning.

Charlie Tucker and I had been planning our excursion to Lakewood for weeks. I'd gotten my driver's license a few months earlier, but knew I could never wrangle my father's car or delivery truck for the trip. So we set to work on Charlie's dad and secured the use of his Pontiac coupe, as long as we filled it up with gas. As Charlie was still fifteen, I was the one driving and he was left to navigate.

That night's dance would more rightfully be called a concert. About sixty percent of the fans stood enthralled in front of the stage, crowding together on the dance floor and leaving the dancers to mark out space they could use in the back.

We paid our $1.25 admissions and immediately set to wiggling our way through the large crowd assembled before the bandstand. We managed to get about halfway through the crowd before Dorsey began and we heard the opening strains of "I'm Getting Sentimental Over You".

Being young, and therefore relatively short, we could only see flashes of the band as we wormed our way forward. During that time, we were seeing more of the Lakewood walls than Dorsey! Lakewood wasn't exactly built to offer a view — this was no elegant state-of-the-art ballroom. It looked like an outdoor dance floor of the kind you might have seen at a Pennsylvania Polish picnic — huge and spreading, the walls and ceiling looking like they were an afterthought.

We edged here and there, as we could, as people shifted or began working their way out of the throng to hit the bar, which was strategically placed by the stage to sell shots of cheaper whiskeys and glasses of locally-brewed beer. Back in 1946, no picnic or dance in coal country could have survived without ready access to hard liquor. The local Catholic churches would even openly sell beer to us teenagers at their Saturday night dances — you'd just hand your dime to the priest and he'd hand you a beer.

Lakewood's bar was positioned to be in everyone's view, which was a good move on most nights, but with the hall crowded, the drinkers and those of us working for a better view must have looked like termites working through wood if anyone watched from above. We paused here and there to watch what we could or applaud at the solos and finales. "Boogie-Woogie", "Marie", "Song of India", "I'll Never Smile Again", "Opus One" — the big, recognizable hits pumped the crowd and made it harder for us to find gaps to squeeze into, but they were so worked up that even the songs they didn't know were celebrated. That helped make for a great show, but it made for lousy sightlines!

Dorsey was an immaculate player and back in 1927 he'd recorded several hot jazz solos on trumpet. In the years since, jazz had changed considerably, moving from New Orleans jazz and Dixieland to swing and bebop, which was just beginning to explode at the time. The perfectionism that led him there was likely what kept him from becoming a notable improviser — he was too concerned with getting things right to stretch out and create music on the fly. As such, Charlie Shavers would jump forward for the brass solos.

When Shavers got his first shot in the spotlight that night, Charlie and I were finally close enough to see. The song was "At the Fat Man's" and Shavers stood up, extremely sure of himself. He started by running up and down the full range of his trumpet, sounding like a runaway roller coaster. Known for his ultra-high range, which was unique and unsurpassed until Maynard Ferguson came along a few years later, he had perfect command of his horn, and had no qualms about showing it. The crowd went wild, and I used the distraction to work my way almost to the stage with Charlie not far behind. Dorsey, never a fan of bebop, still couldn't deny its popularity and appeal. Always the crowd-pleaser, and with intermission almost there, he struck up the band with the fastest piece yet. I've forgotten the name of the song, but the tempo was like a lightning storm! The rhythm section knitted together neatly, but some of the other band members seemed to be hanging on for their lives. Most of the dancers stopped to listen, with the tempo too fast even for jitterbugging. It was a standard-variety, thirty-two bar song, but the playing was anything but standard!

I managed to reach the front of the stage just as Buddy DeFranco left his seat and walked to the microphone, arriving just as the first full ensemble chorus ended. He had been stretching his fingers every chance he got, seeming to prepare for that feature spot. DeFranco had just rejoined the band after a one-year absence, though this was nothing new. He was always quitting or being fired, owing to his musical differences with Dorsey. Only twenty-three at the time, it was a lot to expect him to follow the likes of Dorsey and Shavers. More, he had to deal with the bandleader's strict rules. Public tastes in mind, Dorsey instructed players to play their live solos as they had been recorded, note for note,especially when it came to the best-sellers.

DeFranco was never happy with that approach. He preferred to think of a hundred and one new interpretations each time he played it, rather than remember how he had recorded any particular solo. Tommy, 'The Sentimental Gentleman', stood in opposition to the more modern approaches DeFranco favored, as well as putting commercial considerations first. Buddy, in direct contrast, was Mr. Modern Jazz — the up-tempo clarinet virtuoso of bebop. Buddy stood in front of the microphone tall and lean, straight as a poker. This was his signature style on stage. His posture was that of a classical player — albeit one who was preparing to fly through Chopin's "Minute Waltz" inforty-five seconds. This was his signature style on stage. As jazz critic Whitney Balliett once wrote, "DeFranco is all business when he plays. He stands straight and motionless, and points his clarinet at the floor — unlike Benny Goodman and Artie Shaw, who in exultant moments, would rear back and point their instruments 'directly to God'."[1]

It was clear he was nervous and self-conscious. Stage fright gripped him to the point where both hands were experiencing fine tremors. As well, a slight facial tic was developing into a rapid, bilateral twitch. But the instant after he started his first note he was cool and centered in the music — hands steady, the tic gone. Patients with neurological diseases who display tics, tremors, and other involuntary movements of the limbs or facial muscles as a result often experience none of those symptoms once asleep. Likewise, once playing, Buddy was on automatic — mind to mouth, with the result filling the hall. There was no longer any sign of nerves or discomfort. This was where he was meant to be.

Buddy attacked the clarinet, certainly the most difficult of all reed instruments, with both assurance and a hint of arrogant vengeance. At breakneck speeds — tempos too challenging for most clarinetists — he raced up and down the instrument's three registers and thirty tones. The audience was spellbound. Most of us realized that a new musical master had been born. DeFranco was joining the ranks of bebop's innovators such as Parker, Gillespie, Monk, Powell, Navarro, and Kenny Clarke.

Much later, Balliett would write that "DeFranco, unbearably challenged by Charlie Parker, attacked bebop and mastered it. He developed such fluency and invention and speed, that he was considered the supreme jazz clarinetist. His work has never faltered, and he has kept the instrument alive in jazz simply by playing it so well."[1]

It was standard that jazz soloists would take thirty-two bar solos, or one complete chorus. Only the occasional bandleader, for personal and sundry reasons, would permit or expect more. That night, with the crowd hanging enraptured on every note, Dorsey decided to urge DeFranco on, yelling out *"Take another chorus! Take another chorus!"* It may have been the energy of the crowd, it may have been that, like the crowd, he too didn't want the solo to end, but more likely it was a passive-aggressive move on his part — DeFranco demanded top dollar for his services, and Dorsey wasn't going to let that pass without making him work for it. That isn't to say that while wanting to see Buddy struggle, he didn't *also* want to see him succeed.

What had started, metaphorically speaking, as a race around the block was soon becoming a full-length marathon. Chorus after chorus, never losing the beat, never losing his way, he progressed through one difficult chord change after another. The crowd became ecstatic. They began cheering and

---

[1] Whitney Balliett, *Barney, Bradley, and Max: Sixteen Portraits in Jazz* (New York, NY: Oxford University Press, 1989)

applauding, continuing their acclaim through the entire duration of his final chorus.

The band joined in for the finale and the ovation reached a crescendo that seemed to last for minutes — nothing to compare with the good twenty to twenty-five minutes of Buddy's solo. He didn't bask in the applause, though. Drenched in sweat, washed out and white as a sheet, he just walked back to the saxophone section to take his seat. My eyes were still following him, amazed at what I'd seen, and so I noticed him reach into his pocket, take out a small white pill, and pop it into his mouth. Having talked to him about it later, he doesn't recall putting anything in his mouth, let alone a pill, and to be fair, what I saw may well have been candy or a mint. Whatever the case, I didn't begrudge him the option. Solos of that sort were not unheard of — Louie Bellson was known for drum solos of that length — but they were hardly something we were used to seeing at Lakewood.

Dorsey had a standard pre-intermission number, which followed. Charlie took that as his cue to perform. Noting DeFranco standing alone near the stage, he pulled me over, wasting no time whatsoever. This was something I called 'Tucker Time' — Charlie would come alive and home in on his target. That would be a band member or leader, to whom he'd introduce himself and begin a conversation. At fifteen years of age, he always sported a warm, wide-open, pearly-white smile which could disarm anyone. He was more forward-acting than the advanced guard units of most Marine combat outfits. Having recently started advanced private lessons, he could speak intelligently about drums and jazz. I, on the other hand, was shyer. While I would also talk with anyone, I always had trouble making the initial move and beginning a conversation. I'd later purchase, and would try to master, Dale Carnegie's book *How to Win Friends and Influence People,* but Charlie, I often thought, could have helped write it.

Charlie, in his inimitable manner, looked up at DeFranco, smiling as he always did, and congratulated him on his excellent clarinet solo. This was quickly followed by "I'm Charlie, and this is my friend Steve — Steve also plays clarinet!" At that moment, I was ready to first kill Charlie, and then fall through the floor.

Buddy's conversational rhythm was as perfect as his musical timing. Without losing a beat, the three of us joined in a continuous conversation that at times, at least to two relatively naïve teenagers, seemed to replicate the excitement and intensity of DeFranco's recent solo. Of course, the standard first-meeting clarinet player's questions were quickly run through: What brand of reed do you use? What strength is the reed? What brand mouthpiece? How 'open' is its facing? What make clarinet are you playing? Is a Selmer, Buffet, or Leblanc better for playing jazz — and why? What's the advantage of turning your mouthpiece ligature (the metal reed holder) upside down?

Then on to posture and body language: you keep your fingers very close to the keys — is it best to curl your fingers like you do? You stand relatively still and upright as opposed to Benny (Goodman), Artie (Shaw), Woody (Herman), and so on and so on.

Buddy was personable and gracious, never patronizing or judgmental. His innate friendliness was so contagious that it totally disarmed both Charlie and me, relaxing us. We were prepared to talk as two kids meeting one of the greats — instead, any stranger observing us surely must have thought we three had known each other all our lives.

The shop talk, not unlike Buddy's solos, soon made way for higher and more esoteric riffs. The conversation was stretching out and expanding like true bebop. First, a short introduction, then a full chorus of melody with only minimal changes here and there, quickly followed by the more lengthy body (the 'meat') of the piece composed of quick changes. Talking to Buddy felt like playing music — creative, harmonic, and as free and adventurous as possible.

The excellent book *The Giants of Jazz*, written by Dave Gelly and published in 1987, corroborates my feelings about DeFranco. "His dexterity seemed superhuman and he expressed an endless long and immensely complicated line as though he had all the time in the world." His conversation was as well described by that passage as his music.

Charlie and I shared obsessive-compulsive natures and that, coupled with the intensity of the conversation, kept it largely fresh in our minds. The subject matter literally ranged from A to Z — from amphetamines to Zen. I asked about 'burners', as amphetamines were then called, wondering if they helped with playing and if it was worth trying them.

"No, no, no," DeFranco responded, "they'll get you crazy in the head."

He warned us against alcohol when we were playing. He told us to avoid smoking, as clarinet or saxophone takes strong lungs. He warned us to protect our teeth, as they were necessary to hold the mouthpiece firmly in place.

We started quizzing him about players. I must have asked him about Bird, and Charlie asked him about Gene Krupa, who had been jailed on drug charges for a few months in 1943, and Buddy's answer still sticks out in my mind.

"It was a trumped-up charge," Buddy noted. The police had searched Gene's property and found a small amount of marijuana and then blew the entire scenario out of proportion. It temporarily ruined Gene, but in September of 1943 he had an emotional reunion with Benny Goodman, who was glad to rehire him. Tommy (Dorsey), benefactor that he often was, later increased his salary to $1500 per week and spotlighted his extensive drum solos.

With the subject on the table, I felt free to ask, "Buddy, what do *you* do for kicks?"

"Kicks," he told me, "are your health and money in the bank!"

We talked more about clarinet, with Charlie standing by and wearing a friendly grin as he listened. I asked Buddy about Klose, the exercise bible for clarinet players, and about playing marches, concerned that I might lose my feel for jazz.

"Klose is wonderful," he said. "It's absolutely fundamental. You must master those exercises. And marches! They'll give you a precise sense of timing. Keep yourself open to all types of music."

I told him that I wanted to be a jazz clarinetist, and didn't see how my present high school and private study of marches, classical and other types of music would help me. Buddy replied, "First, study and master all types of music, just as long as they have merit. However, later, if you desire to be solely a fine jazz clarinetist, you must then *eat*, *live*, and *sleep* nothing but jazz! Until that day, continue to study your instrument properly and formally. Master your instrument from top to bottom. Master it in a classical way just as, say, Raphael learned to paint in a classical manner. Then, and only then, will you be equipped to *abuse* your horn, to *bend* the notes, to *syncopate* the tempo, to *defy molto vivace* tempos, to *pepper* and *personalize* your tone, and to stand up *alone* with no written music to guide you other than a few pre-selected and well-established chords. Then you can attempt to create a meaningful and memorable piece of artistic enjoyment not unlike those produced in the field of art by mega-improvisers such as Jackson Pollock, Paul Cézanne, or Pablo Picasso."

At this point, I didn't know about Charlie but, speaking for myself, I was pleasingly lost. I had heard every word Buddy said but he had covered so many topics — things I knew I had to investigate further — that I had trouble returning my mind to the mundane here and now. Time had seemed to stand still, but the best part of my time with DeFranco was yet to come.

Dorsey, the known taskmaster, had already assembled the entire band on stage, minus one. He leered at our trio and with both hands tightly gripping the microphone shouted, "DeFranco! GET UP HERE!"

Buddy at first appeared not to notice, but then he slowly turned and in a calm, loud, and clear voice answered, "ONE MINUTE! I'M TALKING TO SOME FRIENDS!"

Charlie and I returned to the group already assembled in front of the bandstand. We inched our way forward until once again we stood practically eye-to-eye with the band members.

Dorsey wasted no time in striking up the band. The crowd had requested certain hits, and being the crowd-pleaser that he was he began to run the band through one tune after another. The crowd was getting what it came for, getting its money's worth, and Dorsey seemed happy as a clam.

As the end of the evening drew closer, the soloists all got their chance to shine again. Shavers, Richman, and DeFranco took their turns at the center of things. Charlie and I perked up our ears and stood in awe as each of these jazz masters once again displayed their virtuosity. This time, however, the listening experience was anti-climatic. Charlie and I had become so super-saturated by what we had experienced earlier in the evening that what was happening now did not seem to completely register. We needed to come up for air. So, as the band prepared to perform their signature sign-off tune, "I'm Getting Sentimental Over You", Charlie and I decided to beat the crowd and leave.

The thirty-five minute car trip home didn't see much chatter. We both knew that something beyond special had taken place that night — something so unique, we'd probably be talking about it for the rest of our lives. Our virtual silence surely was due to a deep sense of gratitude and worthwhile accomplishment. We had been allowed to enter the temple of learning — so to speak — and the experience had been rapturous and mesmerizing.

Just our luck it had been on a school night. We hurried home to prepare for Friday. My mind was wandering, riffing on various thoughts the night had brought up. I'd never been able to answer that standard question, "What do you want to be when you grow up?" but I always knew I wanted to do something great — something to contribute to society. Having watched Buddy on stage, I knew *that* was music.

Charlie and I didn't talk about the concert until Sunday after church, the telephone seeming too impersonal for the long-winded, soul-searching conversation we were due for. Each of us had heard the music reverberating through our heads since the show. It was chopped and channeled with the advice and goodwill we got from Buddy DeFranco. When we finally got to talk, it was a swirl of memories assembled in a wildly different order than we'd gotten them in. One of us would remember a riff and that would remind the other of another, and here and there something a player did would remind us of a tip we'd managed to pick up.

That concert was the main subject of conversation between us for a while, but it couldn't help but be supplanted by what was on everyone's lips: the war. It was edging onto the horizon of the American consciousness. World War II had ended with peace treaties a few months before, but there was talk of a *new* war. Moreover, a new *kind* of war.

This was the Cold War. Stalin was believed by some to be as bad as Hitler, if not worse, and Russia was beginning to rear its head in a drive for power. The worst of it was that no one really knew what the cold war meant — and that meant we had to be prepared for anything at any time.

We didn't know if Russia was developing a hydrogen bomb, whether there was any end in sight to the spread of Stalin's brand of communism which was blazing like a wildfire through Eastern Europe. As Americans, we knew Russia was now our most dangerous adversary, but in the streets, in the schools, and in the mines, nobody knew exactly what the danger was

— which was the most frightening aspect of it.

Charlie and I were happy enough — we had our music, and maybe the uncertainty was another reason to pursue it *now*, not to wait because there might not be a chance to make it up later. With peace of mind a rare commodity, we reveled in what making and hearing music gave us. From casual enjoyment to serious study of music, we had a grand distraction, and changing the pressure the outside world brought to bear on us felt like changing the world. Indeed, bebop felt like the change the world *needed.*

The lengthy conversation we had had with DeFranco would pop into our minds in snips and flashes, long after the initial experience. We heard his words as other musicians played those ideas on ballroom stages, having saved our pennies for pilgrimages to see every big band that came close enough to our backyards to reach: Jimmy Dorsey, Gene Krupa, Les Brown, Charlie Barnet, Claude Thornhill, Tex Beneke, and Jerry Wald. We avoided the non-jazz bands such as Kay Kyser, Louis Prima, and Guy Lombardo, thinking them too commercial, too unexciting.

Having the words of one of the chosen to guide us through our listening as well as our playing, we became unmistakably assured of what was in store for us. It was as sure as sunrise that music would be our lives. This wasn't taken as destiny, but that we *could* do it, and we had the drive to make it happen. We knew we had to improve our own playing or we might as well just sell our instruments.

That left the question: What must a high-school musician do to move from being the average run-of-the-mill player to being a professional? The answer seemed obvious. We needed the tutelage of a master musician. Not just a great musician, but one of those select few who was also a great teacher — that one-in-a-thousand maestro, likely well-known and highly respected by fellow musicians, a faultless performer who knew his instrument as a part of himself. Among these, we had to find the ones who knew *our* instruments.

This seemed a distant dream in Lansford, where the average hand was more adept at digging out coal than wielding a clarinet or drumsticks. Most great performers do little teaching, and those few who do must be able to switch from working at professional levels to helping the up-and-coming see the road to that place. As such, the great teachers were much sought after, and had their choice of students. Managing to secure one required an audition, and the prospective student would be judged not just on their playing or even on the potential the instructor sees, but on compatibility with the teacher and his methods. The process could easily be cumbersome, laborious, and frustrating. For the student, it could also be expensive.

I knew how high the bar had been set by my sisters when it came to finding a master teacher. Betty was in Philadelphia studying violin at the Hahn School of Music. Jo had garnered a small scholarship for music study on completing high school which she used to take lessons in New York City with Joe Biviano, and even went on to take a few lessons with the outstanding blind pianist Lenny Tristano. While still in their teens, both my older sisters had found their master teachers, and both had set high standards.

Philadelphia was big time, and New York was *the* big time. I'd first seen NYC at the age of ten when our family drove up for the 1939 World's Fair. I can still hear my dad praising Mr. Holland for his masterful accomplishment as he drove us through the then recently completed Holland Tunnel. Philadelphia was home to my grandmother, aunt, and uncle, so I had visited countless times. As well, it was standard practice when our local doctors were unsure of a diagnosis or treatment for my father, in his constant quest for the best, to have us immediately referred to specialists at Temple University or the University of Pennsylvania.

To always seek out the best was, without doubt, the most resonant and important lesson my father ever taught me. I learned the same from DeFranco in conversations over the years. The knowledge would serve me well.

* * *

During the late forties, by following *Down Beat*, *Metronome*, and The American Federation of Musicians' monthly magazine, I could easily keep track of where DeFranco was, as well as numerous other players. Charlie and I weren't the only young students to keep track of where the big bands were and who was playing with whom. Even non-musician youths, listeners rather than performers, kept abreast of what was going on in the big band business. Many of us did so with the same fervor as kids today following their sports heroes.

For me, DeFranco was the one to keep track of and, as he hadn't recorded much, reading the magazines was the best way to stay abreast of his work. Year after year he would win the *Metronome* and *Down Beat* polls as best jazz clarinetist over even the likes of Benny Goodman and Artie Shaw, whose popularity certainly outstripped his. The magazines were read by musicians and the most devoted fans and, among those who knew the music, Buddy was time after time selected as the best. *Metronome* magazine would assemble the poll winners to record as the *Metronome* All Stars. We would quickly snatch up these annual doses of Buddy's playing, listening intently and incessantly for weeks when that time came. His skill was clear and clearly recognized, and provided exactly what I wanted in a teacher. I seemed to *know* that he'd be my coach and guide, even at that point in time. Still, he was kept traveling from one end of the country to the other and so wasn't able to be the consistent once-a-week teacher I needed.

I had my local clarinet teacher of six years, but he took ill and had to stop teaching. For a short while, I thought I'd continue on my own but was quickly disabused of that notion at a regional Pennsylvania State Forensic contest. Each clarinetist performed two selections, about five minutes each, following which written criticisms were presented by attending judges. I'd expected to win but was surprised and saddened when my critique included a few negative comments. Speaking with the young student who did win, I found out that he owed a considerable amount of his skill to studying with a teacher in New York by the name of Gustave Langenus.

All I knew about Langenus from that conversation was that he was an accomplished clarinet player who gave private lessons out of the Dalcroze School of Music somewhere on West 56th Street. Once I had decided to seek him out, it immediately came to mind to ask Buddy DeFranco about him. Now, I think Buddy would have given me his phone number had I asked him, but I had been too shy at the time. I could have phoned New York's Local 802 of the American Federation of Musicians and, as a fellow union member, been given the number, but I lacked the social aggressiveness Charlie had. Recently I asked Buddy how he would have reacted had I discovered his phone number and called him with questions about a prospective teacher. He told me, "Steve, the conversation would have been short and sweet. Something like, 'What did you say that clarinet teacher's name is? Langenus? Well, Steve, if you don't go, *I will!*'"

It was my mother who provided the answer — unsurprising, as with her practical *savoir-faire* she tended to have an answer for everything. She had grown up in America's 'Old West' and learned to accept adversity, which showed daily in her raising five kids while tending the store and keeping up on all the chores expected of a woman of the day. My sister Jo and I had agreed to perform with Mickey's Gypsy quintet at an upcoming wedding at Manhattan's Slovak Hall in the upper seventies, and Mother noted it would be a simple matter to grab a cab from there to West 56th Street, find the Dalcroze School, and speak to Langenus. The wedding celebration would last two days, and we would stay in a hotel Saturday and Sunday evening, as well as being paid well. The band would return to Pennsylvania on Monday evening, leaving me Monday during the day to locate Langenus and arrange for lessons. Mickey picked Jo and me up with the other band members packed into his car along with the instruments, save for the bass fiddle, which was tied to the roof. There was room enough until Mickey stopped the car in Lehighton, about twelve miles away. A young lady got in and sat beside him, and he casually introduced her as the band's singer. Jo gave me a look and told me not to ask any questions. I didn't, and didn't have to — she never sang a note.

It was a month after the competition when we went up to perform, and I followed my mother's instructions to the letter. Monday morning gave me the freedom of New York and time to locate and visit the Dalcroze School of Music. Langenus was absent that morning, but the people I did meet at Dalcroze praised him so highly that I signed up on the spot, sight unseen, with my first lesson one week from that day at 11 a.m. Lessons ran twenty-five dollars an hour, and there was a one-time registration fee for the school of about twelve dollars.

That was a lot of money at the time, but deep down I knew I had done the right thing. At that price, I was sure he *had* to be good! I only made $22 plus expenses for the wedding job. Still, having spent the money was all the more reason to hurry away back to Mickey's band and see about making some more.

To take the lessons, I would have to miss a day of school each week, and I had no doubt I would get my father's permission for that. Even so, I knew that asking him for the money was out of the question, as I'd be told to use my own.

To arrive on time for my lesson I had to take the 7:10 a.m. train from Lehighton, arriving at Pennsylvania Station at about 10 o'clock. That meant a ride to and from Lansford station from Dad or my brother-in-law Ernie Suminski, my eldest sister Betty's husband, but both were always accommodating. I'd ask my mother *not* to get up and help me, but she would be out of bed like a shot at the sound of my alarm clock. Before I left, she'd have fed me breakfast and handed me a substantial lunch to take along, but she wouldn't let me leave without asking that all-important question: "Do you have enough money?"

Whatever my answer, she would reach down into her dress or some other hiding place and produce ten or fifteen dollars.

Post-WW II New York was exciting and wild. Had you asked a Manhattanite of the day to describe it, you'd likely get a glib, lofty, circular response such as, "New York is New York!" And they would be right to say so, as nothing else was. Describing the city to the relatively naïve, unsophisticated, small-town country-bumpkin teenager I was at the time was near impossible. One adult, trying, offered only that it was a twenty-mile-plus rectangle with a checkerboard design. Overly simplistic, but what more could he have said that I would have understood?

It took a few visits with my guidebook and street map in hand to learn the five boroughs, and that that checkerboard was just Manhattan. I quickly acclimatized to the numbered streets running east-west and avenues running north-south, with Fifth Avenue dividing east from west. I learned the difference between Uptown, Downtown, Midtown, and Crosstown. I learned that Broadway was both the theater district in and around Times Square and the street it centered on, also known as the Great White Way, running north-south for the full length of Manhattan Island.

My adolescent existence was far from actualized and the distance between my dreams and reality seemed to be mapped out on the streets of the city. Walking them, as seemed to be the norm despite the heavy street traffic, was like exploring what my life *could* be. Each step was a spark to the yin and yang of my desires and what progress I had made. My goals now seemed loftier, though conversely, more within reach. As my lessons didn't take up my whole day, I had the rest of the time to explore. As it took under a half-hour to walk the width of the island from the East River to the Hudson, or a minute per block to travel north-south, I learned the city quickly.

When I would tire of walking or wasn't sure of a certain address, a cab was always easily hailed and the cost was reasonable. Most cab drivers then were native-born New Yorkers who knew every corner of the city and seemed genuine and sincere about helping an out-of-towner in distress.

After my fourth visit to New York, my mother sat me down and asked, "What kind of a man is Gustave Langenus?"

She caught me by surprise with this — not that it wasn't a fair question. It was just that until that moment, I hadn't tried to put in words the multifarious experiences and emotions that working with Langenus had given me, or the consequent vision I had of the man. She had always trusted me and my judgment and, on the occasions where I did err, she was the model of Honoré de Balzac's "good mother" who "forgives without understanding". As well, she seemed pleased with my daily practice and had noticed the new mouthpieces, reeds, and clarinet exercise books in my practice room, all of his design. She had nothing to worry about, and I was surprised only that she didn't already know this.

Gustave Langenus was the stern, serious-minded, no-nonsense type. In the days past World War II, his name alone was enough to elicit fright, and his attitude was the common stereotype of the German. He was actually Belgian, and any accent he had did not stand out to me. Though stern with high musical expectations, he was also kind, considerate, non-judgmental, non-intimidating, and never petty. I do not remember our very first encounter, or what he asked me to play for him. Whatever it was, this initial audition probably included something from memory, something to sight-read, and possibly a wide assortment of scales, arpeggios and finger-busting technical exercises to reveal my range, technique, breathing, tone production, and overall agility and command of the clarinet.

My mother was pleased to hear all of this. She said I was very lucky to have such a good teacher and, even though he was expensive and even though the trip to New York required one full day each week, it was all worth it. I would have had more to tell her as reassurance had she waited one more lesson to ask. When I went for my fifth lesson Langenus greeted me as usual, but then immediately told me to sit down as he had something to announce.

"You, via my personal recommendation, have been given a $300 scholarship by the Dalcroze School of Music, to be used toward payment of your weekly private lessons with me. Congratulations!"

I don't think I said a word except a flustered thank-you. I was shocked.

He understood my response and what was behind it, adding, "I have other students — lots of them ex-G.I.'s and older than you, but their involvement with lessons and their commitment to the clarinet . . . well, you understand . . . it's not the same as yours."

Having said all that was necessary, he moved straight into the lesson, pausing only briefly to let me thank him again. Initially I had been told to pay that $25 per lesson and did, but the scholarship certificate listed the price as $10 per hour, and so I was actually awarded thirty free lessons. In retrospect, it's clear that Langenus himself decided to teach for less in my case, and who knows if I could have managed the lessons and the travel if not for his generosity.

By the time my train back to Lansford pulled in, I was aching to tell my mother about the scholarship. My father came to the station to pick me up, but I made him wait so that I could call home and tell Mom the news. She was happy for me and congratulated me, but immediately after warned me not to talk so loud on the phone — especially about money. Then she checked off a list of social graces: Did I accept graciously and thank Langenus? Did I wear the clean blue shirt she'd ironed? And of course, she reminded me to send a thank-you letter when I got home. My father, waiting patiently all the while, seemed to be able to fill in the gaps from her end of the conversation for himself.

Keeping something secret in a Pennsylvania town of 10,000 is impossible — you can't. Within a few days of my winning 'the Langenus scholarship', the news was published in our local newspaper. Shortly after, numerous requests for solo appearances came flooding in. My local high school had already been utilizing my talents for their concert band, marching band, orchestra, dance band, solo recitals, clarinet instructor, but now, new demands were being made.

One radio recital sticks vividly in my mind. The nearby town of Hazleton sponsored a weekly Saturday-morning variety show that aired from my town's large department store. The entrepreneur owner was a devotee of classical music. That considered, the three selections I had chosen to play were all classical pieces. I don't recall the other two, but I do remember "Flight of the Bumblebee", always one of my favorites — a fast, flashy tune that always sounded good on the clarinet, and frankly, allowed me to show off.

Faye Balliet was my accompanist on piano, and we were well-prepared for all three pieces. I had finished the first two selections successfully and was finally settling down from my first-live-radio-appearance jitters when the announcer asked, "And for your final selection?" I no sooner got the name Rimsky-Korsakov out of my mouth when all hell broke loose. The announcer got this god-awful look on his face, as though I had uttered some filthy four-letter word, and the live broadcast was immediately cut off.

The dead silence lasted about a minute or so, during which time the radio staff sternly informed me, "Due to postwar tensions with Russia . . . no Russian music is permitted on radio . . . "

Luckily Faye and I had performed together often enough that we had plenty of other songs we could play. We switched from Russian to American, ending my part of this live broadcast with an American classic: Hoagy Carmichael's "Stardust".

I was balancing quite a lot at that time. Along with daily practice and frequent performances, I worked in my dad's store — daily after school, sometimes before school, and if needed, on my lunch hour. I was also playing up to three dance jobs every week, teaching a few students, and of course, heading to New York once a week for my lessons with Langenus. I squeezed in what I could to make up a healthy social life, but my schoolwork was starting to suffer. My peers in the marching and concert bands would often help out and I would frequently sneak in a phone call past the accepted hours to ask about the next day's homework or upcoming exams.

I would apply myself as avidly as possible in English classes, knowing how important it would be throughout my life, but interest by itself is not enough. With everything else happening in my life, I lacked the preparation and attendance necessary to excel. It didn't help that the class took place right after lunch. My father would keep me in his store to sell candy to kids who passed by on their way home or back to school. He would insist that I stay until the very last student had left. Then and only then could I return to school, running to make up the time. In English class my assigned seat was in the front row, as seating was alphabetical, so my absences were always noticeable. One time I came in while Miss S. was facing the board and tiptoed quietly to my seat. Without turning around she asked, "Stephen, why are you late? What's your excuse?"

I was caught completely off-guard and, without thinking, blurted out, "I'm sorry, I have no excuse."

She turned slowly to the blackboard and went back to the lesson. Thinking I had dodged a bullet, I tried my best to act as unruffled as possible, even answering a few questions. I thought I was home free by the time the class ended, but as we were all getting up to leave, she sighed, "Stephen, please wait."

I thought I was in trouble, but she pulled me to a corner, making sure no one else could hear, and slowly asked me, "When is that father of yours going to hire other people to do *his* work so you, a smart boy, can properly attend to his studies?"

I didn't have an answer for her.

My geometry teacher, Mr. O., was also the football coach for the school. He looked peaceful enough, but there were enough rumors coming from the football team that most of us kept our distance. One afternoon, shortly before class was to begin, he approached my desk.

"Stephen," he said. "Yesterday we had a quiz that you missed, so please go sit in the rear of the class and I'll bring you the test to take now."

I had been in New York for my lesson the previous day and wasn't aware of the quiz. Resigned to it, I found an isolated seat in the back and began looking over the test. There wasn't time to get test jitters, and after a quick look over the questions, I began to write. Mr. O. assigned the class a project that he said would take about five minutes, and then, as everyone began reading, he walked to the back of the classroom and stood over my right shoulder. It didn't bother me at all at first, but then my defensive teenage ego kicked in, thinking that he was thinking that I didn't know football or didn't follow the team and he couldn't realize I'd probably be *on* the team if my dad had let me — and more of that nature. My inner monologue proved to be off the mark as Mr. O. smiled and asked, "Is that the *only* pencil you have?"

Pencils were used for practically all class writing, as ballpoint pens hadn't yet flooded the market and no one was crazy enough to try to write a geometry exam with a fountain pen. The pencil I was using was what we called a 'stump' — about one-and-a-half inches long.

"Here, use mine," he offered, handing me a brand-new, nicely sharpened #2 pencil.

Taking it, I thanked him and he was quiet for a moment before asking in a quiet, concerned, but reassuring voice, "And how is your music going?"

My excursions to New York and the reason for them were well-known throughout Lansford, even before the Langenus scholarship cemented the idea that I wasn't just playing with the notion of playing music. It would frequently come up as a topic of conversation, often with some reverence for my discipline and sacrifice to my craft. That said, what New York was like for me wasn't public knowledge. That I was there for a serious purpose was foremost in my mind, but that didn't keep me from enjoying all that I could of what the city had to offer. To the townsfolk, though, I was a busy and dedicated youth only and traveling to the big city was a sacrifice to be commended. I can't deny that I let that impression linger, and not just to strangers and teachers.

One snowy winter Wednesday evening I found myself outside the local high school after band practice let out at 9 p.m., melodies still lingering in my head, having bundled up for the two-and-a-half block walk home. The trip was short, but preparation was still needed, considering the cold. I had barely stepped into the street when a car pulled up alongside me.

A woman's voice rang out, "Stephen! Let us give you a lift."

I looked over to see Maude Tucker, Charlie's mother, smiling up at me. Charlie was sitting between her at the window seat and his dad, George, at the wheel. The car was a coupe, which in those days meant no back seat — some coupes had rumble seats built into the trunk area, but not the Tuckers'. As such, a ride was an imposition and having less than a ten-minute walk, I really didn't want to put them through the bother. As well, I would be off to New York in the morning, and had expected the opportunity to get lost in my thoughts while I could, so I declined their kind offer. Still, I was a close friend of Charlie's and so their hospitality was a given — they wouldn't take no for an answer. As the three of them pressed me to accept a lift, I started feeling that protesting was inhospitable, and I did enjoy the feeling of being someone special to the family, so I gave in.

Maude opened the door and got out. She then asked Charlie to step out, noting that I was a good deal older (by twenty months) and noticeably taller, and so it was decided that he would sit on my lap. We climbed in one after the other and, after a bit of jostling and settling, got as comfortable as we could, my thanking George as we did. Maude then climbed in, offering me another smile as she did. With the slam of the passenger door, George took off through the snow.

As a housewife of the day, Maude had no driver's license, so you never saw her without George. She was typical of the times, highly dependent on her husband and children — in her case, her only son. George was an anthracite coal miner. He made a decent living, but the family was hardly well-to-do. The two of them were music lovers, though they didn't play any instruments themselves. They would usually drive Charlie to and from his club dates, with his drums, and sit through the performances appreciatively. Not only were they supportive of Charlie's playing, but they trusted him implicitly. With that in mind, I should have known what would happen next.

George took the long route back to my house and I can't recall if there was any specific reason or if the route was discussed at all — after all, Charlie was certainly one of my closest friends, and his parents knew where I lived. That route gave us a little time to talk and, unsurprisingly, my trips to New York came up. Maybe Charlie's parents were even thinking it, if too polite to ask, but I suggested Charlie join me on the trip the next day. He'd been searching locally for an advanced teacher but couldn't find one — and an advanced drum instructor was easy enough to find in New York. Even if the idea had crossed any of their minds, the next morning seemed a bit too close. We stayed in the car, talking it over for a few minutes even after George pulled up to my door. Charlie was deep in thought, mulling over his options, and I could tell no quick answer was forthcoming.

Knowing that nothing would be decided until they had the chance to go home and talk it over, I offered that they didn't have to tell me their decision immediately, but Charlie had only to show up at 6 a.m. if he was interested. After we waved our farewells, I started realizing that it was too much, too soon, and that there was no way Charlie would be able to go — no arrangements had been made with the school, for one thing. I thought we could look at doing the trip together the next week, and simply proceeded as usual.

Charlie showed up at the door at 5:55 the next morning. A smile was all that was needed. We would have the train ride for one of our long talk sessions. After that, with two best friends studying music in the city, New York was going to be an even bigger and wilder ride.

Tommy Dorsey

Born in Shenandoah, Pennsylvania in 1905, Tommy Dorsey was only 16 when he joined The Scranton Sirens under the tutelage of Russ Morgan. Playing both trombone and trumpet, he quickly gained a reputation and found work with name bands, notably Bix Beiderbecke and His Rhythm Jugglers. Dorsey credited Jack Teagarden as a strong influence on his trombone style.

Tommy and his older brother, Jimmy, worked in several bands, including those of Rudy Vallee and Paul Whiteman, over the next thirteen years. Following that, the brothers formed the Dorsey Brothers Orchestra in 1934. This didn't last long, with Tommy leaving the next year to form his own band, about the time the group had its first hit with "Every Little Movement".

Tommy's band, which included members of Joe Haymes' prior band, had a hit almost immediately with "On Treasure Island", followed by three more the same year. The band continued making hits, including "I'm Getting Sentimental Over You", "Marie", and "I'll Never Smile Again" — all part of a string of 137 hits on the Billboard charts. The band featured top players including Buddy Rich, Gene Krupa, Charlie Shavers, Louie Bellson, Doc Severinsen, Nelson Riddle, Bunny Berigan, Sy Oliver, and Buddy DeFranco. It also featured notable singers including Dick Haymes, Jo Stafford, and Frank Sinatra, who later credited Dorsey's skills with the trombone as being where he learned breath control.

As big bands fell out of favor after World War II, Dorsey broke up the band in 1946. A hits collection, *All-Time Hits*, quickly became a top-ten album, sparking Dorsey to form a new big band the following year. Also in 1947, *The Fabulous Dorseys*, a biographical film detailing the brothers' early years, was released. In 1953, when Jimmy was forced to wind up his band, he joined his brother Tommy's orchestra, which was then renamed the new Dorsey Brothers Orchestra. The brothers also had their own television program from 1954 to 1956, *Stage Show*, which introduced a young Elvis Presley to a national audience.

Tommy Dorsey died at age 51 in his home in Greenwich, Connecticut, choking in his sleep after eating a large meal and taking some sleeping pills. Jimmy took over Tommy's band until his own death the following year. After that, Warren Covington — appropriately enough, the band's trombone player — took over the bandleader role. Under Covington, the band had its biggest-selling single, "Tea for Two Cha-Cha", which topped the charts. Dorsey's third wife, Jane, formerly a dancer at New York's famous Copacabana club, maintained ownership of the name and rights until her death of natural causes in 2003.

Charlie Shavers

Born in New York City in 1920 into the influential Shavers family of Key West, Florida, young Charlie originally took up piano and banjo, only switching to trumpet later on.

While still a teenager, Shavers performed with Tiny Bradshaw's and Lucky Millinder's bands before joining John Kirby's Sextet, where his solos and arrangements were credited for the group's success. To skirt child-labor laws, he pretended to be three years older than he actually was; consequently, the incorrect 1917 birthdate is still listed in many references. Having established his credentials, he added to his commitments by joining Midge Williams and Her Jazz Jesters. In 1944 he started playing in the CBS staff orchestra under Raymond Scott.

Shavers finally left Kirby's sextet in 1945, joining the Tommy Dorsey Orchestra and remaining with them until 1953 for both sessions and tours on an on-again, off-again basis. He continued as a session player at CBS through this period. He was also tapped to play with the *Metronome* All Stars, and he recorded trumpet solos for Billie Holiday sides.

Leaving Dorsey, Shavers jumped to the Benny Goodman Orchestra, remaining there through 1954. He also took part in Norman Granz's *Jazz at the Philharmonic*, touring Europe as trumpet soloist for the series. Later in 1954 he formed his own band with Louie Bellson, Terry Gibbs, and others. In following years, Shavers played trumpet with Dizzy Gillespie, Billie Holiday again, Roy Eldridge, and Sidney Bechet, among others. His composition "Undecided" is a much-loved standard that has been recorded by singers like Ella Fitzgerald in the 1950s and Natalie Cole in the 1990s.

Shavers died of throat cancer at age 50. His deathbed request was that his trumpet mouthpiece be buried along with his friend Louis Armstrong, who had died shortly before him.

Charlie ('Bird') Parker

Born Charles Parker Jr in Kansas City, Kansas in 1920, Charlie was raised in Kansas City, Missouri. The son of a pianist, singer, and dancer, he took up music early, beginning his study of the saxophone at age 11. Anecdotal histories have him experiencing much derision until he committed heavily to practice — he claimed up to fifteen hours a day. By some reports he would practice every piece in all twelve keys, accounting for his often unusual choices in concert.

Parker began playing professionally with a number of local bands while still in his teens. Kansas City, MO had a vibrant jazz scene, thanks in part to the presence of Count Basie's band. Playing in KC gave Parker plenty of opportunity to develop his style, aided by players like Buster Smith. This led to touring the U.S. and recording with Jay McShann's band in 1937.

He quickly earned the nickname 'Yardbird', later shortened to 'Bird'. This was referenced in a number of his works, notably "Ornithology". In 1949 New York's Birdland nightclub, named in his honor, opened. In 1952 George Shearing composed "Lullaby of Birdland", a tribute to both the man and the club. *Bird* was used as the title for a 1988 biographical film starring Forest Whitaker, directed by Clint Eastwood.

Bird remained with McShann's band despite moving to New York in 1939. Forced to supplement his musician's income, he washed dishes at Jimmie's Chicken Shack, where Art Tatum was a regular performer. Parker left McShann's band in 1942, joining Earl Hines. Owing to the 'Record Ban', a strike by the American Federation of Musicians, no official recordings exist from this period, and Parker became known for playing after-hours clubs in Harlem with the likes of Dizzy Gillespie, Thelonius Monk, Max Roach, Charlie Christian, and many other bebop pioneers.

Renowned for his clean, clear alto-saxophone tone, Bird was also known for creating new approaches that inspired countless other musicians. One of the founders of bebop, he introduced and popularized new styles of melody, rhythm, and harmony in jazz — such as using ninths, elevenths, and thirteenths. Further, he fused the music with classical, Latin, and other genres, both expanding its reach and changing the popular conception of a jazz musician from outsider to artist. This was visible in the adoption of his work by Beat poets and in his studies with the likes of Edgard Varèse.

Hospitalized after a car accident, a teen-aged Parker became addicted to his morphine prescription. To support the heroin habit this turned into, he busked and, at least once, even sold his saxophone. *The Quintet, Live at Massey Hall*, widely considered one of the best live jazz recordings of all time, features Parker on a plastic Grafton saxophone alongside Gillespie, Roach, Charles Mingus, and Bud Powell. The Grafton was all that could be found by the assembled musicians searching Toronto to find a replacement after Bird had sold his horn to buy heroin. His behavior worsened until he was committed to Camarillo State Hospital for six months, which he commemorated in his composition "Relaxin' at Camarillo". Following this stay he recorded material still regarded as classic, including quintet work with Miles Davis and Roach and the album *Bird with Strings*, which he considered his favorite.

Bird died in the Stanhope Hotel, watching Tommy Dorsey on television. The cause of death was listed as pneumonia and a bleeding ulcer. He was 34 at the time, but had lived so hard that the coroner estimated his age as between 50 and 60. In 1984 he was posthumously awarded a Grammy Award for Lifetime Achievement. Every August 29 a Charlie Parker Festival is held in New York's Tompkins Square Park, on a section of Avenue B since renamed Charlie Parker Place.

Chapter 3 New York, New York

The train ride to New York was all business, rather than the fun times Charlie and I were used to, but that was to be expected. Charlie was looking to find his master teacher, and spent the time leafing through issues of *Metronome* and *Down Beat* circling ads. The two of us would discuss each ad, trying to glean what we could to find the right match.

Charlie had spoken at length to many big-band drummers who had toured our area — a veritable list of perfect candidates: Gene Krupa, Buddy Rich, Louie Bellson, Ray McKinley, Dave Tough, Shelly Manne, and various others. For one reason or another, none of these were permanently settled in New York and even if they were, with the grueling schedules they kept — playing one-nighters — none would have had the time to teach.

Charlie was in love with life, always bursting with energy and ready to set the world on fire. Like me, he wasn't interested in dabbling in music as a hobby or sideline — his mission was to *master* music, to experience and execute it fully, to completely understand it, to totally immerse himself in it, with all its rewards, risks, and ramifications. Beyond his natural inclination to rhythm, he was simply a natural — everything he did looked and felt natural. His charm was evident the instant you met him, and his smiles were always perfect and timely. Certainly, this would serve him well in finding the right teacher. It had served him well to date, even garnering him a free lesson from Gene Krupa himself!

We had gone to Lakewood to see Krupa's orchestra, an excellent eighteen-piece swing band. The soloists were top-of-the-line, bebop riffs flying all over the place. Were it not for the familiar facades of Lakewood, we could have easily gotten completely lost in the music.

One soloist in particular stood out. This was Philadelphia's teenaged, puffy-cheeked, bebop trumpet sensation, Red Rodney. His bright red hair, blue eyes, and freckles combined with his short featherweight stature (between 118 and 126 lbs.) belied the fact that this was a force to be reckoned with. In 1946, he was only eighteen and easily mistaken for the band boy — the equivalent of a modern-day roadie, who would have set up Krupa's drums and such — and Charlie and I may well have made that mistake. A common put-down then was, "Blow a trumpet? Why, he probably can't even blow his nose!" No one that night expected anything from this elfin figure, but we were all in for a surprise.

Easily ahead of his time, he was, like DeFranco, a graduate of the Mastbaum Technical High School in Philly. In our previous conversation with DeFranco, Rodney's name had been cited with a certain respect. Krupa, well aware of what he was capable of, would feature Red often. His solos were not the then-standard swing improvisations with a phrase or two of bebop sprinkled in here and there. His solos were *pure* bebop — as we used to say, "as black as coal and right from the soul."

The main difference between bebop and its predecessor swing was that bebop soloists improvised chordally rather than melodically. Often the melody was discarded completely and the chords alone served as the foundation for the solo. As such, soloists were freer to be as adventurous as possible.

Rodney was one of the new and one of the few white high priests of this radical new music. We'd later find out that he learned his craft by spending his every free moment on New York's 52nd Street. There he listened and learned at the feet of bebop's masters: Charlie Parker, Dizzy Gillespie, Bud Powell, Max Roach, and Thelonious Monk. Eventually he was asked to sit in with these greats. With mentors such as these seminal soundsmiths, who needs the melody?

About an hour into the show at Lakewood, Krupa's band took their first intermission. Charlie, as always, wasted no time. Red Rodney had barely jumped off the stage and Charlie was positioned beside him. I was thinking he thought he was going to get Red to open up like Buddy did, and that he was crazy if he thought lightning would strike twice. I had guessed wrong, though.

"Red!" Charlie called out. "Where did Gene go?"

Red was disarmed by Charlie's straightforwardness and replied without thinking, "He stayed backstage."

Backstage at Lakewood was a shabby room immediately adjacent to the main section of the stage. As Charlie jumped onto the stage, it clicked — Charlie had set his sights on Gene Krupa to be *his* DeFranco. Without a pause, he walked straight back to the backstage door. I stayed where I was, thinking it was best to let him do this one alone. The entire band had left and Krupa was resting alone in the little room. The door was open and Charlie just barged in as I watched it all from my position directly in front of the stage. I had to wonder if anyone else realized they were missing the second show.

Krupa shook Charlie's hand and, after a few moments, got up and partially closed the door. I could still see enough to know that Charlie was sitting to the right of Gene, who was demonstrating various aspects of drumming to him. A few minutes in, Gene lifted a whiskey bottle to his lips then paused to offer Charlie a sip, pulling back when it clicked that this was just a high-school kid. Availing himself of a long, healthy swig, Krupa then placed the bottle on the floor on his left, away from Charlie. From that moment, Gene's arms were in constant motion, showing him one technique after another for twenty minutes or so.

The intermission was drawing to a close and each band member came trippingly back to the stage. It was reminiscent of meeting DeFranco at the Dorsey show, but this time it was the bandleader who was missing from the stage, and the sidemen looking around the room for him. The backstage door swung open suddenly and widely, and Charlie walked out with Gene following.

Charlie seemed happier than ever as he made his way up the stage, jumped off the front, and took his place beside me. In his hands were firmly clutched some small books, a pair of drumsticks, a pair of brushes, and a few scraps of paper. Krupa had thrown in some professional goodies along with the lesson.

Everything Charlie had learned poured out of him on our way home that evening. Brands like Slingerland for drums and Zildjian for cymbals were cited. Tips like using metal drumsticks for practicing, types of wrist action, and stick positions were shared. He mimed what he'd been shown — rim shots, rolls, paradiddles, slam high-hats — rattling off the names for each as he did. It was evident that night that Charlie was in his glory.

He had those sticks and brushes with him on our first trip to New York together, as well as a small practice pad and the various magazines to search through for instructors. A couple of ads had caught Charlie's eye. Bill West was taking students at his 48th Street address, and we were familiar with him from articles we'd read. The address alone was impressive. As we discussed the possibility, I noted it was right next to Manny's Music Store, where I once went shopping for clarinet reeds and stumbled upon an impromptu afternoon jam session with Dizzy Gillespie and vibraphone virtuoso Milt Jackson.

* * *

More than intrigued by what we knew from the articles, it was decided that Bill West's studio would be Charlie's first stop.

48th Street between Sixth and Seventh Avenues, we quickly discovered, was not only New York's mecca for highly-regarded music teachers but also a shopping paradise with an abundance of first-rate music stores. Just walking the street from Seventh to Sixth Avenue, you would hear numerous vocalists wailing away, trumpeters using the echo between buildings to accentuate those high notes, saxophonists running over some hot licks, and drummers pounding out one rhythm after another.

The music shops seemed to consider anyone a professional musician if they were simply hip enough to understand how to shop there. Try a number of instruments and mouthpieces with the idea you'll buy later, examine all the reeds in a box of twenty-five then just buy one — it didn't matter, you'd still get treated like you were playing a gig that was the talk of the town.

Charlie found Bill West's studio with no problems, having taken to the city like a duck to water. After a short chat, they scheduled a lesson for the following week, then Charlie came to meet me after my lesson up on 56th Street. He was excited, telling me that he would get along just fine with Bill West and that he was anxiously looking forward to his first formal lesson.

We made our way downtown via Sixth Avenue and then turned east along 52nd St, where we saw one famous jazz club after the other, including the Onyx Club, the Royal Roost a.k.a 'The house that bop built', Jimmy Ryan's, The Famous Door, Club Carousel, and the Three Deuces, where Pincus the doorman was setting up the night's billboard — Charlie Parker and his band, featuring Miles Davis on trumpet, Max Roach on drums, Duke Jordan on piano, and Tommy Potter on bass. Where 48th Street reverberated with music all day, 52nd Street swung with it all night.

We didn't have the night, though. We had to head back to Pennsylvania Station to catch the 5:30 train home for the evening. We decided we'd spend our last two hours that day at a record store, so hailed a cab. This was New York, after all, and even the cabs spoke of jazz history — Charlie Parker was an avid user of them, with a love for them that had him treat them like home, changing clothes, taking naps, purchasing narcotics, and even signing contracts in them. We asked the driver to take us to the nearest and largest record store he could think of. The trip was going to cost us about $1.50, so to get our money's worth we asked the cabbie to point out any and all points of interest.

As we passed them, he indicated Radio City Music Hall, Carnegie Hall, and the big movie theaters like the Capitol, the Roxy, and the Paramount, all of which featured not only full-length movies but stage shows of forty-five minutes to an hour spotlighting famous big bands. He noted that they opened at 11 a.m. and had five continuous programs, so you could go with a lunch at the start of the day and stay until midnight.

Eventually we forgot our original goal, but the cabbie hadn't. He dropped us off at Colony Records saying, "They have everything you're looking for. Ask for Ernest. Tell him Ward Green sent you."

The fare was $1.55, but the quality of the tour we'd gotten got us to add a 45¢ tip.

The Colony was definitely the biggest record store I had ever seen. It stocked everything I could have wanted, and I found myself there without even a dollar to spare in my pocket. I was thinking of this as an opportunity to plan for a future visit, but hadn't reckoned on Charlie's talents.

A clerk greeted us as soon as we entered.

"May we see Ernest?" Charlie asked. "We're friends of Ward Green."

The clerk waved to someone at the rear of the store who started immediately towards us. Ernest was impeccably dressed, extremely well-groomed, and the epitome of 'tall, dark, and handsome'. He took a brief look at me before turning to Charlie, who he carefully scrutinized from head to toe. I'd experienced this earlier today — Charlie and I had had lunch at a YMCA and two men in the buffet line were so enamored with his good looks that they kept tripping over each other.

"I understand you know Ward Green," Ernest put forward in an effeminate voice.

Charlie took the initiative and made up some story that Ernest seemed to swallow hook, line, and sinker. He probably could have said anything considering how enraptured Ernest was with his looks. Seizing upon the moment, Charlie asked if we could listen to some records featuring Buddy DeFranco.

Being a state-of-the-art record store, The Colony had large sound-proofed listening rooms. You could seal yourself off in these booths and take virtually all the time you liked if you had the faith of the salesperson. Charlie gleaned that we already had that, and so moved in for the kill. Shortly, we were listening to Tommy Dorsey recordings, with DeFranco still playing with his orchestra. As Buddy had been voted the top clarinet player by *Metronome*, we also listened to him playing with the *Metronome* All Stars, garnering a full twenty-four-bar solo. While listening, we read through the album's impressive liner notes written by authorities such as Barry Ulanov, Nat Hentoff of *Down Beat*, *Metronome* editor George T. Simon, and Leonard Feather. We used the opportunity to take notes, scribbling down as much as we could as the records played.

This being before 1948 and the introduction of the 33 RPM long-playing record, most jazz recordings were restricted to three or four minutes, hence the unusual nature of Buddy's twenty-four bar solo. The 78 RPM discs were heavy and easily breakable compared to their successors. The short recordings allowed Ernest many opportunities to pop his head into the booth, looking like he wanted to jump in and join us. He finally did, presenting a brand-new Charlie Parker and Dizzy Gillespie release for us to hear. This Gillespie-Parker combo date was their very first recording date together. Hearing them here in Colony for the first time one year later was for me a brand new surprise. Selections included: "Billie's Bounce", "Now's the Time", "A Night In Tunisia", "Groovin' High", "Hot House", and "52nd Street Theme".

Eventually time caught up with us and we had to leave. Our farewells took a minute or two as Ernest quizzed us about where we were staying and the like. We thanked him and guaranteed we'd stop back in, and of course that we'd let Ward Green know what a prince he'd been.

With forty-five minutes until our train, we had just enough time to grab a quick meal. We stopped at Romeo's, the equivalent of a modern fast-food Italian trattoria. We each had spaghetti with meat sauce for the extravagant price of 25¢.

From there it was a good fifteen-minute walk to Penn Station and the 5:31 Lehigh Valley Black Diamond Express, waiting when we arrived. This route offered first-class train service between New York City and Buffalo, connecting at Niagara Falls with Canadian trains heading north. In the other direction it crossed through New Jersey then entered Pennsylvania following the Lehigh River, running five times a day. Often during and after the war, we passengers would see certain coaches with their windows blackened, labeled 'Off-Limits', and heavily guarded by military police. Rumor had it that Uncle Sam was transporting German P.O.W.s from troop ships docking in New York.

The train was quite crowded and it took us some time to find seats, and we were quite glad we were able to. The day had been long and eventful, and we both needed to relax and let everything settle in. Charlie seemed especially reflective, not unsurprising considering it was his first day in New York and all that that he'd seen and accomplished. I was just about to ask him what he was thinking about when he offered it up freely without prompting.

"That Ernest, he sure is a nice guy, and he really does work hard. However, when guys like him talk to you, they always seem to come up real, real close. Why, he was so close I could see every tooth and every filling in his mouth. And his breath! He was chewing teaberry chewing gum! Don't get me wrong — I have nothing against men like him, but they do tend to rattle me when they come on so strong. What's that expression Robert always uses? 'Queer as a three-dollar bill.'"

Our friend Robert was an ex-G.I. with a repertoire of dirty jokes. Charlie mentioning him led to my remembering a joke he had told about a lonely cowboy and some sheep he was tending, which led to Charlie and me exchanging raunchy jokes for a while. Still unable to settle down, we decided to bum a cigarette each from the soldiers sitting across from us. We walked up to the smoking car at the head of the train and lit up, doing our best to act much older than we really were.

While we did, we talked about what 'cool' really meant. And it seemed that everything cool led back to New York.

* * *

Lansford wasn't so small that it was off the map for such institutions as *The*

New York Times, at least the Sunday edition, which made its way to select stores in our county. When we got back, Charlie and I had eagerly run out to grab a copy as soon as the closest store opened. We spent the day eyeing the ads for the various shows at the major Manhattan theaters, discussing the players and what we expected each would have to offer us. One in particular stood out, though — the Capitol Theatre (adjacent to Broadway's Tin Pan Alley) offered a first-run full-length movie, combined with dancers, a comedian, and an enlarged big band. The band would be Boyd Raeburn and his orchestra, with reed players doubling on various woodwinds, French horns, and a harp, a bonus for a reed player such as myself.

In our conversation with Buddy DeFranco he had mentioned the band, noting that it featured some of the most advanced arrangements of the day and stood alongside Woody Herman's band as one of the main places of interest for devotees of bebop in a big band. As such, it came as little surprise when, after two years with Tommy Dorsey, Buddy quit to settle in California and join Boyd Raeburn's band. It wasn't long though until Buddy left Boyd to return to the fold for another year with Dorsey.

DeFranco said it all in an interview with Whitney Balliett, jazz critic for *The New Yorker:*

> *We had our first falling out over my solo on "Opus One", which was a big hit record in 1945. Wherever we went, he* [Dorsey] *wanted me to play the solo that was on the recording because he said that was what people expected — what they came to hear. I was an itchy kid, so I kept changing the solo, and he got more and more unhappy. Finally, he told me he wasn't interested in my creativity, and he fired me. I settled in New York, and things didn't go so well. A few months later he called: "You little shit. You got enough wrinkles in your belly yet?" I told him I was doing great when the fact was I had checked into the Piccadilly Hotel and got the first week's tab — three hundred dollars, which would be like fifteen hundred now* [1989]. *I told him I'd want three hundred a week if I rejoined and five hundred right away* [Buddy told me he needed the $500 for airfare to fly to California, where T.D.'s band now was]. *He turned away from the phone and said, "I knew it. The son of a bitch is broke!" He said yes and I went back. The next uproar, I quit and settled in California, and the strangest thing happened. For six months, I couldn't get work, and I couldn't understand it. Well, I found out later that Tommy, who had a lot of influence and sway, had blackballed me, and to please him nobody would hire me. But I rejoined him again, and we became quite friendly and were close until he died* [Nov. 26, 1956]. *There was no nonsense on the bandstand. There was a ten-dollar fine if you weren't present a half-hour before the show, a twenty-five-dollar fine if you missed the show, and a ten-dollar fine if you smiled on the stand. When you soloed, he'd*

> *never take his eyes off you, and if he felt a little malicious, he'd make you go on and on until you were ready to drop.* [1]

My favorite DeFranco — Dorsey story is one Buddy has shared with me frequently and has also told to British jazz critic Steve Voce, as reported in *The Jazz Journal* and also mentioned by Balliett in *Barney, Bradley and Max*. He and pianist Dodo Marmarosa missed the band train from Louisville to St. Louis — Tommy Dorsey had his own railroad car — and caught up with it by hiring a private plane for $350. Dorsey was in the dining car of the train when they boarded to join the other band members.

"He got up from his seat and suddenly he saw us," DeFranco relates. "It seemed like a full two minutes we watched him. And he went through all the phases of emotion in that time. I grabbed a ketchup bottle, because 'Step outside' was one of his frequent ideas. The veins stood out on his forehead, his face got red, he was flexing his muscles, grunting and groaning, and he came over and glared at us for a long time. Then he suddenly began to laugh. 'You guys are ridiculous,' he said. 'You remind me of when I was a kid. I can't get mad at you. You tried to get there, you hired a plane. Stick around, I'll give you both a raise.'"[1]

Tommy was full of mischief as a young boy. My father, who played clarinet under Dorsey Sr. in our town's concert and marching band, years ago told me two stories. Both Tommy and brother Jimmy, throughout their teens, were required by their super strict and rigorous father to belong to *all* of the town's musical organizations. During one town parade the two youths, marching in the last row of the band and thinking their father was far out of view, began pushing each other, marching in a zigzag manner, and giggling at the girls. Unbeknownst to them their father had slipped back behind them. And in full view of a street full of spectators, he began slapping, shaking, and loudly scolding the two mischief-makers. A few weeks later, following a local picnic at which the band had performed, young Tommy watched as his dad drove off and headed home. Then, as the story goes, trombone in hand, he climbed one of the picnic grove's large trees, perched himself securely on one of the wider branches, removed his right shoe and sock, and with trombone slide cuddled between his big toe and second toe, rendered tender but at times very loud and jazzed-up versions of his father's favorite Sunday-school hymns.

It was a cold December day in 1946, but still bright and sunny, when Charlie and I arrived at the Capitol Theatre. We got there only a few minutes before the second performance of the complete three-part show. We'd planned for the second show, not solely to work around our lesson times, but because we figured the players would have gotten the chance to warm up.

[1] Balliett, *Barney, Bradley, and Max*

Looking back, considering what we saw and heard, it was the right choice.

The theater was quite large and beautifully decorated. It was clean and cozy, despite not being very crowded, especially upstairs in the balcony where we chose to sit, smoking being permitted there. We had our pick of seats and we sat dead-center in front of the stage, in the first row. The seats were wide and well-padded recliners with ashtrays positioned on each armrest. We lit cigarettes, inhaled expectantly, and sat back to await the show.

The movie was a silly piece of fluff about a man who had the 'power' to grow hair, yet through some sequence of events, would find himself totally bald. There were a few laughs in it, and the comedian that followed offered more, but neither was the reason we had come.

The curtain closed, briefly, before reopening with the entire orchestra seated on a special sub-stage built underneath the main stage which rose into full view. The spectacle was impressive, but so was the band — this was a *big* big band. Past the usual instrumentation, seventeen or eighteen pieces, there were French horns, an extremely attractive female singer, a harp with another attractive woman astride it, flutes, a bass clarinet, and, standing five feet tall and positioned next to Boyd himself, a *bass* saxophone.

Almost all saxophone sections had alto, tenor, and baritone saxes.

Occasionally someone like Charlie Barnet would play a soprano sax in a big band, but never before Boyd Raeburn did any big band use a bass saxophone. Raeburn was a pioneer in this respect, unsurprising considering his avant-garde arrangements, in large part the work of pianist George Handy. Handy was a known disciple of the bebop school as well as a pupil of the great classical composer Aaron Copland.

The first selection was "March of the Boyds". Raeburn himself played the bass sax, giving a unique bottom to the band, which was crisp, clean, well-rehearsed, and as modern as a band could be for its time. Solos spotlighted Johnny Bothwell on alto sax and Frankie Socolow on tenor. Bothwell was a great lover of the sound of Duke Ellington and of Johnny Hodges, and it showed.

That was followed by the first vocal selection, "Body and Soul". The attractive woman was none other than Boyd's wife, Ginnie Powell. She had a gentle swing style and was more than capable, presenting some impressive stretches even though this was clearly her warm-up number.

A satire followed, "Boyd Meets Stravinsky", based on the chord structure of "Over the Rainbow" and with multiple key changes. This featured DeFranco's partner-in-crime from his earlier run with Tommy Dorsey. Dodo Marmarosa was rightly considered one of the finest pianists of the bebop era, and he was well showcased this night.

Finally a hush came over the crowd (what crowd there was) as Boyd announced his final selection, a new piece called "A Night in Tunisia". The title itself suggested the exotic, which fit with Boyd's cutting-edge

Steve Botek, age 3

Two generations of Boteks
Stephen Botek Jr and Stephen Botek Sr

Botek Family, Binghampton, New York, 1938
back row: mother Elizabeth, Josephine, Betty, Steve Sr
front row: Agnes, Steve Jr

Boteks Jr and Sr
In Atlantic City

Steve, age 11
In his Lansford High School
Senior Band uniform

Steve in bonnet

**A neighbor plays the bass
on the Botek back porch**

The Botek Duo
Betty, age 15, on violin and Jo, age 13, on accordion

Steve, age 10
In his first Communion outfit

Counselors at Camp Greenwood in Hauto, PA
Including Steve, age 16
(back row, third from right)

Steve, age 14
Climbing a favorite tree

Steve in school band uniform

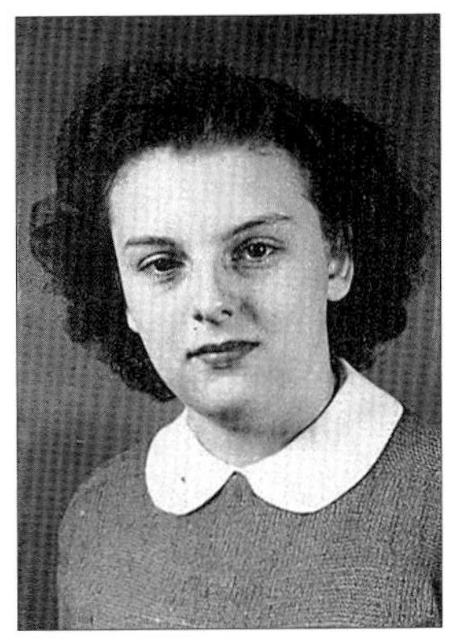

Faye Balliet
Steve's life-long friend, pianist, clarinetist

Charlie Tucker on drums

Pennsylvania Eastern District Band, 1947
Steve Botek as concert master *(first seated row, left)*

P.S. M.A.
RICT BAND

Botek playing his clarinet à la Artie Shaw or Woody Herman

The Modernaires, Steve on left
Not to be confused with the vocal group which worked with Glenn Miller

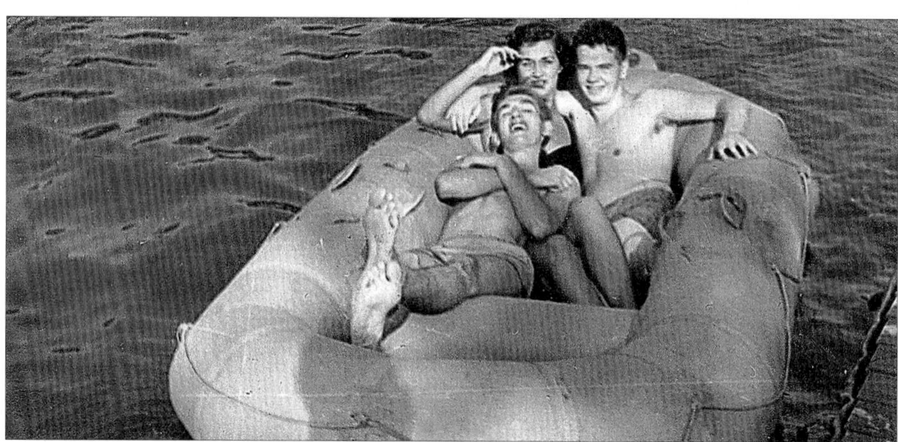

Lake Harmony, Pennsylvania, 1948
Steve, Jo, and Art Rubart

California cool. Afro-Cuban rhythms framed an attention-getting phrase of pure bebop, repeating three times during the first eight bars, resolving at the end of the eight, with the entire eight-bar phrase then repeating. The bridge, or middle section, had eight bars of longer tones descending like steps, repeating twice.

Most standard American jazz tunes are composed of thirty-two measures, with obvious exceptions such as the twelve-bar blues. The final eight measures echo the beginning eight. Despite the unusual selection, the same rules seemed to apply, and being used to this dynamic and following the feverish intensity of a meticulous and masterful rhythm section, the last eight were beguiling.

Usually at this point, the thirty-two bars would immediately be repeated, but in this case, a tag was added to the end. It consisted of the band growing steadily in volume and intensity as they played a simple but spellbinding chant-like phrase. And when the crescendo reached its climax, the entire orchestra simply stopped.

In the brief moment or two of dead silence that followed, a young black trumpet player rose to his feet. The bell of his horn bent upward as if he was playing to the heavens. He began his cadenza on an amazingly high note which he then bent and wove into a masterwork of bebop. We listened spellbound as this unknown horn player made his way through what in retrospect was only a few bars, but a few bars that echoed across the globe — for decades.

Charlie and I were electrified by the performance. Determined to know who that player was, we scrambled through music magazines after the show to find the notice that informed us, "Dizzy Gillespie has joined Boyd Raeburn and will be appearing for some of his Capitol Theatre shows. Gillespie, the co-author of the enchanting tune 'A Night in Tunisia' will be featured soloist."

Sure enough, we had chosen the right show.

* * *

Having seen Dizzy that first time, an early performance for him as well, ignited a lifelong burning interest in his work. Over subsequent years I must have attended at least twenty-five live performances by the man. Two in particular come to mind.

The first was a September 29, 1947 showcase, live at Carnegie Hall. This groundbreaking concert consisted of three unusually long sets, the first with Dizzy leading his big band, the second with Ella Fitzgerald joining the orchestra on vocals, and the third, stripped down to the Dizzy Gillespie/Charlie Parker Quintet.[1] This was no ordinary affair — it was a once-in-a-

[1] Detailed information on this show can be found in the *All Music Guide to Jazz* (see bibliography). Recordings of this concert are available on Artistry Records' *Live at Carnegie Hall* and Natural Organic Records' *It Happened One Night.*

lifetime experience. It was held on a Monday, the night most New York jazz clubs — with the notable exception of Birdland — hosted no live music. With my regular music lesson scheduled for the following day, I traveled to Manhattan early Monday afternoon, having managed to convince both my parents that a concert of this scope might only occur once in a lifetime. I not only secured the additional day off from school, but borrowed an extra $100 from my mother.

Attending the show meant an overnight stay. I checked into the Chesterfield Hotel in the Broadway theater district, dressed in a mod double-breasted suit and wearing horn-rimmed glasses (à la Dizzy, pure bop style). My style didn't get me any special treatment as far as the rate went — just under $60.

At 7 p.m. I was standing in line at Carnegie Hall waiting to buy my ticket, with the crowd inching forward painfully slowly. I was just three people away from purchasing mine when I overheard the ticket seller tell the trio before me, "Sorry, I don't have any. They're all gone."

God forbid, I thought. *I've come all this way and . . .*

As they walked away, I pushed forward with a feverish disregard for anything but confirmation. I nervously repeated what I had heard back to the ticket agent: "They're all gone?"

With the practiced bored indifference of a New Yorker of the day, he took his time before answering. When he did, and he didn't even bother to raise his head, muttering, "I have no three seats together. All I have left is two singles and they're downstairs, row six from the stage."

I knew from the location that the price would be extremely high — the most expensive of any advertised seats. I hesitated, afraid to ask.

"Well, *do you want one*? They're $29 each."

That was a lot of money in 1947, when city buses or subways cost a nickel, as did a bottle of Coca-Cola. A good shoeshine, of the sort you can only rarely find today, would be a quarter including a decent tip. Still, I knew where I had to be that night, so I counted out the cash. Ticket in hand, I made my way to the main floor and found my seat. The hall was abuzz as I made my way through. Those already seated were craning their necks in every direction, conversing enthusiastically with everyone in earshot. Suddenly, it hit me: it was a Monday night.

As I noted earlier, only Birdland featured live music on Monday nights and as such, almost all the jazz players in the city were free that night. No wonder the concert organizers chose a Monday. That explained the lack of the standard New York standoffishness. Genial gestures and cordial conversations flowed more freely than homemade table wine at an Italian wedding. A young man sitting next to me, a skullcap bobby-pinned to his curly black hair, asked, "Do you think Bud Powell will be on piano? You think Phil Woods will be the only white cat in Dizzy's band?"

While we were talking, I noticed it was past 8:15. The band had been scheduled to start at eight, but the audience didn't seem to mind. After all, the place was packed with musicians — no one expected orthodoxy, least of all from Dizzy. It wasn't much longer until the house lights lowered, though, and an emcee hushed thunderous applause for the official introductions, which were of course greeted with the same thunderous applause.

For the next three hours plus, musical history was made.

The second memorable Dizzy Gillespie show I attended occurred much later in my life, a virtually unadvertised free two-hour Tuesday-night appearance with his quintet, maybe one put together just for that night, at upper Broadway's West End Café. This storied venue was a landmark for Columbia University students, having served as a speakeasy and watering hole during the beatnik days, and as a late-night meeting spot for those protesting the Vietnam War.

My wife Ruth and I had stumbled across the news of this performance in a weekly neighborhood publication. We arrived about fifteen minutes before the 10 p.m. start and walked directly to a small table at the rear of the café, about twenty-five yards from a small makeshift stage. There was a small congregation of about twenty students right by the stage, but otherwise the place was fairly empty. No one approached us about ordering a drink and no one seemed in any hurry to have the show begin, with the atmosphere and the conversation both casual and congenial. Looking over the scene, Ruth and I both noticed Dizzy, standing out by virtue of his being past his student years but surrounded by students, laughing and chatting with them — like everyone else, he appeared to be in no hurry for the show to start. Ruth seemed to channel Charlie Tucker, urging me, "Go talk to Dizzy!"

It felt right, so I headed for him without giving it a second thought. Reaching him, I waited for him to finish talking before saying anything. And I definitely had to wait. He was half-turned in my direction and aware I was waiting as he spoke, but I knew quite well that a first meeting with a great like Gillespie, or Davis, or Rich, or Sinatra, could end up anything but congenial. And I knew the stories about Diz.

I personally heard Dizzy, particularly in his early bebop years, make a number of hostile remarks, often while introducing certain tunes. I remember him saying "This one we'll dedicate to the KKK — or should it go to the John Birch Society?" There was one occasion when he was flying economy class to Europe on British Airways. As the story goes, having been seated close to the first-class section, he attempted to use the first-class lavatory. A flight attendant stopped him and told him he could only use the economy facilities. Dizzy told her they were all occupied, and she told him to return to his seat and wait. Dizzy went back to his seat and found a motion sickness bag or something similar and filled it with his urine before pressing the attendant call button. When the same flight attendant showed up, Dizzy lit up one of his famous smiles and, handing her the bag, calmly said, "Here, Miss, please dispose of this."

I hadn't taken any time to think in going up to speak to Dizzy, which was a good thing — this was after all the high priest of modern jazz, and had I taken the time to think, the soul-searching would have inhibited me, if not paralyzed me. Eventually, having finished his thought, he turned to me, asking what I wanted with a silent glare. I quickly launched into congratulations on his lengthy and successful career, and his response was an expression that told me I'd better hurry up. With that in mind, I noted the first time I'd heard him play at the Capitol Theatre with Boyd Raeburn.

His expression changed immediately. He thought it over for a half-second before replying, "Can't be. You're not old enough to remember that."

"Oh, yes," I replied. "I *am* old enough and I very much remember the tune and the solo you played that knocked me out the most: 'A Night in Tunisia'."

On hearing that, he beamed a full, genuine smile that lit up the room. "Well, what do you know about that?"

I returned to my table, and minutes passed with little change. Everything was pleasant, calm, and congenial. No waitress came, and no crowd showed up. Finally, the band took to the stage, the lights lowered, and the chatter ceased. In the silence, we could hear Dizzy tapping off the tempo for the first tune. It took no time at all for me to recognize it: "A Night in Tunisia". While it may well have been his choice to open with from the start, to me it felt like a gracious and heartfelt thank-you for the memories.

Gene Krupa

Born Eugene Bertram Krupa in Chicago in 1909, Gene was the youngest of nine children, all of whom had to start working young after their father's death. Gene found work at the Brown Music Company and took up drums as they were the cheapest instruments in the store. He joined his first band at age 12.

Krupa started his professional career playing in Wisconsin in the mid-1920s. In 1927 he joined Thelma Terry and Her Playboys, the first notable jazz band to be led by a female musician. That same year he recorded for the first time with Eddie Condon, producing the first records to include a full drum kit or a pedal bass drum. The band had to convince the recording engineer to let them record with the full kit, as he was afraid doing so would ruin his equipment, having previously only recorded tracks with snares and cymbals. The next year Krupa recorded with Terry's band.

In 1929 Krupa joined Red Nichols' band in New York. That led to greater prominence and he was asked to join Benny Goodman's band in 1934, where he quickly rose to national fame and garnered the nickname 'The Chicago Flash'. As Krupa's star rose, tensions between him and Goodman erupted and a public fight between them in 1938 led Krupa to form his own band.

The band was a success from the start, but really hit its stride when vocalist Anita O'Day and trumpeter Roy Eldridge joined and "Let Me Off Downtown" went to the top of the charts. However, Krupa was arrested for marijuana possession in 1943 and sentenced to three months in prison. With Krupa unsure how the public would respond, the band folded and he returned to Goodman's band. He did not tour with Goodman because he was still worried about public reaction. Sitting in with Tommy Dorsey at the Paramount Theater in New York, he received such an overwhelming response that he decided to form a new band.

The new band included up to forty musicians, significantly larger than most dance bands of the time. It included a string section, and eventually began to experiment with bebop, bringing in players like Charlie Ventura, Buddy DeFranco, and Red Rodney. The band was cut down over time, to the point where Krupa was playing with trios and quartets from 1951 on. At the same time he toured internationally with Norman Granz's *Jazz at the Philharmonic* series. He continued to play regularly through the 1960s before finally retiring in 1967, though he played occasionally after that point and came out of retirement in 1970.

Krupa is credited with developing the drum kit to what we know it as today. He's also considered to have created the rim shot, and it was his suggestion that led Slingerland to produce tom-toms with tuneable heads. Working with Zildjian, the high-hat stand was developed and the names for ride, crash, splash, pang, and swish cymbals were coined. His book, *The Gene Krupa Drum Method*, set standards for drummers still in use.

Krupa's energy and signature style, along with his popularity, had him in high demand for film work. He played himself in both *The Benny Goodman Story* and *The Glenn Miller Story* and appeared in numerous other films. Warner Brothers even animated over footage of him drumming for the cartoon *Book Revue.* Sal Mineo played him in *The Gene Krupa Story*, which featured Krupa himself on the soundtrack.

Krupa died of leukemia in 1973 and was buried in Holy Cross Cemetery in Calumet City, Illinois. The city of Yonkers, NY, where he died, dedicated Gene Krupa Drive in his memory. In 1978 Krupa became the first drummer inducted into the *Modern Drummer Hall of Fame*.

Red Rodney

Robert Roland Chudnick, born in Philadelphia in 1927, began performing professionally at age fifteen with Jerry Wald's orchestra using the stage name of Red Rodney. He attended Mastbaum Technical High School alongside the likes of Buddy DeFranco and John Coltrane. He went on to play under Benny Goodman, Jimmy Dorsey, and Les Brown. During the earlier years of his career he strived to emulate his idol, Harry James.

Hearing work by Dizzy Gillespie and Charlie Parker, Red soon adapted to bebop. "The moment I heard Charlie Parker, I understood everything," he stated. He began working with more experimental bands, including those of Gene Krupa, Claude Thornhill, and Woody Herman's Second Herd. His skills garnered the notice of Charlie Parker himself, who invited Red to join his quintet in 1949. Red protested that others were more qualified, but Parker insisted that Red was the player he wanted. Working as the quintet's only white member led to a third name — Albino Red. As mixed bands were barred from playing many venues in the American South, Red was presented as an albino to get around the race laws. The following year he joined Charlie Ventura's band, but he continued to play off and on with the Parker quintet until 1951. Red was portrayed by Michael Zelniker in the Clint Eastwood-directed film biography of Parker, *Bird*, but played his own solos for the movie.

Red's career and life were fraught with problems with heroin addiction and run-ins with the police. Through the '50s he was in and out of jails, and his career suffered. With the jazz era fading, and also because he was feeling isolated as a white bebop player, he stopped playing jazz altogether, though he continued to work in music, including a long stint playing in the orchestra pit for shows in Las Vegas. His drug problems continued, his habit supported through theft and fraud, which led to 27 months in jail. Incidents during this period included impersonating a USAF general, stealing classified military papers, and committing insurance fraud. Eventually he overcame his addiction problems, but the damage to his career was done. He studied law, finishing second in his class and completing his studies in just three years; however, owing to his criminal history he was not allowed to take the California bar exam.

A stroke in the early 1970s bankrupted him, and he decided to return to playing jazz. This led to a number of albums with Ira Sullivan, whom he had recorded with in the 1950s. Sullivan convinced him not to stay chained to bebop just because he was used to playing it, and their work together has been called 'post-bop'. Their albums were well-received, *Spirit Within* receiving a Grammy award in 1982. His career re-ignited, Red decided to form his own quintet when Sullivan moved to Florida. In 1990 *Down Beat* inducted him into their Hall of Fame as readers voted him Best Acoustic Jazz Group

Leader; he placed second behind Wynton Marsalis, his former student, for Best Trumpet Player. During this period he toured up to fifty weeks a year, with three European tours per year. His last live performance was at the White House in 1993, recorded for a television special. Red would die of cancer the following year.

Dizzy Gillespie

Born John Birks Gillespie in Cheraw, South Carolina in 1917, Dizzy was instrumental to the evolution of jazz, especially bebop and Afro-Cuban stylings. He played a trumpet with a bell bent at a forty-five degree angle after finding he liked the tone when an accident in 1953 damaged his horn.

Gillespie began playing trumpet at age 12 and won a music scholarship to North Carolina's Laurinburg Institute. He dropped out in 1935 with the aim of becoming a full-time musician, moving to Philadelphia to pursue his goal. He joined Frankie Fairfax's band, with whom he made his first recording filling in for one of his inspirations, Roy Eldridge.

Dizzy moved on to Cab Calloway's band, where he had a tempestuous relationship with the bandleader. Calloway thought Dizzy too adventurous, calling his solos "Chinese music". In an argument where Calloway accused Gillespie of shooting a spitball at him during a concert, Dizzy stabbed him in the leg with a small knife. Dizzy went on to play for the likes of Earl Hines, Duke Ellington, and Billy Eckstine, also arranging for Woody Herman. Eckstine's band reunited him with Charlie Parker, whom he had played with under Hines.

Dizzy and Bird jammed together in Harlem clubs, developing the foundation of bebop. Dizzy taught students like Miles Davis and Max Roach the new style. It was during this time that he composed signature pieces such as "A Night in Tunisia" and "Salt Peanuts". A Los Angeles performance proved too much for the audience, and the negative reaction provided the impetus for their band to break up.

Dizzy went on to lead small combos featuring the likes of Milt Jackson and John Coltrane before starting his own big band which, unfortunately, was not successful. A second attempt also failed to prove fruitful. Fortunately he went to France in 1952, where a lack of other commitments and the French people's love for jazz allowed him to assemble a successful big band. He returned to the U.S. in 1953, and in 1956 assembled another big band to tour the Middle East; the trip would earn him the nickname 'The Ambassador of Jazz'.

Dizzy was also instrumental in the rise of Afro-Cuban music with his fusion of Latin and African elements with jazz in compositions such as "Manteca" and "Tin Tin Deo".

Gillespie's warmth and humor radiated from his performances and his public persona. One notable example is his 'presidential campaign' of 1963, in which he promised to rename the White House 'the Blues House', appoint Ray Charles the Librarian of Congress, and have as his running mate comedian Phyllis Diller.

Dizzy relied more and more on his humor in his later years as his age ate away at the clarity of his tone. In 1979 he published an autobiography, *To Be or Not to Bop*. He led the United Nations Orchestra in the 1980s.

Known for his skilled improvisation and scat singing as well as his distinctive ballooning cheeks while he played, Gillespie was a signature player credited as an inspiration to countless trumpet players. In 1989 he was given a Grammy Lifetime Achievement Award as well as France's Commandre d'Ordre des Artes et Lettres, and made a traditional chief of a Nigerian tribe. In 1990 he was given the ASCAP Duke Ellington Award for his fifty years of achievement in music. He also has a star on the Hollywood Walk of Fame.

Dizzy died in 1993 of pancreatic cancer, survived by his wife, Lorraine, as well as their jazz-singer daughter, Jeanie Bryson, and her son.

Chapter 4
The Song Is You

Every teenager wants to belong.

Belonging to a band is as much an ego builder as is being a member of your school football, basketball, or other officially organized sports team. The teen years are as difficult and filled with soul-searching as they are formative, and no one wants to feel excluded, regardless of posturing and passive indifference. The group becomes the core of things, and forging ahead without one seems next to impossible.

In 1944, Lansford High School had three superior faculty members who were not only 100-percent supportive, but also inextricably bound to the production, promotion, and propagation of worthwhile music programs. Unrestricted academic clout is necessary to inaugurate or advance such endeavors. His position made that a given for John Lauer, the school superintendent, and Howard Jeffries, the school principal, physics teacher, and assistant coach of both the basketball and wrestling teams. Professor Elwood Sprigle, the senior band director in 1944-45, certainly had the support of these two, but was feisty enough to carve out his own terrain had he needed to.

Lauer's word was law. He could comfortably substitute as a teacher for any subject, and he remained a confirmed bachelor because the love of his life was music. Over six feet tall and weighing over two hundred pounds, he was known for demonstrating his anger with screams so loud they could be heard from the school basement to the third-floor classrooms.

Jeffries was built like a wrestler — short, solid, and muscular. In contrast to Lauer, he had a mild-mannered demeanor and rarely, if ever, raised his voice.

Sprigle, in comparison, was certainly no athlete despite his endless energy, as his short stature was compounded by a pronounced limp. On close inspection, one would notice much wear in one shoe — the result of a club foot that, when he walked, would be dragged slightly across the floor. His disability was more than compensated for by his constantly upbeat, contagious, and strong-willed enthusiasm. Not once did any of his hundred band members ever venture a single joking comment about his foot. Everyone loved him and respected his handling of physical adversity.

These were men of great character. They were simple, unassuming, small-town men, sure, but nevertheless creative and driven to contribute to the world around them. They were part of what television journalist Tom Brokaw once described as 'The Greatest Generation'. While our troops toiled in Europe and Asia to bring the war to an end, they devoted themselves unselfishly to keeping the home fires burning. Being part of the hardworking, dedicated, and patriotic American public was something they took as a given. What they allowed, taught, or handed down to us was accepted without question, considered as a gift. When we were students, they were *our* Commanders-in-Chief, and we were easily enlisted to their cause. Wartime had shown us the necessity of working for a common cause, and having earned our respect as leaders, they were given our all.

I was always treated with the utmost kindness and consideration by Superintendent Lauer. After finishing parochial school, I became a full-time student at the public high school, and he facilitated my pursuit of a musical career without complaint. All I needed to do to take my weekly day in New York was pick up a formal excuse sheet from his office and have each teacher for that day read and sign it. There were no grumblings from the teachers and no bickering or backlash from my fellow students. Lauer's word was law, and no one was going to complain once he had offered his approval.

Jeffries was a gentleman's gentleman. A *mensch*. He was Mr. Nice Guy — always polite, always ready to help. He was one of the few physics teachers who was anything but an intimidating prima donna. His model behavior as teacher and principal was inspiring. He made unending efforts to encourage multiple school music programs, and his work ethic inspired us all. It was common among students that they hoped to emulate him when they grew up.

If Sprigle had ever stood still long enough, people would have felt sorry for him. However, he never did, despite his lame foot. He was always cheerful, though pensive at the same time. A creative man, he was able to instill and secure in each of his students a heartfelt and burning desire to practice more, play better, and perform to the highest levels. The band was well-served by him, as well as by its previous leader, Tom Dorsey Sr.

I never had the honor of meeting the elder Dorsey, but Charlie had been a public school kid and, as such, had him as his first-grade music teacher. Dorsey would issue a free instrument to each first-grader, and had given Charlie his first drum and the encouragement to practice, as he did for most of his life.

Sprigle was not originally from Lansford, and the new blood was welcome indeed. Small-town Pennsylvania schools are often so steeped in nepotism that they fall into decay. Different family dynamics were evident in the operation of each school, and Sprigle offered a breath of fresh air, guiding students towards self-actualization. He had an iconoclastic take and was recognized as achieving enough success with it that he was left to it.

He played mostly trumpet and trombone, being essentially a brass man. Still, other instruments didn't scare him in the least, as was demonstrated when he convinced the school board to buy a baritone sax, needing a fifth saxophone for a small school dance band he experimented with. The monstrosity was imposing — four-and-a-half feet tall. I had secretly tried to play it and failed — just finding the wind to coax any sound from the beast seemed to require an extra set of lungs and the staying power of a sumo wrestling champion. At the start of our first rehearsal, Sprigle cordially offered me the chance to try it. I politely refused, telling him, "I'll stick with alto and clarinet. Baritone isn't my bag."

Unruffled, he lay down his trumpet and positioned himself squarely behind the monster, looking like he was about to mount a horse from the rear, like the comedic characters in old serials. Without a moment's hesitation, he was capably running through a few of the standard warm-up exercises. When he finished, he looked up at me.

"Steve, as a true reed player, your approach leaves something to be desired. Look at it through the eyes of a brass man — a large, tangled, twisted piece of tubing just begging to be challenged and conquered."

Hmm, I thought. *Now I'll have to start thinking like a real brass man.*

He always knew how to make his point. Once, he and I were seated alongside each other in the audience as a visiting school's band gave a concert. He was unexpectedly asked to the stage to guest-conduct one of their more difficult orchestrations. For a full five minutes, his direction was precise and unequivocal, though easy to follow. Following enthusiastic applause, he casually returned to his seat beside me and asked, "Well, what did you think?"

I told him that I had enjoyed it and started to expound on the positives when he stopped me dead in my tracks.

"Don't tell me what you liked! Tell you what you *did not* like!"

With a lame conductor, everyone thought that our band would do less marching, but the opposite was true. We were a fixture at football games, parades, and other outdoor affairs once Sprigle got hold of us. In fact, he decided that most of us were too sedentary, and as a result, arranged for us to assemble two hours each Saturday morning to exercise in the school gym. For my part, I enjoyed it because he had spoken to my father to get me freed from strenuous Saturday-morning grocery store chores. Still, no one seemed to enjoy it as much as Sprigle himself, who would join in, running around the basketball court as if he were a kid again, oblivious to his lame foot.

Following the end of a vigorous season of Christmas and New Year's celebrations for the band, including the various Greek and Russian events that followed the standard ones by a few weeks, Sprigle announced that he was planning a mammoth spring concert for May. He already had prepared for most of the selections — the long and varied program would include Sousa, Shostakovich, Victor Herbert, Giuseppe Verdi, Rimsky-Korsakov, and George Gershwin, among others. All of Lansford's different ethnic groups were represented in the song choices.

Each Wednesday, our first period was allocated for extracurricular activities — sports, clubs, chorus, band. Spotting me entering the band's rehearsal auditorium one Wednesday morning, Sprigle immediately pulled me aside to a large mahogany table where he had neatly spread out the music for the May concert. He leafed through a number of them, whistling or singing passages as he went, but stopping abruptly at Verdi's 1851 opera *Rigoletto*. He announced that this was to be my clarinet solo. He handed me lengthy excerpts, all transcribed for B-flat clarinet from solo violin parts. The pages were black as sin. Not just quarter notes, but eighth notes, sixteenth notes, and thirty-second notes weaving together into the most intricate twenty-minute clarinet concerto I had ever seen!

Musicians refer to pages being black to describe how intricate the music on them is. Whole and half notes are drawn open in standard notation, while quicker notes are filled in. The quicker notes are more difficult to perform.

It was a good fifteen seconds before I could answer, "You don't think I can learn to play *that*, do you?"

"Sure," he replied. "You'll learn it section by section and then piece them together."

"Looks like Greek to me," I muttered, still staring amazed at the score.

"Italian, actually. As a Catholic altar boy, you've learned to pray and sing in Latin, so you shouldn't let that scare you."

It was a decent point, decently made. The words were all in Italian, so my comment gave him that opening. And at least I wouldn't have to *sing* it. Still, one glance was enough to make it clear that learning it would take a couple of months at the least. Throughout that morning's rehearsal, I would peek through my new assignment. I found that, in my mind, I could successfully sight-read section after section. Sprigle was right — I could do it, but it would be hard work and I would need lots of time. Still, as soon as I overcame that psychological obstacle, he threw another in my path.

"Incidentally," he told me as I left that day, in a voice that sounded like a malcontent Marine drill sergeant's, "I expect you to memorize the entire piece."

Most musicians, myself included, had no great trouble in memorizing something of a reasonable length. That said, I had heard about certain musicians, highly-trained professionals, who without the written music in front of them couldn't even play something as familiar as their national anthem. That's not a lack of intelligence or even ability, but a block to seeing the larger piece — maybe even a phobia, where the idea of not remembering the note overwhelms the idea that one *can*.

Sprigle reiterated his advice about linking sections together, telling me, "It's like a long chain, with many connecting links. You practice one section and play it to perfection. Repeat it, repeat it, repeat it, until you can't get it out of your head. You may even dream about it. Once you have the piece in your fingers, your brain will have no trouble soaking it up. It's like a sponge and water, a blotter and ink — osmosis! Eventually, you will piece together each link, each segment, carefully reviewing each one of them as you do. Finally, shazam! You've fit all the sections together, memorized everything, and the finished product will be a classic twenty-minute polished clarinet concerto performed by one of my favorite musicians!"

He laughed at his own joke. Still, the confidence he had in me shone through, and I laughed along, a little uncertain at first but quickly assured. He always knew how to reach down into the depths of your soul and motivate you in ways and to extents you wouldn't have dreamed possible. Like Buddy, he was a master at motivation — no ifs, ands, or buts when these men spoke. Though their advice may have initially been unsettling, it came with the will to tackle the challenge set and never failed to settle you into the music. There was something godlike in these men. Sprigle regularly brought me to my musical knees, but always there was the opportunity to genuflect, to learn from the opportunity.

Charlie had an extensive collection of books and records, one that put mine to shame. Hearing the challenge I faced, he presented me with a book on how to improve your memory. It may be telling that I only remember the author's first name: Harry. Still, I had faith in the book then, so knowing I needed time with it, I sought out my own copy and found one for $1 at a large Doubleday store. I returned with not only the memory book, but one by Napoleon Hill about how to properly manage money and become a millionaire and the Dale Carnegie bestseller, *How to Win Friends and Influence People*.

That left me wondering when I could find the time to read the three books, let alone practice what they preached. I immediately began to build my life around my goals, streamlining my schedule and studying or doing chores in set half-hour increments. I became an obsessive clock watcher and disciplined myself to go to bed and rise according to my new daily schedule, eventually becoming so set in the routine that I could virtually eliminate my alarm clock. I would simply tell myself what time I needed to get up before falling asleep and almost without fail, would open my eyes a minute or so before my alarm was set to ring — an ability I retain to this day.

Still, the usual hour per day of clarinet practice was proving to be less than what was needed. Considering I was now not only playing my lessons but memorizing them completely, I found myself practicing two to three hours daily, every day. And thanks to Professor Sprigle, most of these hours were spent trying to master and memorize Italian operatic themes and arias. I was singularly focused on Verdi, his concerto grosso proving to be the largest musical project I had attempted.

Sprigle steamed ahead at full speed. Band rehearsals became longer and longer, sometimes even three in a week. A date was finally chosen, the last Sunday of May, and what had seemed the distant future seemed to be advancing like a hungry wolf.

Pennsylvania winters in the late forties were anything but mild. Temperatures below freezing and frequent and heavy snowstorms began in December without letting up until March. Local lakes and ponds, many of them manmade by the region's coal industry, froze solid. Skiing, sleigh-riding, and ice skating could be and were enjoyed daily, free of charge. The continuous hills of the carbon counties made for perfect ski slopes, but no kid I ever knew had any formal ski equipment. Not a penny was spent on formal lessons and no one thought of buying 'proper' sportswear, other than the ubiquitous American Flyer sled. For us, skiing meant waxed barrel staves, J-shaped metal curtain rods, or whatever household finds would suffice for the job. Some of the 'equipment' was ingenious.

February of 1945 was typical. Up to two feet of snow had been plowed from the streets into long, high piles. These huge mounds, sometimes as high as six feet, formed glistening walls of white separating streets from sidewalks. With no buses in operation, students walked to school and, having no cafeteria, we all walked back home for our lunch before returning to school. The more adventurous students would do so jumping from one mound of snow to the next.

Classes were virtually never cancelled due to weather. The same held true for our Monday-evening band rehearsals, which lasted from 7 to 9 pm with a twenty-minute break at the halfway point. On the last Monday that February, temperatures had dropped into the teens, but the practice was still fully attended. Sprigle had plenty of new pieces to rehearse, so any absenteeism without a foolproof excuse could have resulted in permanent expulsion from the band.

This rehearsal began like all the others, with the emphasis placed on reviewing the ensemble pages. Sprigle was known for throwing curve balls at his students, and in that tradition announced, "Oh, Steve, after intermission, we're going to rehearse your Verdi solo."

We hadn't even attempted that yet at a rehearsal, and the idea caught me totally off-guard and utterly unprepared. Almost immediately, I answered that I had left my copy at home, but even before he answered, I knew that he would have another. What I really did lack and had honestly left at home were my number-one top-notch clarinet reeds. Every good clarinet player swears by the few excellent reeds he discovers. A good reed will permit you to execute everything necessary with nary a squeak or other amateurish sound. An especially fine reed is usually stored away, reserved for performances, and never wasted on anything such as a routine rehearsal.

I was less alarmed at the prospect of trying the Verdi solo in front of the band for the first time than doing a solo on one of my practice reeds. I was too proud and too much a perfectionist to allow this to happen — I had a reputation to maintain, after all. So, when intermission finally came, I quickly slipped on my jacket and then slipped out into the street, running home. I practically flew over the tops of the snow banks.

Sprigle never knew I had left. He was ready for the down beat as I took my place on stage. Somewhat cold and out of breath, I still felt more secure with one of my best reeds at the ready. The extra effort to compensate for not having warmed back up and for my overworked lungs was a small price to pay to avoid the embarrassment of an inferior rendition in front of my peers, and more so in front of Sprigle, risking his disapproval. When the solo came, my playing was not quite perfect, but it was more than adequate for a rehearsal with months left to go before the performance.

March and April came and went, of course, and soon enough, May was staring me in the face, with the red circle on the calendar feeling like a trap ready to spring shut around me. Still, my confidence was growing daily and all the sections were falling into place. Any doubts I had left dissipated whenever Sprigle took his rightful place as conductor. This concert was his baby, no matter how much work we had put in — we had, after all, done so because of his driving force of personality, his vision, and his encouragement. He had taught us to push ahead and, doing so bit by bit, we moved what had previously seemed like mountains. We were all aware of it and knew we shared that bond. Never before had I felt so at one with the band, Sprigle's conducting like a hypnotic spell. Not for a moment did I feel the slightest qualm or doubt, nor did I even remember the intricacies of being Stephen Botek. Here, I was part of a well-oiled machine.

The concert took place on a sunny Sunday in June. The high school auditorium — main hall and balcony — was packed long before the show was to start, and every effort was made to find additional seating. Those who couldn't be squeezed in stood jammed together in front of the doorways to the hall, craning their necks to see what they could.

The band performed brilliantly and the audience responded in kind. That they were impressed was evident in the applause. Not smatterings or polite recognition that faded away at the first opportunity, it came up in waves, each crescendo higher, only slowing when it was evident that the band was waiting to start the next piece. While we heard the applause as justification for our months of hard work, it also served to lift us higher, and drove us to excel even more.

The Verdi solo came around and I lost myself in it. The months of practice and memorization had paid off. Lengthy as it was, it didn't seem to bore the audience. Rather, they seemed engrossed and I was reassured — not that I needed to be at that point — that Sprigle had known what he was doing all along. I basked in the applause at the end of the piece, and it was clear to all the band that while they were applauding all of us, a special place in it was meant for me.

I also had a one-minute-long encore with "Flight of the Bumblebee", perfect for the warm spring day. Also perfect, as always, for me to show off. I was tired by that point, but determined to end the show on a high note — so to speak. The applause that followed lasted longer than the encore itself, spurring Sprigle to do a couple of Sousa marches as additional encores. Finally, the concert ended and it was all behind us, with the school year to follow in a few days' time.

With the final burst of applause for Sprigle, the band joined in, celebrating the man who had led us this far. To us, this was the man — without him, we would not have had a flawless concert to play to the acclaim of our friends and family. It's only in looking back now that I realize there was nothing we knew of the man past his position as bandleader and director. We had no idea where he lived, nothing about his wife and family if he even had any. We never ate with him or bonded socially with him in any way. Likewise, he seemed to respect my existence outside the confines of the school as sacrosanct, but maybe it never occurred to him, like me, that there was any deeper knowledge to be had. Keeping distance from one's private life was the custom of the day and we all respected it.

Still, I learned from him. His work ethic was admirable and contagious, beyond criticism. Proximity to Sprigle bred productivity. Like any great leader, he gave his all and, like one in particular, Franklin D. Roosevelt, he was anything but hampered by his physical handicap.

Now, though, it was over for the year, and things felt incomplete. In my mind, we band members could have used something more, a coda to this long piece — maybe a band trip. No such cap to our great year was to come.

Even so, Sprigle called me forward one last time, approaching me on the last day of school. There were fifteen or so clarinet players in our band and they needed a teacher. He had chosen me, telling me I could charge a few dollars per one-hour lesson, teaching either at my home if my parents allowed it, or traveling to theirs. Noting I had no car, I was told that my bicycle would serve well enough. The student was now to become a teacher. Of all the things that had come to mind to end the year, this was the last thing I expected — the passing of the baton.

I was quite busy through that summer, teaching twenty students in all, effectively a full-time job, shored up by work at my father's store. I worked with pride at having been asked to get the clarinet section in shape for the coming school year. It seemed a task where I was filling Sprigle's shoes.

Unbeknownst to me, Sprigle quit that summer. Later rumors had it that he had asked for more money and was refused, so moved on to be band director seventy-five miles away in the town of York. These were only rumors, however, and couldn't be trusted. Either way, we received no goodbyes, no explanation, nothing — just as quickly as he had entered our lives the previous year, he had vanished without a trace. None of the adults talked about it and the school offered no explanation. Even the music-loving Superintendent Lauer was mute on the subject, though it was certain that he would have fought for Sprigle against the most provincial members of the school board.

We were used to being 'seen, not heard', and as such, Sprigle was discussed only among ourselves, with no calls for answers. Even that lasted only a brief period, as we knew there was nothing we could do. In September, it would be back to business as usual under a new band director.

Nevertheless, I never forgot Sprigle, and told him so in a highly complimentary letter of thanks I mailed to him many years later, searching for some shred of closure. "Sprigle," I wrote, "was one of the two greats to lead the Lansford High School band — Professor Tom Dorsey Sr was the other."

Chapter 5
Teach Me Tonight

If I had it all to do over again, I know one thing I would do differently. I would learn the saxophone as I was learning the clarinet. Preferably, I'd start both when I was very young, perhaps age five. At that age, it's easier to learn a second language, even multiple languages, provided each is taught separately. It's been put forward that later in life, the facility for new languages is simply not the same.

As things happened, I first started playing saxophone at age thirteen, and it was harder for me to learn than it should have been. There are a few good reasons for this. Mechanically, the sax is less complicated than the clarinet — only nineteen notes along one-and-a-half octaves to worry about, padded metal keys rather than open holes which need to be tightly and completely covered by fingers, no wooden parts to crack and warp, and no quick loss of resonance and resilience owing to improper aging of the wood. Still, I had some barriers to overcome.

I was learning on a second-hand horn, one that was far from top of the line and which had *never* been checked for leaks. I struggled by with a stock mouthpiece, rather than upgrading to something better as most players would do. Perhaps most importantly, I had settled for a local teacher who, in retrospect, I can see didn't really know how to teach. Learning any new instrument requires finding one's own rhythm, a comfortable personal tempo with which building on one's ability and understanding feels natural. In finding that rhythm, one can proceed through practice and feel any deviations from the proper pulse. A good teacher patiently helps the student find his or her own pace. All students appear bewildered and lost at times and the teacher's job is to guide them back to safety. My initial teacher gave me none of that, expecting that naming the parts and running through exercises alone was enough.

There was also my own pride. I performed publicly in a large teenage dance band before I was ready. Learning on the job may make sense in some fields, but there's a reason skilled trades used to require an apprenticeship. I had a surface understanding of the instrument itself, and that coupled with a lack of real mastery led to my on-stage sax forays being less than satisfying.

Properly sounding a saxophone takes a considerably larger amount of air than sounding a clarinet. My breath control, metered and measured for the clarinet, lacked the volume to completely fill the sax. What I was lacking was deep diaphragmatic breathing, sometimes called abdominal breathing. I was still taking shallow gulps of air from high in the chest. Critically, male vocalists and wind instrumentalists who breathed incorrectly were labeled as feminine or girlish, while the kids of the day were rougher still, tossing out terms like 'sissy' and 'castrati'.

Again, it came down to finding a master teacher to lead me through the woods.

Persistent patience and endless encouragement — if you look at the lives of the highly acclaimed professional musicians you respect, you're likely to find these two elements prominent. Teachers, whether grade-school or high-school, and even school administrations tend to figure prominently in the development of successful, fulfilling careers in music and the arts. Not that these performers never encountered lax or straightforwardly bad teachers, but it's a safe bet they can name someone influential to their pursuit of their dreams from their school days.

Buddy would tell me about his decision *not* to attend the nearby standard high school, instead opting for Philadelphia's Mastbaum Technical High School, almost like a music school. Alongside classmates like Red Rodney and supportive teachers, he finished in three years rather than the usual four, able to thrive and work on his playing. This was instrumental in his path to becoming a master clarinetist.

Renowned pianist George Shearing credits schooling for lifting him into the career he loves. Born in the slums of London in 1919, the youngest of nine children and blind from birth, he could easily have fallen off the map. In an interview with *Spotlight* magazine in February 1988 Shearing recalled, "I studied piano all the way through school, from age four to sixteen. Thanks to England's public school system, I had a pretty good education, especially for a little blind kid from the wrong side of the tracks."

Maynard Ferguson has always been known to graciously give help, inspiration, and directional guidance to young up-and-coming talent. He credits that partly to *both* his parents being school principals. It was at the Montreal High School that he met Oscar Peterson and first played with him in the school's jazz band. Later, at the French Conservatory of Music, also in Montreal, he would get bi-weekly personal instruction from Benny Baker, who was teaching Doc Severinsen in New York City at the same time.

Maynard and Doc would later end up playing together in Charlie Barnet's band. While he initially dropped out of high school proclaiming that education was not his world, Maynard ended up teaching and founding avenues for musical education from India to New Jersey.

The educational backing was fairly standard among professional musicians, but it would also be built on, or the lack of it compensated for, by working with a master teacher. Counting on chance to provide opportunities would never be enough and wanting to take my sax playing to the next level would mean an active effort.

Once the decision to do so had been made, we found Louis Arfine practically next door to Charlie's drum teacher on 48th Street. This meant of course that my trips to the city were now for two lessons rather than one, curbing my other activities somewhat. Beyond the loss of time, there was also the cost of the additional lessons — another $10 or $15 per week. Still, for all the extra sacrifice, I didn't have my master teacher.

Arfine was more than capable and certainly took me far beyond where I was when I started with him. At the time, I wasn't quite ready to pursue a great teacher for saxophone. Arfine was my equivalent of high school, necessary before I moved forward to higher learning and a vital and invaluable builder of the foundation of my craft. Under his tutelage, my tone improved considerably and my phrasing became much more musical. I had previously had trouble with my vibrato, the rhythmic quivering of the lower lip produced to offer a wavier, more melodic, and more resonant sound. Through these lessons, my vibrato became automatic. Having learned from classical clarinet teachers, vibrato was never brought up. These more professional lessons finally taught me to make the separation — not to simply try and use my clarinet skills on the saxophone, but to treat it as a completely separate thing, after which I was able to adapt what I learned on the one instrument for use on the other.

48th Street was, as I've previously noted, a hub for music stores and, with his studio there, Arfine had some pull in the area. His influence got me a brand-new Selmer sax for around $185, as well as a number of mouthpieces to go with it — Brilhart, Linx, and Long, all discounted. When I strolled through the same area recently, a few major music stores were maintaining the old tradition of the street, but the alto saxes displayed in the windows sold for over $1,000. One large baritone model, a Conn, displayed a large tag daring passers-by to come in and drop $3,800!

As the months went on, it became clear that I was becoming ready to move on and find that master teacher for the sax. Unlike my experience with the clarinet, my horn playing had started in my teens — that alone was a barrier. Canada's piano virtuoso Glenn Gould found his master teacher, Alberto Guerrero, when he was still ten years old. Guerrero, a Chilean-Canadian, mentored Gould in his own personal style, which over nine years became Gould's own: the low sitting position at the keyboard, flat-fingered articulation of the keys, and a unique fluency and clarity of rapid finger passages. Gould stopped all formal lessons at age nineteen, declaring that he no longer approved of his teacher and that he "was equipped with everything except the kind of solidarity of the ego which is, in the last analysis, the one important part of an artist's equipment."

According to rumor, Gould's parents had spent $3,000 a year on his musical education, that in 1940s currency. Beyond that, his mother was a highly accomplished voice teacher who also worked with him consistently at home. Compared with that, my late start on the saxophone left a lot to be desired. If with all that under his belt, Gould still had to search, suffer, and toil to get where he wanted, is it any wonder that the rest of us find reason to rejoice in simply discovering who we really are and the path to our own actualization?

Charlie was satisfied with his lessons under Bill West. He was only paying $5 per lesson. Years later, however, he felt cheated. Bill would often disappear in the middle of lessons to sell drum equipment to other musicians. Charlie would rationalize these episodes by noting he'd seen Ed Shaughnessy, Sonny Igoe, or another name drummer. There was also always something Bill was readying Charlie for that made any inconvenience worthwhile, though, like a Gene Krupa contest where Charlie would compete against other drummers, to be judged by the master.

Looking back now, Charlie wishes he'd made the extra trip from Manhattan to the Bronx to study with Sam Ulano, or to Spanish Harlem or The Juilliard School to find Tito Puente. In his defense, Charlie was just a wide-eyed, sixteen-year-old country kid, and that considered, 48th Street seemed more than cool enough. That was probably a good thing, as Charlie wasn't yet ready for his master teacher, and had he tried then, he might well have been blown away.

While Charlie was happy enough with Bill West, I was feeling ready to move on. The next big leap seemed to be calling, and my legs were getting twitchy. Comfort can be a trap. Being happy enough with Arfine, and having lessons so close to Charlie's was excuse enough not to do anything. Then again, it turned out I didn't have to.

Jimmy's was one of the smaller but friendlier places to shop on 48th Street. There was a twenty-something clerk I always dealt with there — serious-looking, but pleasant and understanding of a musician's life. I mostly talked about instruments and equipment with him, so I remain unsure if he was just staff or owned Jimmy's, in part or outright. I never even got his name — he may well have *been* Jimmy.

Jimmy, which I'll call him for lack of another name, was gracious and generous with his time. He would often open up brand-new boxes of reeds, twenty-five to the box, allowing me to pick them up, bend them to test flexibility and check the grain for that central conical build-up I liked, even check the mixture of tan and yellow that gave it a visual appeal that no one would see but me. These were Vandoren or Rico reeds, cigarette-length pieces of cane, high-quality for my budget. For a clarinet and now saxophone player, this was like getting to taste my way through a dessert cart at a fine restaurant. When someone else would enter during this process, Jimmy would tell me to take my time, leaving me alone with the merchandise while he helped the new customer. Remember, these were reeds that would easily fit in a pocket unnoticed and this was long before video surveillance. I would sift through seventy-five to a hundred reeds to find my perfect matches, choosing maybe three or four when I was feeling flush. Though the process was unscientific and time-consuming, it certainly helped me feel better about the purchase. Even so, the only real guarantee of the sound of any reed is still to wet it in your mouth, apply it to the mouthpiece, and try it *in situ* — a bit more than I felt comfortable asking Jimmy to approve.

Being not only a poor musician, but a poor teenaged one, I purchased mainly reeds. One time, though, I entered intent on a saxophone case. I had heard about a new model called either a tray pack or tri-pack, depending on who you asked. Jimmy asked if brown would be all right, and I said it would be perfect. He left me alone in the store, disappearing through a trap door down a staircase into what was presumably a cellar. This being Manhattan, it was the usual thing for rented space to extend up and down rather than to the sides.

When Jimmy emerged, he was carrying a fairly large rectangular package still wrapped in clean, new brown paper. He seemed as pleased as I was when he opened it and showed me the layout of the case. In a relatively small space, one could fit a saxophone, a clarinet, and a flute — hence the tri-pack name. In addition, there was a separate inner clarinet case that rested compactly inside like a tray — hence the tray pack name. I was smitten immediately and knew I should grab it quickly. However, the price was $38 — more than fair, but I only had $25 on me. I told Jimmy the situation and said I would have to pick up the case another time, considering how much I had and that I had four different groups of reeds to buy at $1.50 each.

He seemed disappointed, but with a clear understanding of my situation. After all, I was not the first or only teenage musician to frequent his store, and he would have known about the limited funds available to such players.

"Are you coming in next week for your lesson?" he asked.

"Yes."

"How about you take home the case now *plus* the four stacks of reeds? You give me the $25 now and bring the remainder to me next week?"

I turned away and feigned blowing my nose. After all, New York was a tough town and no one would be caught dead shedding a tear or two there. I casually noted that my sax was home in Pennsylvania that day, as I'd borrowed one for the lesson, and that I'd be carrying the case home relatively empty. Jimmy got a smile on his face and suggested I take off my heavy corduroy jacket and pack it into the case.

"This goddamn heat is making New York too fucking unbearable to wear that thing!"

He had a point. It was July, and the city was hot as an oven. I needed a jacket for the Pennsylvania side of my trip, in the early morning and evening, and having it with me, was stuck wearing it. Money was tight enough that I couldn't afford a light summer jacket, and so I put up with the inconvenience. I could possibly have afforded one, had I not had the expenses of traveling to New York and my lessons, but without that, I wouldn't be as likely to get the gigs I did and the money that came with them.

I rode home on the train that night with my heavy jacket tucked away in the case, resigning myself to having to wear it on future trips when my sax would be safely packed into the case.

* * *

Jimmy had given me one other thing — the name of a good teacher. This turned out to be the master teacher I needed for the saxophone. His name was Joe Allard, and his teaching and playing were flawless, even god-like. Versed in the most modern techniques, eclectic in style, and beyond reproach, he seemed to be one with his instrument. Anything about the instrument, its players, its history, styles, techniques, he could rattle off on demand, a veritable encyclopedia of the sax. With all that, he was still far from a serious taskmaster — he was a warm, honest man who inspired you at first meeting, even without playing.

As seemed to be standard among those who were first-rate players *and* teachers, he was an iconoclast when left to his own devices, but perfectly capable of fitting in even in the most traditional settings. He proved that by holding a permanent position playing sax in the NBC Orchestra under the tyrannical Arturo Toscanini. Maynard Ferguson's classical teacher also played under Toscanini, who was known for firing musicians for a single mistake.

Back in the forties, the saxophone was still seen as some sort of freak hybrid. Certainly, it was welcome in jazz circles and marching bands, but in classical circles it was the subject of major controversy, with many declaring that it had no place in 'proper' music. While usually made of brass and having keys or valves like other brass instruments, it required a non-metal mouthpiece of hard-baked rubber or even glass, as well as a reed, like a woodwind. Unable to categorize it easily as either belonging with the brass section or with the woodwinds, the very idea of including one in an orchestra led to derision and outrage in many quarters.

This didn't hinder Allard in any way. Despite the controversy, he was sought out by various opera orchestras — where tradition was king. On a few occasions I got to hear him performing with New York's prestigious Metropolitan Opera Orchestra, who thought highly enough of his skills that he was given solos on works by composers as important as Ravel and Debussy.

As comfortably as he fit into a classical ensemble, he could swing and bop with the best of the big bands and jazz players. My lessons would often be interrupted by phone calls from famous names such as Getz, Konitz, Most (both Abe and Sam), Pepper, Quill, and Desmond. Each of these was thrill enough to be silent party to that I simply tried to soak up the atmosphere. And atmosphere abounded. His tiny second-floor studio was at the corner of Avenue of the Americas and 50th Street, a stone's throw from Radio City Music Hall, and you could see the snaking line of people patiently queued on the sidewalk, awaiting admission. Sometimes I would watch them as we played.

Lessons with Joe were a whirlwind tour of everything. Anecdotes about the greats he played with were told as instructional stories, anatomy was discussed to demonstrate how to best breathe and create a resonant sound. The lessons were always given standing up, both of us, in contrast to clarinet lessons. Duets were played at triple forte volume, every moment more challenging than the next, but never a chore. With the volume we played at, I would often sneak a glance out the window to see the response of those in line, gauging my success from their body language. Occasionally it was more than unnerving as I struggled to keep up, never mind that I could tell they could differentiate the striving student from the polished professional.

These were, after all, New York audiences, even if just theater-goers waiting in the hot sun in midday. In the late forties, finding a place to hear good jazz was as easy as finding a good cup of coffee and a New Yorker's ears and tastebuds were usually practiced at discerning both. Morning, noon, or night, one could always feast on good jazz in the city. Duke Ellington, for one, was known to give morning concerts at Harlem's storied Apollo Theater. Once when he was asked why an artist of his stature would bother with morning performances, he answered, "Just to keep the train running," referencing his theme "Take the 'A' Train".

Daily matinées at the Metropole Café, a few blocks over from Joe's studio, began shortly after noon, with performances continuing late into the evening. It was a long, narrow rectangle with a bar running the length of it and a narrow catwalk serving as a stage behind it. In reality, the stage was the top of a long oak cabinet. At first sight the place looked like a stretched-out bowling lane; there was barely enough room to move. Still, it managed to attract the city's finest players. Four or five of them would stand side-by-side single file, high above the restless, shifty-eyed, hustling bartenders, playing the newest innovations. At the Metropole you didn't sit down — you put down a dollar for a beer and, when you'd drained your glass, you bought another or you left. There was no room for anyone to stand around without feeding the cash register.

Standing in a crowded space had been made a commonplace experience for New Yorkers at the famous Nedick's orange-drink-and-hotdog eateries. The experience was becoming ubiquitous, with newspapers recently reporting that American G.I.s returning home from the war in Europe on the *Queen Mary* were forced to stand for every meal owing to severe overcrowding; after rushing through their meal, they had to clear the area to make room for someone else to eat. In New York, though, it was a necessity owing to high rents and low availability of spaces.

Being poor young musicians, Charlie and I would usually be stuck standing outside on the sidewalk, unable to pop for the opportunity to bend elbows with a clear view of the stage. We would have to stretch our necks and occasionally sidestep the gorilla-like doorman to figure out what players were onstage. The opening and closing of the door let us know what songs were being played and offered tantalizing hints of what we were missing, but even those brief excerpts were better than missing out completely.

One notable occasion, I went inside, flush enough to hoist a beer directly under swinging tenor saxophonist Illinois Jacquet. Poor Charlie was stuck waiting in the doorway, though he could have afforded a beer, as the gorilla at the door told him he *looked* too young to be inside — which, of course, was as formal as the ID checks got at the time.

Jacquet launched into "Flying Home", his signature song made famous in 1942 alongside Lionel Hampton. He stood stock still for chorus after chorus, but when he began to really let loose with high-register effects, screaming and squawking on the sax as only he could do, he had to stop more than once to keep from flying off the stage onto the back of a frightened bartender or two. He never stopped for long, though, never lost the intensity of the tune, and the attentive drummer never lost the beat, leaving him a clear road back each time. And to ensure he didn't have to stop anymore, the horn man beside him grabbed his waistband firmly to let him play without having to fight gravity at the same time.

Jazz history was being made 'round the clock in New York, and all it took to see some of it was a brief interlude in the afternoon. Still, it was time to sit down and settle into something less frantic, less frenetic, and a brand-new jazz club by the name of Bop City seemed like the place to go. Especially as that night at nine, the feature would be the Great Satchmo, Louis Armstrong himself with his group, as well as tap-dance duo the Trenier Twins and Buddy DeFranco with his newly-formed quintet.

When I left the Metropole that day, Charlie said we may as well take the six o'clock train back to Pennsylvania. I said yes, then told him it would be the six *a.m.* train the next morning.

* * *

Bop City had no admission charge but, once inside, there was some sort of cover charge and a policy that required you to sit down and purchase a drink. Located on the second floor on the northwest corner of 49th Street and Seventh Avenue (or was it Broadway?), the club was brand-new and sparkling clean but that didn't keep it from being cavernous and drab. In sharp contrast to the many intimate and unpretentious small clubs of 52nd Street, this place exuded a desire for cash made clear by the sterility and utter lack of personality. Still, the only aesthetic that interested me was to be provided by the artists appearing that night.

A tall, well-dressed gentleman greeted Charlie and me the instant we opened the door, ready to show us to a table. We stopped him there, asking first if we could go backstage and speak to Mr. DeFranco. Initially, he seemed taken aback by our straightforwardness, but regained his composure quickly.

"No one goes backstage. We *have* no backstage to speak of."

For a long moment, we stared into each other's eyes, all three of us wondering what our next move would be. Charlie naturally took the lead, explaining that we were old friends of Buddy's who had traveled up all the way from Pennsylvania. While he talked, I took notice of the utter lack of sympathy in the maître d's eyes and knew that the tale of woe was falling on deaf ears.

I ventured, "Oh, man — there must be *some* way you can help us."

It obviously helped that I punctuated the sentence by pulling a crisp five-dollar bill from my wallet and holding it out to him.

"Why don't you telephone Mr. DeFranco backstage and have him come out and talk to you here?"

He was smiling as he offered this, but it was obviously a challenge, expecting that nothing would come of it. Still smiling, he began scribbling on a small slip of paper. I'd spent enough time in New York by then not to betray any anxiety, but my stomach was starting to turn, unsure of how things would turn out.

"If you're wondering where the phone is, it's right there in back of you — that payphone — and here's the number."

He handed me the slip of paper, along with a nickel. This was to become a long-running joke as to my financial skills — a $5 investment which yielded a nickel return. Still, that wasn't all that came of it. Buddy was called to the backstage phone with a minimum of prompting. I was still nervous as I identified myself, hoping he'd remember his only meeting with a small-town Pennsylvania kid on what must have been one of hundreds of stops since.

But this was Buddy DeFranco. Even before I could paint the whole picture, he said he'd be right out and hung up the phone. The maître d' was now unsure, as Charlie and I became fully assured that we belonged. A bit suspicious but unable to question potential friends of the players, he was resigned to waiting with us politely. In less than two minutes, a narrow door we hadn't noticed right beside the payphone opened, and Buddy emerged. A look of surprise flashed for a second across the face of the maître d', but a true professional in his own right, he smiled and nodded to us before returning to his post with a dignified turn on one heel.

So there we were, once again face-to-face with the one and only Buddy DeFranco, dressed impeccably in a new suit. He grinned warmly as he shook our hands. Still unsure, we started to fill out the backstory about our earlier meeting at Lakewood Ballroom and seeing him play with Tommy Dorsey, Charlie and I each expanding on the sentence fragments the other got out but Buddy cut us off, telling us he remembered. In part that may have been owed to our young enthusiasm that night or to Buddy getting to tell Tommy Dorsey to hold on, but a large part of it was simply the personality of the man. The conversation that first meeting had been warm and friendly and, having made that connection, Buddy wasn't the type to let it fade out of memory.

This time, with that first meeting under our belts, he talked to us as if we were old friends, and the conversation had the familiarity of family. He even pointed out the details of his new suit, letting us know his new tailor had made it and that yes, it was expensive. There was no air of superiority — or even sophistication — offered with this, simply a casual observance to fellow musicians who could understand what it meant to reach the point where an expensive new suit was an option.

As we talked, Louis Armstrong began playing and as the audience roared approval at the opening strains of "All of Me", Buddy let a sigh filter through his smile.

"Listen to what I have to compete with!"

We watched together from the front of the club as the crowd went wild at every appearance of Satchmo's famous handkerchief, disarming smile, and at the first hint of his legendary scat singing. We stood in solemn silence as the eminent Jack Teagarden soloed, watching every slide of his trombone intently. With two reed players in our group, the viewing became even more intense as New Orleans great Barney Bigard offered some tasty clarinet passages. Charlie began twisting, turning, and tapping his toes as Chicago drummer Sid Catlett took his turn in the spotlight. No wonder this group was billed as The Louis Armstrong All-Stars.

Still, when we were between songs, Buddy excused himself, noting he was on next and would need some time to prepare. Charlie glanced at me with a ready smirk, a look that I knew meant he would intervene if I didn't do something myself. So I, still not ready to be direct, asked Buddy if he ever taught. He half-sighed, saying that most young people don't really follow through, don't practice enough, and that the families get in the way of their focusing on their instrument. Smiling now, I told him that I wanted to take lessons from him, and he wouldn't have any of the aforementioned problems with me.

He looked me squarely in the eye and nodded, "Okay, how about next Sunday?" Taking the slip of paper with the backstage phone number on it, he added, "Here's my address."

He was writing down the address, already knowing the answer but, not recognizing that, I was enthusiastically agreeing. That streamed into a final question — whether he had any other students.

"Well in fact, I do have *one*," he told me as he finished writing down his address. "A young Italian boy from Queens."

He handed me the slip of paper, which I was still clutching tightly as we shook hands and I assured him we'd see each other this coming Sunday.

After Buddy left, the maître d' came back to us, now treating us with an extra level of care. After all, these were two kids who had casually thrown him five dollars before spending the first few numbers watching the show with one of the performers. The change was subtle but clear, probably having a good deal to do with the great center table he showed us to. Recognizing what was happening, I flashed him my best Sunday smile as he pulled out my chair and handed him another five.

"Take this, and thanks again. One good five deserves another."

Normally the ten dollars would have been a worrying expense, but the treatment, the performance, and the coup in securing a lesson with Buddy make me feel like a big roller in the big city. Charlie was into the groove too, and we acted cool as we could as the night rolled along. After all, beyond our experience coming in, we knew all the players and songs and it wasn't hard to show we belonged.

The Trenier Twins took their turn on stage. They were a frenetic, hyper-manic duo performing various fast-moving dance routines. Buddy recalled later that the crowd was restless at that point, most having come with the intention of seeing Louis Armstrong and having little concern for the rest of the show. Charlie and I watched coolly, still basking in the glow and affecting the air of being the in crowd among the in crowd.

That gave more than a little as Buddy's band took the stage. We cheered wildly, noticeably louder than the rest of the crowd, taking away from the cool image we'd been cultivating to that point, but we no longer cared. This was our personal point of connection — we were in a big New York club, and that guy on stage? We *know* him!

Buddy remembers that the crowd had begun to chatter incessantly by that point, and when he took the stage, it didn't seem to matter a whit to most of them. Uncustomarily, he took the mike and offered the all-too familiar "Ladies and gentlemen" intro to an announcement of about a minute or so. The crowd calmed bit by bit, helped along by a bit of shushing, Charlie and I doing our part to help. By the time Buddy was finished, the crowd was silent. He hadn't said much of note, but something about his manner clicked, and everyone was waiting to see what he and the band had to offer.

The set lasted maybe forty minutes. While we cheered for all the players, our wildest enthusiasm was reserved for Buddy, of course. That isn't to slight the other players in any way. Howard Roberts on guitar demonstrated clearly why he was chosen to play with the band. Teddy Charles, on vibes, had moved to New York from Chicopee Falls, MA to study percussion at Juilliard and it showed. Art Taylor on drums showed us his chops — truly the hard bop drummer's drummer; Charlie, of course, was rapt watching his solo and I had to smile watching him drum along with his utensils in the air. It was quite some time ago, and even Buddy doesn't remember who was on bass or piano that night. Charlie and I had no inkling at the time, but the instant Buddy left the stage, one of the club's managerial staff pulled him aside. With a gruff tone, he commanded, "Lay off the microphone, DeFranco — only Armstrong uses it here!"

Blissfully unaware of the backstage incident, Charlie and I stayed until closing. Beyond wanting to drag out the experience for as long as we could, we also had a night with nowhere to stay before our morning train. Even if a cheap room was within our means, we'd been spending like sailors and any chance of that had been erased.

We went to Penn Station to wait for the 6 a.m. train back home. Having stayed up the entire night, we were both exhausted and decided to grab a little snooze as we had an hour-and-a-half to wait. Having been repeatedly warned about pickpockets, perverts, drunks, con artists, and the like, we sat straight up and side-by-side as we closed our eyes. Still, our judgment being perhaps a bit impaired from lack of sleep, along with the bright lighting of the train station, led us to feel fairly secure that no one would bother us. After all, with the night we'd just had, we felt like this was *our* city. Still, no sooner had we closed our eyes when a train-station cop was banging his billy club against the side of our shoes.

"No sleeping here!" he barked gruffly.

Having gained a sense of importance from the events of the night, we felt ready to tell him off, once we shook off the shock, but he had already walked away. We closed our eyes again and, next we knew, there was that banging on our shoes again.

"No sleeping, I said!"

Still filled with self-importance, I glared as he walked away. He had no idea who we were or what we'd done that night, and he was acting like one of my grade-school nuns — a stick in his hands and he was coming on like God almighty. We might have pushed things too far with the combination of too good a night and too little sleep, but luckily for us, they announced early boarding of our train.

The ride back home was a chance to sleep, but the sleeping was light and every so often one of us would shake awake, and whisper to the other "Do you remember when . . . ?" As much as we needed sleep, that conversation, even in brief flashes, semed more important.

Having been used to my regular city trips, everything seemed off when I left on a Sunday for a change. Most of the passengers were dressed to the nines, maybe traveling to see a rarely-seen relative. A lot of familiar faces from Lansford were there, some eying me accusingly, likely knowing I'd skipped Mass that morning. Still, I paid them no mind, keeping to myself and speaking to no one.

My mind was on the lesson. With the show running and Buddy needing to go backstage to prepare, we hadn't had much time to talk. Among the things I hadn't thought to ask was the cost. Having no idea what I'd be charged, I brought along $25, what I would pay Langenus for a one-hour lesson, plus an additional $10 my mother threw in.

* * *

Buddy had said to be there at one o'clock, and I arrived promptly. His place was on New York's West Side, not far from Carnegie Hall. As I walked in with my clarinet case in hand, my eyes settled on the front desk and a man sitting behind it.

"Oh, you must be here to visit Mr. DeFranco."

Clearly he had noticed the case, and knew Buddy or his visitors well enough. Likely, there were no other musicians in the building if he knew why I was there that quickly. Still, it was possible that Buddy had told him to expect me. He rang Buddy's room and told me to go straight up, giving me simple directions. I felt anxious as I walked the two flights of stairs, not knowing what to expect from the lesson or, for that matter, what to pay. There was also the awe (and fear) I felt playing in front of Buddy. Make no mistake, I knew I was a more than capable player, but this was the big time — playing for the man who had been chosen best in the country several years running.

With all the thoughts racing through my head, I was at the door before I knew it. I didn't even have to think about the directions as he had left it open for me. I walked in and as I closed the door behind me, Buddy stepped up to greet me. Face to face, all my anxieties melted back into nothing, but that wasn't owing to my teenage self-confidence. The warmth of his smile and manner would put anyone at ease, and it all seemed to be mirrored in the room. Keepsakes from around the country were all over — nothing extravagant and not displayed in any particular fashion. It was more like they had found the spots most suited to them, the most comfortable. There was a casual ease to everything which, while not decorated by any stretch of the word, was not messy either. Even the door to what I thought must have been his bedroom was ajar, with a tie hanging on the knob. Looking back, and knowing what I know now about New York residences and rents, it may well have just been a closet.

Buddy was full of questions and, while I had been prepared to discuss the details of my musical experience, he was also interested in my trip and how long it took, what time I had gotten up, whether I needed to use the bathroom, and such. The conversation was personal but light and polite, like that of old friends before settling into the bigger questions.

And then the big question came — he asked me to play something for him. I asked what he wanted to hear, and he made it clear he just wanted to hear me play, telling me to play anything I liked. I played some lengthy warm-up exercises that extended the entire range of the clarinet. Following that, I offered him a home recording I had made of one of the better-known standards — "How High the Moon", if I remember correctly. He listened intently for a couple of minutes, then leaned back, satisfied that he had a handle on my playing. After all, it only took a couple of notes to recognize Tommy Dorsey's playing, and that was the level Buddy was used to playing on.

Switching off the recording, Buddy started into a conversation with me. Nothing was held back, no topic was verboten. His questions were wide-ranging and his answers ran the gamut, nothing easily categorized — some simple and profound, some just short and sweet, some common sense, some so thought-provoking that I was still thinking on them days later.

What we *didn't* discuss was my playing. I knew he had recognized my facility well before he had stopped listening, but he said nothing about it. Instead, we talked about *other* players. He asked why Stan Getz was my favorite tenor player, agreed that Art Tatum was a genius, talked about how to classify Erroll Garner — not bebop, but not anything else easy to peg either. We talked about Artie and Benny and Dizzy and Bird and Bud. A lot of my heroes were first names to him.

Then, just when I was lost in discussion of all these other players, he focused in on one — *me*. He told me he wasn't concerned about my technique or tone, and that we had no need to focus on special fingering, breathing, posture, or the like. He was satisfied that I knew my basics well, and that my facility with my horn was excellent, telling me that my training and disciplined practice habits showed. With that foundation established, he wanted to focus on style, creativity, feeling, phrasing, achieving perfect rhythm — the goal was to attain a personal sound that was free, intense, and exciting, as well as a stage presence devoid of fear and self-deprecation and full of love for myself, the music, and the audience.

Suddenly, the nebulous quality I needed to expand my playing was clear; Buddy was searching for my soul. I knew how to play my instrument, but now I had to learn how to play *myself*. Just as I had to work my body to achieve the best sound from the horn through breathing and posture, he taught me that the opposite could be achieved — manipulating the horn to facilitate *my* sound. I could try different mouthpieces for different pieces, and even file down the lay (bottom side) of some with a carpenter's file to get a bigger bore and the corresponding fatter, more resonant sound associated with big-band jazz clarinet. He framed this as matter-of-fact, noting that I did the same for reeds, sanding them down and clipping them, so why stop there? This wasn't the kind of advice I'd ever get from Langenus. The classical reverence for the instrument was washed away in an instant with the simple revelation that the mouthpiece and the clarinet itself weren't sacred. If anything was, it was the music.

The same applied to my playing. Knowing the rules, I could start abusing them, experimenting with them, bending or breaking them as felt right. There was no need to be rigid. Being hampered by the rules was being square. There was no need to be formal — if I wanted to play jazz, I needed to get over any qualms about playing in an 'illegitimate manner'. He quoted William Blake: "You never know what enough is, until you know what more than enough is."

He told me how to swing. If I wanted to bring my solos alive, making them musical and meaningful, I had to learn to listen. To *everything*. Good players hear the music all around them: nature, birds, trains, rain, footsteps — everything that is often taken for granted must not be. I had to show my soul. And yes, he assured me, that meant suffering, citing the greats like Bird, Powell, Dizzy, Artie, Benny, and even Tommy Dorsey — all of them knew deprivation. He told me to listen to Billie Holiday, but to go beyond "God Bless the Child" and listen to "Strange Fruit". Then there was Dinah Washington, Sarah Vaughan, Billy Eckstine — *wow*, did they wail! The American Negro had suffered tremendously: poverty, segregation, harassment, humiliation, ridicule. They knew what suffering was. And out of that suffering, they needed a voice of their own. The New Orleans slaves developed their own way to sing a song, and out of that, jazz was born.

Syncopated styles and renewed renditions — there you had jazz. The origin of the word itself is uncertain, but one view is that it was Cajun slang from the French verb *jaser*, meaning 'to chatter'. Another view links it to an old slang term, *jasm,* meaning spirit, energy, or vigor. All this is reflected in the music, itself a spirited and speedy conversation between instruments, at least by the view of what went before it. Within a relatively short period of time, jazz produced innovation after innovation on instruments that had been approached largely in the same manner for hundreds of years.

This was new language, needed to tell a story that demanded its own voice. Similarly, the blues, where a mere three chord changes took one through twelve bars, gave voice to a new style. These innovations captured hearts and minds everywhere, and opened eyes to the plight of the American Negro. Those who emulated or followed from their sound never forgot its source, but the story was in the hearts of many of its players who, even when famous enough to have line-ups down the block to hear them, were required to enter and leave through the back door. As such, the music brings tears to my eyes in the hands of those who lived its reason for being.

Erroll Garner makes a sound so full you'd think an orchestra was playing if you didn't know better. You could walk up and see eight fingers on each of his hands and not be surprised if you'd just heard him play. Even so, the man can't even read music — it was his need that drove him to play.

Even the white musicians had their sad stories to play for the world. Poor Jewish families, hard-working fathers and mothers taking care of large families — while their stories were not the same, they recognized what the American Negro had offered the world of music, and set their own stories to it. George Shearing was blind from birth and born to a working-class British family. He eventually moved to the U.S. and formed a quartet with Buddy DeFranco, and even that was a bit of a battle as the two of them were signed to two different record labels, Shearing on MGM and Buddy on Capitol.

Buddy told me not to be afraid of hard work. Even doing my share at home, I had the obligation to my craft if I wanted to make something out of it. He told me to love my father, but to fight him too — to assert myself and teach him to be fair. He suggested I read Sigmund Freud, Wilhelm Reich, notably his *Character Analysis*, and Erich Fromm's *Escape from Freedom* — heavy but necessary reading. He pressed me to keep my body healthy as possible: diet, no smoking (though we both still did, he noted), restraint in drinking, and above all, no street drugs.

There seemed to be no limits to the ground he wanted to cover with me. We talked about his views on the war: "Hitler is indeed evil. War is sick, killing is inhumane. Man often behaves worse than any animal. Yeah, I avoided the army — my asthma was bad and they said I was too neurotic; they didn't want me and classified me 5A, telling me to go do community service."

Hour after hour, we covered topic after topic, until finally the telephone rang and interrupted us. After a brief exchange, Buddy turned to me and asked, "What time is it?"

I told him.

He turned back to the phone as it hit me: we'd been there four hours, and I'd brought money for a one-hour lesson, and that without even being sure of the price. I was wondering how I was going to pay him for all this when he put the phone down and said he had to go immediately. I thought that at least that saved me the indignity of having to end the lesson myself.

Unsure, I asked, "How much do I owe you?"

The word 'owe' was the right one, as there was no way I had enough money to pay him fully. Buddy hesitated for a moment then asked me how much Langenus charged. My face must have fallen to the floor.

"I pay him $25 per hour."

Buddy took a long look at me. I'm sure he could read my mind, if not my pockets. Finally, he asked, "How much do you have?"

The phone rang again as I was answering him. I'm not sure if he heard that I only had $35 or not, but either way, when he finished on the phone he turned to me and told me, "When you pass the front desk downstairs, ask the clerk for an envelope. Put my name on it and $5 inside it. Seal it and leave it with him."

He then shook my hand and showed me to the door, saying, "Nice seeing you. Work hard. We'll get together again sometime, but I don't know when."

* * *

Jazz is now part of the mainstream, but as I was learning it, it was pursued only as an illicit affair, out of sight of the halls of academia. Late at night, away from the eyes and ears of the guardians of music, was the only time to pursue a relationship with jazz and that was true through its heyday, with the defiance of its players resounding in every note. Perhaps that was a source of the passion that players of the time were known for, beyond the poverty and racism that drove them to use the music as a voice. Today, you won't find the by-products of that passion as you did then — no $5 lessons from greats like DeFranco, no $1.75 Birdland admissions, not even adjusted for inflation. There's big money in jazz now, even with an audience not quite as wide or prominent as it once had. There's some loss in that, in not being able to pay that $1.75 to see Parker, Powell, Gillespie, and others playing through the night from 9 p.m. to 4 a.m. While there are still many great players, you don't see the hole-in-the-wall venues with awkward stages packing them in.

Strangely and unlike any other form of music, jazz, as it moved from the public eye, garnered more appreciation and it took *more* money to see it. Shows you could once catch for a buck and a beer at lunchtime now happen only in the larger halls. Where the name Parker once evoked reverence, now at best it recalls a fountain pen. Conversely, at the height of its popularity, the musicians creating jazz were relegated to using back entrances and not mixing with the audiences. They had to look at the world from an entirely different angle. To play as I wanted to, I needed to completely revisit my preconceptions of the instrument, of music, of playing and stagecraft — a complete 360-degree turn.

It was Buddy who gave me the tools to fly solo and chart my own course. While my trips to New York were relatively independent ventures, they were taken to fulfill the goals for my music that had full parental support, with my mother slipping me extra money to be able to get what I did from them. In essence, I was there as the good child learning a skill with his parents' blessing. While there was nothing wrong with that, I hadn't really spent any time exploring what *I* wanted from my music. Talking with Buddy was about that missing link, about what drove me and what moved me — about my *soul*.

We have to step out of the rigid, stiff, boring, conservative lives we know — the ones that are there waiting for us — and chart our own course, make our own maps and, of course, sing our own song. To Buddy DeFranco, all this was natural, innate. It was core to his inability to just play the song as they recorded it for Tommy Dorsey. He wanted to know who I was so he could know how I played. Perhaps today, that might not sound as revelatory as it was at the time, but for a kid who had grown up in a coal town in the war years, just being yourself was never an expectation, even if ever considered as a lark — and *not* following someone's expectations was unheard of. We all carry the expectations of our upbringing until we face them down, either having decided to and making the concerted effort or forced by fate to do so.

Fate handed me Buddy DeFranco.

I'd known and admired his playing, but at that time, had no real grasp of what drove it. Meeting him alone was revelatory — the ease in his manner was his approach to everything, and while it shouldn't be a surprise to see that level of comfort from anyone, it's rare enough that it will always blindside you. That ease seemed an unlikely fit with exuberance, but they meshed perfectly. While I'd been surprised that he had considered me a friend so quickly, it became clearer once I realized — everything about him is upfront and out in the open and it takes no time at all to get to know who he truly is. Maybe the music helped, but it was that approach to life that brought out more in the people he talked to, including me. In a few short conversations, Buddy knew me better than most anyone.

And it was his interest in getting to know me that led me to wanting to know myself better. His honest, soft-sell, straight-from-the-heart style had captured me completely and, even if I didn't fully recognize it at the time, his utter concentration helped me focus. That contagion would leave me walking away from his lessons in a trance. There was a strong hypnotic intensity to being in Buddy's presence that took no swaying watch or deep, intense stare of the kind Benny Goodman was known for. In those lessons — and I consider each meeting, formal or social, to have been a lesson — the focus he put forward was on *me* more than the music, and in that there was an implicit trust that who I was could make music.

Everything about those lessons stays with me. I have always had a strong memory, particularly for spoken words and music — my auditory memory is impeccable. Still, having learned the compulsion during the Second World War that everything was to be salvaged and hoarded, I wrote down most of the important things Buddy would say. Those times he was unavailable, being on the road or overseas, I would leaf through my reams of notes and be able to glean what he would likely have said about whatever was on my mind.

It felt as if I had a mentor I could call to mind at will.

Buddy DeFranco

Born Bonifaccio Ferdinando Leonardo DeFranco in Camden, New Jersey in 1923, Buddy was raised in South Philadelphia. He began playing clarinet at the age of 9, in a family so poor that his blind piano-tuner father had to spend their rent money to buy him his first instrument. By the time he was 14 he had won a national Tommy Dorsey swing contest and played with Gene Krupa on *Saturday Night Swing Club.* At Mastbaum Technical High School, attending classes alongside noted players Red Rodney and Joe Wilder, DeFranco finished in three years rather than the usual four.

In 1939 DeFranco began touring with Johnny 'Scat' Davis. He went on to play under Gene Krupa in 1941 and then Ted FioRito and Charlie Barnet in 1942. It was while playing with Charlie Barnet that he was exposed to Charlie Parker and bebop for the first time, and began to play with and study him. He joined Tommy Dorsey's orchestra in 1944, then moved over to Boyd Raeburn's band in 1946, before returning to Dorsey in 1947. DeFranco recalls one time when Dorsey, who had no interest in bebop, leaned into a basement where his sax players and Buddy were rehearsing and exclaimed, "That's fantastic!" Then, on being told they were playing Charlie Parker transcriptions, Dorsey slammed the door and stormed off, never to mention it again.

In 1950 DeFranco became the only white member of the Count Basie Septet. He toured Europe with Billie Holiday in 1954, then followed that with three years leading a quartet with Art Blakey. In 1958 he worked with Nelson Riddle, premiering Riddle's *Cross-Country Suite* at the Hollywood Bowl and subsequently recording the piece. He also formed another quartet, this time with Tommy Gumina, which explored polytonal music. He toured with Norman Granz's *Jazz at the Philharmonic* series through Europe, East Asia, and Australia. He became the bandleader for the Glenn Miller Orchestra in 1966, continuing with the group until 1974.

Starting his career at the tail end of the era of swing and the big bands, DeFranco continued long past the point when clarinet players such as Artie Shaw, Benny Goodman, and Woody Herman were losing ground in the public eye. If not for the timing, he may have become a much more prominent figure in the jazz world. Still, he's considered the only notable jazz musician who played clarinet exclusively. He is also noted as the only major bebop clarinetist.

Over his long career, DeFranco has performed live and recorded with Art Tatum, Nat King Cole, Charlie Parker, Dizzy Gillespie, Stan Getz, Lenny Tristano, Billy Eckstine, Herb Ellis, Mel Tormé, Louie Bellson, Oscar Peterson, and many others. As well, he was repeatedly voted into the *Metronome* All Stars, playing alongside a wide range of other top-notch performers, including Miles Davis and Frank Sinatra.

DeFranco's many accolades include twenty *Down Beat* Magazine Awards, nine *Metronome* Magazine Awards, and sixteen *Playboy* All-Star Awards. He had his own television show, *The Buddy DeFranco Jazz Forum*, on PBS. He was nominated for a Grammy award for Best Jazz Instrumental Solo in 1998. He has been inducted into the American Jazz Hall of Fame and was the recipient of a 2006 National Endowment for the Arts Jazz Masters Fellowship. As well, there is an annual Buddy DeFranco Jazz Festival held at the University of Montana, which includes clinics for high school and college jazz bands. In 2007 Washington, DC's Kennedy Center honored him with its Living Jazz Legend Award.

Still playing in his 80s, Buddy continues daily practice and performs regularly. His current group is co-led by vibraphone player Terry Gibbs, who he has worked with for many years.

Chapter 6
Body and Soul

During my senior year of high school I saw little of Buddy. I would scour the pages of *Down Beat*, *Metronome*, and other musician magazines, hoping for news about my idol. I'd see pictures here and there, he'd win this or that jazz poll, notes about the makes and models he used would appear. There'd be the professional critics expounding on his playing — mostly positive, but the odd one proclaiming him too cold, technical, or detached. Young up-and-coming jazz clarinetists would cite him as influence or idol, claiming to be hooked forever once they heard him play. Still, when it came to clarinetists, no matter how well-regarded Buddy was, the lion's share of limelight was always split between Benny Goodman and Artie Shaw.

Each of the two bandleaders would act as if the other didn't exist while working to out-swing his opponent. The two would, of course, discuss each other in the lead-up to their much-hyped Battle of the Band contests — live sessions where each group tried to 'cut' the other. They may well have been good friends and admirers of each other privately, but both would maintain the professional hype which kept the crowds pumped and hungry for more. Buddy often noted that he hoped for a chance to be included in one of these public displays, but it was unlikely either bandleader wanted to expand things further. Shaw was living his life in view of the tabloids, with three of his eight wives movie stars — Ava Gardner, Lana Turner, and Evelyn Keyes — and Goodman wanted no competition, even if the hype machine was too much for him to resist.

Terry Gibbs worked with Goodman years back and had ample time to study his behavior. Goodman had either a poor memory for names or simply no inclination to bother learning them, so to him, everyone became 'Pops'. Once, scheduled to rehearse at Benny's apartment, Terry shared a cab with him. As was usually the case, Benny had no money so Terry had to pay the fare (knowing he could expect never to be paid back) and still suffer being called 'Pops' rather than his name. Still, Benny was the boss so Terry bit his lip. But soon he had cause to let his jaw drop. During the break, Benny's wife came into the room with a large tray of soft drinks. Benny continued to adjust his clarinet reed while telling her, "Put them down here, Pops."

Magazine glimpses made up the lion's share of my exposure to new information from DeFranco during that year, as Chester Steinman became the most prominent figure in my musical life. He was the high school's excellent new band director — a tall, thirtyish, handsome but easygoing guy who would never tell us what his major instrument was, feeling extremely at ease teaching any one of the band instruments. One of the times I managed to meet with Buddy during that year, he offered that Steinman sounded like the perfect man to learn ensemble playing from after hearing the man's philosophy on teaching: "Treat students as first-class individuals. The excellent music they then produce will not only echo their thanks but also their bliss."

Steinman excelled at conducting and was easy to follow. Competitive at heart, he would have the best performers compete throughout Pennsylvania. This raised not only the profile of the band, but my personal star as well. People came knocking on my door — the bandleader from Valley Forge Military Academy offered me a full scholarship if I left my high school, went to school there, and of course, played in the band. The bandleader at Cornwall-on-the-Hudson followed close on his heels with the same deal. Both had pen and contract ready in their hand when I finished brief auditions in our parlor. One of the bandleaders had pulled out the first clarinet part of a very standard march and asked if I had ever played it, while the other pulled out one that was black as coal, filled with many difficult, tricky sixteenth notes that stretched over most of the clarinet's range. Deep down, I knew no matter what was offered me, I was *not* going to any military school — life under my father was regimented enough. Still, I was not going to leave this piece of music unconquered. I took a good long look at the march, then without losing a beat or stopping, I cut right through the entire thing, like a chef's knife through a ripe watermelon. The bandleader was impressed, then seemed taken aback when I didn't say yes to his offer. Beyond my aversion to regimented life, any plums he had to offer were mitigated by the stories I'd heard. Buddy had told me about his ruthless draft-board experiences and my ex-Flying Tigers brother-in-law Ernie had more than a few cautionary tales of his own, all with the same moral: *Never trust the army.*

Buddy had faced his draft board head-on. His physical examination revealed: bronchial asthma, multiple allergies, painful hemorrhoids, and an intermittent partial paresis of his right hand — usually functional, but when the condition arose, quite disabling, especially as a clarinet player. Still, he was passed along to the Army psychiatrist, who immediately presumed that, being a musician, Buddy used street drugs. Buddy quickly corrected him, even though the idea would speak to his being unsuited to the military. To make his position clear, Buddy told me he asserted, "I despise war and could never, under any condition, kill another human being. Suppose for example the German boy I shot turned out to also be a clarinet player. Then what? And *you* — how can you claim to be a psychiatrist and at the same time be representing the Army? According to my definition of the word, a psychiatrist is dedicated to relieving people's anxieties. That means a dedication to peace, not trying to enlist people into a murderous machine like the military."

Buddy wasn't trying to get out specifically by saying that, he was simply speaking his mind, but that was enough to do the trick.

"You're too neurotic for military life," the doctor concluded, "and your physical health is not so great. Maybe you can better serve your country as a civilian — buy some defense bonds and donate some of your musical skill to the USO. You won't be drafted and you won't hear from us again."

I had a third, completely unexpected military-linked offer about three months later. It was a Saturday morning in spring, and Mr. Steinman had scheduled a couple of our soloists to compete in a State Forensic meeting. I was to perform two clarinet solos, one pre-selected by the attending judges and an encore selection of my own choosing. There would be no audience, only four professional judges who would select a winner and provide written comments about each player. If nothing else, this would be a great learning experience and an invaluable opportunity to meet other young up-and-coming clarinetists from across the state.

Faye was to attend with me, as my accompanist. By this time, she was quite a good pianist and understood exactly what I needed as a clarinetist, as she and her older brother both played that instrument as well. They were living in the house once rented by the Dorsey family and, like the senior Dorsey, Faye's father was also an anthracite coal miner.

That Good Friday, the day prior to the forensic meet, the local fire alarm sounded at around 1:30 in the afternoon. The alarm was set to sound a different number of rings depending on what block or section of town was the source of the fire. This time, the sequence made it clear that one of the town's four large coal collieries had had a major incident. The sound was familiar to us all — the town had been completely undermined and cave-ins and explosions were common enough. My mother noted the sound as meaning that someone at the mines had been killed. She was right. There had been a major explosion and Faye's father was among those blown to pieces. When we heard the news confirmed, my mother broke down and wept, her brother Joe having died six years prior in the same fashion at age thirty-three, leaving his wife to raise their three children alone.

Faye was a wreck. There was, of course, no expectation that she would still come to the forensic meet to accompany me, but she insisted she would. Sure enough, she arrived looking tired but holding in the pain. I was unsure if she was really in shape for such an important performance, but wasn't going to argue with her about it. Still, the instant she sat on the bench, everything seemed to leave her but the music and she performed both pieces to perfection. Perhaps inspired by her, my playing was likewise note-perfect. I can't recall the first selection chosen by the judges, but the second was a dreamy-but-spirited descriptive tone poem about New Orleans written by my teacher Gustave Langenus.

When we finished, I went backstage to retrieve my belongings, expecting that returning Faye home at the first opportunity would be best. However, there was a man there waiting for me. About thirty years old, he introduced himself as Master Sergeant George Dietz, the solo clarinetist from the U.S. Air Force Band in Washington, DC. I was impressed — here was a fellow clarinet player, an older one at that, and one in a position that said he was an excellent player, and he was seeking me out to tell me he enjoyed my solos. He had more than praise in mind, though. To my surprise, he asked me if I might consider joining the Air Force to play full-time in *the* U.S. Air Force Band in Washington. Now the military schools which had approached me were previously unknown to me, but of course I had heard of the four big military bands in DC! I told him I would need time to think about it, but I was probably going to go on to college, specifically to a music school. He was polite and didn't pressure me, offering me his card and telling me to think about the offer and call him if I was interested. He added all kinds of detail — I would be given a sergeant's rank, receive extra money so I could live off-base, and more. None of this fully clicked with me at the time, but he did note one thing that did — if I liked jazz, the remnants of Glenn Miller's old band were stationed there.

For us kids growing up amongst the Penn state slate and slag heaps, a break was all we wanted — a way out. They didn't come easily or often, with extra opportunities few and far between and extra money nothing more than a pipe dream. Our fathers were all we had, and in those days, a father was like a Catholic priest — just *there*, functional, to be feared, and eventually to be fought. If you lost, you followed in their footsteps; if you won, your best hope was the chance to step into the unknown. It's no wonder Pennsylvania was probably the state supplying the most military enlistees. The armed forces were a way out and, with nothing else beckoning, they seemed like the only chance to many. Sure, some were sincerely patriotic but, even so, many likely preferred the idea of a war abroad to continuing to fight the one in their own home.

On arriving home, I immediately tracked down Charlie for a powwow. That was our term for any serious conversation, as we used whatever American Indian words we knew, partly as a language of our own and partly out of respect for earlier Pennsylvania natives who understood adversity and injustice better than we ever could. Charlie suggested talking to my brother-in-law Ernie. Ernie had survived without a scratch through more than a hundred bomber raids against the Japanese. We had thrilled to his stories about the building of the Burma Road, of flying cargo to southern China over the Himalayas, and of the occasional 'ditching' in jungles infested with Japanese soldiers. His stories and bravery had won our undying respect, but more, his personality won the day. Like Buddy DeFranco, he always treated everyone as an equal, never talking down or looking down his nose at us kids.

When we told Ernie about the offer from Master Sergeant Dietz and the Air Force, he took a while to mull it over before offering, "No. Stay in school. Go to college. The war's over and there's no need to join the military now."

Almost as an afterthought, he added, "What would your friend DeFranco say?"

This was a sign that Ernie had been listening to us and knew how important we considered the advice that Buddy had given us (well, mostly me, but I'd passed every word along to Charlie). Charlie and I looked at each other and knew immediately what Buddy would have said: "Why are you asking me?"

I had to make up my own mind, follow my own bliss.

That evening, I sat down and composed a short letter to Sergeant Dietz, thanking him for his time and telling him how much I respected the opportunity to receive recognition and praise from such a fine clarinetist. I noted that Langenus had suggested schools I was considering — true to an extent, though money would still be a hurdle. A one-cent stamp and it was on its way.

A few months later, near Christmas, I sent off a Christmas card to Sergeant Dietz along with the rest of my circle of clarinet-playing pen-pals. My mother had always underlined the importance and correctness of a heartfelt hand-written thank-you card, note, or letter. The card to Dietz seemed a politeness, and one that would have little impact on my life. After all, I had no interest in the military. My study of music was finally beginning to branch out and show its ramifications. My interests were broadening, my curiosity getting keener, and my senses becoming more acute. Still, it kept open a door I had no idea I would have to look through again a short three-and-a-half years later. With the fury of the Korean War upon us, I'd be composing my third and final correspondence to Sgt. Dietz.

* * *

DeFranco had stressed the importance of taking meticulous care of my health and the repercussions of not doing so were becoming evident in watching greats like Charlie Parker, Bud Powell, Wardell Gray, and Billie Holiday, among others. If it wasn't drug addiction, it was alcoholism; if it wasn't cancer, it was cirrhosis or congestive heart failure; if it wasn't pulmonary edema, it was kidney failure. These insidious and often irreversible diseases were beginning to crop up everywhere and, in a sad and sickening manner, they seemed to be slowly but surely chipping away at our cultural wealth of seminal jazz artists. In a way, this was unsurprising. Beyond the beginnings many of these players had, the life itself wasn't the most conducive to great health. Stress was ubiquitous, and tension and toil considered commonplace. Booze, cigarettes, and drugs were standard relief from it all.

Buddy had spoken at length about psychosomatic illness — how the mind affects the body and the body affects the mind — noting that the two must work together in a perfect gestalt, like a bird and its wings or a locomotive and its steam. He would speak unabashedly about the adversities he faced: his father was blind, his mother had become schizophrenic and needed constant hospital care and confinement, his childhood asthma would still flare up, certain allergies could become quite bothersome, a tic developed in one or both eyes, the paresis in one forearm, a fine tremor in one or both hands, etc. All this would come up in discussing the idea of entropy, and he would note that a good machine produces a maximum of work with a minimum of waste. The goal was to fine-tune your machine so that healthy work would result in as little of a burden as possible.

My apprenticeship in clarinet and saxophone was more than musical. I began reading books by Sigmund Freud, though they were initially too difficult. I absorbed anatomy books, taking in the displays of the body's numerous muscles — a bit more than 650, mostly paired one on each side of the body. Joe Allard, my saxophone teacher, knew this and constantly referred to the largest exception, the diaphragm. Joe had studied some anatomy with a physician who was his New Jersey next-door neighbor. During a lesson, Joe might encircle my upper waist with his arms, pushing on the underside of this most voluminous muscle, directing my attention to taking deeper and bigger breaths. I never thought my saxophone lessons would teach me the Heimlich maneuver.

Where Allard was concerned with function and physiology, DeFranco was alerting me to psychosomatic ills — abnormal muscle tension, various types of pain with their troublesome and perplexing implications, plus proper body balance: centering and homeostasis.

My music lessons were beginning to feel like medical school. And I was finding myself an attentive pupil. Seeing an ad for a book on muscle relaxation called *You Must Relax*, I got my mother to pull out the family checkbook and sent for it. The hardbound book was just one dollar, but I may never have come across it if not for my father subscribing to the *Philadelphia Inquirer* despite our living ninety miles from the City of Brotherly Love. The book's author was Edmund Jacobson, M.D., PhD., a Harvard researcher and occasional doctor to Eleanor Roosevelt. Within less than two weeks, I was immersed in it. In fact, the book was so instrumental to me, I still have my original copy today.

The medical aspects of my learning were not solely about playing. Buddy's physical problems had captured my notice and we had discussed them at length. He'd been so frank and honest about them that it seemed only natural to seek out his advice when problems began to plague me. Since the latter part of my junior year of high school, I'd gotten mysterious chest pains. Our family doctor remained unable to pinpoint the problem, having ruled out everything cardiac. Without a diagnosis, there could be no plan for treatment. The pain would cover both sides of my chest, at times fading away and at others becoming so intense that I felt I was better off not moving. My mother had been able to solve most of my physical ills to this point, but was baffled by this one. Still, she tried everything she could: hot packs, cold packs, Ben-Gay rubs, Johnson adhesive plasters, double-layered flannel undershirts, and hot tea spiked with Christian Brothers brandy before I went to sleep. Sometimes, some of these things would work, while other times, nothing seemed to do any good at all.

I even stopped practicing clarinet and saxophone for a while, thinking I had strained something inside from blowing so much. Rest would help but only temporarily before the dull, heavy, gnawing pain would return whether or not I was playing. I couldn't be sure it made much difference. I became so frightened about what might happen, I decided to maintain my chest as motionless as possible. I wouldn't lift things, I wouldn't stretch, I avoided driving. For a couple of weeks, the fear of moving my upper body became so intense that one of my sisters would shampoo my hair.

Staying in bed was a common prescription of the day. Someone with a broken bone would be confined to a bed with a cast on for four to six weeks. New mothers would be instructed not to move and to stay bedridden for at least a few days. Anyone sick was meant to rest and nothing but — to stay still and stay in bed, immobilized. This was especially true when the illness was unknown, and stress-related diseases or conditions were little understood. What *was* known about them was all too often shrouded in silence, steeped in stigma. The idea that the mind was affecting the body was downright embarrassing. And even where accepted, no one thought a teenager could suffer owing to tension and stress. Ignorance on the subject was rampant.

Lacking such tools as Librium and Valium, 'wait and see' was a common refrain at the time, professionally known as 'intelligent neglect'. The idea was that anything done was not worth the potential negatives until one could be sure. On the other side of the fence were the doctors known for their 'common-sense' cures. What they lacked in objective scientific validity they made up for in subjective anecdotal enthusiasm: "God knows it works, I'd swear to it!"

My brother Robert, born ten years to the day before me, had died as an infant. He succumbed to influenza and pneumonia as doctors waited. Their prescription — plenty of bed rest — had proved useless. My mother and grandmother both suffered from severe arthritis, with aspirin their only medication. The aspirin was eating away their stomachs and triggering bouts of tinnitus. My mother's hands would sometimes assume a claw-like appearance with bumps over the joints. She would bear the pain until she was ready to retire for the night. My grandmother would be so bent over and unsure on her feet that she'd have to descend stairs backwards. For both, nights meant misery.

Not that my family was that unusual. Without treatments, people wore their afflictions without complaint. Infectious diseases could be expected to claim many of our young lives. Polio and other viral diseases were haunting us all. All this was part of life, lives that had an expectancy of fifty-five years. Even our president had been crippled by polio. Still, with his extreme optimism, he was the standard-bearer for all of us. If you had managed to attend the 1939 World's Fair in New York, you would have heard that optimism in his voice before you found yourself among the marvels of the age. Medical, media, and electronic devices were elaborately exhibited and we had the promise that most major diseases were soon to be eliminated. New technical gadgets would revolutionize our homes, turning them into castles. It seemed work and suffering would be terms relegated to the past.

That atmosphere of new hope had made *You Must Relax* a bestseller before I had even heard of it, promising to "tell you all about muscle tension, about how to relax, about how to prevent nervousness and upset stomach, and about how you can have more energy." These were topics suddenly at the forefront of conversations both private and public. Concurrently with the publication of his bestseller aimed at the layman, Jacobson had published *Progressive Relaxation* for doctors and other professionals with his findings more carefully laid out alongside all the supporting research.

In Jacobson's relaxation techniques, muscle control is everything. The action of tightening and loosening our muscles — contracting and stretching — is strictly a reflex action intrinsically linked to the spinal column. The brain has nothing to do with it, according to Jacobson. Much like Pavlov's dogs salivate on cue, or instinct pulls our hands away from a hot burner, we can be trained to relax without thinking. This was the muscular equivalent of hypnosis, which focused on the mind.

As Jacobson's ideas swept the nation, DeFranco was training me to play jazz without thinking, particularly when performing in public. Of course, one must think when initially learning a tune, but after reviewing it a few times you should discard the music and relegate the song to the auditory memory. Once locked in there, it will require no thinking to retrieve it — no voluntary work would be necessary. It takes trust and perseverance to accomplish this, as well as trial and error. Eventually though, we know a tune so well that we can play it in our sleep. Only then are we sufficiently free to revise it, disguise it, and jazz it up. Only then are we *truly* free to improvise.

DeFranco brought up the avant-garde American painter, Jackson Pollock. Pollock had to learn to forget his classical training so he could produce art with no remnants of conscious thought. To do this, he had to relax his mind and body completely — and to be fair, he often used alcohol as an aid. Once he had managed to engage his inner autopilot, he could improvise with paint, exploiting its endless possibilities for artistic expression. Doing so garnered him worldwide recognition.

I was sure that Buddy would not only approve of but be inspired by Jacobson's work. In his absence though, Charlie became my Jacobson confidante. We would practice together, me sitting upright in a chair as Charlie, book in hand, instructed me. After about a half-hour, we would trade places. These sessions were always conducted with classroom-style seriousness. After all, there was so much to be learned and we both had our lives and careers to worry about. I was dedicated to the practice, for my music as much as for addressing my chest pains, and Charlie caught my fever for this new approach. If nervous tension caused excessive muscle contraction, in turn causing anxiety, a sense of failing health, and an unremitting awareness of total body disequilibrium, then, by mastering Jacobson's techniques, we could turn things around, not only addressing pain but spurring ability. This meshed with the conversations I had had with both Buddy and Joe Allard. Learning Jacobson's technique required diligent practice, no less than an hour daily. Some of this practice was done lying down, some while active, some to get a proper peaceful sleep, and some directed towards stopping the mind from unnecessary thinking. My practice was bearing fruit and I was feeling more comfortable with my body. Still, I wanted Buddy's opinion — and likely approval as well. At this stage of my life, I was still somewhat unsure. I couldn't buy a new suit or shoes without first parading them past my fashion-conscious sister, Jo. Even my girlfriends were nervously presented for family approval, though I had little problem choosing them myself.

Jo had presented a number of admirers of her own to the family. One was Ritchie, who supposedly worked on the personal staff of Frank Sinatra in Las Vegas, and was also driving the bus for Tommy Dorsey. It was his connections that garnered me DeFranco's home phone number. This was, after all, a time and place heavily dependent on the favor. It was a necessary part of life, as only some owned telephones and only some automobiles. Past that, many hadn't had time or opportunity to finish high school and were forced to work full-time to support their families. Fear and ignorance kept most people from traveling even if they had the means, and older folk only rarely had learned to swim, to bowl, to read a map or timetable, to play a musical instrument, or even to fall in love. People were hurried through life, moving from their parents to full-time work or to care for a disabled family member — choice was a luxury few had. A life of one's own was nearly unheard of, and most of us lived with necessity nipping at our heels. As such, what one did have was to be shared with others in the knowledge that they likely had no opportunity to gain it on their own. Likewise, it was expected they would be willing to extend their benefits in like fashion if they could and wherever necessary. There was an essence of pragmatism in the favor and any skill, device, or connection one had was freely traded.

Ritchie was one of those who had pulled himself out, but didn't forget where he came from. If he needed help, he would simply ask, and he never refused the opportunity to reciprocate. He would drop in at our house whenever he wished, and my mother would always serve him her specialty — her homemade nut, prune-butter, and poppy seed cakes; my father would offer up a few beers and a couple of shots to go with them. As was the custom for most of our visitors, Ritchie would mention my father's homemade kielbasa, noting he wanted to buy a few pounds to take back to Nevada. My father would almost kill the sale by pulling a sixteen-inch stick of the spicy, smoked Polish sausage from the refrigerator and letting Ritchie have his fill. Kielbasa was odiferous but tasty, and more than a few were known to water at the mouth on mention of it. Pop was probably thinking that one of us kids might need a chauffeured ride to New York someday. Ritchie was 'connected', as we used to say. Dad wasn't really interested in Ritchie as a suitor to Jo, but if Ritchie knew the ropes of dealing with the Vegas mob, he would certainly know how to be godfather to the kids. Ritchie probably experienced it all the time, as everyone wanted favors from someone in his position.

One of my family's perks was our phone. Certainly others had phones, but not all did and so ours was a privilege to be shared with those in need. This was small-town Pennsylvania in the forties, and so our phone number only had three digits: 510. Today that would be an area code, something that didn't exist at the time. Most with phones had party lines demarcated by a letter following the number (*e.g.* 510d) shared by four neighbors — any could pick up their receiver and listen in on another's conversation. Numbers weren't dialed, they were requested of the local telephone operator. Special calls such as long distance, collect, or person-to-person calls would only initially be handled by her before being transferred to a second operator in the long-distance department. Our phone was private because of Pop's business and, as such, it was attached to the wall in the rear of the grocery store.

My call to DeFranco was made as a person-to-person call and, as he hadn't arrived at his hotel (in Davenport, Iowa) when I called, free. The hotel was expecting him in about two hours and the operator relayed the message to me in her most pleasant, upbeat, and professional voice. She assured me she would try the number again in two hours. As was my father's practice, I called the operator by name and schmoozed a bit before requesting the call — Pop always said, "They'll never let you down if you first give them a little bit of innocent gossip to sink their teeth into." And he was right. Operators knew everyone in town, as well as all their business.

The call had been made at nine at night, and the call back was certainly gossip-worthy — it would be 11:30 p.m.! This was something unheard of, barring an emergency. The operator was aware of my music and seemed impressed with the *idea* of Buddy, though I don't know if she had any idea who he was. As sweet as pie, the operator told me, "Stephen, I have Mr. DeFranco on the phone." She was pleasant and helpful beyond expectations. It occurred to me that she might have heard that my dad repays favors with home-made kielbasa.

Buddy sounded great. He had just arrived in Iowa and was relaxed because he didn't have a gig until the next day. He wasn't surprised in the least that I'd tracked him down, telling me he knew we'd connect somehow. I had a list of things to discuss with him, but considering the wait and the lateness of the hour (not in jazz circles, but by Lansford standards), I felt pressed for time and jumped immediately to the Jacobson book. Buddy had seen it advertised, but didn't own a copy. He listened intently as I described the idea of cultivated relaxation as best I could.

"It sounds like a non-religious type of meditation. Meditation that can be scientifically measured," he reflected.

Buddy brought up Dr. Louis Pelletiere, based in New York, who treated mainly musicians and other show business people. Pelletiere's experience with entertainers went back to his college roommate, the outstanding jazz vibes and xylophone pioneer, Red Norvo. Through Pelletiere, Buddy had been exposed to deep breathing and muscle relaxation techniques — techniques the doctor had learned in years of study with Wilhelm Reich, the world-renowned psychiatrist, psychoanalyst, and medical writer. Reich had, in turn, studied extensively with Sigmund Freud in Vienna. In 1939, Reich moved to Forest Hills, Long Island, NY, to escape Nazi Germany. Since then, he'd been confined to a non-prescribing medical practice, having no U.S. medical license. He spent his time training doctors in his methods, treating those patients who didn't require medication, and writing articles and books. Buddy brought up books of Reich's for me to check out, listing *Character Analysis* and *Listen, Little Man!* and one other about sexuality he said I should forget about until I'd made my way through the others. He also said he'd introduce me to Pelletiere, noting, "He's a man who can tie together all those loose ends for you."

Eventually I knew the conversation was coming to a close when Buddy told me to "Keep practicing, keep doing your deep breathing. Learn those Jacobson exercises. Give my best to Charlie. And keep me informed."

I quickly brought up one of the items from my list, offering, "I know a good reed maker in Koscuisko, Mississippi named Luther Hines. He's a good friend of Gustave Langenus. Give me your address, quick, and I'll send you a few boxes."

Beyond being a necessary tool of the trade, I figured boxes of clarinet reeds, about the size of a cigarette pack, were much easier to mail than sixteen-inch sticks of kielbasa.

"I guess we covered everything," Buddy offered after giving me his address.

"Well, we'll have to talk about the glissando another time," I mumbled.

I had taken enough of his time and didn't want to wear out my welcome, but my longing to talk music with Buddy must have been evident to him. He does like to talk and talking about music is what he loves second-best after playing, so he quickly came alive again. I asked him about the opening passage in George Gershwin's "Rhapsody in Blue", which I'd been working on to no avail. The piece begins in the very low register for solo clarinet with a trill. Then, a glissando is the notation for the part that follows. On piano, it's fairly easy to produce: just slide the back of your finger (usually the index) smoothly and steadily over the keys. On violin, it's still easy: just slide one finger over one string as the other hand changes the notes. Performing a glissando on clarinet however requires special skill — you need to slowly raise each finger just a slight bit from the open holes so that each note slides or smears smoothly into the next. Most clarinetists never learn how to do it, and I needed advice. I had been getting by with instructions given me by Joe Allard. Langenus, being strictly a classical player, told me he was unable to help me with this. I was managing to do it for three or four notes but no more, and Gershwin wanted the glissando extended over twenty notes. Buddy verified Joe had given me the right approach, but that it would take serious practice. He told me to think of humming into the horn as I changed the notes, in the way a dog howls — from a very low pitch to a higher one. To manage twenty notes, I should practice three at a time, then expand to four, five, ten, until I could manage the whole glissando. The thing would be to get the sound right as I went rather than trying to fix it after. At that point, it was after midnight, so I told Buddy to enjoy his supper — the one he had postponed to talk to me. No more needed to be said, so we simply said our goodbyes.

It was customary that, following a person-to-person call, one would ask the operator how much it cost. For this call, it was even more necessary as I needed to know how much to reimburse my mother and father, as was the house rule. The same operator was on duty, her voice sweet as ever. She told me the charges, adding, "You'll sleep well tonight, Stephen, with all that music in your head!"

I smiled as I thanked her and wished her a good night. *She should know*, I thought, *she probably listened to every word we said*. It occurred to me that she had just gotten the same education as I had with no effort or connections, while getting paid. Nice work if you can get it.

* * *

The day after talking to Buddy, I visited the high-school band room. Mr. Steinman was quite efficient and known for being organized. A large calendar taped to his wall alerted us to every upcoming engagement at a glance, and I saw it had been updated all the way down to the start of summer vacation. There was even a note reminding us about a yet-unscheduled band picnic to take place before we left.

In March we would be in Lebanon, PA for the All-State High School band competition, playing three concerts in three days. In April we'd be in Shillington with the Pennsylvania Eastern District Orchestra with two concerts in two days; three days after that, I was to compete in the Pennsylvania Forensic and Music League competition in Northampton — he even noted the selections I was to play: Chiaffarelli's "Polonaise" and my old favourite, "Flight of the Bumblebee". In May I would be in New York at, of all places, the Dalcroze School of Music Student Recital with accompaniment by Faye, playing Weber's "Concertino"; six days after that, I'd be at the Pennsylvania All-State Orchestra Festival in Altoona as one of ten clarinetists in a 212-piece symphony orchestra.

The day after that, though, was the date that flared out at me every time I looked at the calendar. Auditions were to be held for solo and first clarinet for various graduating ceremonies, and music students from around the state would be trying out. The song that was to be played for audition turned out to be none other than "Rhapsody in Blue". I smiled and wondered if the operator had heard Mr. Steinman talk about this and stifled a laugh when I was discussing it with Buddy. Or maybe she thought Steinman had already told us and I was just doing my homework.

Through the spring of 1947, the glissando solo in "Rhapsody in Blue" was my goal, ever out of reach. It was the movement of the fingers that eluded me. I had no problem with howling like a dog, as Buddy had told me. As boys, much of our days were spent roaming through the woods — after all, 'Pennsylvania' means 'Penn's forest', in honor of William Penn. Lansford and its slag heaps were completely surrounded by fairly dense forest lining gentle mountain slopes. Our free time was used to explore. As we'd often split up, we evolved a signal, borrowed from Johnny Weissmuller's distinctive jungle call in the *Tarzan* movies. The gang of us — along with my sheepdog, Spotty, our mascot — would often spread out and if one of us lost sight of the rest, the loud, high-pitched familiar wail would sound. It never failed.

My calling skills were mostly put to use in trying to perfect that glissando that spring. It was a busy time and there was less opportunity to go exploring. There were concerts and recitals all the time — as soon as one would finish, another would begin. As such, I developed systems and approaches to mastering whichever pieces were called for. As my mother always said, "If you want something done and done now, give it to a busy person." With my time pressed, I became more efficient using the time I had. Still, with all the musical commitments, high school was losing out on my time with graduation closing in. Out of 186 days of school that year, I missed fifty-seven full days, and was late for many others.

Still, I was enjoying the ride, even with all the work required. For the out-of-town events, we would not only get to see new places, but we'd get to stay over a few nights, well worth the practice and preparation. Steinman always looked after us. He treated us as individuals and in a first-class manner, and in turn we paid him back by working diligently at our music. A master at detail work, he would match each of us up with the ideal roommate. We would stay at the homes of local musicians, with families that were supportive of their children's musical inclinations. Some would put up two or three of us, with Steinman making sure that friends in the band stayed together. The families would feed us and took a close interest in our playing, many of them enjoying a tradition of musicality. The musician children would practice alongside us, and we would share tips and tricks. There was real camaraderie — we were all in it together, and the sentiment seemed to be shared with the musicians we met from other schools too, even when we were competing against them.

One of these musicians, Reuben Heller, became one of my most cherished friends. Reuben was stocky and blond, of German extraction but from Pennsylvania Dutch circles. His band director was Professor Augustine Weinhofer, a pleasant man if endowed with a Germanic work ethic, who knew Steinman. The two bandleaders introduced us at one of the district band weekends. Reuben played an excellent trumpet, but we had more in common than music. He was about my age and his parents slaved similarly to mine in a family-run grocery store in Nazareth, just forty miles away — close enough for similarities in the lay of the land, but far enough away to be an irritation. Sprigel, my previous bandleader, and Weinhofer, his current one, both had a lame leg and were equally pugnacious. Thanks to our respective band directors, Reuben and I would always be weekend roommates when the opportunity arose. We made good company for each other. Reuben knew and loved jazz as much as I did, and had mastered the then-popular show pieces for trumpet: "Hors Staccato", the Harry James number "Ciribiribin", "Poet and Peasant", and many others. After hearing him perform, my father advised me to imitate Reuben, notably his self-confident but laid-back stage behavior.

While deeply competitive, Reuben was no fair-weather friend. Our bond went past music, and we respected and trusted each other completely. In 1940s Pennsylvania men never hugged each other and we were no exception. We were both too shy, proper, inexperienced, and macho to express ourselves overtly, but firm handshakes and paternal pats on the shoulder made the point well enough. We encouraged each other to strive only for the best.

Reuben summed up his take once for me: "When you audition, play so absolutely good that the judges assign you and *only* you to play all of the solos and lead the section. Think big and never let fear get in the way!"

In most competitions, each of us would finish first in our class. On those occasions where we were both competing, we would discuss our playing afterwards, dissecting the lengthy auditions and preparing to play even better the next time. We supported each other and worked well together. Reuben's advice helped me prepare "Rhapsody in Blue" and that imposing glissando that stood before me like a mountain. Bit by bit, the challenge fell before my constant practice and Reuben's support.

Finally the auditions arrived. The guest conductor was one Guy Fraser Harrison, a gracious man, tall and lean with greying hair and soft yet piercing eyes. Those eyes scanned through all of us would-be members of his orchestra, and though his warmth was evident, we all knew that he was the one who would be deciding our fates. Reuben and I had no doubts, however. All the other players were excellent, but we had confidence and each other's support, and I had also been training in New York with masters. Anyone I was competing against would train with Langenus' books, but I was training with the man himself.

Within an hour, Reuben and I each walked away not only a member of Harrison's orchestra, but with a solo and the privilege of first-chair. First-chair clarinet was mine, as was "Rhapsody in Blue". All the work had been worth it.

Those piercing eyes roved like searchlights through the assembled band at each rehearsal. Harrison was straightforward and easy to follow and his conducting demonstrated that perfectly. He wasn't one for pyrotechnics or surprises — he wanted the music to speak for itself, and as such, it needed to be letter-perfect. At over six feet tall, he could easily look out and see what each of us was doing. When something wasn't right, he would correct with gentle grace, offering suggestions rather than reproaches.

Reuben was first-chair trumpet and handled both his solos and section work with relative ease. I could recognize his playing through the rest, soaring above the others and popping out high notes and difficult passages with professional precision. At one point the second-chair clarinet leaned over to me and remarked, "Let's rename him 'Gabriel' — God's divine messenger of music."

High school graduation is for every teenager a rite of passage into adulthood, and the time had finally arrived. We played ceremony after ceremony, and the gravity of the proceedings resounded fully within us. The importance of the day made each of us play our best and even reach beyond it. Each of us knew our own graduation was around the corner, if not just behind us.

The first week of June, 1947 was filled with final exams, speeches, awards, parties, dances, and everything else that could be squeezed in. It was as if the volume on life had been turned up to full — every moment was momentous and packed. All of it building up to the big night of tears, handshakes, and promises. Most of the class was already seated by the time I arrived. I took one of the few seats left and strained to see friendly faces here and there.

It was my first absence from the orchestra and I found myself caught up in their playing, hearing it from the audience. It felt like a different band, one that I was hearing for the first time, and every nuance fascinated me, being on the other side of the conductor for a change. Still, my attention snapped back to the podium the instant the band finished. Our principal, Mr. Jeffries, took the stage; Superintendent Lauer standing stern-faced behind him. Jeffries began calling out names alphabetically, and as each student stepped up onto the stage, Lauer handed their diplomas to them. After a short while I heard my friend Alyce Bokrosh's name and readied myself — having shared numerous classes, we were well aware of how our names fell in the alphabetical list of the students. My name would be next.

It wasn't.

I was stunned. Principal Jeffries was into the D's before I regained my composure. My mind began racing. I was now sure my habitual tardiness and many missed days had caught up with me. I began to feel like I'd been tricked — over years, Lauer and Jeffries had been signing off on my full-day passes to miss class and study music in New York. Jeffries had even sent me home one day to prepare some pieces so I could substitute for a booked show that had cancelled suddenly. I was wondering if they had led me astray — all this time, had they been promoting me as a star player for the school while letting my education slide more than I realized? There they stood on the stage, calmly calling out names and handing out sheepskins without so much as a hint that my name had been absent.

I sat in shock as each diploma was handed to a new graduate. Finally, Jeffries announced "Miss Agnes Zuzu" and we all knew it was over. There was brief applause, following which Jeffries formally ended the ceremony and signaled the orchestra to play the closing hymn. Each note was a knife in my stomach — I now had no idea what would happen next for me.

Suddenly Principal Jeffries broke from the practiced pageantry of the night and, with a flurry of waving arms, called for a halt to the song.

"Oh my! I seem to be late with one final bit of business," he stammered, red-faced. "I almost forgot Stephen Botek's diploma!"

You' d better believe that after all that, I swaggered up to the stage. All the doom-and-gloom that had beset me, silent in the crowd in my pain, had left and I felt light as air. There on the stage I stood, the last student with a diploma in hand. It was enough to elicit thundering applause from the students. Agnes had gotten her fair share of applause too, deserving it for having to be last so often. Reuben was smiling at me from the bandstand, while friends and family were smiling at me from the crowd, maybe all of them as relieved and charged as I had been.

Still, that near-miss counted for something. I now *knew* I had some thinking to do about my future.

George Gershwin

Born Jacob Gershowitz in Brooklyn, New York in 1898, George Gershwin worked with his older brother Ira, a lyricist, for most of his vocal and theatrical compositions. His parents had bought a piano for Ira, but it was George who took to it, inspired by a friend's violin recital. He began taking lessons at age 13; a series of teachers led him to Charles Hambitzer, who taught him technique and classical traditions, mentoring George until his death in 1918. Later George would study with composers like Rubin Goldmark and Henry Cowell.

At 15 Gershwin quit school and began working as the youngest-ever 'song plugger' in New York's Tin Pan Alley, showcasing songs on piano. The next year his first song was published, "When You Want 'Em You Can't Get 'Em, When You've Got 'Em You Don't Want 'Em", earning him $5. At 18 he was employed recording and arranging player-piano rolls, which led to some rolls of his own compositions being released. He also played for vaudeville productions.

Gershwin's compositions began to bring him success, first in 1917 with "Rialto Ripples" and then nationally with "Swanee" in 1919, which he recorded himself with the Fred Van Eps Trio, a year prior to Al Jolson's recording. From there he went on to collaborate with Ira to produce *Lady Be Good* in 1924, which introduced "Fascinating Rhythm". A lifelong friendship began with Fred and Adele Astaire, who starred in the production. A string of well-received musicals followed, including *Oh Kay!*, written about Kay Swift, a fellow composer with whom he had a ten-year affair, *Funny Face*, starring the Astaires, and *Girl Crazy*, which saw Ethel Merman introduce "I Got Rhythm". Co-writing with his brother and playwrights George S. Kaufman and Morrie Ryskind, a trilogy of political satires was produced. *Of Thee I Sing* won a Pulitzer Prize, a first for a musical.

Gershwin's first significant classical work was *Rhapsody in Blue*, which Paul Whiteman premiered in New York. Through this period, he continued to pursue lessons from composers he admired. Arnold Schoenberg refused him, noting "I would only make you a bad Schoenberg, and you're such a good Gershwin already."

Inspired by French composers, Gershwin moved to Paris to study. His idol, Maurice Ravel, was interested in jazz and impressed by Gershwin's work. When Ravel heard about Gershwin's earnings, he quipped, "How about you give me some lessons?" Emulating composers like Debussy rather than the jazz stylings expected of him earned Gershwin some criticism. While there, he wrote *An American in Paris*, a nod to the mixture of styles he was pursuing, garnering mixed reviews. Growing tired of the city, he returned to the U.S. where, in 1929, he supervised the first recording of the piece, sitting in on celesta.

Gershwin continued his studies with Joseph Schillinger as he wrote for numerous films, including *Shall We Dance* and *A Damsel in Distress*. He broadcast a number of radio programs, even hosting his own in 1934, *Music by Gershwin*, featuring originals and arrangements of other composers. He took on the show with the aim of financing his next project.

That project saw light in 1935 as George and Ira worked with DuBose Heyward and his wife, Dorothy, to adapt Heyward's novel and play *Porgy* into an opera. *Porgy and Bess* was a watershed event. Not only was it the first opera with an all-black cast (excepting minor roles), it was written with jazz sensibilities mixed with operatic influences, introduced a number of standards, and still stands as the most important American opera, despite accusations of racist stereotypes being used. Louis Armstrong and Ella Fitzgerald did a duet album of songs from the opera. "Summertime" was also a hit for Billie Holiday and Janis Joplin — it remains one of the most familiar standards today.

Gershwin's recordings are relatively few, apart from his radio broadcasts and piano rolls. He did record with Fred and Adele Astaire and Paul Whiteman. Some of the piano rolls he produced are available on Nonesuch Records' *Gershwin Plays Gershwin: The Piano Rolls*. The Columbia Jazz Band accompanied his piano rolls of *Rhapsody in Blue* for a 1975 album.

Gershwin collapsed in 1937 while working in Hollywood on the score for *The Goldwyn Follies* and died following surgery for a brain tumor. He had previously been complaining of headaches and of smelling burning rubber throughout that year. He is buried in the Westchester Hills Cemetery in Hastings-on-Hudson, New York.

Following his death, Kay Swift took it on herself to complete Gershwin's legacy, arranging and transcribing some of his work in collaboration with Ira. With his early death, the copyrights for George's works expired at the end of 2007 in most countries, though legislation in the U.S. has extended the copyright there until at least 2019, possibly as late as 2027, and his estate continues to collect publishing revenues.

The George Gershwin Theatre on Broadway in New York was named in his honor. The U.S. Library of Congress named their Gershwin Prize for Popular Song after George and Ira in 2007, with the aim of honoring those "whose career reflects lifetime achievement in promoting the genre of song as a vehicle of artistic expression and cultural understanding". Gershwin was granted an honorary Pulitzer Prize posthumously in 1998, his centennial year.

Gershwin was cited as the richest composer of all time by *The Guardian* in 2005, from estimates of his lifetime earnings. His compositions have been recorded by numerous artists, from Al Jolson and Art Tatum to Sting and Herbie Hancock, with Ella Fitzgerald working with Nelson Riddle to produce a songbook album of his compositions.

Chapter 7
All or Nothing at All

The day after graduation Charlie came by to chat.

As we were apt to do whenever we wanted to escape adult supervision, we headed off into the woods. There we were safe to speak our minds, to shake off other people's expectations, to run off at the mouth and forget politeness, and to sneak a smoke or two.

We talked about the end of school and what it meant for each of us. In large part, that was still a huge question mark hanging over each of our heads. Little direction had been decided — and none of it was to be sorted out that day. The conversation became lighter and we started joking, with swear words peppered throughout. Our focus became a Cuban cigar and a bottle of Moxie, 'the super pepper-upper soft drink'. We turned our attention to the topics of the day.

Poster-boy Charles, my old kindergarten compatriot, had gotten his sixteen-year-old girlfriend pregnant and they were marrying tomorrow. After the previous night's graduation, he had pulled me aside and told me in confidence about it — his parents and hers had gotten together and made the decision for them. Not that there was any decision to be made — it was the ways things were: a pregnancy meant a marriage, and fast!

DeFranco had been named best clarinetist by *Metronome* and would record with the other winners: Charlie Parker, Dizzy Gillespie, Lenny Tristano, and other greats.

Still, the big subject loomed and had to be addressed, bringing us back to uncertainty. The Cold War was on and Russia had the bomb, able to easily blow us to bits. Everyone our age felt this sense of impending doom, a future that was dark so soon after the promise of winning the war. One fellow clarinet player, Kenneth Zmuda, talked about both building a bomb shelter in his backyard (in the middle of Miami!), and moving to some remote corner of the globe, naming places like British Columbia, New Zealand, and the Isle of Man. This wasn't unusual for the day but Kenneth, unlike most, had follow-through. In the fifties, I visited his shelter, professionally built at a cost of fifteen thousand dollars and fully equipped in case of any kind of attack. Eventually Kenneth and his wife traveled to all three of the aforementioned locales, staying in each for long periods of time, but finally settling in a remote area of Vancouver Island, near Sidney, British Columbia, where even their address evoked isolation — Land's End Road.

There was a sense of futility, a fatalism in my conversation with Charlie as we went over the scenarios that were being passed around the country. How could we discuss the possibilities for the future when the present seemed so uncertain? Perhaps it was that threat hanging over us that made a difference in our lives — the uncertainty forcing us to live in the present, not able to shelve our dreams when all we seemed to have was the *now*.

I had purposely not enrolled in any college or music school. I didn't have a care for degrees, formal education, or anything other than performing. I didn't want to be a music student, I wanted to be a *musician*. I enjoyed playing most types of music, but jazz was the one I truly loved. Jazz, that bastard child so often shunned by established schools and institutions. Buddy had told me that to play jazz one must eat, live, and sleep it. Jazz was sitting in, hanging out, and kitchening it up with players better than yourself — 100-percent on-the-job training was required, not something any music school or university could teach you. Even if I did attend school, I would likely have to do so on a college band scholarship, and I was through playing for football games and the like. The idea of more immersion in public school music was not enticing. I found myself mocking the idea with comments like, "Those who can, do; those who can't, teach."

Charlie and I had recently seen the film adaptation of *The Fountainhead* which had played at the Victoria, a second-rate theater that was fondly known throughout Lansford as 'The Ranch House', owing to its propensity for screening Westerns. The film had captivated both of us. Charlie and I both paid little attention to movie credits, but as soon as the film ended, Charlie took the lead, bouncing down the theater steps and into the street where he carefully scrutinized the poster. He noted that Ayn Rand had written the book and suggested that we pool our money to buy a copy.

The character of Howard Roark, played by Gary Cooper in the film — were he a musician rather than an architect — could well have been Buddy DeFranco. Both were iconoclasts whose work came first out of a deep conviction in what they did, both commanded twice as much as the next contender but did so with integrity and never disappointed, both created work that will echo through time, and both professed not to believe in any god, but lived a profound and religious zeal and principles.

It was inspirational. Like Roark, like DeFranco, I was due to follow my bliss. Nothing less could be accepted. However, living under my father's roof my choices were not entirely my own: hanging over all my intentions would be an overbearing and inflexible father. Still, graduation already fading into memory, I committed to organizing a summer schedule.

I did so the next day, giving myself a few days grace, with the intention of starting my plans after the weekend. When Monday morning rolled around, I sat at the grand piano that dominated our parlor and began to practice. I'd started taking piano lessons a few weeks prior and had decided my days would be spent in practice, alternating between piano, saxophone, and clarinet. I would do some teaching and play as many gigs as possible. I would aim for a job, likely in New York, with a well-known dance band. It might take a few months, but I figured I could stay at home as long as was necessary to make it happen.

I'd barely begun practicing when I felt my father standing behind me. I stopped and turned and he roared, "If you're going to stay home, you must work — or get out!" I knew precisely how he meant that. He expected me to work six days a week in the grocery store. I wasn't even sure he would grant me the day a week I used to continue my music lessons in New York. It was a catch-22 — those lessons had taken up the most of the money I had earned, leaving me precious little savings. I couldn't afford to leave and I wouldn't get the time I needed to follow my dreams if I stayed. My father was very strict, even dictatorial, with a temper best left unprovoked. His word was law in our house — it was his way or no way. My sisters would be obsequious to avoid his wrath, our dog would run from him, and my poor mother often became the victim of his physical and psychological abuses.

Still, his unyielding attitude led him to appreciate another feisty nature in those who could stand up to him. In preparing to stand my ground and slug it out with him, I had my whole life's experience with his nature to draw on. I knew I'd have to be smart enough to back down some and let him feel he got his way, but then quickly come back with a verbal blow of my own. I'd have to look him squarely in the eyes and convince him that nothing he said or did scared me. I had grown as tall as he was and was ready to break free of the cycle of intimidation. All too long, I had submitted for the sake of family peace, but this time my life was on the line — all my dreams and plans depended on standing up to my father, and I couldn't sit by and let him 'win', as one would do with a spoiled child.

I put on my apron and went into the store. Fixing him with my gaze, the first thing I said was, "On Tuesdays I go to New York for my music lessons."

He nodded.

That was it. I had been building to this moment for years and it was over in the blink of an eye. Maybe it was that I picked my battle and he already knew my commitment to my music, but that brief exchange forever changed our dynamic. Like many significant events between father and son, the importance was in the subtleties, with most of what was communicated left unspoken. I'd staked out my own territory — where my music lessons had occurred with his blessing before, it was now understood that they were not negotiable.

The store, however, was his domain, and I had no desire to fight that. Having allowed that I *would* work there, I did so his way. If I worked eight hours while he worked ten, his body language and an intimidating silence would imply that I hadn't worked at all. The customer, of course, was always right, meaning that I was always wrong, excepting the rare occasions where I could prove otherwise.

While he would pay his workers well, with rewards and bonuses when called for, I was family. He set my salary at $5 per week, no doubt assuming this was more than fair — after all, he was also including room, board, and occasional use of both his delivery truck and his brand-new, eight-cylinder, three-hundred-plus-horsepower Super Dynaflow Buick. My mother recoiled at the idea the instant she heard about it. In full view of the whole family, she shouted, "He'll steal from you if you don't pay him more!"

She knew of course that I would never steal from the store. So did I — I wouldn't need to. She'd do it for me. It wasn't really thievery as she worked in both the store and the house and figured that half the money was rightfully hers. So anytime I was short of cash she would dip into the store register or reach into a pocket or one of her undergarments to pull out a few bills for me. I never had to ask.

My life became a whirlwind — days in the store, except Tuesdays and Sundays; Tuesdays in New York, bouncing between various lessons and learning all I could about the lives and techniques of the musicians there; giving lessons in the evenings and on Sundays; whatever gigs I could manage to land; and of course trying to squeeze in enough practice on *multiple* instruments. Buddy had often talked about how suffering built character and how many of life's adversities would later turn out to be blessings in disguise. I reminded myself of Rand's hero Roark and how he would resort to common manual labor any time his highly personal building plans were blocked or rejected. Still, the work was taking its toll — I felt trapped and somewhat depressed. It was time to phone that Philadelphia psychiatrist Buddy had told me about.

I arranged an appointment for 11:15 a.m. the following Saturday, which included convincing my father that it was necessary and that I needed to miss the day's work. The Reading Railroad, of *Monopoly* fame, ran a daily passenger service from Tamaqua, a bustling coal and railroad center just five miles from my home. I settled into a large, comfortable seat — much better than those on the train to New York — and watched the scenery whiz by for more than two hours. The trip in total was ninety miles and went to the terminus Reading Station in the heart of downtown Philadelphia, all for $4.50 round-trip.

From the station it was just a short subway ride to The Institute of the University of Pennsylvania on West 49th Street. My doctor was Joseph Hughes, M.D., a devout Catholic with seven children, who always reminded me of a military officer — strict and stern, to the point, and always highly capable.

The first session went well enough so I decided to keep coming back, though I would be depending on my father to pay for it. Later on I would learn that Hughes had indeed been a commander in the Navy.

The office was on the hospital's main floor and seemed out of place — the walls were brightly painted, expensive paintings hung there, statuary stood all over, and fine lamps everywhere kept the place bright as a summer day. I often would be shaken from the comfort of these surroundings by the thought that, just upstairs, there might be hundreds of psychotics as colorful as the office, but surrounded by white walls. Even the receptionist, Miss Otterson, a tall, thin woman with perfect posture who spoke in directives, bore a resemblance to Nurse Ratched from *One Flew Over the Cuckoo's Nest*.

I always arrived on time, but always had to wait. Miss Otterson would rattle off a prepared commentary: "The doctor has been detained upstairs. He'll be late. Fill out this questionnaire. He wants you to read this book, but please, it's only a loan. Don't dirty it."

Every session would be interrupted by a bell from the outer office, Miss Otterson's signal that our time was at an end. Dr. Hughes would immediately end the session on hearing the signal. Once he even cut me off in the middle of a sentence, proclaiming "We must end *now*!"

The sessions were $25 each, a pretty penny at the time. Still, Dr. Hughes impressed me. He had arranged a session with my mother and Josephine, not much of a surprise as I knew I had both their sympathies, but he even managed to arrange one with my *father*! My father paid for four sessions total, then, without consulting the doctor, suddenly decided he would not pay for any others. Perhaps it was because of something that happened during his session with Dr. Hughes, but no specifics were given. All-in-all, though, those four sessions helped me greatly.

Dr. Hughes' therapy was anything but subtle. He would ask many direct, blunt questions, ones you wouldn't hear from a present-day psychiatrist. And I, for my part, always offered him the whole truth and nothing but. Today my teenage sexual activities seem normal, but he was often annoyed by them. I was used to telling the same erotic stories in confession, but there I could expect absolution. Dr. Hughes offered strict judgment and no sign of forgiveness. I was to reverse this habit or that or suffer more, and the fault would be my own.

I was instructed to love my father *and* to fight him at the same time, just as Buddy had told me. Dr. Hughes encouraged me to learn what I could from the man while establishing my own life as separate. I was advised to keep working in the store, and *not* to trim my busy schedule at all. Rather, I was to write out my schedule, assigning one-hour increments to each task, each day and week charted and my life sketched out in chart form.

"Keeping this busy will help you to forget the miseries of living close to your father. Do this for the next nine to twelve months and then figure out your own way to leave home — and probably, to stay away for good. This is what maturing means. This is what growing up entails."

Dr. Hughes reminded me of what my mother had told me: "If you want a job done *now*, give it to a busy man." She was right, and however much I was doing, I was not doing enough of what I wanted.

It was time to get busy.

I started to recognize the benefits of working full-time in the family store. It was a great learning experience. I was called on to wear many hats. I handled the money, served the customers, took phone orders, delivered groceries, stocked the shelves, and kibitzed with lonely housewives happy to be away from their home for a few minutes. I also got to schmooze with the salesmen, make orders, and if someone phoned asking for the boss, well, that was me if my father wasn't around. As a member of the family, my training was for the wide view, to see the forest *and* the trees.

My dad's store was anything but typical. Long before diversification became a corporate buzzword, my father was applying it to every aspect of his business. Incorporating his prior professional experience cooking, cutting meat, farming, and merchandising, he brought every skill and idea his history brought to bear into the business. He offered home-made specialties: sauerkraut, kielbasa and other ethnic sausages, and clam chowder. He was known for fresh meats — chickens, ducks, and turkeys lived merrily and noisily in our cellar until it was time for beheading, and all freshly killed to order. Fresh seafood including salted herring and mackerel and freshly opened oysters were a staple for the town's Catholics on Fridays and fast days. My mother, much like Dad, had extensive background in restaurant work, and would prepare various ethnic delicacies which would be featured in the store, including a traditional Welsh dish known as 'faggots', a name unlikely to grace signs in any modern mom-and-pop store. Loose poppy seeds, shelled walnuts, and even cottage cheese were stocked for the area's many middle-European descendants to bake traditional fare. Coffee beans were ground fresh to order. Most unusual by today's standards, during hunting season, my dad would skin and butcher deer and small game in the garage — in November and December, when space would run out in the garage as the town's many hunters would bag many kills, large deer would be hoisted up by rope into nearby trees and secured, waiting until butchering time arrived. The cold kept the meat fresh, and as well, Dad relied on the hungry street hounds that paraded around our house (common enough for a seller of meats), tossing them meat scraps and bones. "Dogs don't climb trees, and those damn cats — well, the hounds will take care of them."

December was an entirely new business in itself. We sold Christmas trees that each morning had to be shaken free of snow in our backyard where they lay overnight and carried around to the front of the property, stood up like proud green soldiers for public viewing and purchase. Once again, the hounds were part of the picture and relied on to keep kids from stealing the trees. The scraps of meat were tossed out to win their continued patrols around our yard.

Following Christmas, there was Epiphany for those whose faith wasn't rooted in the Julian calendar. Easter brought demands for eggs — 'strictly fresh' eggs which, to be advertised as such, had to be no older than one hour by state law. There were a few fussy old housewives who would order me to go to the basement and gather a dozen 'strictly fresh' eggs. At holiday time our hen and rooster supply was enormous, so it took at most ten or fifteen minutes to gather freshly-laid warm eggs, which were then presented to the customer for an extra 5¢ per dozen on their bill.

The store stayed open six days a week from 8 a.m. until 7 p.m., with an additional two hours on Friday evenings. This left me plenty of time to pick up the many facets of the business and to begin to recognize and appreciate my father's protean talent, whatever his shortcomings.

Sundays were not a complete respite from the business. Though the store was always closed, the occasional special customer would call at our back door. Dad would reiterate that on Sundays, he sold nothing. Even so, that rule only remained on a technicality — he would 'give' people whatever they needed and they could make payment on Monday. Though he would always politely welcome them, Dad never waited on them. Instead, I would be called on to find out what was needed and fetch the items. I particularly remember one neighbor who always seemed to run out of saffron. My father would present her with a bright orange tin container maybe half the size of a can of shoe polish. The next day she would bring in the 18¢ it cost. Today that much saffron in a decorative and collectible can would likely cost $18, and I doubt anyone is allowing Sunday shoppers to pay later.

My father may have been foisting these special customers on me to avoid committing some kind of venial sin. Maybe that was one of the benefits of having a musician son — I could be counted on to take on the sin for the family. I would take the customer into the store and once they had their items, I would see them out the front door of the store. Then, alone and assured my father was at the kitchen table, I would reward myself. "Follow your bliss," I'd remind myself, and it would often lead me to the most expensive item in the store. It never took long to decide, and my

Judeo-Christian conscience never intervened. After all, if I was to take on my father's sins, it seemed only fair that I indulge in a few of my own.

As much as I was beginning to understand and appreciate the scope of my father's operations, living and working at home didn't sit right with me. I wanted to be somewhere else, but had no money to be there and no particular place in mind. My childhood Sundays had been filled with car travel to far-away places. Following Mass and a hearty breakfast, we would pile into the car and Dad would satisfy his love of driving by introducing the family to new and exciting places. Often, we would spend little time there, with most of the day from early morning to late night consumed by the drive itself. We experienced New York City long before I began traveling there on my own, also Philadelphia before my psychiatric sessions began, as well as Syracuse, Harrisburg, Atlantic City, and many other places. We visited every tourist attraction within range — Hershey Park, Dorney Park, Wildwood, Cape May. We traveled across the border to the Canadian side of Niagara Falls, we saw the New York World's Fair, we sat in Yankee Stadium. Perhaps it was this wanderlust of my father's and the wanderings it produced that empowered me to seek out what I needed far beyond the confines of Lansford. In the future, my own wanderings would take me to every corner of the globe.

At the time, though, it felt like I might never get the chance to leave. My post-graduation Sundays became a flurry of practice; I worked extra hard to make up for time lost in the grocery store through the week and under pressure to make up the time before my Tuesday lessons in New York. My artistic ambitions had not waned in the slightest, but losing thirty-five to forty hours to manual labor each week was preventing the artistic actualization I needed. With high school over, I no longer had the convenience of cavorting with classmates, and the only incidental social life I had was with the patrons of the store and my family. I could no longer depend on conversations with those who happened to be seated next to me in class or in band practice. I could no longer communicate with a note left on a locker.

I worked to fill my evenings and weekend hours with diversions — additional dance jobs, exciting women, male friends with depth. The alternative was to give in to shyness and end up meek of heart and depressed. Some of my ennui would be relieved when I'd play 'out' with the local big bands. One particular orchestra had fourteen members, with me the youngest. They played well enough and were danceable, but weren't too exciting for a jazz aficionado like me. Still, I was learning how to play in a tight-knit saxophone section. Beyond playing third alto, I garnered *all* the clarinet and sax solos — the first alto player was a superb section leader and also an accomplished clarinetist, but seemed totally inept when it came to improvising. He'd tell me, "I'll play the sweet stuff, you play what's hot."

Some of our stock arrangements included popular note-by-note solos made famous by clarinet greats such as Benny Goodman, Artie Shaw, and Woody Herman. These were so well-known that listeners would often stop dancing and mouth each note. With these listeners in mind, the band's rule was to play every solo exactly as it was recorded, Dorsey-style — though exceptions were made for blues or some more modern bebop tunes, which gave me the opportunity to fly free on solos DeFranco had recorded, among others. On these pieces, I got to exercise my spontaneity and courage, as well as my creativity.

Still, the limits were clear, and I knew in my heart that I had to move out of Lansford. Beyond the musical opportunities I wanted, I had to distance myself from my parents, particularly my father. His work ethic, while commendable, was being projected onto me and cramping my style. There was, however, no middle ground — his take on things was clear: "Work or get out."

Breaking loose was obvious as my goal, but the hows of it eluded me. I didn't know where I could go, what I would do to support myself — I had none of the answers, even as well as I knew the questions. Music was my goal, and though I felt like a big fish in a small pond in Lansford, I knew the opposite would still be true anywhere one *could* make a living playing music. To get to that level, I would need time on my own, more big band experience, and a chance to jam with jazz musicians who played better than I did, never mind a year more of saxophone lessons.

I took comfort in knowing that others had overcome much deeper adversities. Of course I knew about the horrible experiences of the black artists who had pioneered and still played jazz, but the stories I had heard first-hand were those of Buddy's.

Never ashamed of his past, he was free with all the intimate details of his life. I began to think of his name, DeFranco, as meaning 'the frank one'. When I found myself depressed, I had only to think of his blind piano-tuner father who later had to move on to filling vending machines. Buddy and his older brother Leonard, as children, would take turns escorting their father through the subways, streets, and buildings of Philadelphia, sometimes with their sister in tow — the family income was reliant on their navigation, forcing them to miss school. Often the family would have nothing for dinner but candy bars and peanuts. The strain was too much for Buddy's mother and she attempted suicide, finally asking to be institutionalized. She was diagnosed with schizophrenia which, coupled with her severe depression, was too much for her to handle without constant care. Her time in care began just a few years short of the discovery of chlorpromazine, better known as Thorazine, the anti-psychotic medication. This being long before Prozac, Paxil, Zoloft, Effexor, or any of the modern-day standard prescriptions, there was only one course of action — permanent state psychiatric hospitalization. She would spend the rest of her life there, often oblivious to visits by family and friends.

Relying on the inspiration Buddy's background offered helped me to cope with the situation I found myself in, but I still needed a road out. I wracked my brain, but nothing presented itself. Bit by bit, I knew, I would end up resigned to life in Lansford with my musical ambitions stifled if I didn't make some kind of move, and *fast*.

* * *

As June moved into July, Langenus asked me if I was going to take a summer break. The Dalcroze School would close until September, leaving me the choice of stopping my lessons until then or continuing at Langenus' home in Commack on Long Island. We worked out the logistics first of all — I would need to take the three-hour train trip from Pennsylvania to Penn Station, then the Long Island Railroad to Jamaica and change for North Port (another forty-five minutes). He would meet me there and drive me to his home for a one-hour lesson before driving me back.

It was another strike at my plans. Stopping the lessons would mean losing my time in New York and being yoked to the family store on Tuesdays. It would also mean losing momentum, and I had already ceded much ground from my original plan. Continuing with Langenus would lose me much of the freedom of my time in New York and the benefits that offered me. Still, my music was more important than living the lifestyle, and loyalty came first. Adults like him were still looked up to and given the utmost respect, expected to be listened to by any young man or woman. There was reverence for their guidance and there was privilege in being allowed to apprentice at their side. Moreover, the *idea* of the elder was different then — fifty or sixty years old was thought to be ancient, so there was no point in waiting to learn from them at a later date. If we wanted to fill their shoes, we had to take on their knowledge. As well, this was *Langenus* — a name respected by clarinet players of any stripe, classical, jazz, or otherwise.

It didn't take me long to decide.

The lessons at his home showed me another side of Langenus. He would pick me up in his green and tan four-door 1947 Pontiac. His wife would greet me cordially and serve me a large glass of milk and some homemade cookies after I made a trip to the bathroom. Once I'd finished eating, the lesson would begin and, without the trappings of the Dalcroze School, seemed much more intimate. After the hour was over, the ritual of bathroom, cookies, and milk would be repeated before I was driven back to my train.

At one of these lessons, Langenus introduced me to his houseguest, one George Bundy. Bundy was related through marriage to the famous Henri Selmer family. Selmer made state-of-the-art musical instruments and was known worldwide. Their clarinets and saxophones were especially lauded. My own horn was one of Selmer's less expensive models, very good but not the best, and not coincidentally the *Bundy* clarinet. George, then in his middle twenties, also played clarinet, so Langenus decided we should spend the hour playing Beethoven trios.

George thoroughly enjoyed himself, thanking me repeatedly for sharing my lesson time with him. He asked to accompany us on our drive to the train station. As I was boarding, he hurriedly scribbled something on the back of his calling card.

"You're certainly a fine clarinetist, so think of moving up to Selmer's best model. Look up this man at this New York music store. He'll give you a huge professional discount. Good luck!"

I had been told I was ready to move up past my Bundy *by* a Bundy!

On the trip back to Penn Station, I wondered what Buddy would make of that, then thought about those two constant influences on my playing. Though I often wanted them to, Langenus and DeFranco never met. Gustave was almost three times Buddy's age. His typically Teutonic character, born of his time growing up in Belgium, was stern, serious, and pensive. His thinking was predominately left-hemisphere, suited well to the type of music he chose to play. The two men mentoring me differed like night and day in their approaches and performance styles. Still, if they had ever met, their obvious differences would be quickly and politely acknowledged before moving on to what was absolutely uniform to both — their innate, unconditional love for the clarinet and the work ethic that resulted from it. I had seen the separation between the two before, but now that I was glimpsing Langenus' life, I was starting to understand the commonalities between them.

Those commonalities were the lynchpins of what I wanted from my life — dedication to my instrument and to my music. Though each had their own style and direction, both respected any serious-minded clarinet player. Both would have seen the dedication the other held to their craft. Both would have recognized the warmth in the other, even if Langenus held his beneath the surface and Buddy wore his openly on his sleeve.

Langenus came from the colder, more reserved world of the classics where tradition was king and standards were set in stone. While I greatly respected his knowledge and ability, I never looked to him as I did to Buddy — as a teacher of *life*, not just music. Lessons with Langenus were direct and professional. We rarely ever passed the official sixty-minute mark; he was never late and was already there with his clarinet assembled and at the ready. While never condescending or judgmental, he still had that professional air and expected superior results. Still, he never demanded anything of me that he couldn't offer himself, the old master. He would flawlessly play through a difficult passage after telling me to "try to make it sing like this."

Gustave knew that I needed to get away from home and he was doing everything in his power to help. College was the standard solution for those looking to get out from under their parents' thumbs. However, there was no degree in jazz studies. However respected the music was in other countries, no American school offered any training in our indigenous art form. Even the respected four-year degree schools like Eastman, Juilliard, and Ithaca College could offer me at best a clarinet major with a minor in public-school teaching. None of them would offer me the opportunity to learn what I wanted, though — the big bands there would be symphonic ones and football marching bands. A music teaching job would be a nice thing to fall back on, but the training wouldn't give me the shot at my first choice — a life in jazz.

One day, Gustave spied an ad in a trade magazine for a clarinet scholarship and spent weeks helping me prepare the required audition selections. I didn't really think much of it at the time, as I had always been preparing for this performance or that forensic competition. It was only on leaving the audition that it hit me how much we had worked for a mere ten minutes of playing.

The audition was at the prestigious Juilliard School on a sunny spring Saturday. The cramped quarters of the music school surprised me, as I'd played in high school auditoriums which were larger, and I remembered hearing complaints that there weren't enough practice rooms, that there were no dormitories, and that the IRT line in front of the school could be heard regularly inside. I performed in front of a faculty clarinet teacher with piano accompaniment they supplied. He was polite but very matter-of-fact, even introducing himself hurriedly so as to move on to the audition. It went well enough — we began on time, the piano accompanist played well, and I was satisfied with my performance. The teacher, however, seemed bored and inconvenienced. I may have put more into my audition had I realized how much Langenus had done to get me there, but I was distracted by complaints I'd heard about the school and had started to realize that, as much as I loved New York, I had problems with it too, pregnant as it was with noise and pollution. That considered, I can recognize now that I went in with the wrong attitude. Had I been a bit less cocky, I might have seen what an opportunity was laid there in front of me.

I received a letter of rejection from Juilliard the next week — they had awarded the scholarship to another young clarinetist. I was still welcome to apply for regular admission, but would be awarded no money. In my circumstances, that meant simply that that door was closed to me. I was somewhat let down by the rejection, but still relieved, having no real inclination to live in New York, as much as I loved its opportunities and trappings. Looking back, I was in no way ready to live there full-time.

Not long after, Jo was in the city for her accordion lesson. She was browsing through Manny's music store where a well-dressed, middle-aged gentleman was trying hard to pick her up. Jo was used to holding her own with men, and unabashed, she took charge of the conversation, only to find out he was a clarinet player who taught at Juilliard — the same man who had auditioned me and turned me down. "Too bad I hadn't met you sooner," he offered. "I could have done more to help your brother with that scholarship."

In light of that encounter, it became a running joke that Jo should always be present at any of my future auditions.

Gustave was rather calm about the rejection, muttering a few words of condolence and simply raising his eyebrows a bit, not appearing too sad or surprised. I saw his mind shift gears and a slight smile spread easily across his lips. He ceremoniously announced, "The Eastman School of Music in Rochester!"

He went on to sing the praises of the school, noting its state-of-the-art facilities and virtually unlimited financial resources. As part of his philanthropic efforts, George Eastman had founded the school, an addition to a long list of other legendary institutions: the University of Rochester, including medical and dental schools, a section of MIT in Boston, parts of Alabama's Tuskegee Institute, and Rochester's Eastman Theatre, renowned for its acoustical properties and considered by many to be the best in the world in that regard. A renaissance man, Eastman was not only highly skilled in the photographic arts, he was well-versed in banking, architecture, agriculture, and fine arts. The ubiquitous Eastman Kodak camera had helped build him to billionaire status, and I was no stranger to it, having received a classic 'Baby Brownie' for my twelfth birthday from my mother.

Gustave had spent time in Rochester and liked what he had seen, letting me know I would get more than my money's worth if I studied there. There was no scholarship, though, so the next order of business would be to sell the idea of Eastman to my father — after all, he and only he could allocate the family money. As often as Mom would say that half the money was hers, she would have to beg for her share like the rest of us — which was perhaps why she learned tricks like dipping into the store register when she was short. Even if I would have had the gall to ask that of her, there was no way it could finance my education. All of her secret stashes of cash together would hardly make a dent in the couple of thousand dollars I would need for tuition and living expenses. No, I would have to go straight to Dad.

I knew the best approach would be to focus on the positives in an assertive manner, presenting it like a business proposal. He rarely turned down a good business venture, even accepting playing engagements for both my sisters and myself — mostly pro bono ones. We would hear him on the phone saying, "Yes, they'll be there. Thank you for telephoning." Only after that would he inform us of where and when we would be playing.

I turned to applying what I *did* know from the many conversations I'd had with Buddy to the question of dealing with my father. I knew he'd tell me to stand up straight and tall. I should accept my fear, but not let it overpower me. I shouldn't worry, as anxiety would just cause me to cower. I should love my father, and at the same time fight him. I should assert myself.

I had to land that first punch — to be streetwise, avoid being aggressive, and wait for the right moment. This was like a jazz solo. I had to know my basic game plan — the key, the tune, the tempo. That, and my opening had to be rehearsed well to give me that strong entrance so that I would be comfortable enough to improvise. Then, I could let up some, lay back a bit, and depend on my spontaneity and creativity.

I decided to talk straight to my father, but to do so, I wanted to have something concrete to talk about. I got the Eastman School application, mailed it in, and waited for the reply. I had never set foot in Rochester, and so studied it to be able to put forward what it offered, this city that was bitterly cold in winter, yet somehow called the 'Flower City.' Considering George Eastman, I nicknamed it 'Camera City.' The Lehigh Valley Railroad line I used for travel to New York City snaked north about 250 miles and could take me straight to downtown Rochester.

It wasn't long before a brightly-colored oversize envelope arrived with the all-too-telling return address. My mother had been told about my decision and plans, and watched intently as I opened it. She cheered and hugged me as we found out I had been accepted. I was still in shock — there was no mention of a pre-acceptance audition, no conditions whatsoever requiring me to prove my ability. I just had to show up and begin classes — it was a done deal.

I wanted Gustave to know and know immediately — after all, he was the one who had sparked the idea of Eastman for me. We never communicated by phone and, as such, I didn't even have his number. It was our practice when we needed to get information across fast — to cancel a lesson or report illness or a snowstorm — to send a telegram or a special delivery letter. I wrote out a quick letter and sent it special delivery, knowing he'd receive it in two days. A few days later, when I reported for my regular lesson, he greeted me with a broad smile, the letter in hand. He told me was happy and proud of me.

"You'll learn a lot there and you'll certainly get your money's worth."

Gustave was carrying a second envelope, as well as my letter. This one was larger. From it, he pulled out a nicely-framed 8x10 photo of himself — something I had requested of him a few weeks prior. He signed it *To Stephen, a talented musician. Your friend, Gustave Langenus.*

The photograph was worth a thousand words. The picture showed him serious and stern, making the inscription even more potent. I smiled through the entire lesson. It hampered my playing somewhat, but Gustave didn't make any mention of it. He was smiling, too.

The drive from Gustave's house to the train station was filled with more support and accolades as well as thank-you's on my part, though all polite and reserved, as well as often indirect. That was the surface dynamic, the tip of the iceberg we both knew promised there was much more beneath the surface.

Through the rest of the day in New York and the train trip home, I was like some criminal mastermind from the movies. Every moment was dedicated to my big plan. I didn't want to wait, but I knew that late in the evening was not the best time. Instead, I decided to tell Dad the next morning at work. If he wasn't receptive, I would have him in the confines of the store for the entire day to keep trying to convince him. I kept my silence once I arrived at the train station, and through to the next morning.

I told my mother in the kitchen, early in the morning. She was impressed and weighed each argument carefully, including the picture, which she looked at as if she had X-ray eyes. She repeated back everything I had learned about Rochester, and then took a moment for reflection before weighing in.

A sly smile came over her face. "Your father doesn't stand a chance. In fact, go get him now. He's in the bathroom shaving. No man ever says 'no' when they have their pants down and there's a sharp straight razor floating around the room!"

We both laughed, but she motioned to me to head up to the bathroom — she was serious. I turned and went, my stomach dancing, but I was resolved not to show it.

It went exactly as my mother said. He didn't say no to anything, only adding his own conditions: I was to work in the store full-time through the summer until I left for school in September, and every penny spent on my education would be recorded in a ledger, being a loan to be paid back. I ensured I would still have my days off work for my lessons, and Dad offered that the loan was to be paid back "someday" — no time limit was established.

I was ecstatic! Not only did I know I would be pursuing my music more seriously, I would finally be leaving home in five short months, hopefully for good. On top of the rest of my already packed schedule, I started to get ready for the move to Rochester.

Over those remaining months, I began to engage my mother in more open conversations, keeping her apprised of my life and feeling ready for an adult relationship with her. I spent every moment I could playing with my mom's dog, Rexy (my dog Spotty had died ten months prior). Gigs with my sister Jo became celebrations, as we wouldn't be playing together again regularly.

And then there was Faye.

* * *

Faye and I had a long history. Not only were we the same age, with birthdays just a few days apart, we had shared music from when we first met in kindergarten through playing together in the public school senior band. Faye had become my accompanist as well as one of Lansford's best concert soloists. Having decided to put more time into my piano skills, which would be necessary for Eastman, I began taking formal lessons from Faye.

I should have begun piano lessons years earlier. Just as we had learned Latin in high school, and it was the foundation of the languages we knew, piano served a similar role in music. For one, most songwriters worked with and for the piano for basic melodies. It seemed only right that any serious-minded young musician should be encouraged to study piano as well as their chosen instrument. I was well aware of the utility of knowing the instrument well, even if I wasn't planning to play it professionally. With music school on the horizon, it would be an invaluable skill. Faye's skills and ability to delineate the subtleties of the instrument to me gave me a new appreciation for her. I'd seen her as a peer and colleague before, but now she was in the position of being a mentor to me, though I didn't recognize it at the time.

I had been used to seeing my mentors as recognized greats, with other considerations granted by the age we lived in. I had no qualms about learning from black musicians, and in fact, many demonstrated the heights and skills I aspired to, but there was the understanding that we would have less in common — a vicious cycle that perpetuated the separation of the races. It wasn't until later that I would fully recognize all that Faye taught me — my bias had kept me from seeing her as a mentor owing to her gender, as well as her age, never mind her size and shape. She was no Langenus, no DeFranco, not a name I could see in magazines or mention at the music stores in New York. Still, she gave me insight into music and my craft.

There was also a special thrill to taking lessons at her house, since her parents had purchased the old Dorsey home at 227 East Abbott Street which is still there and a few years back sold for just $19,000. Knowing that history made the place resonate with the idea of Tommy and Jimmy practicing, with their father leading them through numbers. As well, after thirteen years of music together, Faye and I had no school band and no shared playing engagements — our communications were now totally of our own choosing. Maybe it was that shift in dynamics between us, but for the first time I began to notice her and find her sexually attractive.

Faye was short and her looks were pleasant, if ordinary — she was the type of person easily overlooked in a crowd. There was one notable exception to this — her ample bosom. By far, she was the best-endowed girl in all of our high school. She was known as Miss Sweater Girl for her predilection for tight-fitting, brightly-colored sweaters and the predilection of the boys in the school to notice them. A sweater, after all, could at least be discussed publicly. Most of my young male friends were sex-starved and never failed to whisper something when Faye entered a room.

We had worked together with excellent results for years. It was high time we discovered each other behind our instruments. Faye was a perfect dichotomy, though — sweet, permissive, and pleasantly flirty when away from her instrument, but strict, demanding, and unforgiving when seated at the piano.

I had my own students, teaching clarinet. One was Natalie Rubart, through which I met her brother, Art, who began taking a very keen interest in my playing and my future in music. Never one to sit on the sidelines, Art became an unpaid promoter, manager, and personal agent. New students began to flock to me at his suggestion, regional bandleaders started inviting me to audition, and musicians would stop me in the streets and inquire about playing together — for the most part, these last were female, and I could tell they'd been playing a different tune with Art.

My mother had a smooth routine for handling the chickens in our basement. When one needed to be readied for a customer's cooking pot she would coax the unsuspecting bird towards her, calmly pick it up, and, soothing it with a litany of *sotto voce* sounds, carefully and securely position the hen's head on the chopping block. The rest was history.

Art's routine with women was very much similar, if ending a bit less bloody. His girlfriends might not lose their heads, but would lose things their mothers taught them to save for marriage. The extrovert's extrovert, he was always in charge and getting just what he wanted.

I never asked why Art jumped on my bandwagon so suddenly. There were no hidden agendas I could see, no unreasonable demands, and he asked for no money. Moreover, he didn't *need* any, as his dad was a successful pharmacist. He seemed to take pleasure in the idea of making me over, repackaging and liberating that part of me he thought was too strict, dutiful, and overly controlled. I had no qualms about that — while I needed the dedication to pursue my music, I also needed to loosen up to be a musician, or at least a *jazz* musician. DeFranco had often spoken to me about "reinventing oneself", and claimed to have done exactly that at numerous times through his long and illustrious career. I knew of this precedent from a man I trusted, and my life was about to change, leaving Lansford, so I had nothing to lose and everything to gain by trusting Art to widen my horizons.

Any shy adolescent could use a friend like Art. He would introduce me to private nightclubs that he could always seem to either just barge into or buy our entry to. He always had spending money, as well as full access to his father's car, a fine-looking, four-door, souped-up Packard. His connections included people with summer cottages in the nearby Pocono Mountains, and got us into parties on the lake with live music and numerous new young women. He decided I needed to see Rochester before going up for school, and so took me on a hitchhiking trip, found me a room for September, and threw in a side trip to Toronto via Niagara Falls. He even took me on a quick scouting tour of Rochester, but we spent our time looking mostly at the girls. All of this was in style, owing to Art's endless charm — one trucker took us forty miles out of his way, and one elderly couple invited us to a home-cooked supper.

As the summer passed, my piano skills were improving and Faye and I were getting closer. It hadn't taken me long to notice more than her sweaters, but with so much on my plate, we saw little of each other outside of lessons. Our schedules rarely aligned, with her free time coming mostly when I was working in the store or out of town to see one of my other teachers, including Joe Allard.

On a beautiful August day, perfect convertible weather, I was due for my final saxophone lesson with Joe Allard. My sister Jo had also scheduled a lesson in New York that day, so we decided to drive. Not the least reason was the excuse for a road trip in her shiny new 1948 Oldsmobile 88 — she was thrilled with her new investment, and I was more than a little impressed. State-of-the-art, it had a Hydra-Matic four-speed *automatic* transmission with no clutch pedal to bother with and no worries about stripping or grinding of gears, and it could go from 0 to 60 mph in just 12.2 seconds. We put the top down and aimed the car towards New York City. I was the model little brother, in large part because I was hoping for a chance to drive on the return trip.

My last lesson with Joe included all he could sandwich into the time we had, knowing it was our last opportunity. Still, it ended promptly at 1 o'clock. Joe wished me luck in Rochester and told me to keep in touch. It wasn't time for farewells yet, though, as a glance out the window told me that Jo was waiting. She sat in the car with the top down, wearing large sunglasses and a bright green scarf that matched the color of the car. Joe's eyes lit up.

"Is that your sister? Oh my, I'll have to say goodbye to her as well!"

Joe had a passion for cars I knew he would have to indulge, though I was unsure what to do if that passion extended to my sister. Sure enough, though, his primary focus was on the car as soon as we reached the street. He rattled off facts like its top speed, horsepower, and mileage.

"Does it handle well?" he asked with a grin, knowing full well what the answer was.

Jo had a passion for highly intelligent men as well as for cars, and wasted no time.

"Get in. I'll take you for lunch."

Joe agreed, but put forward a condition — he wanted to drive. Josephine smiled and nodded approval before sliding over to the passenger side. Joe jumped in and shouted, "Luchow's, here we come!"

He drove like a pro, but a pro taxi driver, dodging and weaving his way skillfully through midtown traffic. When we pulled up to Luchow's on West Fourteenth Street, the doorman knew Joe by name and ordered the valet to take special care with "Mr. Allard's car" and not to forget to put the top up.

Joe knew the menu inside out and ordered for the three of us. As we waited, a strolling oompah band made its way to our table, playing traditional German songs. They gave us more of a show than anyone else, likely owing to three musicians showing more interest than the average patrons — Joe was, of course, focused on the alto saxophonist. They stayed by our table through the finish of the song, and we burst into applause, each throwing a dollar tip into the upright tuba.

Joe turned to me, all business as they walked away.

"Steve, did you notice how much unnecessary lip pressure the sax man used to play those high notes?"

I hadn't.

Joe broke off a small piece of bread, about fingertip size, rolled his bottom lip gently over his teeth and placed the bread firmly but gently between both lips. Then he hummed, arpeggio style, 'singing' his way upward about two-and-a-half to three octaves — the bread never moved and his lips and facial muscles never changed their tension. Jo was grinning and nodding — not her instrument, but she could recognize the skill and finally had a direct idea of what I was getting from working with Joe.

"See," Joe said, removing the bread from his mouth. "It's just like having the sax mouthpiece between your lips."

Jo and I sat there, mouths open, taking in every word as he noted the throat will vary from low note to high and the diaphragm must always support the column of air. He expanded on the importance of the diaphragm, noting to keep it firm and fully expanded, even to produce those high harmonics beyond the normal range of the horn's two-and-a-half octaves. Minimal lip pressure but maximum diaphragmatic support — that would produce the best sound and reduce the work necessary to get it. The oompah player was wasting a lot of effort to no good end — too bad he didn't stay around for a *real* tip.

The lesson continued through the meal, with Jo making comments about music and approach more than specifics, but enthralled at Joe's assuredness and obvious discipline. It didn't hurt when he got passionate either, talking about singing into the sax like Caruso singing to his lover. I can't remember what we ate, but the lesson has always stuck with me. Feeling like I'd gotten an extra lesson for free, I took care of the bill when it arrived.

I didn't get to drive on the way home, but that only freed me up to play and try out what Joe had taught me.

That lesson was another door closing, one of many. There was a final lesson with Langenus, there were gigs that — it being August — were sure to be my last at that particular venue. Customers at the store were aware I would be leaving and starting to treat each visit as perhaps the last time they'd see me.

* * *

1948 was a happy year in the United States. World War II was long over and our 'boys' had come marching home, excepting those brave heroes buried on foreign soil whose sacrifice was not to be taken for granted. For those who made it home the G.I. Bill was providing ample money for college and mortgage loans were virtually interest-free. A quick signature on an honorable discharge paper would guarantee G.I. Joe and his new bride a brand-new private home with all the modern amenities in resurrected communities like Levittown, Long Island. Peace and prosperity seemed ubiquitous, even though the Russian bear was making noises. Soviet saber-rattling was heard everywhere — they claimed to have the hydrogen bomb, announced that they would soon reach outer space, and were openly promoting Communist doctrine in Eastern Europe. The American public had thought we were done with megalomaniacs like Hitler, Tojo, and Mussolini, but we had heard little of Stalin's atrocities — usually the man had been presented in a positive light, with the image of him seated beside renowned peacemakers such as Churchill and Franklin D. Roosevelt burned into our minds.

What had seemed like a golden age finally delivered faded in the fear of the Cold War. Helplessness was replacing our hope for the future. Fear for our safety and that of our country was again casting its shadow on us. We would soon know that Russian missiles were out there and maybe capable of reaching our shores. A slight increase in self-inflicted deaths was recorded nationally, particularly among adolescents and young adults — helplessness coupled with hopelessness often leads to suicide. Still, we found hope in Missouri-born Harry S Truman. This self-made man, president from 1945 to 1953, was not one to be easily scared. His cry "the buck stops here" was heard not only as a call for better organization and administration in Washington, but for the world. With honest and forthright even-handedness, he sent Stalin a message for all of us that there were limits to be respected.

All the posturing aside, the fears of the era weren't enough to weigh things down completely. America felt she had earned her rewards and that it was high time for some 'R&R'. Prosperity was at its peak, and considering what had gone before, it seemed ungrateful not to partake. Progressive jazz was leaving the idea of limits behind, new automobiles were longer, sleeker, and speedier — far from the frugality we accepted through the war years. The car culture was now central to the nation's consciousness, not relegated to being the province of the rich. The old names like Buick, Cadillac, Ford, Oldsmobile, Chevrolet, Dodge, Packard, and Studebaker couldn't keep it all to themselves and had to share the stage with new entrepreneurial rivals like Hudson, Kaiser-Frazer, Nash, Willys, and Tucker, whose unique designs featured a trunk in front, with a rear-mounted three-hundred-plus horsepower engine and triple headlights, the third rotating when you turned a corner. Even Hitler's brainchild, the Volkswagen Beetle, had been resurrected with great success in Great Britain and was soon to hit American shores. The public was quick to forget, now that Adolf was safely buried under the rubble of a battered Berlin.

Even with the opening strains of the Cold War sounding, Americans knew we were a country on the move and what we did would resound throughout the world — at least the non-Communist portion.

Though I had my qualms and concerns and conversations about the Soviet threat, my days were focused on productivity and trying to enjoy every last drop of my youth that I could. Come September, I would be off to Rochester, leaving behind my childhood home along with my family and friends, few of them really grasping what that meant — Lansford was to be resigned to my past, not out of reach of the occasional visit, but certainly not where I would hang my hat in the years to come.

One thing that had been left undone was to get together with Charlie and say our farewells before I left. As my time was spent in the store, practicing, or playing gigs, Charlie and I hadn't seen each other all summer, and he phoned to suggest we get together when my time was getting short. While I had been focusing on my music and my future, lost in the possibilities the age seemed to offer, Charlie, long a history buff and prone to depression, had gone the other direction. The rumors were that he no longer sounded as sharp as he used to, his drumming having suffered as he concentrated on the state of world affairs.

When we met it was just before the Labor Day weekend and I had little time left in Lansford. I expected we would talk about music as we usually did, but Charlie had theories to lay out for me. He postulated big-time future problems and listed off events that year: the assassination of Mohandas Gandhi, the end of the British mandate in Palestine and the formation of the state of Israel, the war between Israel and the Arab League, Yugoslavia under Marshal Tito proclaiming itself independent of Soviet control, the Berlin blockade by the Soviets and the airlifts to the West, and North Korea proclaiming a People's Democratic Republic under Kim Il-Sung. I listened intently, and knew that Charlie was right but failed to see how worrying would do anything. My priority was my life as a musician and all these things seemed so far off, distant in more ways than one.

"Charlie," I told him. "My cold war will be with the Rochester winter, and likely there'll be battles with a slew of excellent young clarinetists. I have to keep my mind unblocked, unlike Berlin — I don't have time for politics! Just keep playing. It's the music that matters most."

Joe Allard

Born in Lowell, Massachusetts in 1910 into a musical family of French-Canadian origin who ran a grocery store and lived above it, Joe Allard was encouraged by his violinist older brother to learn clarinet and bought his first horn at the age of nine. With a minimal amount of training, he joined his brother's Dixieland band.

While Allard attended Catholic school, the public Lowell High School arranged for him to join their band, where he became a featured soloist. Intending to form a dance band, he bought his first saxophone. The band, Joe Allard's Syncopators, built a local following and Allard decided to pursue music as a career. His earlier desire to be a priest, along with his ability to speak French, had church officials looking to send him to Quebec to study for the priesthood until his mother intervened to keep him in Massachusetts. When he told his family that he wanted to be a musician, he met with enough resistance that he decided to pursue accountancy instead, but a short spell in business classes was enough to convince him to focus on his musical career.

Allard joined Frank Roane's Pennsylvanians, a dance band that was offered regular work in town and needed to replace members who wouldn't make the move. At age 16 he began studying under Gaston Hamelin, principal clarinetist of the Boston Symphony Orchestra. The lessons were in French and Allard recalls that Hamelin would correct his language as much as his musicianship. Hamelin demanded that he give up the saxophone, so Allard pretended to comply while continuing to play dance jobs as a saxophonist. Following high school, Allard enrolled at the New England Conservatory of Music but, on Hamelin's advice, soon left to pursue freelance work.

Red Nichols and His Five Pennies were touring when their lead alto sax player came down with ptomaine poisoning. Allard was quickly recruited and toured with the band for the better part of a year. The band had an extended run in Chicago planned, but Nichols convinced Allard to stay on in New York and seek out higher-paying jobs. Allard found work with small dance bands and playing for radio broadcasts. After some time living in the Wentworth Hotel, which doubled as a whorehouse, he was offered living space in Lyle Bowen's studio, a hotbed of active jazz across from Radio City Music Hall, over Whelan's Drug Store. Eventually he started his own studio in the building.

Allard had a wide and varied career. He was part of the orchestra for the entire 22-year run of *Dupont Cavalcade of America*, which moved from radio to television. Owing to his experience with *Calvacade*, he was first saxophonist, as well as a bass clarinetist, in the NBC Orchestra under Arturo Toscanini. He remains the only bass clarinetist to have played in the orchestra not to be fired by Toscanini. He was tapped to be co-principal clarinetist of the Cities

Service Band of America, formed from the various NBC orchestras, as well as the Symphony of the Air, formed to continue independently after the NBC Symphony was disbanded. For both Glenn Miller's and Benny Goodman's orchestras he acted as coach for the saxophone section. He worked with Red Norvo's orchestra and played for the Bell Telephone Hour radio and television shows from their debut in 1940 until they ended in 1965. During this time he moved back to Lowell, then to Manhasset, NY, and to Bergenfield and Tenafly, NJ, where he finally settled with his wife, Anne, and their children.

Allard dedicated the rest of his career to teaching, moving to a studio in Carnegie Hall when the space over Whelan's was sold. Most consistently, he taught saxophone and clarinet at The Juilliard School from 1956 to 1984. Over the years he also taught at the Manhattan School of Music, Mannes College of Music, and at the New England Conservatory of Music, which he had previously attended as a student. He also taught at his various homes, including his retirement home in Haverhill, Massachusetts.

Chapter 8
September Song

The trip to Rochester took about five-and-a-half hours — extremely long ones.

My mother had insisted that my father drive me up to Eastman, likely in the hopes that the two of us would finally get to know each other better. This seemed like a shot in the dark, as she had been trying to get to know him ever since they married, with relatively little success over the years. A car trip could hardly cover the necessary ground. However, my mother knew me well, and I think she realized this might be a last chance, with my future lying far outside the boundaries of Lansford.

I knew that, and I believe Dad did as well, but it didn't make much of a difference. The trip was a solemn one, with neither of us knowing exactly what to talk about and both too schooled in our silence around the other to make the leap to that father-son conversation so mythologized in American culture. Car trips had been a longstanding family tradition, and the conversation that did happen was pragmatic at best — pointing out landmarks, gas stations, and other cars, making comments about driving, guesstimating our arrival time, and such. This was similar to the trips we took when I was a child, but now spotting something interesting on the side of the road or a fancy car was devoid of that innocent joy and just a way to avoid discussing what *needed* to be said. I was going off on my own to be a man, but we were still caught in the mechanics of my youth. For my part, it felt too late to change things, with my focus now on my future.

So there we were, father and son together, I was leaving home, and there was nothing to say.

Though the trip seemed long, a glance at our watches confirmed we had made good time and we congratulated ourselves on that as we reached the city limits. The distance between us faded somewhat then — still there, but just not as prominent as my new city presented itself. Navigating was Dad's job and, out of habit, I kept my silence until he asked me if I was familiar with the area. Looking back, that may have been an uncharacteristic handing down of duty, but I had no idea where we were and had to say so.

We found the place easily enough though. After winding around, we ended up mere blocks behind the school at 25 Joslyn Place. It was a three-storey single-frame house — nondescript, but welcoming enough. I had waited too long to find a suitable room and was forced to settle for what was left — a room in a boarding house for single males. It was sheer luck that it was as close as it was but on first sight I knew it wasn't for me and I would have to move on, first chance I got. It had the feel of a third-class roadside motel — somewhere one might stay out of necessity, but no place you would ever feel at home.

A friendly older Italian woman answered the door in a thick accent, offering her name, Mrs. Tocatta, and a warm smile. She showed us in and walked us up two flights and to the far corner of the house where my room was. By the time we had reached the room, we had bounced my bags against enough stairs and corners that Dad and I both felt justified enough to let them drop to the floor, garnering a slight smile from each of us as they hit. Either an optimist or a saleswoman at heart, she offered that here, I'd get peace and quiet away from the other boarders — there were ten others and I would be the youngest.

"You'll meet them all at dinner," she assured me. "And dinner will be ready in about an hour. It's always served at 6 p.m." She left us to settle in.

The room itself was fairly small, with two windows and a single light bulb dangling on a cord overhead. I looked around slowly, planning where my things would go, especially glad that my mother had pushed me to take my trusty study lamp and extra 100-watt bulbs, as well as my old sheepskin throw rug. My dad had no such planning to do and was finished looking the place over in no time.

He closed the door and told me in a low voice, "It sure as hell isn't the Statler Hotel, but it'll have to do until you get to know your way around Rochester."

Being my first time away from home for any extended time, everything was significant and Dad's comment got me to thinking. I was without any family or friends in Rochester, and while I had spent my summer pondering the positives that would bring, for the first time the negatives of it hit me. I would be truly alone for the first time. Perhaps prematurely, I felt the first pangs of loneliness as I walked Dad back downstairs to leave for home. I was starting to wonder if I had done the right thing, but neither that nor homesickness was a conversation to be had among the Botek men. Dad would just tell me not to be such a sissy and that boys don't think that way.

He simply shook my hand. I kissed him on the cheek, as was the family custom when we wouldn't see each other for a while, and away he drove into the heavy five o'clock traffic. It was as if I was going away for the weekend.

My brother-in-law Ernie, ex-Flying Tiger and G.I., often said, "It's not the army that makes you a man! It's you *yourself* that does it! The military just supplies a roof over your head and then tosses you into shark-infested waters." He'd then start tossing in every cliché he could: "it's sink or swim time", "survival of the fittest", "shape up or ship out", "we've got to separate the men from the boys", etc.

One thing about Ernie — he knew how to drive a point home. It helped that he'd usually had one too many before heading into this speech. Still, his words were echoing through my brain as I looked around my little room and began to unpack what I thought would be most immediately needed. I knew in my heavy heart and sobered soul that my time had finally come.

Dinner was tasty, but being the kid of the household, I was largely ignored other than introductions and a few brief questions. We sat at a long table, and the food was brought out, dish by dish. I sat patiently as the first dishes were attacked, then was warned by Mrs. Tocatta that I should help myself and quickly before the best food was gone. The boarders were all men, ranging in age from 25 to 50. They all looked worn out, like drifters tired from the road but *used* to being tired. As the young student, I didn't quite fit in and it became evident why this room, so close to the school, hadn't been snatched up by some other student searching for their home away from home.

My floor had a bathroom at the far end of the hall. I waited patiently after dinner, checking repeatedly to see if it was free, as the other five men on the floor moved with clockwork precision, never leaving a second between occupants. I finally got my chance, hurrying through my ablutions to minimize the chance of interruption.

My first night in my own room began with a few sleepless hours as I wondered if this was really everything I had been looking forward to for so long. It was sparsely furnished and the simple door lock looked like one hard push could break it. I pushed my chest of drawers against the door, plugged in a night light, and repacked all the food I had brought, fearful of mice. It took me some time, but I finally slept, secure in the assurance youth gives that I could turn this little room into the life I wanted for myself.

* * *

George Eastman was a major benefactor to the City of Rochester. Not only did he fund the Eastman School, but he also constructed the large and expansively furnished Eastman Theatre. He was, however, not just a benefactor offering the city whatever it wanted — he had a vision of his own. That vision had the two institutions directly connected, with large doors on both the main and upper floors permitting free passage between them. As such, patrons attending any of the concerts given in the theater could stroll directly into the school at intermission. Expensive paintings, large sofas, many small, highly-polished mahogany tables, and elegant matching mirrors decorated the upstairs section, formally known as 'The Promenade'.

Eastman had designed, ordered, and paid for every last nail. His considerations were numerous. He was once overheard to say that "A woman needs a place to put down her purse, fix her hair, and straighten her hat", and with that in mind, tables and mirrors were ubiquitous, meant to ease the lives of the women attending shows at the theater or taking courses at the school.

Restrooms were mostly located in the school, ostensibly to save space in the theater and maintain its reverent nature. He may have also had in mind that his large connecting doors should be open during shows and wanted to prevent anyone from closing them and separating the school from the theater. Smoking was always permitted on the Promenade and anywhere else throughout the school, likely a nod to Rochester's severe winters. This was par for the times, with smoking ever-present — in elevators, buses, movie theaters, classrooms, and even hospitals — anywhere other than church and around explosives. But old George may have specifically been thinking of the social element of the habit.

The rest of the building was made up of a few smaller classrooms and a seemingly endless number of small, not-quite-soundproof individual practice rooms. Most rooms had a full-size upright piano, kept perfectly in tune. Most also had a window to minimize the claustrophobic aspects of the tiny rooms, some as small as 4' x 8'. The doors were strong and soundproof with a 6" x 12" glass window to look in through. When playing inside, we knew we were on display to students in the hall, who could move in close and hear what we were playing. This worked as an incentive two ways. First, we would want to meet the challenge of the better players we could hear, and second, we wanted to avoid having remarks made in the hall being aimed at us. These rooms stayed open every day from 7 a.m. to 9:30 p.m., except Sundays. Each evening, the janitor would make his rounds, politely telling each student still practicing at 9:30 that it was time to go home.

The school had a third building, the Annex, which was not physically attached to the first two but stood alone across a very narrow public street. We could avoid walking across the street by using an enclosed connecting walkway on the fourth floor, which would be a great convenience in the bitter winter weather to come. However, it wasn't just the street that kept the Annex standing alone. There was nothing artistic about the building — no way did George Eastman approve its design, architectural fusspot that he was. This was an eight-storey box! My presumption is that the building was constructed as an afterthought, with only pragmatism and functionality to inspire its arrival, and this must have happened after Eastman's death in 1932.

The lower floor of the Annex housed a large, well-stocked library and a huge, loft-style room, one spacious enough to accommodate our entire symphonic band, about 80 members in all. Regular rehearsals took place there every Saturday morning for three hours under chief conductor Frederick Fennell, a clever, affable, even-tempered man with a special affinity for interpreting band music.

On the top floor a small gymnasium also seemed like an afterthought. After all, who puts a gym on the top floor of a building? The Eastman School, being filled with musicians, had little inclination to pursue school honors through sport, like a regular college would. We were still required to take gym once a week, but it wasn't taken seriously by most of the students or staff. The gym and locker rooms were well-equipped though, and everyone was expected to shower following gym class — after all, when we'd be sitting close to each other to play in band, no one needed the smell of stale sweat distracting them from the music.

In my first few days in Rochester, I took in the Promenade without fully understanding what it was that old George had brought to life. Later in my school days, I would find it the ideal place to sit with a girl, enjoy a cigarette, and possibly as George had wanted it, a way for any poor student to get into any theater show.

There were about eighty students in my freshman class, ranging in age from seventeen to twenty-six. The younger ones had come directly from high school, the older ones from serving in World War II. The older students seemed to carry more age in their strides than simple math would suggest. They made up about a fifth of the students and tended to socialize with each other more than the rest of us, though there was no hard and fast rule about who spoke, worked, or played with whom.

Boys outnumbered girls by a slight margin only, which for the time was unusual. Usually, higher education was seen as more the province of men, with many women moving from high school directly to marriage or to work. The war had liberated more than Europe though — women had learned they too could compete in the workplace, follow their dreams, and keep the nation running. And while there may have been some older folks who complained about this new society, none of the boys in the school had any problem with the number of women being close to that of the men. We were, after all, musicians and expected to defy conventions. We were also, of course, young men.

Our first couple of days in school were spent taking various tests. IQ tests were followed by psychological tests, and those were followed by the only one that scared us all — the Seashore Test. The Seashore was a standard test of musical aptitude, but few if any of us had been in a position to take it before. Eastman himself was an avid music lover, not just to the point of funding the school and theater, but playing flute himself. He however admitted that no matter how much he practiced, he never seemed to get anywhere with it. Faced with the test, he protested, "Don't give me the Seashore Test! I'll get nowhere — I'll fail it!"

Each of us there to master our craft had confidence in our abilities — the Eastman School wouldn't have admitted us were we not capable. That didn't mean that taking a test fell in the same category as playing music. I was having the same qualms Eastman did, unsure if my years of playing had at all prepared me for this.

The Seashore made me uncomfortable, but I relaxed when taking it and felt good about my chances. How I did and whether it made any difference were things I never found out — the school never bothered to share the results with the students. There was one student we suspected was asked to leave owing to his Seashore score, but nobody ever asked. We might have been friendly among ourselves, but the students still kept their distance from the administration.

While friendly, there was a certain kind of sophistication about the student body for the most part — unsurprising, considering that it was the wealthier families who could afford not only a school like Eastman, but the indulgence of a family member pursuing music as a career. Everyone played one or more of the standard symphony orchestra instruments and played them extremely well. In the four undergraduate years, there were a total of seventeen clarinetists, and each us sized each other up as we shook hands in greeting. Each time one of those hands clasped mine, I found myself wondering if it could move with as much ease as mine along the instrument. We each smiled as we took each other's measure as best we could without playing. This was to be expected — colleagues of the same age were always the most critical and competitive. With such a large group of talented and serious-minded players, the natural result was that they would, as they say in jazz jargon, try to 'cut' each other. In the end this was a good thing, as we each challenged the others to reach higher and farther than we might have otherwise.

Even as we might try to cut each other, the sharpest blade was wielded by one none of us could dream of cutting: Professor Rufus Arey. As the head of the clarinet department, he would give each of us a weekly one-hour private lesson, and owing to his position made the decisions as to which of us had truly earned what ranking. It was his job to assign each of us our chair in the symphonic band. Most of us newcomers had been solo first-chairs in our high-school bands. Now, as freshmen, like it or not, we were relegated to third parts, much less interesting than what we were used to, while the upperclassmen enjoyed the first and solo chairs. This was standard — freshmen played third parts, sophomores, second, juniors, first, and seniors, the solos. We freshmen were relegated to the back seats.

I sat in the middle of the third clarinets — for the first time in a long time not garnering a special place in the seating arrangements. As Eastman gathered together top-notch musicians from around the country, I was hardly the only one a bit thrown by this demotion. One of my fellow freshmen, commiserating about this shift in our positions, warned me, "If you think this is bad, just wait until they initiate you into the Phi Mu Alpha musicians' fraternity. Then, you'll be addressed by just one name: 'worm'."

Still, the demotion was a relative one. Even with a subordinate status cast upon us, it was exhilarating to play among names like school director Howard Hanson, José Iturbi, Frederick Fennell, and others, never mind Professor Arey and a number of the top-notch pros of the Rochester Philharmonic Orchestra. Even Finnish master composer Jean Sibelius was to be a faculty member, but just hours before he was to leave his beloved Scandinavia, despite having signed the final contracts, he cancelled. That was a disappointment to all, but there was no lack of talent to learn from.

It took just a few days at Eastman for me to know I had chosen wisely. The students were like the Marine Corps, an elite and select group. A lot was expected of us, with every opportunity possible depending on our meeting the challenge. In my previous band experience, we were part of a group within the school, but here, every way I turned I was facing another musician.

The everyday Rochesterians — restaurant owners, music store managers, bank clerks, department store staff, church clergy — all welcomed us with not only open arms, but a genuine respect. After all, we were the children of Eastman, and virtually every adult living in the city earned their living from one of the Eastman Kodak plants or from catering to their workers. The city celebrated not only the camera but felt the need or the desire to return as best they could the philanthropy that George Eastman had bestowed upon them.

The school, being part of midtown, was never more than a couple of blocks from almost every convenience necessary. Sibley's department store was large and fashionable with great prices, and there were banking facilities, a small post office, and pretty salesgirls. As if that wasn't enough to guarantee the patronage of the Eastman students, it also offered student discounts. Bond's offered two pair of trousers with every suit, with especially good prices and selections as Rochester was their home office. There were some less praiseworthy places in those blocks surrounding the school, notably some sleazy, skid-row type bars. Passing them at quarter to eight each morning on my way to class, I'd see many broken-down men lined up against their walls, having spent as long as they could at some flophouse before heading back for some hair of the dog. Some were probably from my Italian landlady's property on Joslyn Place.

There was one notably absent convenience in the area — public laundries. Each week I would gather my dirty clothes, pack them in a specially-designed aluminum 'mailing can' my mother had procured from Wanamaker's department store in Philadelphia, and ship them off home. Yeah, I know — she spoiled me. The can was lightweight, but the size of a modern carry-on suitcase. Large straps closed securely and a window section allowed you to slip in the mailing address. The shipping cost was negligible, maybe two dollars or so. In a week, I would receive the can back with not only nice clean clothes inside, but newspapers from home, some of Mom's home-baked goodies, and a box or two of prunes and other dried fruit. Mom believed in keeping not only the home fires burning, but the plumbing open.

The school had no full-sized cafeteria or men's residence. The girls lived in a dorm on the University of Rochester's East Avenue campus, near the palatial George Eastman House. We boys were forced to fend for ourselves, finding housing wherever we could. For food, there was the YMCA just two blocks away from the school, which served meals every day but Sunday. Prices were perfect for a student budget with 50¢ breakfasts, 60¢ lunches, and delicious home-style buffet dinners for $2 or less. Perhaps they catered to us students in honor of George Eastman, who had once saved the Rochester branch from bankruptcy by donating hundreds of thousands of dollars.

I was occasionally asked if I ever visited the third floor of the YMCA, and would always reply that no, I'd never been above the second, where the meals were served. It took some time for me to learn that the third floor housed a large swimming pool and, according to rumor, everyone swam nude. I never had the time to visit, so never found out if it was true.

Just one block from the school, unsurprisingly, was Rochester's biggest and best-equipped music store. With the guaranteed market of students, it stocked everything from tambourines to tubas, from clarinet reeds to records. On my first stop there, I was overcome with memories of New York and meeting effeminate Ernest with Charlie at that infamous Broadway record shop. Just needing a few reeds, I decided to leave exploring the rest of the store for another time. I waited at the counter to be served, looking over my schedule for the next week. Along with piano and clarinet, I would be taking trumpet. There were courses called History of Music, Theory & Composition, and Sight Singing. Eastman wanted students to have a rounded education, so I would be taking English, Gym, and Psychology. I also had scheduled practice on three instruments and two bands squeezed in.

Sight Singing included a 'listening session' where we would have to identify chords, arpeggios, whatever the teacher played. There would be a private solo exam for clarinet, for piano, and even for trumpet at the end of each semester. The clarinet one would be no trouble, I figured; the piano would require work; and the trumpet, well, that was entirely new territory. It was a requirement though, as the school wanted us to have Music Education degrees as well as our Performing Certificates — our second year would mean taking violin. It was about job security. They didn't expect us all to be able to follow through with careers playing music, but apparently they thought there would always be room for music *teachers.*

I was lost in thought looking at the schedule when the clerk spoke.

"How many credits are you carrying?"

I hesitated a moment, never having bothered to figure it out. "Plenty," I finally answered.

"Too many, maybe?" he ventured.

Not wanting to discuss it, I offered, "Let's see some Rico clarinet reeds."

He quickly produced three boxes, offering, "My name is Steven. What's yours?"

Finding out we had nearly the same name, with only the spelling different, got us to talking. I had too much to do to hang around, but the place had three listening booths and all the latest jazz recordings. I decided to be cool as I could and leave the door to come back when I wasn't so busy — whenever that might be — and schmooze this Steven guy into letting me listen to some DeFranco, Dizzy, and Bird.

As the city became more familiar, my boarding house home began to get me down. I was envious of the girls at the school who got to be housed in a formally-run university dorm. Not only was I missing out on that part of the experience of schooling, but I was spending my evenings and weekends surrounded by adults, and non-musician adults at that.

My opinion changed 180 degrees though when I attended a 'get acquainted' gathering for students one evening at the girls' residence. It was held in the large main parlor, with snacks and soft drinks set out for us. The lights were so bright I thought my shirt would fade! This was likely so nothing could escape the sight of the beady-eyed house mother as she watched hawk-like over her flock. Better than any sheepdog and more vigilant than a presidential bodyguard, she worked the room constantly, one end to the other. She seemed to have eyes that could swivel side-to-side and stare a hole through anyone at will.

Between sweeps of the matron's gaze, I met Louise. My jaw dropped when I saw her. She was a sexy young flute player from Cambridge, Massachusetts, and recognizing me from one of our classes, she asked me to sit down next to her. The first few minutes were the usual formal and introductory banter, but then I asked straight out, "How about going out with me?"

She paused a moment, rolled her eyes from side to side as if planning a prison break, then said, "Sure. When?"

"Right now! Let's get out of this place!"

She broke into laughter at that, lifting her arms high above her head and her legs off the floor. Quickly catching herself, she planted her feet back firmly on the ground.

"In five minutes," she whispered, "a bell will ring announcing that it's 10:25 p.m. — five minutes to closing. Then some of the boys and girls will begin hugging — a few will even work in a kiss before the final bell."

Sensing that I still didn't have the full picture, she added, "No one except the girls who live here are allowed above the first floor. We sign in and out, coming and going. There's a curfew seven nights a week — maybe as late as midnight on the odd Saturday. No overnighters unless both sets of parents say so in writing — and even then, they're still discouraged. And, oh yes, ladies — and that's what we're all called — shouldn't smoke in public or *ever* lift both legs from the floor."

I was taken aback, and suddenly thinking how lucky I was to be living in the boarding house. *What a drag*, I thought. *These poor girls — I mean, ladies.*

"Good night, Stephen," she grinned. Then, conspiratorially, she added in a whisper, "Meet me Monday at one o'clock on the Promenade. I have a few minutes after my flute lessons. Maybe we can sneak a smoke — no one notices there, except maybe the master himself, Mr. G.E. Those portraits of him keep popping up in the least expected places. Or am I just being paranoid?"

* * *

It was 7:30 Monday morning when I got to school. It wasn't that I was anxious to meet Louise — I was — but that I had a private clarinet lesson that day and wanted to be prepared. I searched the basement of the main building where about six practice rooms existed, hoping to find one vacant so I could avoid schlepping over to the Annex. The hallway was alive with music, something that may normally have been a joy but each chord progression, scale, Hanon exercise[1], or Bach chorale meant I was that much closer to crossing over to the Annex with its tiny practice rooms. I had thought of myself as the early bird but I hadn't been early enough — every room had a pianist practicing with an intensity that said his or her life depended on it, and in a sense, it did. These were the keys to their future they were hammering away at, not just black and white ones.

My heart was sinking with each room I passed, but I stopped dead in my tracks at the final door. As much as the sounds of music meant my hopes were dashed, what I was hearing here was too good to ignore, and it washed away all my frustrations. This was serious jazz improvisation. Looking through the door window, I saw a fairly heavy-set black student. There were few enough black students that I was surprised to see one I hadn't previously noticed. I listened, rapt, until he stopped, then tapped on the glass and applauded in front of the window where he could see. He grinned and beckoned me to come in.

"Man, that was good!" I said. "Shearing or Ellington?"

"A bit of both," he answered, "with some Thelonius Monk thrown in."

We introduced ourselves. He was Henry Edmonds from Washington, DC — Hank to friends. We talked about our instruments and experience a bit. He told me he was a graduate student, then stopped short.

"Ah, forget the rest for now," he beamed. "Why are we talking? Get your horn out and let's jam some!"

Hank knew all the standard jazz tunes. No tempo — slow, medium, very fast — seemed to faze him. He could change keys on the fly, shifting like a

[1] a series of exercises outlined in The Virtuoso Pianist in 60 Exercises by Charles-Louis Hanon

showroom-floor Mercedes. He played extended modern chords that were the core of bebop without a second's thought or hesitation. *What a find*, I thought. Considering my previous learning experience, older musicians were always seen as potential mentors. Even at twenty-three, Hank had plenty to teach me, I could tell in that all-too-brief jam session.

And I wasn't the only one who felt the energy. A crowd was gathering outside our room, listening rather obviously. We couldn't tell if they were incensed at our disregard for tradition or if they were cheering us on. We just kept playing, swingin' away at whatever standards were thought of and whatever riffs came to mind. At one of the breaks, one of the listeners came into the room. Hank greeted him warmly. This was a fellow grad student, Frank Hillman, and they had obviously played together before. Hank offered him the piano and he launched into a then-popular George Shearing tune, and the energy was right back there, my jamming along with Frank and Hank cheering us on.

"I'm really a tenor saxophonist and writer," Frank told me when we finished, "but I love playing piano tunes that lend themselves to a block-chord style."

We talked for a while as Hank riffed on the piano. Frank was from Newark, Delaware and had graduated from Princeton with a BA. He loved jazz, and had just entered the Eastman graduate department a few weeks ago. Time flew so much with the three of us there that I didn't realize the time until ten past nine — I had to leave or be late for my History of Music class.

Before I left, Frank offered that we should get together and jam again. Apparently, Monday nights meant there was a jam session at a small but swinging place called Ottman's. A local pianist, Herbie Brock, totally blind, was in charge of it and was pretty particular, but might let us sit in. Frank offered to pick me up at 9 p.m., telling me to look out for his green Willys Jeep with Delaware plates.

One o'clock came and I waited anxiously for Louise. We sat and smoked, chatting casually. She showed me her new Haynes flute and I was more attracted to her than ever. Of course, she was stuck in the dorm and couldn't make it out to Ottman's. My heart sank on hearing the news but following an eye-sweep of the halls, a whispered goodbye and a kiss more than made up for the disappointment.

Ottman's was a converted butcher shop with old meat hooks still standing on the walls, now serving as coat racks. The bartenders were big burly men dressed in white coats and butcher's aprons, and I had to wonder if these were the old butchers learning a new trade. Sawdust covered the floors. The walls were covered with plain but large mirrors and colorful advertising signs that had been abandoned. In the middle of this, Herbie Brock sat perched up on a high narrow stage.

It seemed precarious enough normally, but considering Herbie was completely blind, it seemed almost irresponsible. With this in mind, he was careful not to move around too much, but that never seemed to hamper his playing. He seemed at one with the piano — maybe not a surprise, as together they took up almost all of the stage. The mahogany-colored beauty of a piano was an upright Baldwin with a fine sound to it. Herbie played alone, without the usual drum and bass accompaniment, but he managed to make the piano alone sound complete. The place was packed with all the local musicians, none of whom seemed to notice a thing other than Herbie, with every eye and ear focused on him. According to the rumors, Herbie made numerous trips to Toronto (150 miles away) to study with the master of jazz piano, Art Tatum, himself partially blind. Like Tatum, Herbie could cleanly execute unbelievably fast passages, often with both hands and producing the sound of two pianists improvising together.

Frank ordered us each a bottle of Genesee Standard Ale.

"Drink it out of the bottle," he advised. "This place is kinda filthy."

We lit up cigarettes, grabbed our bottles in our other hands, and edged our way to the foot of the stage. Half the audience stood while the rest sat at rickety old tables squeezed together almost one on top of another. Everyone was enthralled as Herbie moved seamlessly from one standard to another, rapt with a sense of the sacred. His repertoire was enormous and his improvisations amazingly creative and offering brief quotes of other stellar pianists — Teddy Wilson, George Shearing, Bud Powell, and of course, Art Tatum — before flying off in completely new directions.

Intermission arrived and Frank bounded up to the stage. I broke into a grin, flashing on memories of Charlie. Frank cordially offered to escort Herbie from the stage. Arm in arm, they shuffled slowly towards a small corner table. I hustled over, anxious for the opportunity to talk with this great improviser.

"Herbie," I offered, "Your interpretation of 'How High the Moon' would definitely have pleased Bud Powell and what you did with Garner's 'Misty' — wow, man, that was some experience!"

"Thanks, man!" grinned Herbie. "What do you play?" he asked, recognizing me as a player immediately, either from my comments or because I was Frank's friend.

We began to talk about music as Frank was still seating Herbie. Once he'd done that, Frank rounded up two miniature stools for us while Herbie turned and ordered three ales from a passing waitress. Herbie seemingly had an awareness of everything happening around him in the pub and just *knew* she was there.

We talked for a little while, Frank guiding the conversation, and before long he had convinced Herbie to invite us both to sit in next time — all we had to do was bring our horns. *What a golden opportunity*, I thought. Immediately I turned my thoughts to which tunes I needed to review to be ready for this chance. Even before playing with Herbie, I had found another mentor in Frank.

Having established a friendship, Frank came by to see my room, and flipped at the state of it.

"You can't stay in this broken-down dump!" he exclaimed, swearing he would find me something better. "Listen to Bach, man! *Tocatta and Fugue!* You have to fugue from this place!"

We laughed, but I knew he was right. My mind was elsewhere, and I would stall for some time but, eventually, I would listen to his advice.

* * *

The next day, between classes, I darted across the street to the music store where Steven worked. I was looking to buy a few of the illustrated color postcards they stocked, showing the school in the foreground and the city center in the background. I was thinking of my mother, Langenus, Buddy, and that clarinetist in the U.S. Air Force Band in Washington, George Dietz. I thought it would be a good idea to let him know I really *was* in Rochester — that it wasn't just an excuse to refuse his offer, remembering my mother's admonition not to burn my bridges. I was still thumbing through the postcards when Steven spotted me and came over.

"Stephen with the 'ph'," he greeted me. "How are things going?"

I told him about the previous night at Ottman's and how well Herbie Brock had played. There was no doubt that Steven loved jazz and all its trappings. He was quite familiar with Herbie and his work, and we discussed him for some time. Still, I had to get back to class and had to cut things short. I paid for the postcards and was about to leave when he placed something in my hands. It was a stack of new records — Fats Navarro, Woody Herman, the *Metronome* All Stars (including Buddy DeFranco!), and a new young Swedish clarinetist, Stan Hasselgård. He had me hooked, but I told him I'd have to follow through another time. My private clarinet lesson, only my fourth, was coming up in just under a half-hour, and I had to be ready.

My private teacher was Rufus Arey himself, who played first clarinet in the Rochester Philharmonic. A short, white-haired man with a cheerful, rosy-cheeked face, he gave off a paternal air, but underneath I could sense an underlying strictness and a strange tension that seemed to permeate each of our meetings. Only eighteen, I wasn't yet adept enough to understand the psychology of this relationship. What the underlying psychodynamics were, time would have to tell.

In a previous lesson he had confronted me about having a pack of cigarettes in my shirt pocket.

"Does your father know you smoke?" he had demanded in his heavy East Maine accent.

Without hesitation, I replied that he did. Ordinarily, I might have become defensive, saying something along the lines of, "You know, Prof.

Arey, the school *does* allow smoking," but something held me back. It wasn't only that I wasn't assertive enough, but making a comment of that sort would have been inappropriate, unproductive, and answering back would have set the tone for our future lessons and been unwise. Still, his question grated somewhat — I was hardly the only student who smoked. In fact, many of us sat up front in our History of Music class and puffed away during the lesson, with Miss Watanabe never saying a word about it. There were ashtrays along the Promenade and in the Student Lounge. And past all that, it wasn't any of his business anyway.

In return, Arey was somewhat unnerved by my silence and quick answers, which put him on the defensive. He was obviously wondering how to end the conversation, and fumbling in trying to do so. Maybe it was because of that uncertainty that he finally gave me the hint I needed to understand the tension in our lessons to date.

"You were undoubtedly one of Gustave Langenus' better students. You came highly recommended."

Ah, I thought, *that's it! A bit of professional jealousy, and me the student who didn't have to audition for him owing to Langenus' recommendation.*

"You use his model," he continued, "The G.L. concave-bite black rubber mouthpiece. Don't you notice how shrill the clarinet sounds with the G.L. as compared to what I have here: a three-star glass O'Brien?"

Frank Hillman had said something along similar lines just a few days previous, but without considering the instrument — he had asked me if I didn't think *my* tone was too shrill. I told Prof. Arey that I had never really taken time to meticulously examine the differences between clarinet players' tones, but had been thinking about it lately. Sure, I had noticed if they were really sugar-sweet or horribly bad. Considering Frank's comment — which was still stinging — I needed no convincing, but it did feel like a betrayal of sorts *not* to use Langenus' mouthpiece. It didn't take me long to decide — I just wouldn't tell him.

"Does the music store across the street sell O'Briens?" I asked.

By now, the thoughts of professional jealousy were gone, but if they weren't, what Arey said next would have made me forget about them completely.

"No," he replied. "But I've been saving a three-star 1948 model just for you!"

That pretty much ended our lesson. By that point we were out of time, but this act of faith and generosity would have left me unable to continue anyway.

With the new mouthpiece and a little practice, my tone turned from shrill to Benny Goodman mellow. As well, I made that mental leap from the Long Island Langenus school to the Rochester Arey school. I was recognizing that I had taken much of my approach to music for granted.

The same, of course, applied to my life in general.

George Eastman

Norma Ellis
Rochester TV host and singer

Stephen B. Sextet, The Annual Eastman Christmas Dance
Steve Botek (clarinet), Jack Loftis (bass), Hank Edmonds (piano),
Norma Ellis (vocals), Dan Ettinger (trombone), Bob Livingston (drums)

Eastman School of Music Woodwind Teachers, 1949
Including Rufus Arey *(second from left)*

Orchestra Conductors Paul White and Frederick Fennell

Eastman School of Music band, 1950

The Eastman Dormitory for Women
Eastman had no men's dorms

Eastman Freshman Class of 1949

Top row of upper photo includes now-noted composer-pianist Ron Nelson, Steve's roommate Clint Thayer, Steve, and Barney Mallon *(fifth to eighth from left)*

Botek Family, 1952

back row: Betty, Steve Sr, Elizabeth, Jo

front row: Betty's husband Ernie, their children Charles and Carol, Francis

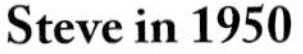

Steve in 1950

Steve in 1980

Ruth Botek in a Rochester garden

Shigo Family
Al Shigo with wife Marilyn (Ruth's sister) and children Judy and Bobby — Shigo would become one of the world's most famous plant pathologists and arbourists

Elizabeth Botek
Steve's mother

Walter Mallon, Meme Mallon and Steve Botek

The Mallon family, Botek family and accordionist Joe Knutt *(in suit)*

Ruth Botek and her dog, Buttons
Maine coast, 1979

Gustave Langenus

Born in Malines, Belgium in 1883, Gustave Langenus graduated from the Brussels Royal Conservatory at the young age of 17. He then emigrated to England, where he was hired by John Philip Sousa for European tours in 1902 and 1903. Once Sousa returned home Langenus joined the London Queen's Hall Orchestra.

In 1910 Langenus emigrated once again, this time to the United States, where he quickly became the solo clarinetist for the New York Symphony Society under Walter Damrosch. He remained with the society for nine years, then spent the next four years as the soloist for the New York Philharmonic.

Langenus taught clarinet at the New York Institute of Musical Art, the New York College of Music, and New York University, among others. He regularly taught, and was a featured conductor, at the National High School Music Camp in Interlochen, Michigan. He regularly performed with his own woodwind ensemble throughout this period.

Langenus' compositions and arrangements for clarinet are widely used and recognized for their innovation. His original works include "Indian Mother Song", based on the pentatonic scale that the pre-Columbian music of American Indians was largely based on.

A master teacher in every sense, Langenus died in 1957, his books of exercises already established as the standard for clarinet students and professionals. To this day, they are still widely in use.

Chapter 9 Anything Goes

Saturday nights were the loneliest night of the week. I had gotten used to a weekend social life which revolved around my playing dance jobs, and now without that, I had not only no social events to fill my weekends, but no money to compensate. I could certainly use the extra bread as a young student. It occurred to me that I hadn't even touched my saxophone in a month. The solution seemed to be obvious: join Rochester's musicians' union. With that, I would have not only the opportunity to snoop around for some weekend work, but some new contacts in the city.

The fee was less than twenty dollars, as I was registered as a transfer member from the Lansford local. The secretary of the Rochester local was a pleasant, grey-haired gentleman who, like most Rochesterians, it seemed, had an Italian-sounding name. That I attended Eastman came up almost immediately and sparked further conversation.

"Do you play sax?" he asked.

"Yes, I play alto — but my main instrument is clarinet," I offered hopefully. "I've done a lot of big band work — usually playing third alto and doing all the clarinet solos."

He lifted a finger and I was unsure if he was telling me to wait or be quiet, so I sat in silence as he lifted the receiver and dialed a number. I listened curiously as he spoke in sentence fragments, none of which seemed to make sense on their own: "You needed . . . the rate was . . . mm-hmm, someone new. . . ." Suddenly, he hung up the receiver and fixed me with one eye.

"Okay, I just got you at least one job. The second Saturday night in December, there's a big dance at the Buick garage." He stopped to take another second to size me up. "That's three blocks behind the Eastman Theatre. This is an annual affair — all the big staff and spouses. Society stuff — there'll be an eighteen-piece band."

He took another uncertain look at me before continuing: "You read well, don't you? You'll sight-read the book with no trouble, I'm sure. Twenty dollars for four hours. 8 p.m. to midnight. Any overtime is double pay. Wear a dark blue suit with a white shirt. The leader will fix you up with a bow tie."

He put out his hand to shake mine, and as he did, almost as an afterthought, he added, "It was nice meeting you."

I can't remember if I even managed to speak a word between saying what I played and saying goodbye. No one ever made me sew or draw or catch a football or take any kind of dexterity test — nothing was done to see if my hands were steady and sure. Talent definitely helps, but you don't even need all ten fingers to be accepted. What makes the difference is the commitment, and that commitment is shown in practice. No chops, no gigs. I can only presume that the Lansford local spoke well of me.

* * *

My Eastman buddies were an appropriately serious lot. Their tenacity flowed freely, as did their unfaltering devotion and consummate dedication. Music and its mastery was all that mattered. Anything less and they never would have been selected for the school.

Eastman had a focus on practice, demanding no less than four or five hours each day. The simple reason: it works. There have since been many studies of elite performers, from concert violinists to chess grandmasters, from competitive ice skaters to professional mathematicians — whatever the discipline, researchers find the difference between the greats and the lesser talents simply boils down to the amount of practice they've notched up under their belt. Indeed, the most important talent may be the talent for *practice itself* — not everyone has the will to maintain a routine. K. Anders Ericsson, a cognitive psychologist and an expert on performance, notes that the most important role that innate factors play in one's success in their chosen field is the willingness to engage in sustained training. For example, he found that top performers dislike practicing just as much as others do — which is why even great athletes and musicians quit practicing when they retire. Still, they persevere, and that will to keep at it makes all the difference.

I would spend up to two hours daily practicing my clarinet, another hour practicing piano, and maybe fifteen minutes more practicing trumpet. That would be tripled if I had a test coming up. Through much of that time, I was effectively practicing my sight-reading.

That said, I had mastered clarinet even more than sight-reading — but it felt like piano and trumpet were mastering *me*. And the next year, I would have to tangle with the violin! I would be judged by the same people judging those who had played all their lives on those instruments, and so I had to catch up.

With the Thanksgiving break fast approaching, I would be returning to Lansford and visiting my family. The break was little more than a long weekend, but it was going to be the first real day off any of us had had since school began. It was at the forefront of everyone's thoughts, but we had little time to discuss it. Practice was still the watchword, and the school was buzzing with activity. Empty practice rooms were rarer than gold. The Annex reverberated with a mix of vocalists and instrumentalists, each trying to shut out the others and concentrate on the music in front of them. It was a madhouse in some ways, with individual practice seemingly impossible with the music of other students spilling over you wherever you were. Still, we managed. Like commuters driving in noisy rush-hour city traffic with its snags and slowdowns, we acclimatized and learned to focus on our goals and ignore the distractions, mostly with a sense of courtesy to those of others.

Likewise, we managed enough small talk to make our plans for the upcoming long weekend. Heavy snow was predicted, which would be a difficulty, but Frank had a four-wheel-drive Jeep and offered a solution: he would drop me off in Pennsylvania on Wednesday evening, then continue on to see his family in Delaware. He'd then pick me up on his way back Sunday afternoon. In New York State, in Pennsylvania, in Delaware, it snowed the entire length of the trip. Were it not for the Jeep, we likely wouldn't have been able to make it. I felt a little bad leaving Frank on his own for the last leg of his trip home, but he assured me that the Jeep had seen worse and he would have no problems.

Thanksgiving had always been an extra-special holiday for our family. My parents had married on Thanksgiving, so the last Thursday of November was always a double celebration. For me, there was an added bonus in being home for the first time since leaving. There was not only the comfort of family itself and the old home, but in the traditions that were our own, such as feasting at noon on Thanksgiving Day.

After we ate, my father cornered me to ask about my clarinet playing: "Has your playing improved?"

It was clear to me that he wanted to be reassured he was getting his money's worth. Recognizing this, I was smiling as I opened the clarinet case and began assembling the five sections assuredly.

"Yes," I said, just avoiding being cocky. "I'd say it has. Particularly with this new glass O'Brien mouthpiece."

I held it up as I noted it, then in silence I chose my very best reed, moistening it well for as long as a minute or two, savoring the build-up. I adjusted the reed and mouthpiece firmly, bringing the clarinet to my lips in almost the same motion. The first sounds from the instrument were low notes, loud and vibrant. I danced through the full range of the instrument with lightning dexterity, presenting the tones in familiar scales and melodic arpeggios.

The expression on Dad's face said it all. He was impressed. His clarinet case was nearby, and while he initially seemed to be thinking of joining me in a duet, the idea was quickly and quietly scrapped following my brief but convincing warm-up. He was at a loss for words. I felt *great* — not only at getting some measure of recognition, but at the knowledge that I had left him speechless.

The silence was short-lived as he found another avenue of attack.

"I see you're smoking now," he challenged, motioning to my pocket. "You know it's bad for your wind."

Without hesitation, I returned, "But *you* smoke occasionally. I only smoke a few each day and will probably stop before long."

There was no comeback offered. We simply left the parlor and joined the others still feasting on our Thanksgiving banquet. My eldest sister, Betty, had made it in, along with her husband Ernie and their children Carol and Charles — the latter only one month old and meeting his uncle Steve for the first time. Jo was there, as were our younger siblings, Ginny and Francis.

Having the warmth of family around me again was great. This was my first Thanksgiving coming *back* instead of being part of the group at home. For the first time, I had stories that no one else had heard. Moreover, each morsel tasted juicier, fresher, more vibrant with the knowledge that I had finally completely asserted myself. I had finally dealt with my strict, punitive, and hard-to-approach father without surrendering my own individuality. And while it wasn't said, I knew there was respect now in the silences between us.

Unlike traveling back home, no extra effort was needed to return to Rochester. The highways were plowed clear but the roadsides were bright thanks to a foot-thick blanket of still-fresh snow.

Frank drove me directly to my new home. He had decided that I could do better. He had found me a room on University Avenue, a mere ten-minute walk away from school. For my part, I was anxious and nervous at the same time. I had never shared a room before, but while I had privacy at the boarding house, the atmosphere was beginning to get to me and I knew a change was necessary.

"No more boarding houses of broken-down men for you!" he had proclaimed. "You'll be sharing a large room with an upperclassman friend of mine, Don. He's quite the genius — an ex-G.I., a viola major who plays jazz trombone, and comes from a family of artists and sculptors. He'll be one heck of a mentor."

The door was opened by a short and heavyset woman in her forties. Another Rochester Italian, she seemed pleasant enough. She told me she had been expecting me and, without ceremony, picked up one of my suitcases and began walking up the stairs.

"You and Don will share the upstairs," she noted. "My daughter and I share the downstairs. No girlfriends overnight. You may practice until 7 p.m. No unnecessary noise or radio playing after 11. Don will explain everything else."

She seemed to be finished, but then seemed struck by an afterthought. "Oh, yes. You'll take your meals outside, but on certain Sundays you're invited to a home-cooked Italian dinner with my daughter Rosa and myself."

I shut the door behind me as quietly as I could, feeling some sense of stillness in the room. Sure enough, in the far corner of the room, Don was lying sprawled out on the bed. Flat on his back and motionless, he seemed so tranquil I had to wonder if he was still breathing. After a moment more I thought, *If he isn't dead, he must be in some kind of trance*. But then he gently opened his eyes and without any other movement, greeted me.

"Welcome. You must be Steve. Your bed is over there — make yourself at home. I'm practicing my Jacobson relaxation exercises. We'll talk tomorrow."

With that, he slowly closed his eyes, his mouth drooped open slightly, and the room filled with a peaceful calmness that exuded from his entire body.

Unlike any moment at the boarding house, this felt like home.

The next morning I got to talk to Don freely. He told me that he had learned about Jacobson exercises from a course at the school offered to help students perform without being nervous and to rid themselves of the unnecessary tensions that arise in everyday life.

The teacher was George Amarandus, a local masseur. He had stuttered most of his life, and gone to Chicago to study relaxation techniques for the sake of applying them to his handicap. He did so with complete success and wanted to share what he had learned so much that he had offered to teach for free at Eastman. He had a natural link to the music school in that his wife was a cellist in the Rochester Philharmonic. As a side note, she was pregnant and studying Jacobson techniques to help her undergo natural childbirth.

Howard Hanson, the director of the Eastman School, was not only a brilliant conductor and composer, but a great advocate of any technique that musicians could employ towards a better performance and as such, granted Amarandus free classroom space and unrestricted guest-teaching privileges. I was amazed to find out about all this. Langenus had been right — where else could a musician find a free college class in formal relaxation?

Of course I immediately signed up. My first class was in the morning, at 10. About twenty-five students were there, with the girls slightly outnumbering the boys. Of course, everyone was interested in enhancing their performance skills. We all had high hopes of successfully mastering a technique that once and for all could put our stage-fright demons to rest. Luckily for me, the only text required was the book I already owned: *You Must Relax*.

Tall, serious, and soft-spoken, Amarandus talked with a metronomic rhythm — short sentences, perfectly enunciated. After a while it became clear to me that that the timing of his speech was part of a technique to overcome his stuttering. At first it didn't even occur to me, and if I hadn't previously known, I never would have guessed he had ever stuttered.

He asked us to close our eyes and continued talking, his voice becoming softer, more soothing. Each in their turn, he focused on various muscles, starting with the scalp and working his way down to the feet. For each, we were asked to consciously tighten the muscle and maintain the tension for a few seconds. This way, we could consciously establish what that tension really felt like. Following that, we would release the tension and coax the muscle to relax, and understand the difference.

It only took two classes — with some diligent practice in-between — for me to become aware of complete tightness and total relaxation in any individual muscle. Other students were reporting a ripple effect — feeling *groups* of muscles linking together and relaxing as a unit. Having been previously exposed to Jacobson techniques, I seemed to have mastered a level of control that eluded many of the other students.

During our fourth class, something new occurred. After each body part was mentioned by Amarandus was tightened, then relaxed, it floated away. That is, each body part felt weightless and seemed to disappear into thin air. It was like leaving my body, like having an out-of-body experience. I felt like I was floating high above the heads of my classmates, and others reported the same experience. All the muscles of our bodies were relaxed enough that we felt we could abandon our bodies and all its learned stresses, including the propensity for stage fright. The new out-of-body self would be able to get the job done peacefully and naturally, without the weight of all the anxieties and the anxieties those gave rise to.

Following a few more weeks of training, we were asked to bring our instruments to class. I remember standing in front of the class, clarinet in hand. Amarandus led me through the same process, and I allowed each muscle to become weightless. Unlike other times, I kept my eyes open, which seemed the natural thing to do when facing an audience. Before too long, I felt my body floating, and slowly placed the clarinet into my mouth. Confidently, I played through a long series of standard warm-up exercises, feeling no tension, no self-consciousness, no stage fright. Jacobson was right — with all my muscles relaxed, no anxiety could exist, be it the everyday ones or those specifically attached to performance.

Jacobson's techniques had come my way at little expense. His book had cost me a measly dollar, and Amarandus never asked for so much as a penny. It seemed too good to be true — never before had I paid so little to gain so much.

I had always considered Jacobson's techniques something arcane which only close confidantes like Charlie could share in, but at Eastman I was part of a group that shared this knowledge, and everyone took it seriously. I knew I was in the right place.

Gym at Eastman was the polar opposite — an utter joke. For an hour each week, we'd change into our gym trunks, parade up to the gymnasium, then stand at attention while the 'coach' would take attendance. After that, he might hang around another five minutes before disappearing to the lounge for a game of bridge, while we played an informal game of basketball. Despite this utter lack of concern for the course, it was mandatory though it was a non-credit course. I often thought about cutting the class, but was too intimidated to do so — my Judeo-Christian background coupled with the lack of information as to where we stood grade-wise kept me going, as much as I could have used the time to practice. Instead, I would display some passive-aggressive behavior, and simply show up late.

It was during one of these episodes that I met Barney. It was the first week of December — much too cold to run around in shorts, and too cold to shower in the facilities offered. Even had the shower room been warm, walking around in the bitter Rochester winter damp was an invitation to a cold. I was in the change room hurrying to make up for my tardiness when I noticed the student beside me taking his sweet time.

"We're late," I told him. "We're going to miss the roll call."

"No sweat," he replied. "If the coach leaves, I'll go find him in the student lounge and give him our names."

Almost as an afterthought, he added, "What *is* your name, anyway?" Smiling suddenly, he offered, "I'm Barney. Barney Mallon. I'm actually *from* Rochester. I play string bass and tuba."

Thus began a friendship that has lasted my entire life. That day we never even left the locker room, instead sitting down and sharing stories. We had many things in common — the large part of the conversation was about jazz. Barney was also a devotee of bebop. We also discussed the school and Rochester itself and Barney, having grown up in the city, promised to take me around and show me the local jazz scene. He also invited me to dinner at his home that Saturday evening. Not having sat down to a good home-cooked family dinner since Thanksgiving, I immediately said yes. The YMCA and White Castle may have served well enough, but they couldn't compare.

Still, as an Eastman student, my view of Rochester was a small circle orbiting out around the school. Going to the Mallon home took me off the paths I had gotten used to, taking thirty minutes — and a dime for the bus. Nearly everything in the city bears either the Eastman or the Kodak name, some carrying both. The Mallon family lived off Lake Avenue, in Kodak Park, a nice residential section which suggested that Barney's parents could easily afford to have sent him elsewhere, but didn't. In those class-conscious times, that was easily seen as a ringing endorsement of Eastman.

Barney's parents greeted me at the door, though Barney himself was nowhere to be seen.

"Walter and Meme," they offered. "Don't dare call us Mr. and Mrs. Mallon — that sounds way too old and stuffy."

I had a pang of jealousy for a moment — these seemed like proper parents for a musician.

They apologized for the condition of their house, which was in the process of major repairs. Barney's sister Barbara appeared and introduced herself, apologizing for not being more energetic — she had just recently recovered from a long bout of mononucleosis and this was her first full day out of bed. I felt immediately at home — or *not* at home, as the case may be. In Lansford, admitting such signs of weakness to a stranger so openly on first meeting would be unimaginable. Here, the Mallons didn't give it a second thought. They were so warm and welcoming that I never even thought to ask where Barney was.

Meme flooded me with questions about my parents, Pennsylvania, and my thoughts about Rochester. Barney's name came up and she asked if I would go up to the third floor and awaken him for supper.

"It's the room at the very top," she told me. "The one where that good jazz is coming from."

The door to Barney's room was partially open. I could hear the music from his radio along the entire length of the double staircase. It was hot and new bebop and I knew that this was no Rochester radio station — not at 5:45 in the afternoon. It had to be from that Toronto jazz club I had read about. I'd heard that broadcasts of their shows could sometimes be tuned into on this side of the border. Apparently the club featured the latest and greatest in jazz, confirming for me that Dizzy and Blakey were right when they'd say that jazz is too good for the Americans.

Barney's room was cluttered with ashtrays. He was an indulgent smoker, with Camels his brand of choice. There were also beer bottles around the room, also his brand of choice, Genesee Ale. As the drinking age in New York was eighteen, Barney, myself, and the most of my freshmen classmates could legally drink ourselves into oblivion any time we so desired. Still, he was drinking, smoking, and listening to hot jazz in his room, never mind staying in bed all day Saturday — no way would my parents ever allow me to do any of that in their house, legal or not. I found myself immediately envying his fortune in having such open, understanding parents.

Apparently I had been the subject of discussion among the Mallon family, who had decided that I would be the perfect clarinet teacher for Barbara. As soon as I roused him, Barney asked me but I took no time to even think about it before answering no. My schedule was already jam-packed, especially now that I had taken on a steady Saturday-night job. The subject came up again over dinner, and Walter wasn't prepared to take no for an answer. A successful and highly-respected insurance agent with a full family life, he was used to juggling chaotic situations. He presented me with a plan.

"You arrive at our house at 4:45 on Saturdays, teach Barbara for an hour, then I'll pay you, we'll give you dinner, and I'll personally drive you to your dance job."

This stopped me in my tracks. A home-cooked dinner, some money, and a ride to my gig — it was too good to pass up. As we were already eating, I knew Meme was an excellent cook, and the meals would be a huge leap forward from the student fare I was surviving on. Beyond that, I was being invited in to a happy and music-loving Rochester family. In direct counterpoint to the apprehension and anxiety I was used to in dealing with the head of a household, I was being treated with warmth, respect, and generosity. I agreed quickly, making sure to note that Meme's cooking helped to seal the deal.

It was a good decision. Barbara was a conscientious student. Though having only about one year's experience with her horn, she still had a background in piano, so knew the basics. She listened well and progressed nicely through the lessons. A good student makes a teacher's job easier — and decent pay and a home-cooked meal don't hurt either.

* * *

The Buick gig had no rehearsal, and I had to sit and read the book alongside seventeen other guys who had played it all before, hundreds of times. It would have been impossible had I not spent my entire life sight-reading and keeping that skill in practice. This was no swing band, as I was used to, or even classical. This was a *society* band. The lead alto player told me to stay with him through the night and to use a wider vibrato than usual — they wanted to be Guy Lombardo! Not my scene at all but, having practiced my sight-reading to the point of it being second nature, I was more than able to fill the spot.

Time may fly when you're having fun, but it streaks by when your plate is full. Before I knew it, Christmas had come and gone like Frank's Jeep cutting through the snow en route to Lansford and back for another visit. My New Year's Eve gig was a huge success, netting me a cool $22. The spring semester had begun, and with it came an inordinate amount of work — more time dedicated to practice, harder studies, more jam sessions, and many more well-paying weekend dance jobs. My schedule was exhausting and so tight that it seemed my every second was planned, but despite the breakneck pace, everything felt like a perfect fit.

I managed to squeeze the time for a weekend trip back to Pennsylvania to meet up with Charlie and see Benny Goodman play at the Hershey Park Ballroom in Hershey. Charlie and I went over what we knew — Sonny Igoe of Bill West fame was on drums, and superstar Wardell Gray was on tenor sax. Stan Hasselgård was a nineteen-year-old Swedish bebop clarinetist whom Benny admired so much that he put him up in his apartment. Chico O'Farrill had written the arrangements, and they were sublimely advanced.

We were surprised to see that Hasselgård was not there. It was only later that we would find out that he had been killed in a car crash the previous November. Being a clarinet player and knowledgable about Benny's career, I wondered about trying to talk to him. Now, I have to wonder what Benny might have said had I known and asked about Stan. Likewise, had we known that Wardell Gray would die mysteriously in the Nevada desert just six years later, we may have sought out some time with him first.

However, we didn't know about Stan, and couldn't know about Wardell, so our focus was on the players who we had an instrument in common with. Charlie assured me I had plenty to talk to Benny about as the intermission neared, and he resolved to go find Sonny Igoe.

With the intermission on, the eighteen band members filed quickly off the stage, wasting no time, as if they couldn't get away from their leader fast enough. This left Benny standing all alone on stage, slowly leafing through some music, likely uncertain what else to do or where to go. Nobody approached him or went near him. I noticed this and wondered what it all meant — were people scared of him, and if so, why?

I got an answer decades later. After a concert at the Metropolitan Museumof Art in New York, I had the opportunity to ask Phil Woods, "What was it like, being the fine clarinet player that you are, playing in Goodman's band, being on the road with him, touring Russia with him, et cetera?"

Phil had played alto saxophone for Goodman's band, though he was a clarinet major at the Manhattan School of Music and at The Juilliard School. There was no saxophone major available at Juilliard at the time, so he was coached privately to be able to pursue his goals on sax. Still, with Goodman, he got cemented as a sax player, not a clarinetist.

His answer showed why. Without missing a beat, and with an abrupt change in his demeanor, he clearly, loudly and angrily shot out, "Why Goodman, that son-of-a-bitch!"

On one of his tours with the King of Swing, he said, the band was staying in a motel and he took the afternoon to practice his clarinet. Almost immediately, Goodman who was staying on the floor above, was at his door. He told Woods in no uncertain terms that in *his* band, there was only one clarinet player who should be heard — Benny himself.

Goodman's father was a strict, struggling Jewish immigrant tailor with a no-nonsense command of his nine-child family. The elder Goodman worked long hours at a meatpacking company and would return home dirty, exhausted, and reeking of lard — a scent which Benny died unable to tolerate. Benny's restrictive, orthodox, lackluster youth certainly explains much of his adult penchant for pettiness, parsimony, and interpersonal ineptitude. Born into abject poverty, he worked hard to move himself onto the right side of the tracks, and left the slums of Chicago once and for all when in his teens. Historian Ken Burns notes that he "willed himself to greatness." Goodman dropped out of school at sixteen in August, 1925 to join Ben Pollack's Orchestra. Traveling to the West Coast, he earned enough to support his entire family, while his father made only fifteen dollars per week. While his father was proud of Benny, he was too proud to see him play sophisticated places without a new suit. He was still saving money for that suit when he was struck by a car and killed — he never did see his son perform in public. The mere mention of his father was enough to reduce Benny to tears after this.

Considering his origins, it's little wonder that Goodman's eccentricities and often sullen manner were so deeply ingrained in his personality. This of course wasn't common knowledge in his heyday.

I gathered my courage and set to finding out why he was left alone on stage. Benny was willing to talk to another clarinetist, but unlike talking to Buddy, the conversation stayed firmly planted around the instrument. I kept my questions short, sweet, impersonal, and polite — after all, this *was* the King of Swing and there were rules to follow when talking to royalty.

I had always been fascinated by his big, pure resonant tone, and asked how he managed it. How was he able to project a tone so it was heard at the distant end of a dance hall without using a microphone?

Benny was soft-spoken, congenial, and in no way condescending. He used simple, declarative sentences packed with advice, answering all my questions. He talked about establishing or visualizing a certain sound before ever even picking up your clarinet. Locking onto that image like an archer sighting the target, only then would you place the horn in your mouth. Without thinking of anything but that sound, take a deep breath from your diaphragm, blow everything through the clarinet, and fill up the entire room.

This was in sharp contrast to a later meeting with Artie Shaw, who loved to answer one question with another.

* * *

With regular gigs, regular student hours, and good friends, I was feeling a sense of accomplishment and the inner peace that comes along with it. Everything seemed like being in the right place at the right time and, moreover, doing the right thing. To use psychological terms, things were ego-syntonic (offering a high degree of emotional responsiveness to the surrounding environment) and I was experiencing a sense of self-actualization to the fullest degree. Not only was I playing the music I loved and thriving doing so, but I had a new, ever-expanding circle of friends — each one a mini-mentor, offering me new ideas, styles, techniques, opportunities. They all accepted me as I was, with no judgment, and all expected that I had endless room to grow as a musician. That dynamic being so widespread was something new to me, and perhaps I never could have adjusted if not for all I had learned from Buddy. Rochester seemed a haven for DeFrancoism, as I had started to think of his approach to music and life.

Barney seemed to know every serious jazz musician in Rochester. He loved the music, played it well, and was much sought after for paying gigs. In contrast, though my paying jobs had been increasing, they were relatively scarce. He decided to change this and began inviting me along on some of his gigs wherever there was room for a clarinet player. At these gigs, I'd be introduced to all of the band members, most in their twenties, with Barney and I usually the lone teenagers, though there were only months left before that would be a thing of the past. Being Barney's buddy was a foot in the door for most of Rochester's rather exclusive jazz scene, as well as a window to information about the whens and wheres of the best jam sessions and paying gigs.

One steady Friday night job of Barney's stands out in my mind. It was unusual because, even though he was considered a full member of Hank Berger's sextet, playing double bass for the group, he received no salary for those Friday gigs. While the club's budget allowed for paying six players on busy nights such as Saturdays and even Sundays, Friday crowds were never too big and with that in mind, the management offered to pay for only five men. Barney was asked to come along and play anyway, receiving his fill of free beer and food for his efforts.

Barney liked to drink and could down good food like the starving student he wasn't — remember that he, unlike the most of us, lived at home while attending Eastman. When I tagged along, he would order a free beer for me at each intermission, downing two or three on his own. Once I saw this, I understood why he was sleeping late into Saturday that first night I ate dinner with his family — he was in recovery from his 'pay' from his unpaid gigs!

"Bring your horn to the club," he would tell me each time I came along. "But leave it in the trunk. Later in the night, when Herr Berger loosens up, I'll ask him if you can sit in for a few numbers."

Berger was an excellent trombone player, loose and free, but as a bandleader, he ran a tight ship. I never could figure out if he liked me or not, or even if he liked my playing. Nevertheless, Barney's tactics always worked. It helped that he could suggest letting me sit in was compensation for his not being paid.

Barney always came across as hip, cool, and in control. After a while I discovered that the ease I felt around him was standard when hanging out with string players and even brass players. It was when I met another reed player that posturing and personal stabs would ensue.

This happened shortly before the Easter break. I accepted a well-paying four-hour gig with a fifteen-piece band organized specifically for the occasion. Three of Rochester's saxophone stars were included in the band. There was Johnny Lewis on lead alto, Sam Ansuini on fourth tenor and all the solos, and the up-and-coming sixteen-year-old local bebop sensation Joe Romano on second tenor. I pulled the position of third alto sax, as well as garnering *all* the clarinet solos. There was a fifth reed man as well, very competent and supplying depth and a solid bottom to the section with his baritone sax.

Romano resembled Flip Phillips, but sounded like Dexter Gordon. Ansuini had a super sweet sound and could phrase a ballad so beautifully that couples often stopped in mid-dance to listen. Lewis had such a full, rounded, voluminous tone that, if and when called for, he could easily project it not only over the top of the saxophone section, but also over the entire orchestra with precision control.

It was a pleasure and a privilege meeting and playing with these saxophone giants, but it lacked the ease and camaraderie of working with Barney and other string players. Still, the one-upmanship made it clear to me that I would never excel as a saxophonist; clarinet was my forte. At intermission, though, all the posturing was over, each of us knowing each other's strengths, and complimenting each other on them. Joe Romano summed it up, "Sam's the sweet one, Johnny sounds super-strong like Willie Smith or Johnny Dankworth, and Steve plays one helluva clarinet!"

Having felt left behind in my saxophone playing, I was more than grateful for the compliment, but he didn't stop there.

"And where did you get that groovy double-breasted suit? If Bond's sells them, I'll be waiting outside their door when they open in the morning!"

* * *

Easter vacation finally arrived. While none of the myriad ways I was keeping busy felt like a burden, the idea of actually having five full days to myself was too much to pass up. As well, Rochester's wicked winter was finally calling it quits and spring fever was infecting the student body. There was also that the Easter landmark meant only six full weeks remained before I would have a full year at Eastman under my belt.

It wasn't to be that easy, though. With Easter vacation on the horizon, I was called into the office of the assistant to the dean. Although I was doing well enough in most of my subjects, I was close to failing Theory of Music. The theory course at Eastman was worth four to six credits, was a core requirement, and was spread over two years. The course was based in large part on the works of J.S. Bach, that prolific master of musical composition. I had underestimated Bach's genius and had failed to fully apply myself to understanding and imitating his style of composition. A failing grade in any of the other academic subjects or in one of the applied music courses (piano, trumpet, band, or orchestra) might have been tolerated, but to fail theory was to court expulsion.

I rode the Lehigh Valley Railroad from Rochester to Mauch Chunk, PA (now known as Jim Thorpe). Normally a pleasant five-and-a-half hour trip, I couldn't enjoy it trapped in a web of soul-searching sparked by this news. Melancholy quickly gave way to resolve and I spent the most of the trip rehashing my past problems and planning strategies for the future, knowing that Bach would have to receive my full attention for the remainder of the school year.

I had my course of action planned out by the time Dad met me at the station to drive me the rest of the way home. I kept quiet about the grades, suspecting that it would lead to arguments about how worthwhile my time at Eastman was. However, as soon as we got home, he announced that the school had written to him as the financier of my education about my trouble with theory. I was quick to explain that I had misjudged my time, and needed to play out less at night and stay in more and study. I told him I would get a tutor, one steeped in Bach, would change my class seat to one at the front of the class, and I would participate more — ask many questions, do extra work outside of class, and always be in my professor's face.

Dad was really listening to me, so I decided to hit him with something new.

"I need more time in Rochester, so may I please stay there for the summer? I can profit musically from the opportunities there and of course, I can get a head start on theory for my second year."

What I *wasn't* saying was that I didn't want to be working for him through the summer.

Dad thought a while and then told me, "Okay, you can stay for the summer, but I'm not going to support you for those three months."

I was ecstatic — though I hid it well. I knew I would never work for him again. I would be totally free in Rochester, but I would also be absolutely broke. What I needed now was a steady paying gig to get me through the summer in Rochester.

Easter passed quickly, with my time spent on planning the details of my recovery in Theory of Music class and plotting ways to get that summer gig I needed in a city full of musicians. I had to concentrate more on the former, so the latter would be left fairly open. Still, I felt relaxed, refreshed, and eager to return to Rochester.

Beyond my self-appointed tasks of learning theory and Bach, I had two important concerts coming up, both to be held in the Eastman Theatre and both open to the public. Frederick Fennell would conduct the symphonic band while the junior symphony orchestra would be led by someone as yet unnamed, but certainly equally capable. As a freshman, my chair in the symphonic band was of secondary importance. I had no solo or first clarinet parts to perform, those being reserved for the upperclassmen. With that in mind, the concert would not be a major distraction from repairing my Theory of Music grade. Or so I thought.

At our last band rehearsal, Fennell realized that he had no saxophone player to perform the sax solos Bizet had written for his signature piece, "Bolero". Fennell faced the clarinet section, almost twenty strong, and asked if any of us played E-flat alto sax. I was the only one to raise my hand. Certainly there were others that did, but most of them were so rigidly trained in classical clarinet playing that they were afraid that playing sax would ruin their clarinet embouchure (lip formation), as was the thinking at the time in many circles. Possibly, some simply didn't want their final grade based on their saxophone playing when they were already comfortably ensconced in position with their clarinet. Fennell may have been a fair and decent laid-back gentleman, but he would expect a flawless performance.

The concert, held just a few weeks later on a pleasant spring night, went well. Fennell was called to take more than one bow, and was more than pleased with our performance. He even pointed to me, asking that I stand and be acknowledged for my saxophone solos on "Bolero". I too was more than pleased — my final grade in band was assured to be a good one. More than that, I had reassured myself that I could excel on the saxophone in the right circumstances, not too long after considering myself an also-ran on the instrument in the face of playing with some giants.

However, there was still Bach burning a hole in my head. How had I let myself overlook his importance, his greatness, his genius — never mind my grade? We had studied his life the previous semester in our History of Music class under Miss Watanabe. She presented him in her usual didactic manner, with a supremely serious schoolmarm look on her face, as she did for others like Scarlatti, Beethoven, and Mozart. Her approach may have been to compensate for her seeming somewhat scared. She had good enough reason. Though it was 1949, the war was still in our consciousnesses. For my part, I was no exception, treating anything Japanese with passive-aggressive behavior. Eastman saw her differently, of course, and she would stay on their staff for decades, constantly advancing through an illustrious career.

Despite my attitude towards the Japanese at the time, I still took in enough to pass the course, but I remembered more about the cigarettes I sat there smoking than any of those classicists. Thinking back, I realized I had fought complete immersion in the class, evidenced in my final report. We had to write 1,500 words on the classic musician-composer of our choice and I asked for special permission to write about one of my idols, Benny Goodman, pleading that he was classic within American music. I may have been the only student in that class whose paper wasn't about a composer who is immortalized in plaster busts sitting atop pianos around the world.

Needing to immerse myself in Bach didn't change much of my routine, though. One evening I sat down to listen to Symphony Sid, a hip New York City radio announcer who played nothing but jazz from midnight to 6 a.m. I had a six-tube table model Zenith Bakelight radio which, while small, was nevertheless powerful enough to pick up stations that far away. This particular night, though, I was unable to tune in Symphony Sid, his station being drowned out by another. The announcer identified the station as being from Toronto, sixty-five miles due north across Lake Ontario and the Canadian border. I stayed tuned, hoping to hear some jazz, but instead heard something I needed to hear all the more. The program that night was to be a two-hour concert recorded in the auditorium of Toronto's Eaton's department store. I reached over to change the station, but stopped when the announcer introduced a young Canadian pianist, Glenn Gould, crediting him as the world's youngest expert interpreter of Bach.

Jazz was what I wanted, but I knew I needed to become more familiar with Bach for the sake of not only my future at Eastman, but the independence that came with it. Settling for classical seemed like homework, but I knew I *had* to do my homework and understood what the consequences would be if I didn't. I settled back to listen, and found that listening to Gould was anything but work.

He seemed to have perfect timing and be totally engrossed in everything Bach had written. There was such intensity in his playing that time-worn melodies sparkled and became magically new and fresh. Even in the extremely fast passages, his technique was amazingly clean. Regardless of the speed, he was able to separately enunciate each note — something every instrumentalist, yours truly included, struggles for years to perfect. I was enthralled to the point where tears came to my eyes at one point. I found myself yearning to be able to articulate as well. For the first time, I heard a classical performance as I did jazz — certainly it helped that, like jazz pianist Erroll Garner, he hummed, grunted, sang, and groaned along as he played, all of it a *sotto voce* accompaniment to his piano artistry.

I wondered why no one at school ever played Bach this way. I was sure that Bach himself would have nothing but praise on hearing Gould's interpretation, and may well have even admitted that he himself could not perform his own music as well.

Gould finally ended a laundry list of Bach variations that lasted for nearly half an hour, and I sat stunned — he was more precise than a metronome and more rhythmically strict than the majority of drummers. He could begin a piece at a certain tempo and *twenty-five minutes later*, end it in exactly the same tempo without losing even a millisecond of a beat.

I fell in love with Gould's playing that night. His uninhibited and exuberant expression of Bach moved me so much I was wondering why it had taken me so long to get hip to old J.S. I devoured the composer's work after that. Tuning in to Gould's concert by chance was a turning point for me, one which helped me find new enthusiasm to study Bach.

* * *

May left no moments to breathe. Everything was necessary, this commitment or that one, and much of it with my entire future hanging in the balance. I had strictly compartmentalized my time and inwardly I *knew* that I would succeed, no matter how much I felt spread out in every direction.

I felt confident enough that I managed to start up a relationship with Phoebe, an extremely tall, buxom Liberal Arts major with a minor in piano at the University of Rochester. She was a jazz fanatic, and that I was a jazz player, combined with my 6' 2" height, bonded us immediately. She was six feet tall and preferred taller men, and I was one of the few who fit the bill. We'd met when she attended a jam session I played in — she noticed me and my playing, and I noticed her and the way she came alive to the music. She stared into my eyes while we talked and that was it. Most of the time, she was proper and ladylike, but the instant she heard jazz, she was a wild woman. It was the best of both worlds for both of us.

The school held a semi-formal dance and I found myself stuck. I wanted to take Phoebe, but didn't have a car to pick her up in. Walter Mallon came to my rescue. As an insurance agent, he had connections and contacts all over town, and arranged with the owner of the city's largest Chevrolet garage to let me rent a brand-new 1949 sedan for just $19. The owner handled the transaction himself, being unsure of renting to a nineteen-year-old and wanting to look me over. Still, I had Walter Mallon's recommendation, and he just gave my driver's license a cursory examination before saying, "Walter Mallon must think well of you. Enjoy yourself."

I did. The night with Phoebe was perfect and I finally felt like I had found someone who understood me. She had no problem taking part in the conversations between the students of a music school and even impressed some of my friends with her knowledge of jazz. The dance was however just a brief interlude between practice and school. I had to scramble even more to make up the time I had spent at the dance, preparing for it, and arranging for the car.

All the work was made all that much easier with the idea that managing it meant I would have a full, free summer with no worries about working in my father's store or living under his rules. With that, though, came the worries about how I would pay for it, so time was spent inquiring about work. These inquiries sandwiched between all my other commitments meant that I could hardly do justice to the search. It was a catch-22. If I took the time to look for work, I might not put in the time necessary to pass Theory of Music and throw my entire Eastman experience out the window — and considering they would again write Dad, that might kill the idea of staying in Rochester to do the job anyway. If I gave Bach the study he deserved, I would be outflanked by one or another of the countless other musicians in town looking for the same jobs as I was.

I had to deal with what was in front of me and hope that getting a job would take care of itself. I changed seats, moving to the front of the Theory classroom and started raising my hand every chance I could. The teacher was a cold, standoffish man who was a bigwig on the faculty, and the most I could ever raise from him was a half-smile. In the end, the combination of making myself more visible and immersing myself in theory and Bach worked, and I passed the course, though without comment one from the teacher. My grade was certainly owed in part to Glenn Gould, who likely made the difference between my failing the course as I was otherwise destined to, and passing it. Without Gould, I may never have found my passion for Bach.

The grade was all well and good, and certainly took some of the weight off me, but I was still without work for the summer. Barney came to my rescue. I found a note from him in my student mailbox informing me that Johnny Lewis, now the lead alto man in Bill O'Brien's band, was looking for someone to replace him. O'Brien's band worked three nights a week — Mondays, Wednesdays, and Fridays. Bill had recently been discharged from a military band and was anxious to continue playing in civilian life. A devout Catholic, he was a natural choice for these gigs — tri-weekly parish hall dances paid for by one of Rochester's largest Catholic churches, a full cathedral operating under Bishop Fulton Sheen who would soon win nationwide T.V. fame with a weekly show. The church had enough money to support three gigs a week for a fourteen-piece band, large enough to have the standard big-band instrumentation.

The note went on, not only offering how I could get the gig, but pushing me to take it and save myself from working in Dad's store for the summer. He noted that three months of nothing but jazz would be the best thing I could hope for.

I left him a note in response:

Barney,

It's done! I'm staying for the summer!

Man, he'll pay again for Eastman come September, but the summer bread will have to come from my horn.

Save me a Genesee — we'll down a few!

Steve.

Benny Goodman

Born Benjamin David Goodman in Chicago in 1909, Benny was the ninth of twelve children of working-class Jewish immigrants from Poland. At age 10 he started music lessons at a local synagogue, joining a boys' club band the following year. He moved on to take lessons from Franz Schoepp but soon became influenced by New Orleans jazz musicians playing locally.

Goodman began playing professionally while still in his teens, working alongside Bix Beiderbecke at age 14 and dropping out of high school the following year to concentrate on his music career. He joined Ben Pollack's orchestra in Los Angeles at 16, which moved east to New York in 1928. He recorded with the orchestra in 1926, and a bare two years later was recording under his own name, though continuing with Pollack through 1929. During this time he recorded not only with the full band, but with various subgroups under a variety of names.

Late in 1929 Benny's father died in a traffic accident. Benny had previously urged him to retire, but the elder Goodman was unwilling to live off his son's success. It would haunt Benny for the rest of his life that his father never got to leave the job he hated so much or to see his son play professionally.

Through the late 1920s and early 1930s Goodman garnered a reputation as a session musician, recording with the likes of Red Nichols, Ted Lewis, Paul Whiteman, and both Dorsey brothers; he also played for film and Broadway. Working off this success, he assembled his first big band, a twelve-piece group.

The new band won a slot on the radio program *Let's Dance* in 1935. Wanting a 'hotter' sound, Goodman hired Gene Krupa and, on agent John Hammond's suggestion, purchased Fletcher Henderson's song catalog and hired the bandleader to write arrangements and his bandsmen to teach them. The show aired late and had little effect in the East, but helped the band develop a following on the West Coast, though they were unaware of it at the time. When a strike led to the show's cancellation that May, the band decided to embark on a national tour.

Audiences were unprepared for the hot jazz stylings Goodman presented, and the negative response left the band on the verge of collapse, both financially and in terms of morale. In August they reached Los Angeles for a tour-ending three-week engagement at the Palomar Ballroom. A recording of "King Porter Stomp" backed with "Sometimes I'm Happy" had been released the previous month to rave reviews, but had little effect on earlier shows. However, combined with the West Coast radio following it made a powerful turning point for the band. Following a lukewarm response to their first set, Gene Krupa announced, "If we're gonna die, Benny, let's die playing our own thing." The crowd broke into wild applause on hearing the hot jazz stylings, cheering through Bunny Berigan's solos. The audience was there to hear the Goodman band they knew from radio, and Benny only found out because he thought the gig was a lost cause. The rest of the engagement was historic, with newspapers featuring the new musical phenomenon prominently. Audiences sparked a new dance craze, the Jitterbug, which also received national attention.

Goodman's success boomed, playing with the full big band as well as in a trio, a quartet, and a sextet. He was dubbed 'The King of Swing' by Krupa. His popularity allowed him to forego touring the Southern states where Jim Crow laws prevented integrated bands from playing, and so he was able to hire Teddy Wilson in 1935 and Lionel Hampton in 1936, incorporating both into a quartet with him and Krupa. In 1937, *Camel Caravan* became a prime-time radio showcase for Goodman, running for three years. The highlight of this period was a then-unheard-of swing concert at New York's Carnegie Hall in 1938. Recognizing the importance of this date, Goodman cancelled other engagements and arranged rehearsals inside the venue to ensure the band knew the acoustics. Recordings of this concert were found in 1950 and have remained in print ever since.

In 1939 Hammond snuck Charlie Christian onto the stage during a break in a show, after finding out Benny thought the electric guitar wouldn't work with the band and Christian himself was too flashy. On seeing him there, Goodman chose a song to stump Christian but was pleasantly surprised by the result. Christian was hired and played with the band and the sextet for two years, also writing arrangements. Fletcher Henderson himself joined the band during this period.

In 1942 Goodman married Hammond's sister, Alice, after dating her for just three months.

With swing on the wane, Goodman took on bebop, hiring Buddy Greco, Zoot Sims, Stan Hasselgård, and Wardell Gray among others. Though Goodman was initially taken by the new style, he began to see it as the wrong approach and returned to swing. He then began to seriously pursue classical music, recording first with the Budapest Quartet. In 1949 he began studying under classical clarinetist Reginald Kell, learning to change his approach entirely from embouchure to fingering techniques, even going so far as having his finger calluses removed. He went on to commission and premiere works by composers such as Béla Bartók and Aaron Copland.

A rift developed between Goodman and Hammond owing to an ill-fated 1953 tour of a new swing band alongside Louis Armstrong's All-Stars. The two men would only reconcile in the 1980s, though Benny played a 1975 PBS tribute to Hammond alongside George Benson, who later guested on a Goodman album. He continued playing into his later years, recording and touring with various bands of varying sizes.

Goodman was known to be quite the taskmaster, Helen Forrest recalling that her twenty months with him "seem like a life sentence". His disdainful glare became famed as 'The Ray'. Despite this reputation, he managed to attract top-notch musicians including Harry James, Ziggy Elman, Stan Getz, and vocalists such as Anita O'Day, Martha Tilton, Billie Holiday, and Peggy Lee.

Goodman appeared with his band in a number of feature films, including *Hollywood Hotel, Syncopation, Stage Door Canteen, Sweet and Low-Down* (his only starring role), and *A Song Is Born*. Steve Allen played Goodman in 1955's *The Benny Goodman Story*, a heavily fictionalized biographical film.

Goodman continued playing clarinet until his death at age 77 from a heart attack. He was survived by his two daughters, Benjie and Rachel, and interred in the Long Ridge Cemetery in Stamford, Connecticut. His personal collection, including rare recordings, was given to the Yale University library. That same year he was named the recipient of the Grammy Lifetime Achievement Award. He was named to the Kennedy Center Honors list in 1982. "Sing, Sing, Sing" was named one of the NPR 100, the public broadcaster's list of the hundred most important musical works of the 20th Century.

Glenn Gould

Born in Toronto in 1932 to musical parents, Glenn Gould began playing piano at an early age, with his mother (a relative of Norwegian composer Edvard Grieg) his first teacher. At age 3 he was determined to have absolute pitch, able to identify and reproduce any tone. He started composing original works very young, performing them for family and friends, even at Emmanuel Presbyterian Church at age 5. At age 6 Gould attended his first live performance and was inspired by featured soloist Józef Hofmann, considered one of the greatest pianists of all time. At age 10 he began studying piano as well as organ and theory under Alberto Guerrero at Toronto's Royal Conservatory of Music. At age 12 he won the piano trophy at the Kiwanis Music Festival, his first and only competition — after that he remained vehemently opposed to competition, especially among young musicians. He achieved his diploma from the Royal Conservatory with highest honors at age 14, but continued studying with Guerrero for ten years.

A child prodigy, Gould quickly became known for technical proficiency, absolute accuracy, and his unique technique, swaying and humming as he maintained fast tempos while playing each note with crispness and clarity. He used a special chair built by his father, allowing him to sit lower than standard seating and to pull the piano keys down rather than striking them from above. The chair now is displayed under glass at the National Library of Canada.

Gould studied music largely by reading it rather than practicing, a technique learned from Guerrero. He practiced very little, focusing on articulation when he did, even refraining from playing pieces until mere weeks before recording them. He eschewed what he called 'hedonism' — showmanship and theatricality — preferring to concentrate on playing. His arrangements and interpretations were recognized widely for their brilliance and originality.

Gould gave his first notable public performance in 1945, playing the organ. In 1946 he performed with the Toronto Symphony Orchestra, and in 1947 he gave his first public recital. Three years later he would give his first radio recital, beginning a long association with the CBC (Canadian Broadcasting Corporation) as both performer and producer, the latter role resulting in his Solitude Trilogy, three hour-long documentaries about regions of Canada that employed overlapping voices in a fugue style, what Gould termed 'contrapuntal radio'.

Gould became the first North American to play the USSR, touring the country in 1957 and playing music previously restricted under Soviet Communism. His last public performance was in April 1964 at the Wilshire Ebell Theater in Los Angeles. Following this, Gould no longer performed live, restricting himself to recording and broadcasting, where he had a greater sense of control and intimacy — he even considered tape editing as part of his creative arsenal.

Gould's recordings include the celebrated *Bach: The Goldberg Variations* in 1955 and an also-acclaimed, though markedly different, 1981 version of the same piece — his first time re-recording the same work, spurred by advances in recording technology. Bach was a particular favourite and Gould recorded most of Bach's keyboard works, becoming particularly associated with the composer. He also recorded all of Beethoven's piano concertos and most of his sonatas, as well as all of Mozart's sonatas, despite criticizing him fiercely, even saying that the composer "died too late". He recorded numerous composers and works that were not well-known to North American audiences.

Gould was known for his eccentricities almost as much as his skill. He was secretive to the point where Yehudi Menuhin once noted, "No supreme pianist has ever given of his heart and mind so overwhelmingly while showing himself so sparingly." He wrote under pseudonyms, allowing him to criticize his own work. He was extremely particular about the arrangements and conditions in studios he would record in. He refused to play concerts without the chair his father built, using it even when worn through. He hated applause, arguing that the tradition should be abandoned. When Gould soloed with the New York Philharmonic, Leonard Bernstein warned the audience that he took no responsibility for what was to follow. Even so, Bernstein has noted "There is nobody quite like him, and I just love playing with him."

Gould won three Grammy Awards for his music, and another for his writing on album notes. Toronto's Royal Conservatory of Music founded the Glenn Gould School in 1997. The Glenn Gould Foundation was founded in 1983 and awards the Glenn Gould Prize every three years for a 'highly exceptional contribution to music and its communication'. The CBC established the Glenn Gould Studio in their Toronto broadcast center. A celebrated film, *Thirty-Two Short Films About Glenn Gould*, is structured to reflect Gould's playing of the thirty-two *Goldberg Variations*. His recording of Bach's "Prelude and Fugue in C Major" from *The Well-Tempered Clavier* was selected to be included on the Voyager I spacecraft, now the farthest man-made object from Earth.

Gould had planned to give up playing piano professionally at age 50, with his later years to focus on conducting, composing, and writing about music. However, just two days past his fiftieth birthday he suffered a stroke which paralyzed the left side of his body. In hospital his condition deteriorated quickly, and he was removed from life support just over a week later. He lies buried in Toronto's Mount Pleasant Cemetery, his gravestone engraved with the opening notes of *The Goldberg Variations*.

Chapter 10 Summertime

I welcomed June 1949 with open arms. Rochester had become home, and now I was free to live in the whole city, not just stretch out from the confines of Eastman when my commitments allowed. Not that Eastman was by any stretch a burden, but pursuing my course work limited my time and consequently my access to the rest of the city. Sure, I had seen a number of the jazz venues and met a number of the people of the city, but life as a student is invariably centered around the campus.

Rochester was both small town and big city at once, its people unpretentious and unassuming, and thanks to Eastman sitting in its midst, there was an almost universal love of good music. 'Kodak City' may well have been called 'Music City'. It seemed the perfect place for a struggling musician to hang his hat. And I *was* struggling — practically penniless and still searching for a more specific direction than simply *music*. But all Rochester asked of me was that I remain immersed in music and dedicated to my career, something that was my goal in the first place. A musician in Rochester was not quite royalty, but the news that one played was always greeted with enthusiastic warmth.

I was not just happy, I was ecstatic. Phoebe could tell by just looking at me when she stopped by on her way home to New Jersey for the summer. Over the past month, she'd been learning more about jazz from me and I had been learning about her wide range of subjects — geology, astronomy, sociology — but more importantly, we could talk about personal affairs with each other comfortably. It hadn't taken long before she could read me like a book.

"Steve, you look great!" she told me. "Why, you're full of energy! Are you dating someone else?"

Phoebe, perceptive as always, knew I needed no other women. Perched politely at the door to my bedroom, she didn't wait for an answer, instead pulling me close into a long and intense embrace. The only thing that treated me better than Phoebe was jazz. I loved both and could never seem to get enough of either. We were still locked in a kiss when the downstairs phone rang. More permissive than most landladies, Mrs. Arfino allowed us to have girls visit our bedrooms, even if only in the morning. My roommate Don had a buxom blonde girlfriend who never missed a day, showing up early each morning, standing over his bed, shaking it a bit to make sure he was paying full attention, then jumping in with him. I called that the 'morning matinée'. Don had nicknamed her 'NF', short for 'nymph'.

Mrs. Arfino called up to say my mother was on the phone. My final report card had arrived and she told me gleefully that I had passed everything: theory, composition, and all three solo performance exams — clarinet, piano, and trumpet. She congratulated me before turning serious for some parting motherly advice: "Now you rest some, eat more, and fatten up. You'll need to be in good health for a full summer of jam sessions, bebop, and those big band gigs."

I told Phoebe and we celebrated until we realized that it was getting late and she had to go. We kissed a long goodbye and she left, making me promise to write.

Later that day Don decided it was time for him to leave for home. He would be gone all summer, and I would have twice the space for the same price. He left me with instructions to tell NF to call him when she showed up the next morning, as he had forgotten to tell her he would be leaving. Finally I was alone. But the next morning, as expected, NF showed up. It was a bit awkward telling her that her boyfriend had forgotten to mention he would be leaving for the summer. She was surprised and upset, but quickly regained her composure and sat on his bed, eyeballing me, with the unspoken message being more than clear. With Don gone, she was willing to give *me* a try. Unwilling to cross that line, but unsure what else to do, I said nothing until she got up and left of her own accord. *Theater closed*, I thought. *No more matinées until September*.

I took some time to readjust to the place as mine. Mrs. Arfino was great, and even sharing the place had been good, considering it was Don. All of us Eastman boys had interesting living situations. The girls got their own dormitory, but male students were simply given a list of assorted off-campus housing and expected to fend for themselves. Rooms were readily available and easily affordable, but seventeen- and eighteen-year-olds could hardly be expected to choose well. Few of us had ever lived apart from our parents before Eastman and many made bad choices, such as my earlier rooming house or the kids who ended up staying at the YMCA. There was a similarity to the military in attending Eastman — in class, during rehearsals, or on stage, absolute perfection was expected, but when off-duty, we were left to adapt to any and every type of adverse living condition.

That said, the girls were living in the cold and uninviting dormitory, their comings and goings monitored in minute detail by frowning house mothers. As boys, we could live happily in loosely-run private homes, such as my University Avenue rental. We had no formalities to live by and, considering the times, we boys were almost expected to be promiscuous and wild in our free time.

Maybe the cold atmosphere of the girls' dormitory owed partly to history. School founder George Eastman's mansion was directly up the street. Once it had always been full of festive events — organ recitals, chamber music concerts, dining and dancing, parties, etc. All that ended with Eastman's death by suicide. The house was now a photographic museum, but the shadow of his demise still hung over it, and we all knew it as 'George Eastman's house'. Biographers attribute the suicide to severe depression, with no single notable pivot for his decision. His death being otherwise senseless, the sorrow of the loss of such an inventor and philanthropist permeated everything he had once owned — which in Rochester was quite a lot.

In contrast, I was quite happy in the Arfino house, out of the reach of the shadows of Rochester history. There was easy access to the school and amenities, I liked Don, and I liked the Arfinos.

Maria Arfino, the landlady's only daughter, showed up at my door that Sunday morning, stretching her neck in to see me lying sprawled face-up across the bed, stripped to the waist, eyes closed, and totally motionless. I was of course practicing my Jacobson exercises. While endorsed by Dr. Jacobson's alma mater, Harvard University, and dignitaries like Eleanor Roosevelt, the idea was still unknown to most and Maria didn't know what to make of it. I felt her presence, though she said nothing and made no sound.

"Stephen, are you okay?" she suddenly blurted out. "You're hardly breathing! Open your eyes — I have something to give you."

I waited a few seconds before opening my eyes and taking in the picture of her in the doorway. I wondered if this plain Jane twenty-five-year-old living with her mother really understood what a sex-starved nineteen-year-old like I was at the time would make of that.

"I've a piece of homemade cherry pie for you," she grinned. "You're also invited downstairs in about an hour. As you are is good. Well, it's always best to cover yourself. You don't want to catch cold and the body's temperature can drop . . ."

I took her in as she talked. Sexy she wasn't. Still, a penniless, starving student living in an attic could be immediately attracted to a woman who could bake a pie — though Maria was too sisterly for me to even think of her sexually, even if I didn't have Phoebe.

* * *

My new gig with Bill O'Brien's band came with additional perks.

To fill Johnny Lewis' shoes required specific training, and Johnny himself was providing it. We got along well and I found out he was yet another Rochester Italian — 'Lewis' was his stage name, with his birth name only having the 'L' in common, the rest being long and Italian. Though he was a sax man he was built like a lead trumpet player — short, stocky, and very wide-chested. He managed volume like Maynard Ferguson and I knew it would be a lot of work filling in for him.

"Bolero" had restored my self-confidence with the saxophone, but I had to be ready to play with a professional band, as well as catch up with all its other members. Unlike Johnny, I was tall and lanky so producing the volume he wanted wasn't easy.

"The lead alto," he told me, "has to be able to soar above the trumpets and the rest of the brass."

To help, he had me try a new mouthpiece, a five-star Brilhart with a very wide bore. It helped, but alone it wasn't enough. I had just seven days to prepare, and filling his shoes would mean playing triple forte for hours on end — an easy matter with his big lungs, but a huge leap forward for me. Still, there was no backing down. Not going ahead would mean losing my source of income and the freedom of Rochester for the summer, never mind showing O'Brien and his band that I wasn't up to the professional standards they needed. In one week I had to make the leap from an insignificant third alto player, blowing only moderate volumes and always following four other saxophones, to being at the forefront of a big band.

There were three gigs left for Johnny with O'Brien's band, and I tagged along for each one, positioning myself directly alongside his chair. I paid no mind to the audience or what they must have thought seeing me sitting there with no instrument. In hindsight, I found a cure for stage fright: fear. The idea that I might not be ready let me put everything else aside and focus on the task at hand. I analyzed and memorized everything Johnny did as best I could. Even so, when away from the stage, occasionally I would be gripped by nagging questions. Why was I trying so hard to perfect my sax playing when it's always been my second instrument? Had I learned clarinet *too* thoroughly, making it harder to adapt to the sax? Why had I taken this gig instead of the clarinet gig I'd been offered?

Sax is generally easier to learn for a newcomer, but for me, it was hard work — much harder than the clarinet. I had to unlearn my clarinet skills to relearn them for the sax. Clarinet I could play without thinking. To this point I hadn't had any problems being overly conscious when playing the sax as it wasn't something that came up all that often. The clarinet gig I had been offered was with Russ Ives, playing Dixieland jazz two or three nights a week for up to $18 a gig. However, with Bill O'Brien I would be playing bebop and earning up to $21 a week. It would be a stretch for me, but it was the right decision musically, which was more important than financially.

No matter how much I could have used the money, no matter how much easier it would have been to stick with my clarinet rather than take on a regular sax gig, Dixieland would always lose out to bebop. Dizzy Gillespie had called Dixieland players "moldy figs", and the last thing I was going to do was disappoint Dizzy.

It was easy enough to forget my doubts when playing along with Johnny, as much as I had to work to keep up with him. He was warm and easygoing. The other orchestra members however kept their distance, giving me a polite but cool reception. It was understandable. Johnny would be gone next week but they would still be there, and their bread and butter would depend on this young, untested Eastman kid who would have to not only play well, but fill Johnny's shoes. That I was an Eastman student was probably a larger part of their reticence than my relative youth. Despite my experience, there was an animosity and even jealousy that existed between some professional jazz players and the Eastman students. We were seen as elitist classical players, too high-brow to play jazz, while the local home-bred musicians were seen as populists, playing whatever the public wanted: big band, swing, Dixieland, and the latest thing, bebop.

I stood with one foot in each camp. I knew I would need to overcome that distance to work well with the band. Any well-knit saxophone section needs to phrase together, breathe together, and even make their mistakes together. Like military planes flying in close formation, if the leader went a little off, the rest of us would need to follow or there'd be a wreck. Bill took me aside and helped quell my anxiety. He had no doubts — I would be his new lead alto man. With Bill's endorsement clear, the rest of the band would fall in line, even if it meant this skinny Eastman kid would be making more than they would.

For the Wednesday, Friday, and Saturday night shows, 8:30 to 11:30 pm, leads would be paid $7 a night, those who doubled (played bass and guitar, or second trumpet and vocals) would get $6, and the rest, $5. I quickly agreed, but put my foot down when he told me that we would be paid by check, once a week, at the end of the week. I told him I needed to be paid cash and paid for each gig that night. He coolly asked me why.

"Because this summer, thanks to you, I will only earn $21 each week — plus another $3.50 for Barbara Mallon's private lesson. With only $24.50 a week, I'll be broke most of the time. Like tonight. I spent my last dime to get here on the Lake Avenue bus."

He didn't flinch and didn't say a word, but the look in his eyes said enough. Sure enough, he paid me cash after each gig. I guess he couldn't really agree to do so out loud as then he'd be on the hook to do the same for all the others, but he understood my situation being a struggling student as well as a struggling musician and so never said another word about it, just quietly handed me the cash each time we finished playing. With that settled,

I eased my way into the idea of lead alto and quickly made the position my own, earning the trust and camaraderie of the rest of the band.

What a life I had that summer! I was playing music for a living, had no roommate, no classes, my daytime free, and a nice landlady. Two nights a week, I got home-cooked meals — one at the Mallons', and one at home from Mrs. Arfino. The rest of the time was mine to fill. Mine and my trusty Zenith Bakelite radio's. My mother had found it when radios were scarce during the war years, the last one available in Pottsville, not far from Lansford where none could be found. Barney may have introduced me to jazz from Toronto stations, but Symphony Sid from New York City was my own find. Easily the Big Apple's most hip and avant-garde jazz show, it required a little fine tuning to pick up, but with some work, it came in loud and clear. Sid played only the best modern jazz, be it swinging big band or state-of-the-art small combos, never anything commercial. Sid specialized in the new, and echoed Dizzy Gillespie in calling Dixieland players "moldy figs". Bop was the thing for Sid.

Often broadcasting live from Birdland, "the Jazz Capital of the World", Sid would showcase every worthwhile modern jazz artist. The club itself was at Broadway and 52nd and was simply jazz heaven. For only $1.25 admission, you had three choices of seating: tables with waiter service, the bar, and a bleacher section where, unlike the others, you didn't have to buy any drinks and there were no age restrictions. Once I sat in the bleachers with Charlie and my teacher's son — only fourteen or fifteen years old but a jazz aficionado — and listened to a non-stop show that ran from 9 p.m. to 4 a.m. The first group featured Bud Powell, the second Dizzy Gillespie, and the third Charlie Parker — a priceless experience for an unbelievable price! Though Rochester was feeling like home, I was missing my forays to the Big Apple and Sid provided a decent substitute, not to mention astounding jazz late into the night.

So my nights were filled with jazz, thanks to Bill O'Brien and his band, Sid, and those times Barney and I could get together. My days had their fair share of music, as I practiced and jammed with friends, but they were also the days of a poor musician. Thank God I grew up in a grocery store — hell, I was almost born in one!

As the story goes, my mother had slaved all day waiting on customers — it was Christmas Eve, a busy day for a grocery store even in the middle of the Great Depression. Towards evening, she turned from helping a customer, dropped her apron, hustled upstairs, and delivered an eleven-pound baby boy. My dad, proud as a peacock but still a businessman, passed out free cigars to all the last-minute shoppers.

"The sign in the window says it all," he was reported to have announced. "We deliver!"

My time in the family business had taught me to shop for food. I could find quality goods at the best prices. Further, my father had once been a professional chef, and between his and my mother's culinary talents, I had picked up more than a few tricks. I knew how to properly prepare many foods, and also how to keep costs down by coaxing the last bits of run-of-the-mill edibles into sumptuous meals.

That said, I had no fridge or stove of my own, and no access to Mrs. Arfino's prized kitchen — she may have been simpatico with the students, but she wasn't crazy, and opening up your kitchen to students was a recipe for disaster. As a result, lunches were conceived and consumed in my room, cold. Breakfast and supper, excepting my two weekly home-cooked meals, would be at the 'Y' — fifty cents for breakfast and under two dollars for supper, all including tip. Lunches were eaten on a tablecloth of yesterday's newspaper, and only small cans were viable choices as large ones would go bad before I could eat my way through them. Sardines, tuna fish, mini-sausages — these were staples for me. I could have gone a notch cheaper and eaten Spam, but I still almost vomit when recalling the explicit stories I'd heard about G.I. cuisine — even K-rations were preferred to Spam and its vile sister, S.O.S. (known to servicemen as 'shit on a shingle'). Tomato sandwiches became a standard at mealtime.

Even with practice time down, the days were mostly about filling time. I lived for the nights. That was my time to shine. Either I'd be playing a gig or there'd be a jam session somewhere. They were plentiful and easy to find. Small clubs abounded in the city and they would often hire a top-notch pianist to lead jams for the week. In a city full of musicians, this was a brilliant business move — they would pay one player and get the rest for free!

With so many musicians around, you would be *invited* to sit in (for free!) at these jams. Less than total mastery would be forgiven, but without it, you would be asked to sit back down once the song ended, if not sooner. On the other hand, if you knew the latest tunes, their usual keys, and had great chops, you would be expected to stay for the evening. The expectation to join in lay somewhere in the middle. You needed to show a strong understanding and total involvement in jazz, and at least *some* of the time sound like the greats you were emulating.

The audience came in all shapes and sizes, from all walks of life. Music was a fact of life in Rochester, and its citizens treated it like sports fans do their game of choice — they knew the stats, the greats, and a great play when they saw it. We never got into it too much with the non-players, never knowing how square or hip they might be. It didn't really matter. They came in droves, and that was the main thing. In doing so, they were paying the bills, supplying the applause, and sometimes even bought our drinks or food directly. And of course, no musician ever refused.

For us players, it was jazz, jazz, jazz seven days a week. We adopted our own speech, whether to separate us from the crowd or to link us to the greats. A car was a 'short', money was 'bread', someone outstanding was 'the living end', and the word 'like' got inserted almost anywhere in a sentence — *like he did this but like he really wanted to do that.* With speech as a marker, we knew each other even without an instrument in hand.

"That gig went well."

"Cool, man. But like my axe needs repair."

"He swings and she wails, man. Great chops. They're the living end."

'Chops' originally meant a very proper embouchure for a player to blow into an instrument, but evolved to mean playing any instrument well. While many of these terms are standard today, at the time, they were the secret code of the initiated. It was how you knew someone as a serious player — someone who lived and breathed jazz, rather than picking up a horn on weekends.

I immersed myself totally in the scene. I was in love — with the music, the improvisation, and the life that went along with it. It was fresh, creative, fast-paced, and challenging. Bebop was brand-new, state-of-the-art, cutting-edge stuff, but in Rochester there were enough players around that I could be inundated with it. Flatted fifths, extended chords, and breakneck tempos were replacing worn-out jazz styles and all the old corny copycat clichés. Parker and Gillespie were leading the charge, and I felt proud to be marching in their footsteps.

With almost nothing but jazz filling my time, I steadily improved over the summer. My fingers followed faithfully the tunes that were playing in my mind. I finally really knew my way around the horn. I could do everything I wanted to on clarinet, and my sax playing had taken huge leaps forward. Feedback was getting more encouraging day by day — and not just from the fans, but from my fellow musicians who knew the music inside out.

I was so steeped in jazz that September looming seemed an unnecessary imposition. This surreal, orgasmic existence would have to end. It would be back to Eastman, back to the rules and regulations inherent to classical music, back to strictures and structures, teachers and tradition.

Why not break completely loose and fly free as a bird? Why not lose myself totally in this Dionysian world of jazz? After all, as those near and dear to me would tell me repeatedly, "jazz was your first love".

The answer was simple. I was living on $24.50 a week, and as much as I loved jazz, I wasn't quite ready to starve for it — well, not completely anyway. With that in mind, I committed to one more year of classical before I could cut loose. That of course meant I had to drain every drop of what remained of the summer. So I would complete one more year at Eastman, but just that one more. After that, I would never have to play anything classical again.

One other thing became clear that summer — I had to move. As much as I liked Don, I didn't need to get caught up in his drama. Sooner or later, the Nymph would end up pregnant, and even if she didn't, I didn't need my roommate's girlfriend sprawled across my bed whenever he went out of town.

An opening came up in a private home, sharing with seven other students, all highly respectable. As a bonus, there would be home-cooked meals each night but Sunday. I shared a room with Clint Thayer, a trumpet player from New London, Connecticut, who was our class secretary. The class president, Bud Scherley, lived there as well. Ron Nelson was a composition major who asked me to perform one of his compositions, "Sunday Morning", for my final piano exam.

These weren't jazz cats, but that's what I wanted. I needed to get into the headspace of Eastman and be able to devour the classics for the year. I needed to let some of the rich-kid, old-boy know-how rub off on me. There would be plenty of time playing gigs to immerse myself in bebop — before the new year began, after it when I would leave classical music behind me, and probably the occasional gig through the school year.

And in every club, every performance, every jam, I savored that taste of bop to the last drop until the doors of Eastman were open again.

Adolphe Sax

Born Antoine-Joseph Sax in Dinant, Wallonia, Belgium in 1814, the eldest of eleven children of an instrument designer, Adolphe was involved in music his entire life. His father, Charles Sax, gained such a reputation that he was appointed instrument maker to the Belgian court. Adolphe apprenticed at his father's workshop, showing an aptitude for and a love of the work. He went on to study flute and clarinet at the Royal Singing School in Brussels.

Sax designed his own instruments from an early age, even entering flutes and ivory clarinets of his own design into competition at age 16. When he was 20 he patented a design for the bass clarinet which was lauded, but a popular soloist in Brussels swore publicly never to use it because Sax was its creator. Sax challenged him, "Play your clarinet then, and I shall play mine." The ensuing competition attracted four thousand people, with Sax the clear winner. That triumph led to his becoming a soloist. As a measure of his skills, pieces were written for him that were abandoned when he left as no one else could play them.

After relocating to Paris in 1841 he developed a set of valved bugles that quickly garnered attention and became known as saxhorns — still used widely, these became the basis for the flugelhorn and euphonium. His greatest success was, of course, the saxophone, which he invented while he was in Belgium, though he only patented it in 1846. He had demonstrated it in Brussels in 1841, but from behind a curtain, fearing that it would be copied. It garnered widespread attention and praise, notably from composer and conductor Hector Berlioz. The Paris Conservatoire hired him to teach based on this success, even offering a class in saxophone under its inventor. Adolphe hired his father to supervise the manufacture of saxophones from 1853 until the elder Sax died in 1865.

Constant litigation threatened his patents, forcing Sax into bankruptcy three times. Even after a successful battle against lip cancer using herbs, he kept producing instruments but nothing matched the success of the saxophone.

By the time of his death in 1894, legal battles had left him poor. Though he had never married, he had five children with Louise-Adèle Maor, one of whom continued his business until it was taken over by the Selmer company of Paris. His body was interred in the family mausoleum in Montmartre Cemetery in Paris. His image was used on the Belgian 200-franc note from 1996 until 2002, when the currency was replaced by the euro. The street where Sax was born was renamed in his honor in 1896.

Chapter 11
But Not For Me

Artie Shaw was coming to Eastman.

The news spread like wildfire. The classical fans were intrigued, the hard-core beboppers had to give him credit for his creativity, and *every* jazz clarinetist was pumped up beyond belief. All of us knew at least some of his solos, notably the one on "Stardust", which even Buddy admitted was probably the greatest clarinet solo ever recorded.

I had often spoken with Buddy about Shaw and never a bad word was said. Buddy credited Goodman with more facility and more swing, but noted that Artie was by far the master creator. Looking at Artie's life, it becomes evident that jazz solos weren't the only thing he excelled at. Beautiful women flocked around him, and every so often he'd marry a new one — after divorcing the old one, of course. Unsurprising, considering he was not only famous and known for his creativity, but also the classic idea of tall, dark, and handsome. Still, jazz was first and foremost in his life.

Frank Hillman, my friend and Eastman colleague, once told me about the day he heard Shaw's band playing at New York's Capitol Theatre. Admission back then was $1.25 and included a full-length feature film, a short novelty act usually with a comedian or two (even Dean Martin and Jerry Lewis), and thirty minutes of live name-band music. When the band finished, the house lights would go on, and most of the audience would leave. Some of us diehard fans never moved, other than maybe a trip to the washroom. Instead, out came the lunch bags or a cigarette and we'd wait to do the entire thing over again. No one would ever ask anyone to leave, so you could stay the day from morning 'til midnight, when things finally ended. It was in this scenario that Frank saw Artie Shaw and his band play. Each time, the rendition of "Stardust" was different — five completely different solos in all, with the midnight show adding no less than *six* additional encore choruses. According to Frank, each featured Artie improvising more brilliantly than on any of his recordings, hard to imagine as that is.

Standing over six feet tall, like DeFranco, Shaw also dabbled in psychology, psychoanalysis, and Ayn Rand-style philosophy about the individual. I was thinking of their similarities for a very specific reason. Four years earlier, a brief comment at our initial meeting earned me thirty minutes of Buddy's time, and now I was planning to try for a repeat. I wasn't expecting the same kind of friendship with Artie, but managing to swing some quality time discussing music with him would be enough of a triumph — one I was looking forward to. This was, after all, Artie Shaw, whom jazz writer Scott Yanow once described as "One of jazz's finest clarinetists who never seemed fully satisfied with his musical life . . . constantly breaking up successful bands and running away from success."

It would be a while until Artie graced Eastman's halls, and meanwhile the Eastman grind was back on. I was doing an hour daily of practice on violin, an hour on piano, and two to three hours on clarinet, as well as preparing my weekly lesson for Barbara Mallon, doing my various written homework assignments, attending band rehearsal and orchestra rehearsal, and on top of everything else, attending daily noon assemblies required of all fraternity pledges. I was tired enough from bouncing between my various responsibilities but, beyond that, violin was taking an extra toll. Practicing the unfamiliar instrument was wreaking havoc with the muscles of my left hand and my right shoulder — to this day, lingering sub-acute pains still persist. Knowing I'd have enough on my plate, I gave up Bill O'Brien's band.

Phi Mu Alpha was an honorary national fraternity. This being Eastman, there was no frat house to live in and public areas were par for the course. The noon assemblies had us initiates ('worms' to the upperclassmen) on the main steps of the school's busiest walkway wearing silly costumes and singing ancient madrigals. Being that it was Eastman we were all musicians, so abrupt tempo changes from the various senior members conducting the chorus were tossed in to throw us off-balance, along with jeers. Of course we resented this, but we *were* Eastman students and nothing would stop us from rising to a musical challenge.

This, however, was only the *public* part of our initiation. The private part was to come after four weeks of 'worm-like' behavior. The final initiation ceremony would be held on the last Saturday evening of the month. No one would say what would take place, and we were told not to ask. The rumor was that certain students might be stripped nude, tarred and feathered, then set loose in downtown Rochester, but no one could say for sure.

During this time I felt I could take on some more and started a regular Saturday dance job. The band revolved around a cocktail-style piano, and though it was a bit prissy for me, it paid well and the singer, sax, and clarinet were given lots of liberty. Bob Very, the bandleader, was one of the sometimes sweet, sometimes sadistic upperclassmen in charge of initiations. He had me excused from the initiation to work in his group, but was quick to note, "Your turn will come some other night. And we'll do you alone." He chuckled as he said it.

More than a month passed without me hearing one word from Bob about it, even as we did the regular Saturday gig. I went from worrying to thinking, *Hey, Bob's really a nice guy — surely he's just allowed me to slip through the cracks.* I figured he needed me for those Saturday-night gigs so I was home free.

Then one day I opened my student mailbox and inside, on official fraternity paper, was a formal invitation for the following Friday — of course, Bob needed me for the Saturday. I was to report to the school band's rehearsal loft at 6 p.m.

When I arrived I was greeted by Bob and two other frat members. No one else seemed to be in the building. There was a sinister sense in the air. First they questioned me for ten minutes about the structure, rules, by-laws, and such of Phi Mu Alpha and I began thinking this would be easy.

Then I was told to undress.

Bob said, "Oh, you can keep your shorts on." It had the feeling of a personal favor.

That feeling promptly disappeared as they began applying molasses and feathers to my bare skin. Finally I was seeing the proof of Bob's rumored sadistic streak. I suspected something sexual, but no one back then ever talked about homosexuality, except to joke. We barely even talked about heterosexuality. Sadism, however, was open territory, and made a good outlet for other things left undiscussed.

Big deal, I found myself thinking. *You've covered me with goddamn molasses and feathers. Now, can I go home?*

It wasn't going to be that easy.

"Put your clothes on but leave everything in your pockets here," was the next command.

After I did so, they led me down the stairs to the side street. I felt ten pounds heavier.

"Get in the back seat," Bob ordered, pointing to his huge four-door Hudson sedan.

Once inside, he blindfolded me, asking me to swear that I could see absolutely nothing. The car started. I had gotten to know Rochester well, but I couldn't even tell what direction we were headed in. The street noise faded away and I knew we were out in the country. Bob was a native Rochesterian and probably knew all kinds of obscure places I'd never so much as heard of.

It was close to an hour later when the car stopped. I could smell the country air and it was chilly. Rochester was always cool, but the outskirts even more so. Bob removed the blindfold, and one of the others double-checked my pockets before reporting, "No wallet, no change, no wristwatch, nothing."

It was so dark that I could hardly tell the difference with my blindfold off.

"Your job, Botek," Bob grinned, "is to find your way home. Oh, and don't forget — tomorrow night, we begin at eight!"

They jumped in the car and sped off.

I took a moment to assess my situation. *Feathers!* I thought. *And after all the chickens I cleaned. I'll never sleep on another feather pillow.*

A car came whipping by and brought me back to the problem in front of me. The instant their headlights hit me, they began going even faster. I had no mirror, but was sure I couldn't blame them. I was moving slowly and stiffly, like Frankenstein. There were feathers sticking out of my clothes, and pasted all over my neck, face and hands — probably even in my hair.

As the car passed, its headlights reflected off a nearby road sign. It seemed to be positioned at a large curve in the highway and pointing north. That seemed a bit of a triumph until I realized that I had no idea which direction Rochester was.

I decided to hitch-hike. I'd done enough of it in the past — the only difference was that I'd never done it in feathers. I positioned myself at the entrance to the curve, standing erect and close enough to the road that any sympathetic motorist would get a chance to study me before pulling over. The first few cars flew by. I had no real idea of the time, but I was sure it was getting late.

I was just about to give up when a couple pulled up beside me. I approached cautiously, thinking I had best explain the situation before trying to get in the car. The woman passenger, an older lady, rolled down her window and on getting a good look at me seemed startled. I immediately blurted out the whole story, hoping they'd believe me and being sure to note that I had no money, no ID, nothing except what they could see.

I asked which direction Rochester was in, and if they would be kind enough to help me out. They asked me a few other questions, mostly about music and Eastman, until they seemed satisfied I was telling the truth — what other possibilities they might have imagined I couldn't begin to guess at.

"Get in," the man said with a sigh.

They agreed to take me to the far eastern periphery of Rochester, thirty miles away, where the East Avenue bus begins its route. Once there, I could wait for the bus and be home in twenty minutes. They would even give me bus fare, which I offered to repay but they refused, likely wanting to be done with me as soon as they could. The heat of the car felt wonderful and I even welcomed the woman's cigarette smoke after my ordeal, despite it being some odorific brand like Fatima. I had bigger things to worry about. By this point my jockey shorts had absorbed a good amount of molasses, and the feathers that had migrated along were beginning to give me one hell of an itch!

Eventually we arrived at the spot where the East Avenue bus began its route. The area was well-lit, but there was no bus to be seen.

"Wait over there," the woman told me. "The bus will arrive in no time."

I thanked them both repeatedly, telling them what kind and considerate folks they were.

Walking away from the car, I noticed a new problem. The back of my pants, from the knees up, were now completely stuck to my skin. When I got home, I would have to cut off the trousers, trim the feathers, and scrape off the molasses. I thought that maybe I could convince my roommate Clint to help me when I got back.

I was thinking about how I would manage to clean the gunk off me when I noticed a lone parked car in the distance. Its parking lights were on, and a closer look revealed a glowing amber 'TAXI' sign on the roof. I waved frantically and got the driver's attention. Luckily no one else was around to see me flapping around, covered with feathers. When he pulled up, I explained the story again, finishing by letting him know that though I had no money on me, I could pay him if he drove me home and would even guarantee him a $10 tip. He smiled and waved me in.

We chatted as we drove. He was yet another Italian but from nearby Fairport. He was also an avid jazz fan, even knowing Buddy's name immediately. We got along incredibly well. So much so that when we arrived, I ran up and returned with a twenty, telling him that not only was his $10 tip in there, but that he could keep the change.

"You may not play an instrument, but you and Buddy would get along great," I told him. "You're as simpatico as he is."

The next day I would laugh and joke about the experience with Bob at our gig — after all, what else could I do? But that night, I wasn't laughing in the least.

If anything, the experience had told me that I didn't want my musical future in the hands of the likes of Bob. I resolved to buckle down and get that second year under my belt and to explore my other options. This was my future I was building, and as much as I wanted to fly, it wasn't going to be with feathers.

* * *

My final semester was enlightened by the assistance of Mr. Arey, my clarinet teacher. An old-timer, he played Jean Sibelius' music many times. I told him I would be performing a lengthy clarinet solo in Sibelius' tone poem "En Saga", and he jumped into action. He explained numerous things about the Finnish composer and the country itself: how Sibelius and Finland suffered during World War II, how oppressive and sad life was under the Stalin regime, and how Finland finally gained its freedom and became a full-blown democracy, in part due to the world-wide recognition of their number-one composer, Jean Sibelius. Yes, his music is sad and soul-wrenching, but that's what he had to write about.

Sibelius in mind, I needed a new practice area. The Annex was crowded and full of noise at any and all times. Up to sixty students side-by-side in rooms that weren't *quite* soundproof, all playing as loud as they could so as to drown out the others — this wasn't conducive to playing such mournful music. Sure, it could serve for hot jazz where I could simply play loud and overcome the Dixieland, Bach, and countless other tunes leaking from one practice room to another. Sibelius needed silences and whispered tones not interrupted by a sudden trill or solo. When I confided my problem, a friend let me in on a secret.

"Certain upperclassmen," he whispered conspiratorially, "have just taken over the 'attic' dressing rooms in the Eastman Theatre and practice there during the day."

Security was nearly non-existent throughout the school and theater, and the idea made a simple kind of sense. After all, old George Eastman had designed the school and theater to open to each other for a reason — they weren't meant to be thought of as separate entities. All I had to do was make my way up a few staircases, inquiring about the dressing rooms as I did. There was already someone practicing in the first room, so I nonchalantly continued down the narrow hallway, and finding room three vacant, I claimed it as my own.

Each morning from then on, I could practice in peace without interruption to my heart's content. No one ever asked me if I had permission to be there, but Eastman was always about the students and it was unlikely anyone would take issue as long as the reason I was there was music.

While I was working on Sibelius, I was driven to do well by the man but not to the point where I would forget my first love, jazz. Nor my current love, Phoebe, for that matter — we both had busy schedules, but we went out together whenever we could find the time. On nights when I had managed to secure a gig, she would be sitting in the audience, cheering me on. One of these nights was a local dance for Eastman freshmen where I had been hired to play clarinet with one of three combos playing. We went on first. Once we were done, Phoebe yelling out encouragement throughout our set, I started making my way across the dance floor to find her. She found me instead, not letting me off the dance floor. Where I had just been in the spotlight on stage, now it was her turn. On the floor, she pirouetted and capered, garnering the attention of everyone around — not hard for a six-foot-tall woman. One of the things that attracted her to me was that I was taller than she was, part of a fairly small pool of men who fit that qualification. As such, the two of us stood out on the dance floor and, in an unfamiliar spotlight, I struggled to keep up with her.

She exhausted me in no time and we returned to our table for a drink. No sooner had we sat down than we were joined by the freshman class president, a vibrant and energetic voice major from New York City. He was planning a freshman Valentine's Day dance and wanted me to form my own small combo to play it. He felt I had stood out in the current group, and was looking for the kind of music I played in my solos. He offered $90 and I immediately agreed, Phoebe beaming as she watched us negotiate a deal.

The February 14th Sweetheart Ball was held in the school's long second-floor Promenade. The majestic spacious hallway would for the first time give me the opportunity to let loose and play jazz at Eastman — other than in a practice room, of course. It was a beautiful setting, covered in marble and dotted with expensive oil paintings and large mirrors placed above shining mahogany tables. There were comfortable long sofas along the wall, and altogether it offered an elegance that was unmatched. Of course, looking out over it all was George Eastman's portrait, hung high above the entrance.

I had been impressed by Hank Edmonds since that day in the practice room and had immediately secured his services on piano. Then I got Jack Loftis, another graduate student, an American Indian from Oklahoma, who played bass. Bob Livingston was a local drummer, the only non-Eastman student in our group. My old friend, Dan Ettinger, played trombone — he was a viola major and played classical music, but he had an equal love for jazz, which he expressed through his horn. There was also Norma Ellis, a voice and piano major who had garnered her own weekly T.V. show. And finally there was me on clarinet and leading the band. We were billed as the Stephen B. Sextet, and we had gelled in a relatively short time. We played hot jazz and the students swung with us, cheering along to our bebop licks. The dance was an unmitigated success and would lead to many more gigs for us over the next few months.

* * *

Artie Shaw arrived in town on a cool early spring evening. The show was well-attended, no surprise considering the buzz through the town the preceding months. To everyone's surprise and delight, this jazz clarinetist did a superb job of Mozart's classic "Clarinet Concerto". The crowd yelled for an encore, which took little prompting, and I took the opportunity to sneak out of the main hall.

I climbed the stairs to the dressing rooms, and smiled when I saw he had been given room three — the same one I had claimed for my morning practices.

I didn't have to wait long before he showed up — tall, full of energy even after the long show, and somehow with his tuxedo still immaculate. He entered the room, propped himself up on one of the large dressing tables, and curled up into almost a lotus position. We were alone but I knew that soon, hordes of people including reporters would be at the door. I knocked, entered, and quickly introduced myself. I complimented him on the Mozart and told him it was just as well-executed as his "Stardust",

"Frenesi", and other masterpiece solos.

He sat up straight as a poker and listened intently to everything I said. We ended up talking shop, each asking the other what kind of clarinet, mouthpiece, and reed we used. All of it felt special, but nagging at the back of my mind was the idea this would still be somewhat of a wasted opportunity if I couldn't think of that really *special* question to ask, something that I couldn't find the answer to in a magazine and that maybe no one had ever asked him.

"Artie," I ventured, "what do *you* think of bebop?"

He got a funny look on his face, and his eyes got wide. I got the feeling it was a question he was waiting to answer. And I was right. Unlike a lot of other jazz players, Artie was an intellectual and his answer lost me in more than one place. He went on at length, and there's no way I could remember it all.

"Bebop, you see, is an intellectual concept. It's a special state of mind. A type of advanced thinking. Like Goethe. Like Schopenhauer. You see, to properly perform bebop, the individual involved must first consider . . ."

That part I remember well. Not just because I was struggling to follow along, but that was when five reporters with cameras at the ready stormed the room. The conversation was over, but I managed to shoot out one last question.

"Do you have any photos?"

"Not right here," he said, grabbing my hand and shaking it. "But John here is my manager. He'll take your address and mail you one."

John had come in with the reporters and pulled me aside to take down my information. As he did, fans started pushing their way through into the already crowded room. Artie could always draw the crowds and though he was known to disappear from them and go into hiding, there was one thing he never seemed to run from — a well-meant, serious, intellectual tête-à-tête.

Two weeks later a large manila envelope arrived. It was securely sealed and carefully packed, with 'PLEASE DO NOT BEND' neatly hand-printed in one of the corners. Inside was a large glossy photo of Artie, with "Best of luck to my friend Steve" written across the bottom. The picture wasn't even the standard 8" x 10", this was an 11" x 14"! The conversation had meant something to him.

The town was still abuzz about the show and the press clippings were quoted constantly. Adjectives thrown out constantly included: tall, dark, handsome, sexy, suave, brilliant, astute, charming, charismatic, and gifted. How could anyone *not* be enamored of such a giant? That certainly goes for all the beautiful women who pursued this enigmatic pied piper, often abandoning all else to do so. While everyone else was still talking about the show, I had the photo pinned to my wall, a reminder of the conversation that followed it — the encore no one else got to experience.

My own adjectives never got to see print (until now, that is). They include: engagingly introspective, constantly searching, perpetually restless, but *never* insincere.

This quintessential giant of the clarinet wasn't the only genius on my mind at the time. Sibelius was still a pursuit of mine, and though my morning sessions in room three were now conducted as if Artie Shaw was still there with me, the Finnish composer was taking more and more of my time. Not only did I want to perform "En Saga" properly, I wanted to evoke what I now knew went into this beautiful tone poem. Beyond my sudden affinity for the composer, there was another connection.

A few years previously, Eastman had offered Sibelius a full-time job. A contract had been signed and he was expected to begin at the school, but he cancelled at the last minute. The rumored reason was failing health. Finland had only recently gained full independence from Russia and, prior to that, Stalin and his henchmen had been extremely harsh with both Russian and Finnish composers. Much like the work of Shostakovich and Prokofiev, Sibelius' work cries out with anger, defiance, and unresolved sorrows.

World War II had done more than uproot poor Jean and his family. Another major disruption like picking up and moving to Rochester may have proved at the last minute to be physically and mentally impossible. It may also have been that with Finland finally free, he felt a need to stay and be part of the re-emerging nation. Or it could have been, like many who have stayed strong through trial and tribulation, that come the moment of peace, all the strain finally settles on them and they need to retreat from the world.

Even with Sibelius' connection to Eastman being that tenuous, I felt the need to do right by him and his work. As the Spring Junior Symphony Concert was about to get underway, I told myself that I wanted to play each note pitch-perfect. The long, cadenza-like solo was so practiced that it constantly reverberated through my mind; it had even haunted my dreams. Sitting about halfway through "En Saga", the solo floated beside me, waiting for its chance, never out of my field of vision. The full orchestra had been building up speed and volume as the conductor flailed away, seemingly in every direction at once. Then, sudden silence.

The conductor became calm, and after the silence had sustained for a few seconds he pointed to me. I knew as soon as I started that I could finish the whole thing and do it justice, regardless of any anxieties I might be feeling. This was my usual modus operandi — I might be nervous about performing a certain piece, but once in the moment, I was *only* in the moment, and I produced.

The solo began as a lament, just as Sibelius intended. I projected my full tone throughout the auditorium while maintaining a constant intensity. Everything was going fine, the solo sounding exactly as I had wanted it to.

Then it seemed that I lost consciousness for a second or two. The clarinet continued though, through some sort of mental reflex, and the cadenza never lost a note. Soon enough it ended, and I could relax through the remainder of the piece.

Once the piece was finished, the conductor acknowledged me and I took a bow. The concert was over, but I was unsure of what had happened. Various colleagues congratulated me, but I couldn't be sure they weren't just being polite. To be sure, I would need to hear the recording. Or so I thought. Confirmation of my success came the following day in an unexpected way. While waiting to order a sandwich for lunch in the cramped student coffee shop, a professor I had never seen before approached me. The friend I was sitting with informed me, "That's Professor Remington, the head of the trombone department."

Remington introduced himself and asked if I was Botek. After I had confirmed I was, he showered me with beautiful compliments about last night's playing. Later, I learned that he was never afraid to speak his mind, good or bad. Thank God he spoke to me. I had been living under uncertainty, sure that I could never get past niceties in finding out how well the solo actually went.

Visiting Eastman in the year 2000 I found that the recording had indeed been made, and that I could have had it at any time had I so wished — but it had just been discarded. I had been too timid to ask about a copy for myself, and since no one told me specifically I could have one, just left the matter alone. At the time, I was probably glad enough to have played it well and didn't really realize what keeping that record of it would mean down the road.

There were only a few weeks more until school closed again, and I would have a second year under my belt. Most sophomores who had survived to this point were likely to pass. Eastman had a very low failure rate and a very low drop-out rate as well — students had to prove their dedication and sincerity in the first place, so most who were accepted fought through until the end, whatever it took. These last weeks would be busy, busy, busy, but everyone was stealing moments to reflect. Each of us would miss many of our fellow students; having not only had standard school experiences together but having played together, we knew each other in a way that most college kids couldn't. As a result, my circles at Eastman had no phonies, no false flatterers, no dead wood — just sincere and genuinely good people.

To be fair, the richly productive and enterprising atmosphere seemed to prevail throughout the entire U.S. in 1950. We had been through the Great Depression, followed by a World War, and the country was more than ready for some peace, prosperity, and cultural advancement.

The general feeling was that we had worked hard through the first half of the century and it was time for our just reward. Little did we know that, come June, President Harry Truman, once an aspiring concert pianist himself, would make an announcement with the potential to alter every young American life, certainly those of us at Eastman looking forward to our June graduation.

Blissfully unaware of what was to come, there was still time for some fun, even with school winding down and all the pressures those last weeks brought with them. Maynard Ferguson and his big band would be appearing for one night at a local public auditorium. My roommate Clint, a *classical* trumpet player, showed some minor interest, but shrugged it off as he was unable to afford the $7.50 admission charge. I liked and respected Clint, but I could never get into his head or relax with him. I told Clint he couldn't afford *not* to go, and bought his ticket for him. The concert was superb. Maynard 'the Fox' was humble and congenial while blowing away the audience. He even jammed with local musicians late into the night after the show.

Throughout the years, and in many diversified concert settings, I have had the privilege of conversing at length with Maynard. While his fans may have known him as 'Maynard the Fox', I consider him 'Maynard the Magnanimous'. I've never seen another band leader as generous with solos for his sidemen. In Harry James' big-band days, you could count the trumpet solos played by musicians other than the maestro himself on one hand.

Maynard seems to have mastered the art of human bonding. At a November 8, 1974 Lehigh University concert his big band sparkled with excitement. His trumpet section consisted of Stan Mark, Dennis Noday, Lynn Nicholson, and Bob Summers. Besides showcasing each individual trumpeter, Maynard quite often did exceptionally high duet passages with twenty-one-year-old Ohio-born Nicholson. We all know that imitation is the sincerest form of flattery. But does the student honor the master by soloing not only in the unique high range but in purposely popping off a few *extra* high notes — ones even Maynard marveled at? I'm sure that with Maynard's secure ego someone playing even higher than him, rather than being a threat, becomes a creative thing to be encouraged.

My trumpet-playing boyhood buddy, Reuben Heller, and his colleague, expert drummer Bobby Grasso, organized the Lehigh University Jazz Stage Orchestra, conducting the group as well as performing with it. That night they opened for Maynard and his band. As the orchestra played, Maynard and his men stood on the sidelines, listening, obviously impressed bythese college kids pumping out hot jazz. The crowd strutted, shook, and swung to the orchestra and you could see Maynard and the boys noting the appreciation and involvement of the audience. Maybe that was what inspired them to perform to their utmost limits that night and give a show that still ranks in my all-time five best jazz concerts.

Maynard the Fox again displayed his magnanimous generosity at a semi-private Monday-night concert in a high school auditorium in Frackville,

Pennsylvania in 1982. Frackville is a small, economically-depressed north-eastern Pennsylvania town located a stone's throw from the anthracite coal-mining community where the Dorsey brothers were born. The ticket price was a measly $6, twice what was charged at the Lehigh University concert eight years before. The Frackville auditorium was relatively small, as was the attending audience. How, I wondered, could Maynard make any money schlepping his thirteen-piece band and everything that goes with it to this god-forsaken burg?

Just a minute or two of intense listening, and the crowd appeared transfixed as crisp, exciting, tasty, and well-rehearsed big-band sounds transformed this humble and shabby school setting into a listener's paradise. Suddenly everyone was dancing and shaking, yelling out encouragement as outstanding ensemble work and impossible solos boomed out from the stage. I was finding myself wishing I played trumpet!

It became evident as the night progressed that money had little if anything to do with this appearance. Following each and every selection — and this is something Maynard does so masterfully — he introduces the performing soloist, giving a short rundown on where each artist has studied music and what city or town he hails from. This particular night The Eastman School of Music was mentioned a lot as was Frackville, and other Pennsylvania places. Yes, this was a homecoming for some — a chance to have local folks and friends witness what it's like to be featured, be sincerely encouraged, and be professionally allowed to creatively contribute to jazz and big band mastery at its best.

Following this particular concert — possibly because of the disarming unpretentiousness of the setting — Maynard appeared even more affable and ingratiating than on previous occasions when I had spoken to him. We chatted for what seemed like a good twenty minutes; our conversation ended with his offering me a chance to travel with the band. In good taste and with an astute sense of humor, he jokingly alluded to some of the band members' social and professional idiosyncrasies. He was a little time in saying, "If you really want to write about my band and psychologically study us in depth — then get on the bus and join us for a week or so!"

Man, what a missed opportunity!

I had a second missed opportunity with the Fox. Rumor had it that the very band we'd heard that night at Lehigh could be hired for about $15,000! I married shortly after that, and to this day I regret not having begged, borrowed, or stole the money to have them play the reception. Who knows, maybe Maynard, proud Canadian, might have discounted his fee on learning that my bride-to-be, Ruth, was Toronto-born and raised.

And how could I forget a few years later when he was appearing at Manhattan's Blue Note? Maynard, even though that day he had two valuable mouthpieces stolen from his midtown hotel room, allowed me to invite myself to his hotel and granted me a one-hour interview. As always, he answered all questions and made me feel perfectly at ease.

That night in Rochester, Clint loved the concert, but only thanked me on the last day of school. We were closing up our room after everything had been moved out, and we would likely never see each other again. In those last five minutes in the deserted house, we shook hands in silence for a final goodbye. We both held in our emotions and refrained from a warm embrace, as that wasn't 'hip' for men to do in 1950.

Clint broke the silence.

"Thanks again for that Maynard Ferguson concert. Maybe someday we can be friends again."

I remembered how Clint had helped me acclimatize to the Rochester winter, even being able to sleep with the window open while the cold froze fresh fruit and the ink on my desk. I reminded him of that, adding, "Thanks for the *cool* experience!"

We laughed and shook hands. That was the last we saw of each other.

There were many other last words, not only to fellow students, but to landladies and staff at the stores during the days and local musicians and staff at the clubs during the nights. Walter Mallon was one of those other friends. He was the first parent of a friend who was a friend himself, not a 'sir' or 'ma'am' to be treated with polite deference. Like DeFranco, he was open and always helpful, never ceasing to surprise me. Despite his bouts of respiratory problems — he had beaten chronic tuberculosis a few years earlier — he made sure to help me with moving and packing, and even found a friend to chauffeur me home.

Those last days were filled with many a restrained goodbye, as emotional as we could get while following the rules for men at the time. All the sorrow was mixed with joy, though — we had done it. Not only had we completed another year at Eastman, but we had grown as musicians, found many trustworthy friends, and many of us, myself included, had broken away from home. I had accomplished what I had set out to, as had many others, and we all recognized it, even if the mores of the time kept us from fully expressing it. That said, it *was* a school full of musicians, and as much as we held back according to the standards of the time, our goodbyes and farewells were still more open and honest than you would find at most any other school of the day.

We all had one thing in common: the music. And still, every now and then, I'll hear a riff or a solo that reminds me of how someone I knew in those days played it and they'll come immediately to mind.

Artie Shaw

Born Arthur Jacob Arshawsky in New York City in 1910, Artie Shaw was raised in New Haven, Connecticut where anti-Semitism exacerbated his introversion. He picked up the saxophone at age 14, moving on to the clarinet several months later.

Not long after, at only 15 years old, Shaw left to tour with his first band. In Cleveland he worked with Austin Wylie's band until he won an essay-writing contest and a trip to Hollywood. That led to a stint with Irving Aaronson's band, which took him to Chicago. Not only performing, Shaw was learning about music as he toured. In Cleveland he was introduced to black artists and their stylings, notably Louis Armstrong, and as well absorbed symphonic works. Leaving the Aaronson band, he settled back in New York, where he played as a session musician and with various bands until his own work began to receive attention.

Shaw's debut as a bandleader was at a show at the Imperial Theatre in New York, noted as the first-ever swing concert. A natural innovator, Shaw received critical accolades for his "Interlude in B-flat". Backed by a string quartet and rhythm section, this is often cited as an early example of 'third stream', the fusion of jazz and classical. With attention focused his way, Shaw assembled his own big band. Drawing on his experience playing with symphonies, he came up with unusual arrangements and instrumentation that earned him critical praise as well as popular acclaim. He served as bandleader for George Burns and Gracie Allen's radio show, outearning the popular duo by himself. In fact, at one point he was estimated to be earning over $60,000 a week.

Shaw's band featured a number of stellar performers, including Buddy Rich on drums. Billie Holiday was hired as a vocalist, the first time a black female singer worked full-time for a white bandleader. According to *Lady Sings the Blues*, Holiday's autobiography co-written with William Dufty, there was also a behind-the-scenes affair between her and Shaw, but that account is known for its inaccuracies. Either way, audiences in the American South were not ready to tolerate the mixed-race group, and they decided to part ways, by all accounts amicably.

Shaw, dubbed 'King of the Clarinet', compared his nickname with Benny Goodman's 'King of Swing' and insisted they were wrongly applied: "Benny Goodman played clarinet. I played music."

An innovator first, Shaw was not interested in pandering to the public taste — even his theme song "Nightmare" wasn't a popular hit, though his band did rack up a number of hits, most notably "Begin the Beguine", "Frenesi", and "Moonglow". He not only brought elements of classical music to jazz, but played with bebop, incorporated Afro-Cuban elements, and included instruments such as harpsichords in successive groups that ranged widely in size and style. These groups featured notable performers such as Helen Forrest, Ray Conniff, Tal Farlow, and Mel Tormé.

Shaw enlisted in the U.S. Navy during World War II, forming a band that played to servicemen and women in the Pacific theater. The move was foreshadowed by Time magazine, who noted when the United States entered the fray that Germans saw America as "sky-scrapers, Clark Gable, and Artie Shaw." He was eventually given a medical discharge owing to exhaustion, having played as many as four concerts a day, often in the middle of battle zones.

Always a chameleon, Shaw played classical music after his return, working with the New York Philharmonic under Leonard Bernstein. He formed a series of small combos under the name the Gramercy Five, named for his home phone exchange, which had their biggest hit with "Summit Ridge Drive". Despite the name, the combos weren't limited to quintets.

Eventually, in 1954, Shaw quit playing clarinet, saying that his perfectionist approach would have ended up killing him had he continued. He noted, "In the world we live in, compulsive perfectionists finish last. You have to be Lawrence Welk or, on another level, Irving Berlin, and write the same kind of music over and over again. I'm not able to do that."

Shaw moved to Europe and remained there through the 1950s, turning his hand to writing. His autobiography, *The Trouble With Cinderella: An Outline of Identity*, was released in 1952, its title referring to the idea that "nobody lives happily ever after". His fiction writing began with a collection of three marriage stories entitled *I Love You, I Hate You, Drop Dead!*, followed by a collection of short stories, *The Best of Intentions and Other Stories*. His autobiographical novel, *The Education of Albie Snow*, remains unpublished.

Finally, in 1981, he organized a 'legacy band' under his name, the Artie Shaw Band. Clarinetist Dick Johnson served as bandleader and soloist. Shaw ended his retirement from clarinet with occasional guest-conducting stints.

Throughout his career Shaw had a tempestuous private life as well. He married eight times, most notably to Lana Turner and Ava Gardner. He had two children, both boys, and when asked why he didn't maintain contact with them, he quipped, "I didn't get along with the mothers, why should I get along with the kids?" He was called before the House Un-American Activities Committee for his involvement with the World Peace Congress.

Shaw was the subject of two documentaries, Canadian filmmaker Brigitte Berman's *Artie Shaw: Time Is All You've Got* and a BBC documentary, *Artie Shaw — Quest for Perfection*. He received a Grammy Award for Lifetime Achievement in 2004. He wrote his own entry for *Who's Who in America*: "He did the best he could with the material at hand."

Shaw died of complications from adult onset diabetes at age 94.

Jean Sibelius

Born Johan Julius Christian Sibelius in Hämeenlinna, Finland in 1865 to a Swedish family, Sibelius adopted the French variation of his name while a student, and is still known as 'Jean' today in Finland.

Sibelius began studying law at Aleksander's Imperial University in Helsinki but soon quit in favor of music. He studied at the Helsinki Music School, since renamed the Sibelius Academy, until 1889, when he moved to Berlin and then Vienna for further studies.

Returning to Finland in 1892, Sibelius married Aino Järnefelt, with whom he would have six daughters. He was operated on for throat cancer in 1911.

Wagner was an early strong influence on him, but Sibelius eventually rejected his techniques, preferring Tchaikovsky, Ferrucio Busoni, and Anton Bruckner. His contemporary and rival was Gustav Mahler. The two composers disagreed on overall approaches, but addressed similar themes, both drawing on folk music and literature.

Sibelius is a source of Finnish national pride. His compositions include "Finlandia", "Valse Triste", "Karelia Suite", and "Lemminkäinen Suite". He scored thirteen plays, the opera *Jungfrun i tornet (The Maiden in the Tower)*, and numerous other pieces, including over 100 songs for voice and piano. Most notable are his seven symphonies, following the completion of which he composed the tone poem *Tapiola*, music for Shakespeare's *The Tempest*, and then little else. He produced no works for the thirty years prior to his death and even refused to discuss music.

Sibelius is known to have remarked, "If I cannot write a better symphony than my Seventh, then it shall be my last." A rumoured eighth symphony may have been produced, though the only concrete evidence of its existence is a bill for copying of the work. The assumption is that Sibelius destroyed any copies of the score, likely considering it unworthy. He is known to have burned much of his work, with his wife a witness to the act.

A brain hemorrhage ended Sibelius' life at age 91; he is buried at his family home, Ainola, named for his wife. In 1972 his daughters sold the property to the Finnish government, which currently maintains it as a museum. A thirty-minute drive from Helsinki, Ainola is open to the public from May to September each year. His image was used on the 100 markka Finnish banknote until the currency was replaced by the euro.

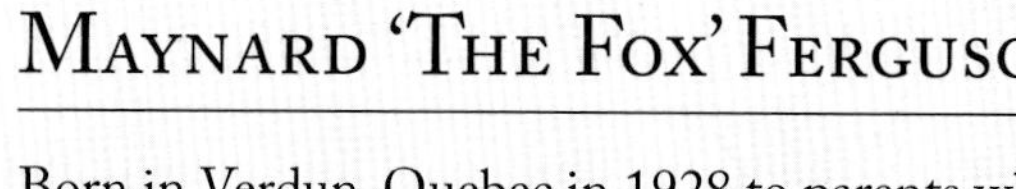

Maynard 'The Fox' Ferguson

Born in Verdun, Quebec in 1928 to parents who were both school principals with a devotion to education and music, Walter Maynard Ferguson was playing both piano and violin at age 4. He moved on to cornet at age 9, and within four years he was soloing with the Canadian Broadcasting Corporation Orchestra. He became a fixture on the CBC, performing for a variety of shows.

At 15 Ferguson dropped out of high school to play in dance bands, primarily on trumpet but also on a range of brass and reed instruments. He would play until 2 a.m. six nights a week, with his parents picking him up at the end of the night. He replaced his brother Percy as bandleader in a popular Montreal band that included Oscar Peterson, who lived about eight blocks away from the brothers, and played in the Montreal High School jazz band with them. He opened for numerous visiting U.S. acts, his ability to play clearly in the high register winning him many offers. He also won a scholarship to the French Conservatory of Music, where he studied under Bernard Baker from 1943 to 1948.

In 1949 Ferguson returned from France but quickly moved to the U.S. to take advantage of previous offers from name acts. He played under Boyd Raeburn and Jimmy Dorsey before joining Charlie Barnet's band, where he worked alongside Doc Severinsen in a renowned trumpet section. The band's rendition of "All the Things You Are" angered composer Jerome Kern's widow, and was pulled from sale. Not long after, Barnet decided to retire (which didn't last), and Ferguson accepted an offer from Stan Kenton.

Playing with Stan Kenton's forty-piece Innovations Orchestra led to work with a more successful, less experimental, follow-up band where he played third chair, but had many solos and developed a notable following.

Ferguson left the Kenton band in 1953 to do session work for Paramount Pictures and he performed on forty-six soundtracks. He was contractually bound not to play in jazz clubs, but continued recording. Wanting to play live, he left Paramount in 1956.

The Birdland Dream Band was Ferguson's next project. As bandleader for an all-star fourteen-piece ensemble assembled to play at the legendary club, he met the players who would follow him into his own band in 1957, which had hits including "Maria" and "Olé". As big bands declined in popularity, Ferguson felt audiences were more interested in hits than innovative playing and so moved to playing more and more with smaller formations, most often a sextet. With the success of the smaller groups, he disbanded the big band in 1967.

Then, seeking spiritual renewal, Ferguson moved to India. While there he taught music and founded the Sri Sathya Sai Institute of Higher Learning's Boys' Brass Band. He studied under Bhagavan Sri Sathya Sai Baba, pursuing his spiritual goals. He would later incorporate Indian instruments into many of his recordings.

Upon leaving India Ferguson moved to Manchester, England, where he began designing his own trumpets and mouthpieces. He played widely, first with a group called Top Brass, then assembled various ensembles to tour Europe. He quickly secured a record deal, assembling a big band to perform originals and new arrangements of pop and rock songs. The group became a part of the BBC's *Simon Dee Show* in 1970, and the repartee between Dee and Ferguson established itself as a core element of the program. This happened as Maynard's old bandmate Doc Severinsen was establishing himself in a similar position on *The Tonight Show*. The new band began playing North America the next year. In 1973, Ferguson moved to New York and, over time, American players replaced the British ones, the band being reduced over time to a twelve-piece.

Ferguson performed a solo trumpet piece for the closing ceremonies of the 1976 Montreal Olympics. That year, he began work on a series of albums that saw a fair amount of commercial success, including a #28 pop-chart with his rendition of "Gonna Fly Now", the theme from the movie *Rocky*. He was the target of acrimony from critics who felt his aims were too commercial. Ferguson, for his part, was frustrated over Columbia Records' unwillingness to let him include any jazz songs on his albums. After his final contracted album with the company he moved on to smaller labels and a new big band. He followed that up with the fusion septet High Voltage, which recorded two albums.

In 1988 Ferguson formed Big Bop Nouveau, a nine-piece band that focused more on mainstream jazz, playing original compositions and standards. This band, which would continue the rest of Ferguson's life, recorded with the likes of Michael Feinstein and Diane Schuur.

Ferguson played trombone, saxophone, clarinet, violin, and piano, as well as trumpet. He also created two hybrid instruments, the Superbone and the Firebird, the latter with Larry Ramirez. The Firebird fused the trumpet with the trombone, and the Superbone combined a valve trombone with the more common slide version.

Ferguson was a winner of the *Down Beat* Magazine Award for best trumpeter three years running, and was inducted into the *Down Beat* Hall of Fame. He was a three-time Grammy nominee. Considered second in popularity only to Oscar Peterson among jazz musicians in Canada, he was inducted into the Canadian Music Hall of Fame in 1997 and received the Order of Canada in 2003. His bands have included the likes of Chick Corea, Wayne Shorter, Joe Zawinul, Don Ellis, Joe Farrell, and Chuck Mangione. New Jersey's Rowan University runs the Maynard Ferguson School of Jazz Studies as well as an annual jazz festival dedicated to Maynard.

Ferguson died in 2006 of kidney and liver failure resulting from an abdominal infection. He was survived by his second wife, Flo, their three daughters together, and a stepdaughter. His obituary in the Washington Post declared, "He nailed the upper registers like Shaq nailing a dunk or Lawrence Taylor nailing a running back — and the audience reaction was exactly the same: the guttural shout, the leap to their feet, the fists in the air. We cheered Maynard as a gladiator, a combat soldier, a prize fighter, a circus strongman — choose your masculine archetype."

Chapter 12
Wrap Your Troubles In Dreams

With Eastman behind me, it was back to Pennsylvania for June. It was delightful. Spring had been cool, but numerous deciduous plants and trees were slowly coming alive. Wild huckleberries bloomed first, followed by raspberries, blackberries, and finally, elderberries living up to their name. As kids we would scour the woods, discover their hiding places, and spend countless hours collecting them. Part of the appeal was the work — hard and tedious, sure, but meeting the challenges of penetrating mountain brush, wild animals including snakes (including poisonous ones: the rattlesnake, water moccasin, and copperhead), and the hot summer sun made the triumph all the more sweet. We didn't just eat them. The region was loaded with expert cooks and bakers all anxious to buy our wares.

That was in the past, though. This time I was back as an adult, and moreover, this wasn't home anymore. Now I was a visitor en route to my real destination: New York City.

Charlie Tucker heard I had returned and immediately showed up with the latest issues of *Down Beat* and *Metronome* in hand. He informed me that Count Basie had broken up his big band and formed a sextet — with Buddy DeFranco on clarinet!

"What a switch!" Charlie gushed. "In Dorsey's band, Charlie Shavers was the only black, now Buddy DeFranco will be the only white in Basie's band."

We talked about Buddy at length that day, about how his experience with injustice and affliction kept him from being separate from the black players, unlike many other white players who had privileged upbringings. Having had to look after his blind father and escort him on his vending-machine rounds, he consequently gained none of the class issues that were at the basis of race divisions, and ended up 'color blind'.

Charlie and I decided over lunch to make a trip to New York. Basie's sextet, Buddy included, would be playing at a club there. I decided I would also try to set up an appointment with Buddy's personal physician, Reichian therapist Dr. Louis Pelletiere.

Not wanting to sit in Lansford waiting for the trip, we took the 6:10 a.m. train the next day. It was like old times, even if the fare had risen slightly — the two of us on our way to New York, too short on cash to take advantage of things like the dining car, jazz on our minds and at the forefront of our conversation. We even carried packed lunches from our mothers. It was like we were kids again.

I had managed to set up my appointment with Pelletiere. He had a small apartment annexed to the Woodward Hotel on the corner of West 55th Street and Broadway, an area I knew well from my previous travels in the city. Even his apartment number was resonant — he was in 802A, and 802 was the number of the local of the American Federation of Musicians union for New York City. There was no formal office. We sat down in what appeared to be his living room, and he proceeded to ask me numerous questions about my parents, siblings, and myself. Although he took very few notes, his concentration and focus was evident.He was an impressive man, even at first glance. Short-statured with a medium build and in his middle thirties, his dark hair framed deep, vibrant, penetrating eyes and a pleasant smile.

After we talked for about ten minutes, he pointed to a small side room and told me to disrobe. I was ready for this, as Buddy had told me of the process, but he then told me, "You may keep your shorts on," and I flashed back to Bob Very using those words at the Phi Mu Alpha initiation. I shook it off. I had liked Bob, but had never trusted him as much as I did Pelletiere, even after so little time.

During the exam that followed, he looked at, touched, and thumped practically every part of me. It was like an expert jeweler examining a precious gem — he turned me every which way to see every aspect of me, to ascertain every possible flaw. He pointed out numerous areas of my body that were tense, questioning me about pains and flexibility.

"I do get frequent neck pains," I told him. "Once in a while, I get headaches plus these stomach pains that sometimes make me think I'm getting an ulcer."

"Your intercostals are very tight," he said, pointing to my ribs.

I was afraid I had more of a pathology than he would want to handle, and began a defensive tirade of explanations to avoid being rejected as a patient. He saw right through me.

"It's okay," he assured me. "I don't need to know all the reasons, but I'm sure your strict father, your stern Catholic schooling, and a deeply hidden desire for a full and free sexuality all play an important part."

For the remainder of the session, he led me through deep diaphragmatic breathing exercises. I caught on more quickly than most, being used to similar exercises to enhance my clarinet and saxophone playing. He took me farther though, my breathing becoming deeper, longer, and more intense.

"Think of the oxygen flowing into every corner of your body," he instructed me in a low whisper.

I diligently followed his instructions, and felt my body slipping into a kind of overdrive, reflex bringing in the Jacobson relaxation techniques I had studied at Eastman. He was pleased with my responsiveness. The session cost me $15, and I left eager to tell Charlie about it.

I hurried down Broadway to 48th Street and made my way over to Manny's music store, where Charlie and I had agreed to meet when I was finished with the session. Sure enough, he was standing there in front of the drum display, having a lively conversation with one of the clerks. Pure and classic Tucker: he could strike up a productive conversation with anyone, any place, at any time.

He turned to me as I approached.

"Steve, I've got bad news," he said straight-faced. "Basie's group is not going to be at the Brass Rail tonight. My friend here, a fellow drummer, waited on Gus Johnson, Basie's drummer, when he came in to shop a few days back. The group was calling off both the gig at the Rail and a return engagement they had at the Strand Theater on Broadway. Apparently, the band is off to Chicago, then California. Wardell Gray might be substituting for Bobby Graf or Charlie Rouse."

"Best we try phoning Buddy," I said, rummaging through my pockets for a nickel. "On second thought, let's save five cents and walk over to his hotel — it's in walking distance."

The hotel clerk was very helpful. A clean-cut young actor who was a serious jazz buff and an ardent fan of Buddy's, he seemed to know everything. Buddy had checked out earlier in the week.

We kept talking. He described some of the story I had missed. Buddy had joined Basie in February, 1950, after his own combo folded. He had thought of starting his own big band but his manager, Willard Alexander, said the time wasn't right, noting that even Basie's big band couldn't survive the present climate. Alexander was also Basie's manager, which may have been how Buddy became part of the new sextet. He told us Clark Terry was now a permanent member of Basie's group. As well, they often had guests like Freddie Green on guitar, or a trombone — J.J. Johnson, Kai Winding, or possibly Slide Hampton.

He excused himself as a customer came to the front desk, and Charlie and I said goodbye. We decided that without the Basie group, we may as well catch the earlier train back to Pennsylvania.

The Lehigh Valley 6 p.m. Special from Pennsylvania Station was extremely crowded. It took some work, but we found two seats together. The seats then were large, wide, well-cushioned, and offered plenty of room to stretch out. They were tall-backed, enough that our row of two made a cozy and private niche — and all this was at the economy fare! Charlie decided to hit the restroom, knowing that we couldn't use the train's washrooms while in the station. The toilets at the time simply flushed human waste out onto the tracks through a large cylindrical hole at the bottom of each. They were locked up when in a station so as not to provide any evidence to the passengers of the results.

Charlie raced back with a copy of *The New York Times* he had found in the washroom.

"Look!" he urged. "Look at this headline!"

It read *North Korea Attacks South Korea: Seoul Under Siege. Truman to Broadcast — Tonight at Nine*. It was June 25, 1950, and armed Communist troops had brazenly crossed the thirty-eighth parallel. The United Nations was assembling to discuss aiding the South. I put the paper down.

"Charlie, how is this going to affect us? We have our music to focus on, our careers. Who has time to think about some civil war in some little country far away? It's the Russians we have to worry about, and if they ever drop the bomb on us."

Charlie disagreed, and the conversation became somewhat heated. Across the aisle, a middle-aged Catholic priest turned his head and leaned over towards us. Without introduction, he fixed his gaze on me and asked, "Son, if I may, how old are you?"

I hesitated. This wasn't the first time that a Catholic priest had engaged me in conversation on the train. There was the time three years prior when one had been bombarding me with questions like, "What do boys your age do for kicks?" Remembering that experience I was wary, but Charlie, extrovert that he is, jumped in with an answer.

"Father, Steve is twenty and I just turned eighteen a few months back."

"The reason I asked," offered the priest, "is that the president is planning to introduce a military draft for young men of your ages."

It was time for a break. As if missing Basie and Buddy wasn't bad enough, this capped our reunion trip to New York!

"Father, Charlie and I are going up to the smoking car for a quick cigarette. We'll finish this conversation when we return."

Charlie wasn't much of a smoker, but he took my cue and followed me. Perhaps in light of the news we'd just received, he asked me for a cigarette the instant he saw my pack come out of my pocket. I was still more focused on the messenger than the message, not wanting to believe the priest.

"Why do these vagabond priests insist on playing with our minds?" I demanded.

Always quick with an answer, Charlie retorted, "Better they play with your head than any other part of your body! Remember the parochial school definition of a kiss? 'Higher persuasion for lower invasion'?"

We laughed, and our conversation became lighter. Behind the smiles, though, was uncertainty. Neither of us knew what any of this meant. Of course, it wouldn't be long until we found out, now that the war was beginning to encroach on our lives at home. Still, there was plenty to divert us. The evening we got back, Charlie would go out while I begged off home. That night, he would meet Cecilia, who would end up his wife. They're still together, and she now takes care of him, as he's partially paralyzed and confined to a wheelchair.

* * *

Mother was a staunch believer in eating a full breakfast. As such, the morning table was always laid out with juice, bacon and eggs (or pancakes if the mood struck her), toast, butter, marmalade, coffee — the works. She was always the first one up and the one in charge of all the cooking. Her kitchen was her palace — a special, almost sacred place where she set the rules. Virtually anyone was welcomed as long as they minded their manners and appreciated the good food. Mother was also one to keep tabs on every aspect of life, including current events. While I'd dismissed the priest as trying to play with our heads, I knew I could count on her to know the full story. As much as I'd shrugged off the news, it nagged at me all night: what if it was true?

Newspapers were a secondary source for my mother. Working in the store, she talked to everyone in town, and heard everything. She'd know how trustworthy every source was and who to talk to for confirmation. The store was more of a source of information than any of the county's radio shows. If only reporters knew to consult my mother! She'd know about any possible draft. Regular customers included all the draft board for World War II: the elder statesman of the group, a local senior citizen, a Lutheran minister, the town mayor, the Catholic priest, and the local judge. These and maybe one or two disabled veterans would be included among the current Selective Service officials. With my high school band, I had furnished the music to which healthy young local boys marched off to war the last time, with most of the board sitting comfortably in prestige seats. Sure enough, Mother had already checked with the officials. She noted that since I was no longer enrolled at Eastman, I'd likely be drafted by Christmas.

"Why don't you jump back into school?" she suggested. "After all, you left on good terms after completing your second year. You could easily go back for another, and then the draft board would probably leave you alone . . ."

"I'm no sissy," I interrupted. "I quit to go to New York and follow my professional music career. And that's exactly what I'm going to do!"

I knew I could go back — the dean of students had even asked me why I was leaving, but her surprise was in my wanting to play jazz rather than long-hair music. I wasn't going back to classical, and it could be heard in my voice that my mind was made up on that point. There was a look of sorrow on Mother's face in response. I recognized it immediately and shifted gears.

"Look, Mother, my eyesight is poor and my teeth are all patched. They'll probably classify me 4F anyway. Let's wait and see."

Pennsylvania, with its unique place in American history, breeds patriotism like no other state, and it was rumored that our state had one of the highest numbers of enlistees. Every day, our local newspapers would report at great length about some civic-minded patriot who had just enlisted. The story they left untold was that many fine young men — and some women, too — saw no future in the dilapidated and depressing coal towns they lived in and saw the military as their road out.

I talked about this with Art regularly over that summer. We both figured that with the large numbers of enlistees, they wouldn't need us. It wouldn't be long until we were eating our words.

* * *

When the summer ended, I returned to Rochester. I was still against re-enrolling in school, but I wanted to get together with Phoebe and plan for my move to New York. We'd both talked about moving there after school, and while she had time left in her formal education, mine was finished as far as I was concerned.

I took a single room in a Victorian-style mini-mansion right next to the Mallon household. The landlady lived in the house with her only son, Roger, a doting, complaining, cantankerous, unmarried, and unattractive guy in his late twenties. The house was too big and there was very little heat. Usually around 65°F inside, the temperature wasn't conducive to me practicing my instruments. Furthermore, when Phoebe visited, she'd immediately put *on* more clothes while I was urging her to take some off. I used to run next door to warm up at the Mallons. Meme was always home, and would greet me by asking, "How are things over there in the Deep Freeze?" before inviting me to stay for lunch.

September turned into October which, to my dismay, was still comfortable. Sure, the nights were chilly and the house always cold, but the bright sunshine in the daytime would compensate for that. Phoebe had relaxed her Protestant Puritanism enough to unleash her sexual energy in my direction and, me being a connoisseur of creature comforts, she more than satisfied. All this was making Rochester *too* comfortable, when I wanted to push ahead and forge my own path in New York.

Things changed in mid-month when Art's letter arrived. I knew it had to be important — Art *never* wrote. I was worried opening it, hoping nothing extraordinarily bad had happened to him — with Art's wild approach to life, everything moderately bad happened regularly enough and would certainly be nothing to write about. Like mine, Art's parents owned and ran their own store. His dad was a successful pharmacist and their store, like my parents', was a treasure trove of information. The rear of the pharmacy was used in the evenings for poker games with a number of locals, including the chief of police. Art was famous for pumping poker guests for information. He'd find out if he was *really* in trouble with the police, or which high school senior had to get married because she was pregnant.

The letter was short and sweet:

> *Dear Steve,*
> *Reverend P. was playing poker here last night. He said you and I should visit the local county courthouse* [where the Office of Selective Service was located]. *Mention his name. They can tell us almost to the day when we will be drafted. Probably, it won't be until December, but we will definitely have to go.*
> *This gives us about two months to decide which branch to enlist in. I'll try naval aviation, you should enlist as a bandsman.*
> *Hurry home. We have to look into this now!*
> *Your pal,*
> *Art.*
> *(P.S. Still dating Mary, but also seeing Evelyn on the side.)*

Art had proven to be a real buddy. Not only was he warning me of the dangers that lay ahead, but he was trying to provide me with a solution. Art loved life — specifically the good life, one jam-packed with excitement, diversity, and pagan self-satisfaction. Nothing scared him, nothing surprised him, and nothing ever seemed to stop or even shock him. At times he seemed possessed by Dionysian devils, while at other times he could charm the toughest of teachers or the strictest parents and authority figures. With his good looks, glib tongue, and winning smile, he could talk his way out of anything and, as an amateur boxer, he could fight his way out as well. His entire life was hedonistic — in search of fast cars, fast women, airplanes, and the new experience. This, however, was something new — Art was being serious.

The thrust of it wasn't a surprise. Art was fiercely loyal to his friends. There may have been some necessity in that, as every act needs an audience. His no-holds-barred narcissistic id needed companions who were the opposite, and who could fully appreciate his uniqueness. His cadre of friends was small and devoted, and there was an unspoken deal with all of them — Art provided the excitement, while we acted as superego, providing the caution and common sense. That included me, of course. Where Art would counter my Catholic guilt, I showed him the value of restraint, caution, and sacrifice. Now here was Art looking out for *my* well-being. The devotion to a friend was nothing new, but planning and preparing? *That* was.

The clerk at the Mauch Chunk office of the Selective Service department knew Art. For all I knew she may have shopped at his dad's pharmacy, been an old family friend, or dated him. Even before I asked the question, she knew what we needed to know.

"Both of you will be called up sometime late in December," she said, studying our records. "Good luck," she added, showing us out with a polite smile and turning her attention to the next anxious face.

Art knew where to go from there. We drove to the adjoining town of Lehighton.

"I know the Navy recruiter there," he said conspiratorially. "I'll speak to him about flying and the Naval Cadets. You find the Air Force sergeant and pick his brain about enlisting and becoming a bandsman. Don't promise them anything and don't fall for any of their bullshit. If and when we do enlist, it'll be for three or four years instead of the two we'd be drafted for.

"The war is young — they need us as much as we need them. So, let's try to get a good deal — and get it on paper. We want to pick our base and the jobs we want. It can be done, but remember: don't trust the military! Don't fall for any of their false promises, their never-ending bullshit."

I wondered how long I'd been away. Art always knew how to assert himself, never fearing anyone. He always would take us meek quiet types and turn any of us willing to follow into independent free-thinking adults. The caution and planning was new, though, unlike the Art I had known.

The afternoon hadn't ended before Art had worked out a potential three-year hitch as a naval pilot, to be stationed at nearby Willow Grove. If he passed the physical and had no police record other than minor traffic and speeding infractions, he'd be enlisted and promptly begin officer's boot camp. After being commissioned and trained to fly the Navy way (he already knew how to fly, but was told he'd need to forget everything he knew), he could then select the adventure he always dreamed of: flying from aircraft carriers.

I was more than lucky to have tagged along with Art. The military had only one office: the Navy and Marines used it during the day, and the Air Force and Army took over for the evenings. Art being Art, he had the Navy recruiter eating out of his hands — almost literally. He had ordered lunch for the three of us from a nearby pizzeria. I was thinking that if the recruiter had been female, he might have been General Rubart by that point.

Five o'clock brought a changing of the guard, with the Air Force and Army recruiters settling into the office. It was my turn now, and Art simply sat back in silence, smoking a Camel. The message was clear: do what I did. I was there to smile, probe, ingratiate, listen carefully, and above all, lead the session without falling for any of the recruiting propaganda. I imitated Art's attitude and approach, and soon had all the information I needed.

Yes, the Air Force was interested in enlisting me. Being a bandsman meant I could enlist for a three-year stretch rather than the customary four. There were about ninety bands stationed around the world. My vision wouldn't be an issue as long as it was correctable with glasses; as for my teeth, they could pull whatever needed to be pulled, fill and repair the rest. In any case, it wouldn't present a problem. Once enlisted, the draft board would leave me alone, regardless of my ship-out date — however, if they grabbed me before I enlisted, then the recruiter wouldn't be able to do anything for me.

This left me wondering how long I could wait. Did I really have until late December to decide? One way or the other, I was certain of one thing: I was *not* enlisting just yet, and definitely not in October.

I was just about to leave when Art finally spoke up. He mentioned that I had a friend I corresponded with in *the* Air Force Band in Washington, DC. If I auditioned for them and was accepted, what enlistment procedure should I follow?

The sergeant was impressed.

"If they will accept you there," he told me, "have them give you a formal letter. Everything in writing. Bring me the letter, enlist here, and I'll send you for ten weeks of basic training after which, letter in hand, you'll be shipped to Washington for permanent duty."

That was all I needed to know. We stood up and shook hands.

Art however had two more questions.

"If we hadn't both dropped out of college, could we have avoided the draft, for maybe a year or two? And how soon might the Air Force or Navy *close* enlistments — say, if they get an overabundance of recruits?"

The sergeant stared at us in silence. Was there something he knew that he wasn't telling us? Or wasn't allowed to? After a few seconds, he spoke.

"Boys in college now won't be allowed to finish the year. Two semesters, that is. It's different than in World War II. At the end of this current semester, all eligible college men will probably be quickly drafted."

Again there was silence. Art and I looked at each other, but no one spoke. The sergeant had revealed something that probably only a few people knew at this point. If I had bothered to re-enroll in school, as my mother had suggested, I would have been drafted anyway. In a sense, Art and I were lucky to have left college when we did — it gave us the opportunity to check out all the angles while the students wouldn't have the time, even if they had any idea they should. And checking things out now meant that we could choose some of the choice spots before all hell broke loose at the end of the semester. Getting into the Air Force Band now was a possibility, but if I had been trying alongside all of the students at Eastman, my odds would have been considerably lower.

Driving home, Art said that we deserved a drink after all that. We weren't twenty-one yet, the legal age in Pennsylvania, but Bugsey's had served us even as seniors in high school. Bugsey knew our ages anyway — he played poker with Art's dad and hunted deer with mine. The beer was cold and good. The toast was to friendship. Normally, that was something that didn't need to be said, but considering the day's events, the two of us could literally end up a world away from each other, so underlining the point seemed right.

Back home, dinner was waiting with Mom anxious for news. She had seen more than her share of young men whisked off to war, to never return. The political rhetoric about Korea wasn't fooling her. MacArthur's bravado might have worked in the Philippines, but his claims of being able to clean up the mess in Korea by Christmas were more than suspect. Mao wouldn't sit idly by as American troops advanced toward his borders. Truman must have been anticipating a longer drawn-out fight if he was prepared to pull so many young men out of college as well as other walks of life.

It was agreed that I needed to contact Sergeant Dietz, who had asked me to join the Air Force Band in Washington in 1947. Hopefully he would consider me suitable in 1950, with my improved skills. A first-class letter cost three cents, but would possibly take three days to be delivered. Mom pushed me to make a person-to-person call instead — it would cost three to five dollars but that was a small price to pay, all things considered.

Each second seemed like a minute as the long-distance operator dialed a few Washington numbers before finally finding Sergeant Dietz. While we waited for him to pick up on his end, my mother cautioned me, "Mind your manners and compliment him on those clarinet solos of his that we heard on the radio when they broadcast from the Capitol steps. Oh, excuse yourself for not being more formal and writing. If he does tell you to come to Washington, tell him you'll be more than happy to do so, at any time convenient to him."

"Sergeant Dietz," a voice came on the phone. "To whom am I speaking?"

Spending the day with Art had prepared me for the call. I stayed cool, calm, and collected as I traded banter with the Sergeant. All of Mother's advice was followed to the letter and the conversation ended with an invitation to audition on the Monday following the Thanksgiving weekend. He even promised to verify the conversation with a formal follow-up letter.

The instant I got off the phone Mom let out a loud scream of joy. Everything had gone perfectly. The joy turned to wariness when the phone began ringing a minute or so later. It was Mildred, the long-distance operator. She told us that the call lasted almost eight minutes, cost $7.10, and that she couldn't be happier about my audition. Mildred may have been happy, but my feelings were mixed. Avoiding fighting in the war would be something to celebrate, but it was not yet a sure thing, and even if it was, all I could think about that night was the oft-repeated warning from my brother-in-law Ernie, "Never trust the military."

Both Art and I had our work cut out for us. He left for Willow Grove while I returned to Rochester. Before he left, though, he promised to accompany me to Washington. It helped that I had secured permission to borrow my dad's brand-new 1950 Buick for the trip — Art was anxious to try it out and experience first-hand what a straight-8, three-in-the-tree, three-hundred-plus horsepower engine could do.

The train trip to Rochester was six hours, plenty of time to think things over. My pen-pal Donald M. from Lititz, PA, had joined the Marine Band in Washington directly after high school. We had met as competing clarinetists in one of the Pennsylvania state competitions and had continued writing to each other, with him occasionally asking if I ever thought of joining the service. His advice was always the same: if I did try to join, I should try for one of the big four bands in DC — Army, Navy, Marines, Air Force. I should stay away from the field bands or some small band aboard a ship. I would always write back telling him that I wasn't going to join, but if I did, it would be the Air Force Band for me. I had heard too many horror stories about the Army from ex-G.I.'s; the Marines were too gung-ho and you could lose your identity once you were in; and ships and water didn't excite me, nor did the tradition, vocabulary, or uniforms of the Navy. That meant the Air Force — the officer pilots were usually cool and human, there was the simple dark blue uniform that could pass for civilian clothes without the jacket and hat, and the attitude was comparatively fresh and unassuming. I wondered what Donald would think when he received my next letter.

Despite feeling I had made the right decision through the train trip, the instant we pulled into downtown Rochester a wave of doubt and fear overcame me. It lasted less than a minute, but left me wondering if I had done the right thing in dropping out of school. Wasn't the idea of the audition just putting all my eggs into one basket? Rochester had been good to me and, after five more weeks, I might never live there again.

All the soul-searching came to an abrupt halt as I spied Phoebe anxiously scanning the crowd in search of me. When our eyes met, she rushed forward and without a word, took me in her arms and kissed me passionately. It seemed to last minutes until, finally, she broke away and grabbed me by the shoulders, standing eye-to-eye with me.

"This Air Force thing," she began, "are you really sure about it, Stephen? I have some ideas about the military. Let me tell you . . ."

She was off and running, back to being her usual pedantic self. I grinned, knowing that my only chance to calm her down would be when we got back to my bedroom.

The following day I visited Eastman. The school felt strange, like I no longer belonged. I stayed clear of the main building and went towards the Annex. I knew Frederick Fennell would be there rehearsing either the Symphonic Band or the Junior Symphony. I wanted to discuss my upcoming audition with at least one of my former teachers.

Looking back, I guess I didn't go to my clarinet teacher, Rufus Arey, as he could be overly rigid and quite judgmental. On one occasion he had mocked Fennell, noting that he went by straight 'Fennell' when he entered the army, but when he came to Eastman he added an accent to his name and became 'Fénnell'. Arey had a provincial mindset, once having proclaimed that "there's more horse's asses around this school than there are horses!" The one experience that probably made the most of an impression was his quick dismissal of Benny Goodman's recording of "Poor Butterfly" when I played it for him — it wasn't his type of music so he didn't even bother addressing Benny's tone or phrasing.

Fennell in comparison was more open-minded, and he *did* have military experience. He was just finishing his rehearsal as I approached the podium. He had a towel wrapped around his neck, a trick learned from Leonard Bernstein to take care of perspiration. Arey would have thought this an affectation. Me, I appreciated the dedication to detail it showed. By break time, the towel would be so soaked that you'd think he'd worn it into the shower.

He greeted me by name and asked how my playing was coming along. I knew that he knew I was no longer a student, and got the impression that he wanted to avoid discussing that. Nothing unusual — I was used to the same from former classmates. In those cases, the sentiment was that I was no longer one of them. This was four months into the war and few students seemed at all concerned with Korea or the draft. Little did they know that, come January, a large number of them would be following my lead — stopping school and hurrying to enlist in any military band they could to avoid being drafted for two years in the infantry.

Fennell wasn't judgmental — it just seemed an uncomfortable subject, and not one I was interested in hashing out anyway. I explained my situation, and he listened intently. He thought a moment before giving me his advice.

"First, be able to sight-read everything and anything they put before your eyes — but don't expect to ever sight-read *perfectly*. It can't be done. Try not to lose your place, keep up the proper tempo, and observe the dynamics — inject as much musicality into the piece as possible. The first run-through is always the hardest. Do the best you can. Avoid excuses and apologies.

"Second, prepare a standard familiar clarinet piece. Practice it until you can play it perfectly. You don't necessarily have to memorize it — you can take the score along. Pick an extremely difficult work, but by all means, master it.

"Third, have an encore piece ready, and ready from memory. Something you can execute perfectly, fast and furious. Something like 'Flight of the Bumblebee', 'Perpetual Motion', 'Dizzy Fingers' — you know the kind of piece I mean.

"Fourth, when warming up, they'll be listening, so prepare some

Tommy Dorsey

Charlie Shavers

Charlie Parker

Red Rodney

Dizzy Gillespie

Buddy DeFranco

Buddy DeFranco
Publicity photo for the
Buddy DeFranco Orchestra

Buddy DeFranco
During Buddy's first tour with
the Glenn Miller Orchestra in 1968

Buddy DeFranco
Soloing at the Düsseldorf Concert during the 1954 "Jazz Club USA" Tour

George Gershwin playing piano

Adolphe Sax

Joe Allard with Mrs. Maud Bonade
At party for Daniel Bonade's retirement from Juilliard, May 1959

Joe Allard's studio
Daniel Bonade in window, 1959

Benny Goodman

Gene Krupa

Benny Goodman (clarinet) and Gene Krupa (drums)

Leonard Feather

Phil Woods *(left)* and Gene Quill

Maynard Ferguson

Autographed photo of Artie Shaw
Sent to Steve after their meeting at Eastman

Glenn Gould performing with string section for CBC broadcast
Note his unique playing style and the chair built by his father

Glenn Gould
CBC broadcast, 1964

Glenn Miller

The Airmen of Note, 1950s, led by Fred Kepner

interesting and intricate scales in various keys — even various modes. Include some tricky arpeggios and the like.

"Fifth, from your high school band, you should know any and every Sousa march. Be ready to play them.

"Sixth, be very polite and soft-spoken. Don't be nervous. Say 'sir' at least part of the time, but not after every sentence or they'll think you're trying too hard."

Good ol' Frederick — and I'd never called him that before — had said it all. There was no need to write any of it down. I remembered every word then and can repeat practically everything verbatim now, fifty-three years later. When Frederick spoke, he did so sincerely, deliberately, and without a trace of malice. He could silently stare into your soul, feel the suffering that was there, and spontaneously create a course of action to eradicate it. Much like Buddy, he was an unpretentious giant.

We shook hands enthusiastically. I wished I had some parting gift to leave him, but I knew there was no need.

It would be eighteen years before we would shake hands again. I happened to be spending a few days in Miami on business when my life-long friend Ken Zmuda, a native Floridian, invited me to attend a morning rehearsal at the University of Miami. The orchestra was composed of various bandleaders from the military, high schools, and colleges across the country. I asked who the bandleader would be and Ken answered with only a sly, "You'll see."

We entered the auditorium and I scanned the orchestra. Soon the conductor came into view. Sure enough it was Fennell, flying through some breakneck overture, flailing, gesticulating, and perspiring profusely. The break was only a few minutes later and I hadn't had time to think. Tucker Time came back to me and I grabbed Ken, shouting "Let's go," and headed for the stage.

Before I made it all the way, Fennell spotted me and yelled out, "Botek! Yes, Botek — that's it, Stephen Botek!"

He greeted me with open arms, happy to see me. Treating me more like a friend and peer than some insignificant former student and drop-out, he talked with me through the break. I showed him the schedule of the events I was attending and he reared back.

"My God," he said. "Even a full, free concert tomorrow night by Stan Kenton!"

I remember thinking how Rufus Arey would have dismissed that, if he had even noticed.

Back in 1950, though, there was more of a sense of propriety preventing Fennell and myself from fully expressing ourselves. We had to read into the subtleties. No slouch at interpretation himself, I'm sure it meant a lot to Fennell that, even after leaving the school, I came back to him for advice.

Likewise, I recognized the way he treated me and the scope of his advice — not a quick comment to ease the life of a stranger, but all he could offer, given with a true spirit of kinship.

Barney Mallon had become even a closer friend, now that we were living next-door to each other. I no longer had the camaraderie of Eastman or my old roommates or even Phoebe, who was busy with her studies, so Barney became my primary confidante. He had begun his third year at Eastman and could fill me in on all the gossip and goings-on, but he was under no illusions that his student status saved him from the draft. Of course, I had filled him in about the things I had learned with Art on our trip to the base, and he was starting to get more than nervous about the possibility.

Loose talk around events in Asia didn't help. There was talk that China could possibly enter the war, and that General MacArthur was feuding with President Truman, wanting to use either the atom or hydrogen bomb if the war became serious enough. The actual news that reached us was sparse and inconclusive — radio broadcasters weren't saying too much and newspapers seemed to be just copying each other, offering nothing new. With a lack of information, people were beginning to fill in the gaps themselves. In this case, no news was *not* good news.

Barney was encouraging me to keep up my daily practice, and going out of his way to find me an extra dance job here and there. The work was needed desperately, my father's support having ended along with my career at Eastman. It seemed to me that I could try to do my part for Barney by becoming *his* Art Rubart and pushing him to act before it was too late. Sure, Barney would *talk*, often mentioning a trip to nearby Samson Air Force Base in Geneva, NY and trying to get into the band there. His chances would be good — not only had he become one of Rochester's most respected jazz bassists, but he also played tuba, even if he preferred not to. Unfortunately, Barney was all talk when it came to his future, and he wasn't inclined to action unless something was right in front of him. It helped to demonstrate to me one of the downsides to having his free-thinking, open-minded parents — he was so used to support, he never *had* to go out and do anything. He was able to live on lethargy and daydreams with a room at his parents' and all meals provided. Pushing him forward the way Art pushed me would take some time and effort, time neither of us had. After all, I was still learning the lay of the land.

Weeks flew by, and soon I'd be heading south for Thanksgiving in Pennsylvania. Walter Mallon had offered to drive me down, but I said no when the opportunity came to travel down with Phoebe instead. This would be the last of these train trips — Rochester was no longer feeling like home. I was noticing the overcast days, chilly nights, and occasional snowflake. While I was playing some, it wasn't the life steeped in jazz I had been expecting and coveting, and it didn't seem worth bearing the weight of the Rochester winter.

This would be goodbye to good old Rochester.

Glenn Miller

Born Alton Glenn Miller in Clarinda, Iowa in 1904 and raised in Nebraska and Missouri, Glenn attended high school in Fort Morgan, Colorado. Given a mandolin by his father as a child, he began playing music, soon trading the instrument for a trombone.

In high school Miller was introduced to dance bands and he started one of his own with classmates. In 1923 he attended the University of Colorado, where missing classes regularly to go to auditions and gigs in Denver led to his failing three courses in one semester. He dropped out to focus on music.

Studying under Joseph Schillinger, Miller developed his signature sound and approach to composition. He toured with various groups before Ben Pollack hired him and gave him the chance to write arrangements. Seeing success, he sent for his college sweetheart, Helen Burger, to join him, and they married shortly after.

Miller joined Red Nichols' band and, from that association, got work playing in orchestra pits for Broadway shows, alongside Benny Goodman and Gene Krupa. He continued to get freelance work as a trombonist in dance bands through the 1930s, finally landing a spot in the short-lived Dorsey Brothers group, where he also served as arranger. From there he was hired by British bandleader Ray Noble to put together an American orchestra — it was in this group that he first tried arranging a lead clarinet in front of four saxophones, a format which would resurface in his own band.

Miller formed his first band in 1937, a dismal failure. He returned to New York and decided to return to the clarinet-and-four-saxophone arrangement he had tried with Ray Noble's band. The band became a hit, featuring the likes of Billy May, Ray Anthony, and Bobby Hackett, as well as singers like Marion Hutton and Ray Eberle. Tex Beneke and the Modernaires were also featured performers on a number of their recordings.

"Tuxedo Junction" set a record in 1939 by selling 115,000 copies in its first week. "Chattanooga Choo-Choo" became the first-ever gold record in 1942. "Pennsylvania 6-5000" was based on the phone number of New York's Hotel Pennsylvania — it remains their number to this day, making it the oldest continuing phone number in the city. "Moonlight Serenade" was Miller's theme, and a vocal version was later recorded by Frank Sinatra, among others. Other hits include "In the Mood", "String of Pearls", and Miller's arrangement of the traditional "Little Brown Jug".

From 1939 to 1942 the band broadcast three radio shows weekly, sponsored by Chesterfield cigarettes — Harry James took over the broadcast when Miller joined the U.S. Air Force. The band also appeared in two films, *Sun Valley Serenade* and *Orchestra Wives*, Miller demanding a strong script and that the band be integral to the story. During this time he was accused of being too commercial, to which he answered, "I don't want a jazz band." He did place high emphasis on his arrangements, but allowed room for some improvisation, notably by Tex Beneke.

In 1942 with the U.S. entering World War II, Miller joined the U.S. Air Force as a captain and director of the band. He treated this band as a separate entity, rarely performing the hits from his civilian band. Traditionalists fought his reworkings of military music in modern styles, *Time* magazine noting that the military was now "swinging its hips instead of its feet". However, the soldiers and public responded with approval and Miller's approach won out.

To be closer to the troops, Miller had the band transferred from its original base at Yale University to London in 1944. There it took on an international stature and a name to match: the American Band of the Allied Expeditionary Force. As well as regular vocalists Johnny Desmond and the Crew Chiefs, the band had numerous guest vocalists such as Bing Crosby, the Andrews Sisters, and Dinah Shore. Miller was promoted to major, owing largely to the band's positive effect on morale.

On December 15, 1944, Miller was scheduled to play for soldiers who had fought in the liberation of Paris. Flying in poor weather conditions, his single-engine plane disappeared over the English Channel, and what happened remains a mystery. His remains and the wreckage of the plane were never found.

Miller was portrayed by James Stewart in *The Glenn Miller Story*, a biographical film. Legacy or 'ghost' bands continue to the present day after starting in 1946 with Tex Beneke as leader. Beneke wanted more recognition and, in an acrimonious break from the Miller estate, renamed that band the Tex Beneke Orchestra. The estate asked Ray McKinley to lead a new ghost band after the success of the film, which is the band that continues today, having seen leadership by Buddy DeFranco and currently led by Larry O'Brien. A separate Glenn Miller Orchestra for Europe founded in 1990 under Wil Salden continues to tour. Glenn's brother Herb had a band that continued through the 1980s, and his son John now leads a band playing music in the Miller style.

A memorial stone for Miller lies in Arlington National Cemetery at his daughter's request. Festivals celebrating his music take place annually in his birthplace of Clarinda, in Fort Morgan where he attended high school, and at England's Twinwood Airfield, where he was last seen alive. Miller received a posthumous Lifetime Achievement Grammy Award in 2003.

A wealth of recordings exist, from the hugely successful civilian band's releases through the recorded radio programs they did to the sessions the Army Air Force band recorded with and without guests.

Chapter 13
Do Nothin' Til You Hear From Me

My parents received me with their usual welcome-home warmth. My mother was overjoyed to see me again, greeting me with a barrage of questions about my health and plans, her concern about the draft barely disguised. My father, in contrast, coolly challenged his drop-out son. I knew the grocery store was about to close for the holiday, so he wouldn't be able to reduce me to being a clerk for the weekend, forcing me to work for my supper. Instead, I greeted him with new confidence, telling him that I would be practicing clarinet on Friday and Saturday, then borrowing his Buick to go to Washington.

Despite his numerous faults, Dad was a man of his word. Possibly it was some learned Catholic fear: breaking his promise would amount to bearing false witness, which would leave him open to possible damnation by the Devil. He had previously mentioned that I would be able to drive down to try my chances in Washington. No doubt my mother pushed as well, wanting anything but to see her son head off to war.

So Sunday came and Art and I began the 190-mile trip to the capital. Both of us were unfamiliar with the city. Despite our numerous road trips when I was a kid, the furthest south I had visited was Cape May, New Jersey. We'd made no hotel reservations, but we spotted a bed-and-breakfast a few blocks west of the Capitol building. The landlady was sweet, the price was right, the room decent enough, and there was even Sunday parking on the street, so we decided to take it. The woman who ran it immediately became all business when we made our decision, demanding cash in advance.

"You wouldn't mind if I practice my clarinet a bit?" I asked.

She changed her tone completely then.

"No. Absolutely no practicing an instrument in this house!"

Art and I retreated to our room. We griped a bit, nicknaming the woman 'No-Practice Priscilla'.

"It'd be futile," Art reasoned, "to argue with this old bitch, so let's think of another plan."

"I could take the car," I suggested. "Drive it to some quiet out-of-the-way place, practice — yes, inside the car — then return. Better if you stay here — you'll just be bored."

"No," he countered. "After you're done, I'm taking the car and driving to Baltimore."

I didn't even question it. It only took a moment to remember Art mentioning a new out-of-town girlfriend. Baltimore was about 125 miles round-trip from Washington, certainly out-of-town. It had to involve a woman, or Art would have dragged me into it. That must be why he had been so willing to accompany me to Washington. Still, it was late enough that it wasn't worth delving into the details. Art told me he would probably stay in Baltimore for most of the night. *Aha!* I thought. *It* is *a woman!* He would be back at the B&B waiting with the car at 7:30 a.m., ready to chauffeur me to Bolling Air Force Base.

We drove out and found a park in sight of the Washington Monument. On seeing the monument, Art pushed me to get closer, and we kept moving towards it — me stopping at one spot after another, and Art urging me to move closer. Finally we ended up parked right in the shadow of the monument. It being about 8 o'clock on a Sunday evening, the monument itself was closed and the park deserted. I was concerned about police running us off, but Art said they would at worst send us on our way and we could find another spot. The idea of practicing for my military audition underneath the monument was too poetic to ignore, so my qualms were set aside. I practiced diligently inside the car while Art napped in the back seat — after all his pushing to get closer! Being beneath the monument seemed to spark my playing, giving me the right mind-set for the day to come — I had something to thank No-Practice Priscilla for! When I felt I had played as much as I needed, I drove us home and woke up Art. He then drove off (in my dad's brand-new Buick!) without even leaving me the girl's name, address, or phone number. Considering how impulsive, selfish, driven, and horny Art was, I had to wonder why I was worried about trusting the military.

Trying to sleep, I tossed and turned for awhile. There was so much riding on the next day. It could make the difference between my being on the front lines or having a relatively cushy band job in Washington. Beyond my own doubts and fears, I had to worry about Art not showing up on time. Still, I fell fast asleep before too long.

Come morning, I was awakened by the smell of coffee. No-Practice Priscilla, full of smiles, had a complete breakfast ready and waiting. I told her Art was already outside and didn't need breakfast. I hadn't checked, but faith was all I had. If Art wasn't there, I wouldn't make it to Bolling Field. So I figured, rather than spend the extra time worrying, why not just enjoy breakfast and deal with it when the time comes?

At 7:30 sharp I stepped outside and was surprised to find the car was actually there. Art was slumped over the wheel asleep. *Good*, I thought, *the son of a bitch kept his word.*

"Move over, asshole," I said, shaking him awake. "I'm driving us to join the United States Air Force!"

Master Sergeant George Dietz hadn't changed much in three years, still the picture of health, still extremely polite and mild-mannered. Being the first-chair clarinet in a band of this caliber was certainly a prestigious position, but made all the more so by his age — about thirty-two. He was in command of the full clarinet section, numbering as many as twenty-five for a concert band formation. A full symphony orchestra would have twenty-five to thirty violins and violas replacing that clarinet section. The Air Force Band used the standard concert-band instrumentation but added some symphonic elements including a few cellos, a harp, two or three string basses, and a piano. Frederick Fennell had augmented the Eastman concert band with cellos and basses to form a 'symphonic band' and, as such, I was already somewhat used to the arrangement.

As Sergeant Dietz showed me around, I realized how unique this made the band. It would be the only one of this kind in Washington, maybe even around the world. I was seeing more of the big picture, and it was one that spoke to me. Bolling Air Force Base had a reputation for being home to many outstanding, innovative, creative, and distinguished musicians. Someone had skillfully gathered together many of America's most promising musicians under one umbrella as an enormously large Air Force family. This included the remnants of the late Glenn Miller's Army Air Force Band, who had recently regrouped as the eighteen-piece dance band The Airmen of Note and had a rehearsal hall just one building away. The Air Force had since split off from the Army, but that tradition was still theirs even if the band now played mostly originals and only maintained a few Miller arrangements, as Glenn's wife had organized a ghost band to tour under the Miller name. Buddy would later serve as leader of the reorganized Glenn Miller Orchestra from 1966 to 1974, having taken the job only on condition it made money, and under his direction, it did. If I hadn't moved on to a career in medicine, I could have bugged Buddy for a job with the band.

That this base was built around music was underlined by Sgt. Dietz and his deferential, courteous attitude. This wasn't the military standard as we knew it. Even without thinking of the threat of being drafted into the infantry, I was feeling that I wanted in.

Art and I were there with ample time to spare for the audition. We were greeted pleasantly by short, overweight, and out-of-shape Master Sergeant

Ed Grace — also far from standard military issue. He played tuba in the band (which apparently some extra weight helps with) and was in charge of all the paperwork for the band. He was friendly beyond belief and thoroughly disarming. He first offered me a cup of coffee, which I refused. He seemed to know quite a bit about me, enough that I was starting to feel a bit disturbed by it. I searched my memory, but couldn't remember ever meeting him. Suddenly he stopped abruptly by a phone and told me he had a roommate from Pennsylvania who wanted to speak to me. Without another word, he picked up the phone, dialed, and handed me the receiver.

"Hello," I ventured, "this is Steve Botek. To whom am I speaking?"

"Steve! This is your old friend Gary from high school. Remember me? From the district and state bands in Pennsylvania? The trombone player? You remember, I'm sure — there was Reuben Heller, Reading, Shillington . . ."

"Gary," I was still flustered, "what in the heck are you doing now?"

Gary had enlisted in 1947, shortly after graduating from high school. He hadn't played the trombone much since then, but had taken to studying arranging and was now the chief arranger for the band and the symphony orchestra.

"In fact," he added gleefully, "I even write occasionally for the Airmen of Note, the old Glenn Miller dance band! They're looking for a lead alto man. Are you interested?"

I was. So much, I could barely speak.

"Is anyone nearby listening to our conversation?" Gary asked me.

"No," I answered, puzzled. "I'm alone here in a far corner."

"Okay then, listen carefully. The commander-in-chief is one big fusspot. He's totally in command here and his word is law. He'll interview you as part of your audition after Dietz decides how well you play. Dietz is a great guy and you're a fine musician, so that shouldn't be a problem. Howard, though, is a neurotic son of a bitch. He'll size you up from head to toe, trying to disarm you, discourage you, dissuade you. He'll try to expose your weaknesses, break down your ego, even make you angry, and if he does, he'll prove to himself that he better not enlist you because you'd never survive his neurotic power-hungry need to be top dog.

"Just stay calm, don't threaten him or get angry. He's a former clarinet player and though he's very envious and critical of young, talented, tall players, he needs them at the same time. I hope your hair is still sort of long — he hates crew cuts. I know, go figure. It'll also help that you're from Pennsylvania — that's his home state and he has degrees from Penn State colleges: two earned and three honorary. Our band and orchestra is overloaded with PA boys. So that's one thing in your favor.

"And please: mention nothing of any of this to Ed Grace. I don't want to lose *my* happy home! Good luck, Steve! Bye!"

I put down the receiver. What had been looking like an Eden had a snake in it! Now I needed that cup of coffee. This bastard Howard sounded like my father — exactly what I was trying to get away from. Thinking about Pelletiere's advice about power-hungry men, I decided to start practicing my Jacobson exercises. I took a few deep breaths, then ran to the men's room and checked my hair. I had to look smart, and moreover, *be* smart to face the colonel. So resolved, I returned. Grace handed me a cup of coffee before saying his farewells and adding that he hoped to work with me in future.

Sgt. Dietz showed Art and me to the rear of the main rehearsal studio and asked us to sit down. The full band, eighty strong, was assembled and ready to begin their last selection of the morning. I got my first glimpse of Colonel Howard as he stood center stage perched on a long, wide podium, baton in hand and ready to conduct. On sight, I knew Gary was right — the attitude oozed from him. The downbeat given, the band proceeded to fly through the piece, one of Rossini's semi-popular race-to-the-finish overtures. The music sounded crisp, precise, and perfectly played. The overall effect was utter professionalism as each and every member played letter-perfect. No one got lost, no one seemed to hesitate — with one notable exception. Every so often, Howard would forget to cue in some soloist, but the players would all compensate for his lapses. These guys were completely capable of handling their own section or solo entrances unassisted.

Great conductors such as Bernstein, Ormandy, Hanson, or even Fennell seem to follow every measure of a piece. It's been said Bernstein memorized and followed *every note* of a selection.

Players watch conductors of this caliber constantly. The directors know, follow, and cue each and every soloist and section, never lose their place, and use their baton in such a simple, straightforward up-and-down manner that performing under their leadership is a clear, peaceful pleasure rather than an anxious and painful guessing game.

Howard wasn't really leading the band. The band was leading itself and just letting him think he was in charge. These astute musicians had learned *not* to watch him too closely, *not* to expect help with their entrances, but rather to depend totally on their own musicality. They were following the leader, but their *section* leaders — the first-chair trumpet, first-chair clarinet, or first-chair trombone — knew what they were doing. Large dance bands almost always function in this manner, with the bandleader there for show more than anything else — think of 'bandleaders' such as Guy Lombardo or Lawrence Welk, and probably 'pop' summer symphony conductors like Arthur Fiedler. Even so, these bandleaders understand the musicality at play and you wouldn't see the numerous gaffes evident in Howard's so-called leadership. The overture finished, the band stopped in unison, perfectly synchronized — followed by Howard's final downbeat, one beat too late. I held in the derisive smirk that wanted out. Too much was depending on the day to take pleasure in that moment.

Art stayed put as Dietz and I edged our way to a small room directly behind the stage. I assembled my clarinet and took a moment to wet my reed — it takes a minute or so of sucking on a clarinet reed to properly wet it. I asked if I could have another minute or two to warm up.

"Of course," Dietz replied.

With Fennell and Gary's advice on my mind, this was not going to be any helter-skelter, notes everywhere, ordinary warm-up. Beyond their advice as to the audition here, Fennell had constantly pointed out the utter importance of a proper warm-up, as had Langenus, Allard, and DeFranco.

"Remember someone, if only yourself, is always listening," Buddy used to warn me. "Each note that you play from the first to the last must sound musical. The concert actually begins backstage, so don't waste your time, don't waste your talent. Play each note to your fullest capabilities, like your entire life and career depended on it."

Buddy should know. Often he would listen attentively at a distance to some yet unintroduced musician as he or she warmed up. Buddy claimed to need no more than a good minute or two before he could jot down various things about the player from what he heard: their gender, approximate age, how long they've been playing, who they possibly studied with, what area of the country they came from, whether they were an introvert or extrovert, if they were passive or assertive, and countless other things towards a psychological profile of the player. Buddy notes that on numerous occasions he would present his blind analysis to a total stranger, only to be met with anger and accusations of spying.

Dietz, sure enough, listened intently as I pounced on the first note, full throttle. I maintained a full, rich, resonant tone — one that I knew a fellow player had to notice. I flew through various scales, arpeggios, and even one mode or two, all while trying to maintain a balance of good taste — to show off without being seen as a show-off. Dietz leaned in, his eyes widening, fighting back a tiny, crooked smile and I knew I was sounding good to him. I stopped and simply nodded. He reached for some pages, and produced a score I had never seen before — he asked if I had, and even if I hadn't answered, the look on my face would have told him no. The piece was black as coal with innumerable sharps and flats, and was written in one of the more difficult keys.

"Read," he commanded, with all the softness gone from his voice, reminding me that he was indeed a sergeant.

Sight-reading never scared me so on I read, playing as many notes as possible. I missed a few here and there but never stopped, never lost the rhythm, and never apologized. It was like skiing down a long and fairly steep hill full of moguls — some you'd fly over top, others were best approached from the side, and still others were best avoided altogether. The approach was the same. If I hit something wrong, I tried to stick the landing, avoid wiping out, and never stop. I continued for about five minutes with this manic, double-time drill, and it was clear that Sgt. Dietz was convinced I could properly handle myself under pressure.

"Enough," he ordered.

I stopped and he handed me a Rossini overture — the same one that the band had just performed. This time he didn't bother to ask if I had played the piece before, simply presuming that I had — or that I should have. He counted off the tempo, notably faster than Colonel Howard's. Rossini always appealed to me, with his "William Tell Overture" a personal favorite. I had battled with it many a time, its violin parts transcribed to clarinet as a tongue twister, with the difficult staccato passages needing to be tongued — produced by a rapid rhythmic touching of the reed with the tip of the tongue. It's akin to speaking with perfect articulation at breakneck speed without any stammering or stuttering. I wasn't familiar with this piece but, as with all of Rossini's music, it galloped along in a similar fashion, used the same figures, demonstrated his love of staccato, favored a fast tempo, and never failed to constantly challenge and surprise the performer. I found this appropriate as Gioacchino, Rossini's first name, is similar to the word *giocoso,* which in music is an indication to play with a gay, playful quality.

Halfway through the overture, everything seemed to be going very well. My tongue was nimble and my fingers flying. My eye-hand coordination was more than adequate. Still, the good sergeant wanted more. About five minutes remained in the piece and there would be no letting up. He had the whip out and was beating me on, waiting to see if I'd trip and possibly break my neck. I flashed on Buddy telling me about Tommy Dorsey requiring him to play chorus after chorus — not liking bebop and taking it out on Buddy by egging him on outwardly while waiting for him to stumble. This wasn't much different from the teaching style of Dorsey Sr, the only music teacher either Tommy or Jimmy ever had. In Lansford, the stories were ubiquitous about the Dorsey wrath, and how the sons dared not fail lest they end up being slapped across the room or subject to beatings with their father's shaving strap. I kept all this in mind and refused to let up. There were only minutes left, so why not suffer it for that short while more? When the piece ended, I felt I had done a respectable job on Rossini and hoped the good sergeant would agree.

He didn't even acknowledge it, instead telling me, "Now for one last encore type selection. Do you have some short thing you've memorized and possibly you like to play or have played a lot?"

Fennell was dead right, and I inwardly thanked him for his advice.

"Do you remember when you first heard me play?" I asked Dietz. "'Flight of the Bumblebee'?"

"Fine," he said.

I knocked it off in under one minute.

"Thank you very much," he said. "You may pack up now. Then, wait here. Someone will come to fetch you."

He was in military mode and, unlike his previous warmth, I could glean no clear idea of his feelings. Still, what had leaked through was all positive and I was feeling good about my chances. Little did I know that I was about to meet one of the most rigid, vindictive, power-crazed, sadistic, and psychologically ill individuals of my entire life. Many years later as a psychiatric professional, I would encounter other such non-psychotic men — although ones officially diagnosed with Personality Disorder. They would all be confined to a psychiatric institution or assigned to a compulsory and strict psychotherapy regimen.

No such luck with Colonel Howard.

Having seen him conducting earlier, I had been led to expect a self-deluded fool — a buffoon who everyone hid the truth from out of necessity. I had no idea the levels of self-importance the man commanded. I had been warned, but I figured it was exaggeration, not underplaying of the man's temperament. I was taken to meet him, like a slave before a king. Howard oozed self-righteousness and reveled in the power of his position. He never even offered me a seat, cautiously looking me over from far behind his polished mahogany desk — certainly not G.I. issue, but certainly kept in pristine shape by G.I. labor. We bantered for a while, my being careful not to overstep any of the unwritten bounds as well as the ones that were clear. I remained cool and suppressed any traces of fear, anxiety, and nerves. He was ready for me, and gave the impression that he would garner as much satisfaction from crushing me as he would from gaining a talented clarinetist for his band. He hung on my every word, searching for anything he could pounce on, but I left him no openings. He dropped names, I countered with names of my own but phrased them deferentially.

I praised him and the assembled band I had heard earlier, trying not to let my awareness of his inadequacy as bandleader show.

"Sure, I've heard the others," I cooed, "but none except yours would suit me."

It was, to be frank, bullshit. Certainly, this band was where I wanted to be if I had to be in the military, but there were likely more than a few others that would have served to keep me out of Korea, ones that likely had bandleaders who knew what they were doing. Still, I was here and as such, being obsequious, polite, and respectful, all in an effort to get into the good graces of a man whose very presence made it clear that he was a pompous son of a bitch.

This was another strength gained from my years in Dad's grocery store. My sisters and I grew up knowing how to sell. It was second nature. I was resolved that I would not go home without a contract in hand. The trick here was to pump my virtues, but align them with what he perceived as his.

Each of his sentences was transparent enough that I could glean more about the man — none of it pleasant — and speak to it. Thanks to my experience at the store dealing with salesmen, I could gracefully counter his parries and thrusts, while letting him think he had won a point. Through all this, I worked to suppress my disdain for a man who couldn't even recognize that a band of *eighty players* were all working to compensate for his shortcomings. That became harder as I noticed his one foot peeping out from the side of the desk. *Elevator shoes!* I thought. It was hard to forget that while he went on about my height, but I managed.

The tête-à-tête was over fairly quickly and I felt drained, but resolved not to show it. He offered me a half-assed smile. I had won his approval, at least for the time being. Having done so left me sick to my stomach, but I held it in and showed no sign of it. I knew his Captain Queeg paranoia would always keep him from trusting me completely, but judging from the interview, I was sure I could handle him.

Howard offered me neither advanced sergeant's rank nor off-base rations and quarters, enticements Sgt. Dietz had offered me back in 1946. He told me my two years of college weren't enough to earn me officer's status. There was a war raging and, as such, it was a buyer's market for all the branches of the military. Coming begging with my hat in hand, I had to gladly accept whatever I could get, and I knew this was not the time or place (or person) to push for more.

The interview complete, I was escorted back to the auditorium where Art was still sitting patiently in the same place we had left him. I hadn't been thinking about it while I was gone, but I was surprised to see this when we returned. Art was known to be a slave to his high-energy impulses and his amateur boxing training. With nothing else to do, it would be no time at all before he was dancing all over a room, bobbing, weaving, shadow boxing. Seeing him sitting there patiently with this spark of his completely held in made me realize exactly how serious things were.

Of course I had taken the audition seriously, but until that moment, I was largely seeing it as an audition — and auditions always had their own peculiarities that one was forced to adapt to. The interview had seemed like an accompanying formality — nothing unusual when applying for a gig or to work with a band. Though I knew it, the idea had been pushed to the back of my mind and only seeing Art sitting there brought it home: our lives were on the line here.

Still, there was nothing left to do but wait at this point. I was exhausted anyway and needed the rest. We sat in complete silence in the huge auditorium, waiting. Not a word passed between us. Art didn't even ask about my audition and how it went — he could see my face and that was good enough. We both knew, though, that however well the audition went, my fate was in the hands of another. *Either way*, I thought, *the work is over.*

Five minutes passed before the silence was broken. A small, thin man wearing glasses and in uniform entered the hall. He introduced himself as Warrant Officer Robert Landers, the choral director of the Air Force's glee club, The Singing Sergeants. *That's nice*, I thought. *Why are you telling* me *this?*

"Your clarinet audition went very well, Stephen," he told me matter-of-factly. "We'd love to accept you on that merit alone, but it so happens that we need good clarinetists who can also sing a bit — to double, so to speak — and fill some of the secondary singing spots in our choir.

"Can you sing?"

Can I sing? The phrase resounded through my head. Two years at Eastman taking piano, trumpet, violin, saxophone, but *damn it*, not one voice lesson. I had dated many female vocalists — why hadn't I studied with them? Catholic choirs, school glee clubs, sessions with band singers, girlfriend vocalists — all flashed before my eyes in counterpoint to visions of Korea at war.

"Yes, I can sing!" I answered *sotto voce*, knowing I had to fill the silence before it became awkward and before it got me shipped off to Korea as infantry.

"Fine," smiled Mr. Landers (warrant officers are addressed as Mister). "Get up on stage and I'll audition you now."

I made my way up to stage wondering how I'd got myself into this mess. I'd have been glad to double on saxophone or another reed instrument, but voice? I'd only really sung at camp and in church. Never had a single voice lesson and never took part in an organized choir or formal group — it wouldn't have been that hard and it would have made the difference. Singing songs at camp and in church where I could easily be drowned out would mean nothing. Still, I had no choice. One way or the other, it couldn't be worse than the interview with Colonel Howard.

Once I was on stage, Mr. Landers told me to sing anything. I took a moment, searching for something I knew and could perform. Finally, I settled on "Down by the Old Mill Stream", which I knew from camp.

It was bad enough struggling through the song, earnestly as I could, but Art was twisting in his seat, trying not to burst into laughter while Landers was glaring at me in a less-than-military fashion. Art knew I couldn't sing, and as much as the situation called for a serious approach, he had reached his limits. His face was turning beet-red watching me, and I could see him struggling, out of the corner of my eye. I stopped after one verse, knowing it was a valiant enough effort and all of us had suffered enough.

Landers looked up at me, raised an eyebrow, and with the utmost gravity asked, "And where did you say you sang?"

"I sang in camp and in church," I sheepishly replied.

I have to give credit to Art. I think he hurt himself throwing himself to the floor to avoid laughing or being seen after that.

Landers was visibly perplexed, his jaw moving in indecision. Something about me had gotten to him, despite my singing. Was it my refusal to give up? Could it be that he didn't want to tell Dietz, Grace, and Howard that he had failed me? Did he know it was unfair to expect a professional-level clarinetist to *also* be a vocalist and perform extra duty in his fucking glee club? I studied his face as he was studying me, and suddenly his jaw stopped moving and I sensed he'd made a decision — and from the look on his face, it wasn't in my favor. Art had sensed the gravity of the moment and was peering over the top of a chair back, waiting. Landers sighed and excused himself. He went to the main office, I gleaned, likely talking to Dietz, Grace, and Howard about me. Had I impressed them enough to justify taking on someone with my singing skills? Landers returned in about ten minutes, no sign of expression on his face. If we'd been playing poker, I would have left the table.

"If we promise," he began slowly, "to bring you back here after Basic to play in the band, will *you* promise to then also study voice, say for six months to a year, and at the same time help out by singing with our glee club?"

He hadn't even finished the sentence before my 'yes' leapt out of my throat. I quickly regained my composure, though, asking for a formal letter stating what we had discussed. I claimed it was for my father, a cynic who would never believe that I had been accepted. This was partly true, but the real reason was the obvious one, and Landers knew it as well as I did: never trust the military. He couldn't have gotten where he was without knowing that. As for me, the day in Washington was enough to confirm that for me: Gary's warning, Dietz's change in demeanor for the audition, the visible self-importance and buffoonery of Colonel Howard, the assembled band pretending he was conducting properly, and this latest, the surprise vocal audition. It was all too clear that in the military, anyone could turn out to be a wolf in green wool.

Sgt. Grace gave me the letter and it was large, impressive, and flat-out beautiful. Looking at it, I saw my ticket out of Korea but, beyond that, it was on heavy bond parchment, with the various colors, seals, and signatures of an official document. I could hardly wait to wave it in my father's face — it showed that I had made the right decision in leaving Eastman when I did, as well as going there in the first place, that I could run my own life, and that I wasn't just following whims as they came along.

No one mentioned the vocal audition, in or out of the letter. Landers had likely not told anyone of our arrangement, so my embarrassment was to be kept between him, Art, and myself. Appreciating his tactfulness and discretion, I knew I would keep my end of the bargain. I would train my voice and sing again for him and that next time, it would be something soft, sweet, and satisfying.

After we were done at Bolling I just wanted to head north and get home to my folks. Art, however, was in no hurry. He wanted to see Washington while we were there, so we drove around downtown. He insisted on visiting the Washington Monument.

"It'll be open now," he urged. Afterwards we headed out on our way, stopping for gas near Gettysburg. While I was pumping gas, Art disappeared. I was just starting to curse him under my breath when he reappeared, about ten long minutes later. He was carrying sandwiches and two very large paper cups.

"Time to celebrate!" he announced. "I poured three bottles of Ballantine Ale into these two cups, and I thought these pork sandwiches looked good."

Art was always the soul of generosity, but he could afford to be. He was never broke. If he needed money, he would simply reach into his dad's cash register and take whatever he wanted. It didn't surprise me that he had procured food and drink — that was to be expected of Art. The only thing I wondered about was why it had taken him so long — but I should have known the answer before he blurted it out. It was Art's way to fly in, grab what he liked, and make it his, and there was only one thing he ever bothered to take his time getting.

"Look what else I got," he grinned, holding up a piece of paper. "The name and phone number of that cute little teaser who makes the sandwiches."

Ahh, right! I should have known it wasn't just the sandwiches that looked good.

* * *

It was close to 9 p.m. when I carefully parked Dad's Buick Super next to the house. I tried to be quiet but I was quickly reminded that it was impossible to arrive unannounced. My mother's dog, Rex, could hear a pin drop and knew quite well the powerful whine of the Buick. On hearing it, he let out his own whine in response and a barrage of barking. My parents were at the door before I was. Mother greeted me with a warm hug and kiss, both more heartfelt than usual — I knew she was anxious for news. Dad simply shook my hand. The longest greeting, though, went to Rex — it was as if I'd been gone for a year. He ran around the three of us in circles, refusing to relent until he got hugs, kisses, and paw shakes.

With greetings out of the way, we didn't bother with small talk. I didn't even get the standard maternal questions about whether I'd been warm enough. There was absolute silence as I pulled the parchment out from its large manila envelope. I didn't bother explaining a thing, simply handed the letter over to my parents.

My mother read it first, becoming wide-eyed and grinning widely. She ended with a tearful, "Wonderful! Wonderful!"

My father didn't really need to read it after that, but did so as Mother hugged me unmercifully. He stayed silent for a moment, his eyes welling up as he turned slightly to the side to mask his emotion.

"Well," he murmured. "How do you like that?"

"This calls for a celebration," Mother exclaimed.

To celebrate, porterhouse steaks were brought out from the store and my mother set to preparing a feast. The meal was, for a change, centered on me. Mother was basking in the knowledge that I wouldn't have to go to the front lines, while Dad was recognizing that I wasn't just some drop-out — my accomplishments were such that they could be recognized, by the United States Air Force at that. The conversation was very matter-of-fact, and even sparse, but the mood was light, joyous even, and for the first time in a long time it felt like the entire family was on the same page. Well, the household, anyway — Betty was of course at home with Ernie, Jo was out on a gig, Agnes was out on a date, and it being late when I arrived, Francis was up in bed. Still, I couldn't see any of them not being happy for me. The meal was outstanding, Mother having outdone herself in honor of the occasion. Even Rex got a piece of steak and joined in the festivity.

The following day I showed off my letter to the Lehighton recruiting sergeant. He seemed happy about it. Of course, to him I was another enlistee and a bit more money in his monthly paycheck. I knew not to trust the military, but even so, he seemed friendly, helpful, and honest. If I trusted no one, how could I know when and where to sign? I never learned the recruiter's name. At the time, no visible name tags were issued and his name would only be on his dog-tags. I have no idea why his name never came up, but I assume his being a recruiter used to dealing with civilians left him free to skirt standard military protocols. Personal name tags have now become part of the standard uniform, but in those days, address was largely by rank, learned from looking at someone's sleeve. Looking back, there were superior officers like Colonel Howard who never addressed me by name. Like Benny Goodman addressing everyone — including his wife — as 'Pops', it made position clear and kept things simple for the higher-ups. My youngest sister Ginny married a colonel, Col. Robert Gates, and his two teenage sons from a previous marriage always answered their dictatorial dad with a 'sir', even on the afternoon I visited as we all stood on the beach in bathing suits, preparing to water ski.

The recruiter, by virtue of his rank, would generally have his name learned by those of lesser (or no) rank, but he never mentioned it, nor did anyone else. Maybe a bit of a code of secrecy helped recruiters, as no one would then be able to pass along the names of those who had tricked them. Still, this one even pointed out to me that, as a bandsman, I would only have to enlist for three years rather than four. I already knew that, but I took his mentioning it as a sign that he was being forthright. I decided to trust him. He told me that I would probably *not* be doing my basic training at Samson Air Force Base in nearby Geneva, NY, which had recently been converted to an Air Force base after many long years as a Navy boot camp center.

The expectation had been that I would be doing my Basic there, reasonable driving distance from the family in Lansford.

"No," he assured me. "Samson is not quite large enough to handle the influx of new recruits expected to enlist right after Christmas."

I knew now he *was* being honest. He had just given away the secret about the upcoming draft and its fallout.

"Your sign-up date," he continued, "will also be around then. Possibly December 28th — Wilkes-Barre, PA for your physical and swearing-in, then come January 2nd, you'll take the train to Lackland Air Force Base in San Antonio, Texas."

Texas! I thought. *Washington, DC had seemed like a far trip south!* The idea felt like adventure, like further distancing myself from the expectations and ties of family and establishing myself on my own. And with my being treated as an adult in mind, it came back: never trust the military.

"Will you put that in writing?"

He smiled and nodded.

"What will happen," I ventured, "if the draft wants me before December 28th?"

"Have no fear, Stephen. Air Force sergeants have more political pull than you can imagine. Trust me. I'll take care of everything."

Never trust the military rang through my head again. But there was no alternative. I would get it in writing and *if* the draft tried to get me before it was settled, I'd have to go by his word that he could get me out. I *had* to trust that the Air Force was fairer than the Army that Ernie always warned me about, more egalitarian and more trustworthy. It wasn't as if I really had much choice.

Schedule in hand, I raced home. I knew Mother would be waiting for news. I had about a month before I became official military property, and I would have New Year's Eve for my own even after that.

* * *

December in Lansford was a religious celebration. Not only was the town predominantly Catholic, but in a coal town, prayer is always a part of life. Special ceremonies including extra masses and processions would run the length of Advent, on each of the four Sundays preceding Christmas. Early in the month, St. Nicholas' Day was celebrated. School became bearable for kids, with the break in sight and days off for blizzards, football and basketball victories, even the first official day of deer season. Christmas Eve was naturally celebrated widely, but it had special significance in the Botek home. Not only was it my birthday, it was also the birthday of a brother born exactly ten years prior. He had only lived about eighteen months, dying during the great flu epidemic of the early 1930s.

There was Christmas Day following, of course, which meant a flurry of activity and the one day when even the most desperate neighbors would make do with what they had rather than stop by to plead for the goods they'd forgotten. St. Stephen's Day follows the next day, and then there was nothing — and almost nothing to do — until December 31st.

New Year's had its traditions as well. People would stay up past midnight not only to welcome in the New Year, but to finish off the old. Any open bottles were to be drunk dry, any open food to be consumed, and in honor of the coming year, new bottles had to be opened as well.

I planned my December very carefully. Not only would it be my last month as a civilian for some time, but I would turn twenty-one. This would be my last month living with my parents, and I would soon be going through the humiliating hell of basic training. I wanted lots of rest, to stay perfectly healthy, and to maintain my practice. I'd want to avoid those drunken nights with Art, any entanglements with the law (always a possibility during a drunken night with Art), any accidents (another possibility during a drunken night with Art), and any pregnant girlfriends — Phoebe might not be nearby, but who knew what could happen during a drunken night with Art!

Apart from the celebrations, for me this was a month for quiet time with friends and family. I channeled all I learned as a God-fearing Catholic and minded my P's and Q's. I didn't even mind helping out in the store, knowing that past that month I would never have to again. Each time in the store was a chance to see and speak to townsfolk whom I would be leaving behind, a goodbye for me even if they didn't know it.

When it was time to leave for Texas, Mother helped me pack. My independence as an adult wasn't threatened even by that, as it was allowing her one more gesture before I went off completely on my own (except for Uncle Sam, of course). She chose two pairs of my best underwear, an extra shirt, a pair of socks, and a couple of handkerchiefs, using only a small zip-up cloth bag for my things.

"You won't need much," she told me. "This note from the sergeant says they will issue you all necessary clothing on arrival.

"So you'll have room for these." She demonstrated the foodstuffs to me as she packed them. "Dried apricots, prunes, raisins, a few chocolate bars, my homemade nut-and-poppy-seed rolls — enough to share if you like. And here's fifty dollars, just in case. Keep it in a safe place."

Ernie drove me to the train and Mother insisted on coming along. I had said my farewells to Dad before leaving and, as I leaving for who knows how long, a handshake and kiss on the cheek was the crux of it — more than enough emotion for 'the old man'. It was an extremely cold morning and I was wearing my fleece-lined ¾-length jacket, as unnecessary as it would be once I was en route to Texas. Various young men lined the platform and mothers milled about, looking sullen. Mother left to speak to another mother in the same position, and Ernie pulled me aside to talk.

"Steve," he chided, "you never told me about your physical. Did it go like

I told you it would?"

"You know, Ern," I smiled, "you were 100-percent correct. They counted my eyes, checked if I was breathing, listened to my heart for ten seconds, felt my groin, had me bend over and cough while they shoved a finger up me, and they virtually ignored my teeth.

"The second doctor was a psychiatrist, I think. He asked if I liked girls, and I told him I love them, that I have two or three right now. That I can't get enough of them. Then he asked if I liked boys, and I said, 'Sure, doctor, but not like *that*.' He asked if I ever slept with a boy or a man, and I told him my brother and I had to share a bed when Uncle Paul came to visit. 'Dismissed' was all he said."

Ernie laughed.

"But guess what, Ern," I continued. "Later that afternoon, about thirty of us were standing in front of the judge to be sworn in. He started with a few facts about the Air Force, which we were supposed to say 'yes' to, and we did, in unison.

"Then he read the part about us swearing to loyalty and bravery and serving the Air Force for four years. I interrupted and said, 'Your honor, I'm only enlisting for three years.' The judge remained silent for a moment, then a voice came from backstage: 'The Air Force changed bandsmen enlistments from three to four years two weeks back.'

"And guess who it was, Ern? That same sergeant who recruited me!"

"See," Ernie sighed. "*Never* trust the military — those sneaky bastards."

Mother was running back towards us along the platform, so I ditched my cigarette. We saw others all looking past us, so we turned around to see.

"Oh God, Steve," Ernie whispered. "Here comes the train. Y'know, in a way, I wish I was also going. Somehow, sometimes, I miss those good old days."

We were shaking hands goodbye as Mother ran up to us, tears streaming down her face. Seeing her cry, I started crying too. Considering my military rep started with this train trip, I was glad she'd packed the extra handkerchiefs. We hugged goodbye and I didn't think she would let go for a minute, almost having to pry myself loose. I wiped my face and lined up with the others.

My old recruiter had appeared and was all smiles. He announced that our group had thirty-one men — yesterday we were boys, today we were men — and would be riding in a special Pullman car all the way to San Antonio. The coach had individual sleeping compartments, a small kitchen and dining area, plus a porter and others to attend specially to us.

"And quickly now, before the train leaves — since I am not going to be going with you, I need a volunteer to be in charge."

Bullshit! I thought. *You already pulled a fast one on me — four years instead of three. Drop dead!*

"Also, you heard me say there are thirty-one of you? Well, I'm sorry to say but we only have thirty beds. Who wants to volunteer to double up?"

I couldn't believe my ears! Was this son of a bitch serious? The military was absolutely paranoid, super-strict, utterly unyielding, and totally intolerant of any behavior that in the slightest manner might even *resemble* homosexuality, and now it wanted some of us to double up? Say my friend Michael and I volunteered, just to help out. What would the drill sergeant in San Antonio say when we arrived, never mind the other guys? Would we be labeled fags, sissies, or queers for the next four years? Probably everyone was thinking the same — no one dared volunteer. So to avoid being selected, which likely would carry the same stigma, as we boarded the car I excused myself to go to the washroom. It was nothing but a dodge, as I knew the lavatory door would still be locked as long as we were in the station. I hid myself out of sight in the last section of the coach and waited until we were well on our way before going to my assigned seat.

Once I sat down, I asked who volunteered to be our new commander. Surprise, it was Michael! I'd known Michael since parochial school and his new position changed nothing between us. It wasn't long after I sat down that he popped over to ask me to join in the poker game about to begin.

Who volunteered to bunk together? No idea. I never asked and never heard. Considering we were from Catholic country, that was standard even before we had signed our enlistment papers. And even back in 1951, as new recruits we knew the drill: don't ask, and even more importantly, don't tell!

Chapter 14
The G.I. Jive

How bad could the Air Force be? Enlist and get four days between your physical and going off to basic training. Board a Pullman coach and get four more days free of work, with continuous poker, excellent food, and a clean bed to myself. And the trip itself — the train headed north (!) first, then west, then pulled over to a remote side track, waited for an hour until another train flew by, then finally headed on to Texas. A four-day trip for a military starving for new recruits when a flight from Allentown International would only take four hours — it was just as Ernie had described the Army: "Hurry up and wait."

Through the windows we got glimpses of famous cities, and when the train stopped we actually got the chance to step out and see them. From Chicago we finally headed south to St. Louis. It reminded me of Art describing his experience with a Navy recruiter. "Join the Navy and see the world," the recruiter said. Art nodded, "Yes, see it but never get a chance to explore any of it unless your ship ties up and shore leave is granted." Here, we were actually getting the chance to disembark and see a little of the cities we were heading through. In the same day, we set foot in both Illinois and Missouri!

Franklin, our porter, was black and probably accustomed to being treated like a second-class citizen by train travelers, but our group was friendly and joked with him — if anyone had any problems about his race, they kept it to themselves. The morning after St. Louis, we would be pulling into his hometown, Texarkana. He told us, "If any of y'all had two really long legs, you'd be able to spread out over two states: Texas and Arkansas."

Sure enough, Franklin was all smiles the next morning as we neared his old home. Each of us wrote out our orders for the chef, as was the standard. The reason offered was that there would be no mistakes if we wrote out our own orders, but I think in part, the real reason was that Franklin was unable to write the orders out himself. I had this suspicion confirmed when he produced a Texas roadmap and pointed out Texarkana to me.

"Read here, Mister Stephen," he politely encouraged. "Doesn't it say that Texarkana has a separate municipal government in each state? 20,000 people in Arkansas and 30,000 in Texas. I told you, Mister Steve, that in Texas, everything is bigger — and I do mean everything!"

Franklin was happy to be nearing home, not just because of some homesickness, but it would be his last stop with us. He was going home. I wondered what his life in Texarkana would be like. I was sure he couldn't read or write. Calling me 'Mister Stephen' was ordinary enough for a railroad employee, but I had noticed something else. Once our train had left Chicago and headed south, Franklin had begun addressing Michael, eighteen years old, as 'sir' — with no one asking him to do anything of the sort. Remember, we had no military clothing or even rank at this point. It was clear that we had reached the South — the *Deep* South — and things were as my brother-in-law Ernie had often told me.

The map was an Esso one, and Franklin told me to keep it.

"A souvenir," he cheerfully offered.

I shook his hand in thanks, palming a $10 bill gained in the previous night's poker game.

"Here, buddy, is *your* souvenir. A thank-you from up North. Pennsylvania — our good ol' Keystone State."

Saying it made me wish I had something truly Pennsylvanian to give him, and then suddenly an idea struck me. I unzipped my bag and fished around and produced one of my mother's homemade nut-and-poppy-seed rolls for him, apologizing that he couldn't try one fresh from the oven. I didn't see him eat it, of course — no railroad employee would eat in front of a passenger, no matter how friendly things had gotten — but the last time I saw him before he left the train at Texarkana, Franklin beamed a huge farewell smile at me, which I returned. I didn't know if it was my gesture or the taste of my mom's baking that had widened his smile.

There wasn't much of the trip left after that, and we only saw Franklin's replacement as he cleared up our breakfast dishes. Breakfast finished just before the train pulled to our final stop.

It was 8:45 a.m. and the temperature had already risen to 55°F. The San Antonio air felt warm and dry. A mild breeze scattered dust and debris around rows of parked blue Air Force buses. We were just taking in the scene when a voice boomed from between the coaches.

"Look alive, airmen! Grab your gear and line up, double file, outside!"

We scrambled, all eager to make a good first impression. A brief roll call followed, and we boarded a bus headed towards the outskirts of the city. None of us knew the rules at this stage of the game, and so no one dared speak for the fifteen minutes it took to get to our destination. There were a few nods, gulps, and 'ahh's as Lackland pulled into view.

It was immense. A large gate crowned with a semi-circular wooden sign — *Welcome to Lackland Air Force Base* — greeted us. Dry, dirty, dusty, and flat as a pancake, the grounds seemed to go on forever. Lackland had its own streets — some paved, some just dirt roads, further adding to the idea of its size — it had its own back roads! There were two-storey wooden buildings everywhere, obviously barracks soon to be our new homes. Men marched as one in groups, filing by with no notice paid to us green recruits. A few may have been muttering condolences or laughing at us under their breath, but their gazes never wandered.

We entered a large, empty field, maybe the length of a football field but the width of five. It was completely bare except for clusters of men every thirty feet or so. The bus driver found an empty spot, screeched to a halt, and shouted, "Last stop! All out! Find a place to sit down. Stay put until someone comes to fetch you. Smoke 'em if you got 'em."

We followed the orders to the letter. Looking like cattle left to graze, Michael and I found a patch of grass, threw down our now-useless Pennsylvania winter jackets, and pulled out our cigarettes.

"I'll trade you one of my Sir Walter Raleighs," I suggested, "for one of those Old Golds."

It was a deal. We sat and smoked, saying little, everything being too big and new to be reasonably discussed, including the rules of conduct. Hours passed until someone came. He called Michael's name and Michael hopped to attention and followed along, pausing only to throw me the rest of his pack of Old Golds. It was an unexpected gesture, and maybe the warmest one possible under the circumstances. It was practical too — at least it offered a way to fill the time.

By 6 p.m., with names being called and faces disappearing, the field was emptying fast. Everyone else from my original group of thirty-one had been collected. I wondered if I had been forgotten, or worse — they had missed my name! Were there FBI agents dispatched across Texas searching for the scoundrel Botek, traitor to his country? I wondered who I could ask to be sure, but then I had no idea if I should be asking anyone anything — maybe that would get me in trouble.

Hurry up and wait, I remembered. Sighing, I lit another smoke. And another. And another. They were not only filling the time, they were taking the place of everything else. I had been sitting in the hot sun since breakfast without being given food or water. By 7 p.m. the sun was setting and the temperature was dropping fast. There was an ominous chill and I remembered what little I had heard of freezing-cold desert nights. Funnily enough, they had never come to mind when I was packing for the warmth of Texas in the midst of a Pennsylvania winter — at the time, thinking I would ever be cold in San Antonio seemed absurd, or would if it had ever come to mind.

Finally I saw someone coming towards me. He was young with a medium build, dressed in a one-piece grey overall with matching cap tilted back and to the side — a uniform I was still too green to recognize as what I would be wearing. At first I thought he must be a bus mechanic — most of them were black and they had been moving around the field through the day. It was still the fifties, and that he was black meant that he would have no power, and couldn't be the one I was waiting for. Still, a friendly enough face at first glance made me smile — which I quickly retracted when it occurred to me that smiling might be against protocol.

He introduced himself as Basic Jackson Jones, or 'J.J.' to friends. He explained that Basic was the term used for newcomers such as me — and him. Having no rank, we would display no stripes either. I told him my name and that I would be a Basic should anyone ever come to fetch me. He laughed, telling me Corporal Wiggans had sent him to find me and bring me to the barracks. I breathed a sigh of relief, having thought that I might be left out for the night.

"I've been here a week," he told me, "in this godforsaken hellhole. We're both Basics, lowly Basics. We get all the shit, we're always on the defensive, and we must always salute first."

I was glad to hear a friendly, *real* voice, but shocked at the same time. How did he know he could trust me to let loose like that? Sure, I was glad that he did, but I had to wonder if I looked too out of place in the military.

"Botek," he suddenly wondered out loud, "Like Brubeck. Do you like jazz? I'm from Brooklyn and this Texas hillbilly bullshit is hard to take."

I grinned and we began talking. He led me to a large two-storey billet. The front door was wide open and every light in the place appeared to be burning. Through the many windows, I could see numerous young men, some in their underwear and some with towels around their waists scurrying around the building.

At the entrance we were halted by a short, stern-looking man in his late twenties wearing fatigues and a helmet with two stripes painted around it. Jones stood to the side, remaining dead still and perfectly silent.

"I'm Corporal Wiggans," the short man pronounced. "I'll be your Basic Flight Chief for the next ten weeks."

I extended my hand, saying, "I'm Stephen Botek. Glad to meet you, Corporal Wiggans."

He refused my hand and eyed me sternly.

"Repeat what you said," he commanded, "but like this: 'I'm Stephen Botek, *sir*. Glad to meet you, Corporal Wiggans, *sir*.'"

I did as he asked and, noticing Jones cuing me to salute, added the salute to the end of the introduction.

"Now — both of you — double-time it upstairs. I'm going to show you how to make a bed."

J.J. nearly pushed me up the stairs.

"Remember what I told you," he chided. "Salute everything that moves!"

He snickered before continuing: "Okay, I should have told you to say 'sir' after every sentence when speaking to anyone higher in rank than a Basic. Later, when Basic is completed, only officers will be addressed as 'sir'."

Upstairs, a huge open bay greeted us. There were two long rows of double-decker steel cots. Large footlockers filled the floor — one per person.

"One bed, one box per Basic," said J.J., the phrase obviously having been repeated many times. "You're in the Army now! Hey, according to the roster they gave me, you're from Pennsylvania. Close enough to New York to make us Yankee cousins."

I smiled and took in the scene. The joint was jumpin'. It *was* Saturday night, after all. Could this be the usual end-of-the-week party? There was guitar music and someone else was practicing the flute. Others were seated on their footlockers busily writing letters. Some were heading for the showers while others seemed to be returning. About four rows of beds away there was a slender boy in his Jockey shorts lying spread-eagle across the bed, puffing away on a large cigar and reading a *Captain Marvel* comic.

"He's from Texas," J.J. commented. "He's fresh out of high school, innocent as a daisy, and not very streetwise. But otherwise, he's a good kid. You'll be introduced tomorrow morning, when they parade us off to Sunday service."

Guitars, cigars, and camaraderie — I was beginning to think maybe the Air Force wouldn't be so bad after all.

"Here comes John," J.J. whispered. "He's from West Virginia. He'll strut straight down the center of the place totally naked without a care in the world. If you look, you'll see why the group has already nicknamed him 'Long John Silver'."

Then Corporal Wiggans appeared. J.J. snapped to attention. Our benevolent leader took center stage and all else fell by the wayside — the music stopped, letters were placed on footlockers, and everyone stood to attention, including John. Wiggans went to the nearest bed to me and vigorously tore the bedding away from it.

"Two sheets, two blankets, and one pillow!" he barked. "Make a one-in-four tuck here, place this there, shove that here . . ."

From my face, it must have been obvious I was lost, but J.J. cued me to play along and I knew that meant he would show me later. Obviously Wiggans needed to think whatever he was doing was teaching me, so I had to feign understanding. Wiggans tightened the upper blanket 'til it was as taut as possible, then turned to me. I was doing my best to look attentive and focused.

"Botek," he yelled, "give me a quarter!"

"Yes, sir, Corporal Wiggans, sir!" I fished through my pockets. "Here's a shiny new one. Uh, sir."

"Unless it bounces, the bed isn't made correctly," he added.

His attention was back on the bed, and I shot J.J. a puzzled look. He shook it off, trying to restrain a smile. With a flourish, Wiggans threw the coin down onto the middle of the blanket. It bounced up slightly one time and the Corporal turned to me straight-faced but with glee in his voice.

"See, I told you so."

He looked me over, and must have noticed how tired I looked.

"Have you eaten, Botek?"

"No, sir. Not since this morning. Sir."

"Jones, take him to the mess hall. Stay with him so he doesn't get lost. But hurry back. Lights out at 9 p.m. sharp and 5 a.m. comes quickly."

Over supper, with no one else in the mess hall, J.J. had some choice words for the Corporal: mother*this*, mother*that*, asshole (his favorite), and fusspot.

"That bouncing-quarter bullshit!" he moaned. "Why, in the National Guard, we always used a half-dollar."

He looked at me and grinned, seeing that I was somewhat overwhelmed.

"Don't worry, man. A little food in you and a good night's sleep, and you'll be on your way. All that jazz can wait for tomorrow.

"Now, let's talk about something *important* — what was it like seeing Bird and Dizzy in person?"

* * *

J.J. was a true buddy — much like Buddy himself. He was the type that makes life secure and interesting at the same time. We went to Catholic mass together, and it stood out by its sameness. When everything else around me had changed considerably in the last few days, the service was the same. This was in the days before Vatican II, when masses were still in Latin and as interchangeable as a McDonald's, no matter where you went. The service felt like an anchor — not as a weight, but like a touchstone, a sign that despite the distance between Lackland and Lansford, or even Rochester, life was still the same. Once a week, regardless of my feelings toward priests, things were back to normal. 'Normal' at this time in my life was a change and a welcome one.

My group numbered only twenty-three, and apparently ninety were needed to begin a formal basic training — not that any of us had a problem with a lack of formality. Our group was composed completely of future bandsmen, and there was some good in that. I was surrounded by musicians and, as such, felt at home despite all the strangeness the military had to offer. After all, strangeness was, in a way, home to a musician. That said, 'musician' was a relative term. Of those of us at Lackland, I was probably the only one who had been auditioned in advance. Of the others, many would find they didn't make the grade and would be sent out into the field. While we all played to some extent, at Lackland we never discussed it. That was partly owing to having enough in front of us we had to deal with, but we also had to protect our positions, and knew better than to play our aces this early in the game.

For my part, I was positive of my future position but avoided mention of it to avoid jealousy. The rest of the flight (Air Force terminology for our group) had not yet auditioned, and so were not assured of theirs. Not wanting to rock the boat, I not only skirted around mention of my audition, but didn't mention my selection for the Air Force Band. At least, this knowledge of the musical connection explained the billet — the guitar and flute I heard that first evening. We were different, special — not to be grouped with the rest — and there was comfort in that. Despite the betrayal over the length of my term, at least that I was a bandsman was secure.

Each day, a few new members would straggle in. That they were assigned to our billet made them suspect as musicians of one sort or another. Some, like our cigar-smoking Captain Marvel fan, were straight out of high school while others, like myself, had completed some college, though we hadn't graduated — anyone who had would have been placed in Officer's Candidate School. Only a few of us even had our instruments. I practiced for ten or fifteen minutes each evening, but those who played brass had no such option and those who played larger instruments didn't even have the option of bringing them to the base. Still, I kept to myself about my music, as you never knew which of the new guys were trustworthy. My clarinet was kept locked in my footlocker and, like many others, I slept with one eye open.

It took three weeks to build up a full contingent. Each of us hailed from a different part of the United States but, once we got to know each other, we began to get along beautifully. About a quarter of the group were Texans who initially acted cool and detached to us Yankees, but it didn't take long for that barrier to be breached once it was established that we were all on the same side — we were not only all Americans, but we were all musicians, or all *supposed* to be. Some may have simply played the cymbals in their high school band, others may have just lied trying to get the three-year enlistment rather than the regular four. Auditions would determine who would be assigned to bands around the world and who would end up as cannon fodder in Korea. Still, we built camaraderie around the idea that we all played. Myself and a few of the other Northerners even made the switch from speaking fast, slowing our tempo considerably, some of us even adding a Texas twang and some 'y'alls' to our speech.

Basic training was a study in the geography and the psychography of the nation. I got to sample the wit and humor of boys from not only Texas, but Oklahoma, Alabama, Mississippi, Florida, New York, New Jersey, Ohio, Michigan, Illinois, etc. I learned dirty stories from across the nation, and how filthy language varied from place to place. More seriously, I learned what teamwork could do, as well as brotherhood. All the differences aside, we were citizens of the same great nation, and the size and scope of that nation became clearer as we all met boys from every corner of it. Our group clicked, working together easily and happily — only one or two 'washed out', the rest of us were no slackers, no quitters. It wasn't the military making men of us — we were doing it ourselves by standing firm, staying strong, and not allowing our innate manhood to be stripped away.

There were two other things we all shared. We were all always constipated, and we all rarely got erections. The first was put down to a lack of bathroom privacy — toilets sat side-by-side with no dividers in-between. Men can usually urinate and shower alongside each other, but it takes some advanced social retraining to empty your bowels in your buddies' presence. The second was blamed on the cook. Rumor had it that saltpeter was being cooked into our meals, though we never found out for sure. Still, ninety young men rarely getting erections was more than suspect. Even so, with no privacy and no women around it made little difference.

Sunday afternoons, we were told, was a time to sit down and write letters. This is something that normally would be left to the recruits to do on their own, but Lackland was eager to get out word to our parents. We had no T.V.s, radios, or newspapers, so we were unaware that the base, built to house up to 30,000 men, was rumored to contain around 200,000. News was trickling out that conditions were close to, if not already, unbearable, and even a few deaths were reported. We were, unknowingly, being told to provide some good PR. Maybe our group was treated softer than most, being musicians — I can't say for sure — but most of the letters were upbeat. I know, because most of the guys would ask for help with spelling or writing.

The major gripe we had — that we wrote about; no one was telling their parents about the saltpeter or constipation — was the Texas winter. It was warm enough during the day to go around bare-chested, but a freezing 32°F at night. Then there was the dust. It was omnipresent. Once a week I would report for sick call, standing in line with loads of other coughing young men to be given relief in the form of A.P.C. tablets (Aspirin, Phenacetin, and Caffeine — the military's all-purpose feel-good cure) and up to a pint of codeine cough syrup (which we'd nicknamed 'G.I. gin'). I always had my meds with me during daily marching. Even the Texans would show up for sick call. They had little problem with the dust, but one or two A.P.C.s washed down with a generous swig of codeine was usually an unforgettable high.

Clothing was another issue. Weeks had passed and we still hadn't been issued any. My mother had decided to pack minimal, yet I was still ahead of many of the others. The Air Force had over-recruited and their cupboards were bare. Not only were we short our fatigues, but we had no shoes, socks, underwear, rain gear, hats, belts, or dress uniforms. I had luckily brought along a sturdy pair of Florsheims, and marched in those daily until they were worn to a nub. Those recruits with less sturdy shoes sometimes found themselves marching practically barefoot out of necessity. We Northerners had the winter jackets we had left in to protect us from the rain and cold, but the Southerners were out of luck. With the pace of Basic, what little clothing we had was falling apart by our fourth week when all of our Air Force clothing was finally issued.

Ken Zmuda, who would become my friend, joined our flight from Miami, Florida. Like the rest of us, he'd been told to dress light and take only the clothes necessary for a two-day trip, as he would be issued clothing on arrival. Everyone laughed when Ken wandered into the barracks dressed for a Miami cookout in a short-sleeved print shirt, light trousers, loose-fitting loafers, and sunglasses. Ken soon got the joke. He was forced to march for weeks in those dumb loafers. Luckily a few extra shirts andtrousers were around — Ken got to borrow those, and use them until they were nothing but rags.

Mail call happened each afternoon. Corporal Wiggans would stand himself atop one of our footlockers and gather the entire flight, who would circle around him like adoring fans. He would shout out a name, and once we answered, the letter would come flying in our direction. Names would be more about the pronunciation that was convenient to Wiggans at the time. Ken Zmuda, for instance, became Zaw-ma or Suh-mud-duh. Wiggans was from Ohio, where countless Polish people live, and surely he had encountered tongue-twisting Slavic names before. This was basic training, though, and the rookies needed to be roughed up. Like Rodney Dangerfield, we got no respect. I was often Bow-check and occasionally Bow-teak.

One afternoon Wiggans noticed one last piece of mail — a large cardboard box. Everything else had been flung wildly into the crowd. He picked it up, almost dropping it as he read the name.

"Bow-teek!" he yelled.

Without waiting for a reply, Wiggans sent the parcel flying in my direction. I dove for it and took the brunt of its weight, with only a corner creasing the floor. It must have weighed twenty pounds! This was the first parcel anyone had received, and I started wondering why. Were parcels against the rules generally? Were they subject to inspection? It was against regulations to sit on our beds or footlockers before 7 p.m., so I stashed the parcel beneath my bed. 7 to 8 p.m. was the 'free hour', jokingly referred to as Show Time. We could do our own thing. Trumpet players were able to practice; Dear John letters were read aloud and dissected; Long John Silver could display his wares; Caldwell could lie nude in bed with a Havana cigar and his latest *Captain Marvel;* and I could finally open my package.

There were born comedians in our group, like Herky Skiles from California. Rumor had it that his parents were professional vaudevillians. Herky knew more jokes and funny stories than the Pope knew prayers. If our flight felt down due to some unfair gung-ho military bullshit (Caldwell's favorite phrase), Skiles could always resurrect spirits with a side-splitting story. Some of these were ridiculously stupid, and then other master joke-tellers like Ken Zmuda would chime in with their own in response. Caldwell would announce it as a contest between states — "Florida vs. California" — and it would become a fight-to-the-finish joke fest, a matter of honor.

Now feeling the full impact of military indoctrination, the flight began exhibiting passive-aggressive behavior. Close quarters and strict regulations were beginning to take their toll. The wide temperature span was hard for the most of us to adapt to, let alone the dust and wind. Illnesses abounded — in fact became commonplace: pinkeye, acute conjunctivitis, ocular foreign bodies and hemorrhages, nosebleeds, impacted ear canals, otitis media, acute bronchitis, sinus infections, allergic reactions, chronic laryngitis, acute gastritis, intestinal cramps, diarrhea, Charley horses, tinea or jock itch, athlete's foot. It seemed that it wouldn't take much to push the group over the edge.

One such near-crisis occurred when a large number of our flight showed the signs of food poisoning. The rumor came to us that some angry recruit assigned to K.P. duty had thrown a bar of yellow soap into the large vat of mashed potatoes. Company morale dropped to an all-time low. Wiggans was good about allowing us to sign out to go to sick call (in ten weeks, I had to go at least ten times). The morning following the tainted-potato scandal, about twelve of our group headed for the hospital, but no one could enter. Gathered outside on the road, in long serpentine lines, were hundreds of sick young men. Not one stood at attention, instead they were bobbing and weaving, with some vomiting, others bent over in pain, and some just passed out on the ground.

I'll never forget the frightened look on the young doctor's face as he and his aide darted in and out of each row, ignoring those that seemed the least sick and searching for those ones ready to keel over. Luckily, none of my friends needed hospitalization. We were given Donnatal liquid, compazine suppositories (known to us recruits as 'ass plugs'; most men refused to insert them), antacid tablets, and, as always, A.P.C.s. Later that day a new rumor circulated: a few deaths had been reported — some from food contamination, others due to complications from pneumonia and tuberculosis.

It was in the days after the potato incident that my mother's parcel arrived. Everyone, myself included, needed some good news. When free hour arrived, I quietly sat on my bed unwrapping the heavy brown paper and cutting through thick grocery-store twine. There were newspapers, family photos, letters from friends — all more than welcome and longed-for. Less welcome were the dried prunes and apricots, considering the events of that week. More welcome was a large bottle of Milk of Magnesia and some of Mother's trademark poppy-seed-and-nut rolls. Of course there were fresh underwear and handkerchiefs — but there was a surprise when I started to pull them out of the box. Lovingly concealed inside them was a large bottle of my favorite French wine.

"*Ooh la la*," came a whisper from behind me. Frank Britt had been watching. "*Merci beaucoup* to your Mama!" he exclaimed.

Frank and I had grown quite close. He had unexpectedly lost his father a few years earlier and had to, in his words, "grow up fast." A native of Birmingham, Alabama, Frank had the gracious Southern hospitality that came with that upbringing, as well as a personal charm whose radiance few could resist.

"Liquor is illegal," I whispered back. "How in the hell will we even get rid of the fucking bottle?"

"You damn Yankees," he drawled. "Why, back in Birmingham, we never sweat the small stuff. Just hide the little bastard until lights out. Once that asshole Wiggans goes to his private room, you bring it out and the party will begin."

9 p.m. came quickly. I jumped up top to where I had hidden the bottle and Frank, knowing what was to come, slowly and quietly eased himself into the lower bunk. The night guard began his four-hour shift by turning out the lights and spitting out, "Sleep tight, you worthless little mothers."

He retreated into the latrine. Corporal Wiggans had long since gone upstairs and closed his door. Frank waited a few minutes until he was sure the coast was clear, then made his announcement.

"Listen up, y'all! Botek has something special that came in that big box. Booze! Fancy French wine! He'll drink first, then me, and I'll pass it around. Just remember — everyone who drinks will come down on anyone who snitches!"

I popped the cork, took a deep swig, then handed it to Frank. He did the same and passed it down the line. Everyone was excited but no one talked in more than the occasional low whisper. The bottle moved fast. A few giggles, a whispered joke or two, a number of resounding burps, and it was empty. Frank ordered its return.

"Steve," he whispered, "tonight, you'll sleep with that sweet French thing. Then tomorrow when we march off to breakfast, we'll figure out how to get rid of her."

Luckily there was no inspection that night. There had been one a few nights earlier. The overhead lights had come on around 2 a.m. and everyone ordered out of their bunks. A captain I recognized from my hospital visits had ordered us to form two rows, strip, and stand at ease. Remaining at ease while bare-assed naked and an unknown hand inspects your privates must have been meant as a joke. No one told us what they were searching for: venereal disease, crab lice, hernias. Twenty minutes later, they had left empty-handed, apparently having found nothing.

At 5:30 the morning after we drank the wine, we lined up in front of the barracks for our morning march to the mess hall. Forming rows of six abreast, we would be marched double-time and chanting would begin, with every member singing at the top of our lungs the responses to the calls of our leader. The back-and-forth always reminded me of Catholic mass. However, when we were asked to invent a verse, we would always come up with something raunchy.

It was still dark and visibility was low. We sang and moved in perfect unison. I was in the middle, trying to hide the fact that I had a wine bottle hidden under my clothes. I was starting to worry about getting rid of it, as taking it into the mess hall would leave me open to discovery. Then I became aware of someone switching places with the man running beside me, doing so in flawless cadence. The new man sang out, "Where is the bottle? Give me the bottle! Where is the bottle?" perfectly in time with the song of the others. Here was a benefit I'm sure he never expected from his musical training.

It was Ken Zmuda. He never even turned his head, simply extended his left arm in my direction. I handed the bottle over, in perfect time, wondering what Ken would do with it. Without losing step and with his head held high and eyes focused straight ahead, this former little-league southpaw somehow got the speed in his arm to pitch the bottle high and far into the Texas night. The crash of the bottle smashing into a thousand pieces resounded through the morning air.

"What's that? What's that?" shouted Wiggans.

But ninety airmen continued to march. Ninety airmen continued to sing. And ninety wonderful guys proved that collective secrecy is the truest sign of real brotherhood.

* * *

My mother knew me well. Her gift box had included a few much-welcomed magazines: *Down Beat*, *Metronome*, and the musician's union monthly, *International Musician*. DeFranco's name was mentioned in a few places and I wondered what advice he might have for my present situation.

The afternoon mail brought an answer, if not the one I wanted. I had asked that question of Charlie Tucker, and his response was prompt.

Dear Steve,

Don't tell me Basic is getting unbearable! Why, if Buddy was there, he'd breeze through it like it was one of his ten-minute solos!

Yeah, I know you have to 'sir' all your superiors and sure, they call you names: babies, little girls, queers, assholes, and worse. But it's a show kind of existence. It might be surreal for ten or twelve weeks but it's necessary, and it's easy to figure out.

It's all written down on paper in those chain of command books. Why the absolute obedience? It has to do with war — jumping over a cliff if you're ordered to, dying for the cause, and all that kind of stuff.

The military doesn't hide anything. Everything is black and white. Their motives are so simple and straightforward that even a child could figure them out.

Take Buddy's first professional boss — Tommy Dorsey. What a fucking enigma that man was. Remember? He always called Buddy 'shithead', at least for that first year or so: "Hey shithead, come here", "Hey shithead, do this", etc. Buddy was nineteen and still had a phobia about microphones. Dorsey just made things worse by mocking Buddy's bebop and solos and forcing him to do chorus after chorus.

So much for 'The Sentimental Gentleman'!

You know this stuff! He used to drive Buddy into exhaustion. Despite ol' T.D.'s public image, he was an ill-tempered, foul-mouthed perfectionist. Sure he was sadistic at times, but he could also be benevolent. He ran hot and cold, just like his father — I saw the way his dad was when he gave me my first drum lesson back in first grade.

Tommy's meanness lacked any rhyme or reason. The military makes complete sense in comparison. You know that, right or wrong, everything they do is geared towards winning a war.

What you have to put up with is child's play compared to what DeFranco had to deal with when he began his first job. So stop your fucking bellyaching before I sic Tommy Dorsey on you.

Stay cool. Work hard. And stop bitching.

Your Friend,

Charles.

I was incensed! Where did Tucker get off, preaching to me that way? Still, it didn't take me long to cool off and realize he was probably right. Buddy put up with things much worse than I'll ever have to experience. I settled into that knowledge, knowing that things could be worse, and it helped some. The instant I did, though, things got worse. Lackland was already bursting at the seams accommodating more than six times the enlistees it was designed to. Wiggans came up with a solution.

He decided that he should take on the weight of the problem. Which in reality meant that *we* should. We were ordered out of our cozy, steam-heated wooden barracks and assigned to live in six-man unheated canvas tents. The tents had previously been stored with some chemicals, producing a distinctive and pungent odor I remember to this day.

I should have figured this was coming ten days earlier when a few of us were 'hand-picked' (meaning no one was dumb enough to volunteer) to erect tents. We worked like dogs that afternoon. The temperature reached 70°F and, without Wiggans around, the group of us stripped out of uniform. I earned the nickname 'Sledge' that day, owing to my impressive work with the sledgehammer. More importantly, the Texan youths assigned to the detail stopped being standoffish and warmed up considerably to the Yankee in their midst once I proved my work ethic. One short young fellow from Waco broke the ice and gave me my nickname by pointing me out to the others.

"Look at that 'Sledge' go! He sure is quick with that hammer. Almost as fast as he used to talk when he arrived! Now, after a few weeks around y'all, his mouth has finally slowed down, but he's still got that speed in his arms. All he needs now is a bit more of a Texas twang and maybe some Texas poontang then y'all could adopt him as your country cousin."

I had never lived in a tent before. Even the Boy Scout camp I attended in my teen years had had cabins. Before adolescence, many a winter evening was spent 'living' in a hand-built backyard igloo — mostly to escape my parents. As to tents, I had no idea what to expect.

"Maybe living in a tent will be fun," I offered.

"Are you kidding?" Zmuda shot back. "These fucking tents have no wooden floor, and we'll be sleeping on those flimsy canvas fold-up cots with the thin straw mattress. We'll be less than a foot above the cold winter ground with no heat except a small coal-burning pot-bellied stove! We had those in the Guard — they usually won't stay lit at night.

"No latrine, of course. We'll have to run to a barracks, identify ourselves, sign in, then piss or shit, sign *out* again, and identify ourselves to the tent sentry before returning. Oh, *right!* We'll probably all get four-hour shifts on sentry duty freezing our asses off outside *before* getting the chance to freeze our asses off *inside* the tents!"

Ken sounded bitter, but everything he predicted was dead-on. It was good to have him in my tent at bedtime, though. He knew how to handle the stove, which we constantly struggled with to keep lit. On our first night in the tent, Wiggans popped his head in through the flap, throwing two extra khaki-colored blankets at each of us.

"That fucker!" Ken muttered after he left. "Four blankets each because he knows it's going down to freezing tonight!"

Ken showed me how the National Guard did it. We each rolled our blankets together like you would roll up a rug, leaving a space just large enough to slip into. Instead of taking off clothes, we added all we could: two pairs of underwear, socks, and trousers, both shirts, a cap, and whatever else might be on hand. I followed his instructions to the letter, then extinguished the lantern, and slowly wormed my way into the cocoon of blankets.

Ken yelled from the other end of the tent, "How is it, Sledge?"

"Tight," I yelled back. "And for some reason — still cold!"

I had dysentery at this point and that meant a few times a night I would be worming my way out of the blankets, running to the barracks, and following the sign-in and -out procedure, just as Ken had described. And each time, I would return to find the blankets cold again. Never before or again in my life did I feel as cold as those tent weeks in *Texas*, of all places. Even Rochester felt tropical in comparison.

Reuben Heller confessed to a group of us at lunch, many years later, how he and his tent partner handled the same situation when they were stationed at Lackland.

"We did the same as you guys did," he recounted. "Still, neither of us could get warm. I think my teeth were chattering. Then, one of us got the crazy idea to share just one bed, so we huddled together body-to-body, fully clothed. It was just beginning to get nice and warm when the tent guard — one of us Basics — stuck his head through the flap, shined his flashlight on us, and screamed out 'Oh my God! Two men in a bed! Two men in a bed!'

"We had a lot of explaining to do. We almost got thrown out. I think the only reason we weren't is that the officials knew *they* were to blame, not us. They knew how ridiculous and intolerable the sleeping conditions were, but they just turned their backs and left it up to us to find a solution. They couldn't make any noise about it without having to admit their own failure.

"Hey, Steve, didn't you tell me about your recruiting sergeant in Lehighton? The thirty-one men, but only thirty beds?"

"Yep," I grinned.

"Too bad he wasn't there on those below-freezing Texas nights. He probably would have *ordered* us all to buddy up by twos!"

The closest thing to consolation we had was that we finally got our fatigues. Only a one-piece khaki-colored outfit and a soft cap, but it was at least a sign that we actually were in the military and this wasn't some elaborate hoax. However, there weren't enough to wear day in, day out, on work detail, and for inspection, so as official policy we alternated between our fatigues and civilian clothes. A number of us had our clothes nearly reduced to rags by this point, and the fatigues were also quickly getting worn down. Between the clothing situation and living in tents, at no point did we look like a cohesive group of soldiers *or* civilians.

One evening we were all told to dress, leave our tents, and march to the movie theater. Some of us joked that the only reason we got to see the movie, the only one in two weeks, was that the officials were afraid we would freeze to death otherwise. The theater was small and filled to capacity. Worst of all, it was completely inundated with that Texas dust. The film was one of Bill Mauldin's classic satires about Army life. His two signature characters Willie and Joe had us all in stitches, but no sooner would we start laughing than some of the laughter would turn into coughs. Even between the jokes, there was a constant soundtrack of coughs, sometimes making it impossible to make out the dialogue. Between the dust and the illnesses brought on by the cold, the coughing was non-stop. This *despite* most of us having brought our G.I. gin — the military-issue codeine cough syrup. G.I. gin came in vest-pocket-size ten-ounce bottles which were freely circulated among us. Air Force physicians were frustrated by the number of sick recruits and the 'gin' was prescribed to near everyone. I often wonder how many of those enlistees became full-fledged G.I. gin junkies.

At the time, though, not one of us cared a whit about the future. Whatever the downside of the codeine high, it seemed better than fully experiencing the sick and surreal existence the military was handing us. Help was on its way, though. Recruits had families and concerned mothers had Congressmen. Pressure was brought to bear on the military for its mistreatment of enlistees. Whether that was the deciding factor or not, we can never be sure, but certainly no Congressman was going to sit still while hordes of angry mothers threatened to organize their own solutions, with or without them. Changes came quickly and we all packed up our tents and moved indoors.

Ken and I worked together assembling two-decker metal cots in our new billet. The experience was a joy — not only did it mean that the days in the tents were over, but Ken was always good for a laugh, especially when camp conditions were at their lowest. An entire school of comedy revolved around *Eine Farte*. Some fellow jokester had mailed Ken a copy of this German magazine. No one could read it as it was written entirely in German, but even beyond the title, there were articles on Germany's World War II concentration camps and Russian gulags, and Ken made many a sardonic comment about the supposed similarities to Lackland. Pointing to the pictures, Ken noted, "Lackland, in part, utilizes some of these 'camp' techniques. No, not the truly tragic Holocaust parts or the work-to-your-death business. Nah! None of that heavy-duty physical torture shit. Our Air Force is too smart for that approach. Here, instead, they go after us psychologically. They fuck with our minds and keep us on our toes with twenty-four hour unpredictability and irrationality. Push us to our limits. Brinksmanship, it's called. Get us collectively to surrender, subjugate ourselves, and above all: never disobey!"

Gallows humor, perhaps, but it was all we had.

When our tent living ended, Wiggans, closet egalitarian that he was, announced that we could choose our own bunkmates and set up anywhere throughout the new, heated, open-bay barracks. I chose Frank Britt — a tall, laid-back Alabamian — whose only fault was sleepwalking. Spotting the long (and hot!) steam pipes sitting not far above the upper cot, I quickly claimed it as my own. Frank, never less than generous, wanted me to have it anyway.

"It's bad enough I roam the ground floor at night. Put me up high and I'm liable to break my neck!"

We were no sooner established in our new home when we were marched off to the quartermaster. Zmuda, jogging alongside me, joked, "Here we are, half-finished with Basic, and only now am I getting my full uniform allowance. Making me march in civilian loafers — should I sue the bastards?"

I laughed, but was smiling for another reason when we returned. Another pair of fatigues, new underwear and socks, a field jacket, work and dress shoes. As well, we each got a complete class-A uniform including a hat (and it fit!), plus our brass insignias, even a stylish dark blue raincoat. It was like a second Christmas in February. It took only a few hours to transform this ragtag bunch of street-clothes soldiers into a slick and sharply dressed marching machine. Morale soared with the new clothes.

It helped even more that we were all excused from duties for the following afternoon. Instead, we were off to some distant assembly hall to be lectured on G.I. insurance, death benefits, veteran claims, and other military services. Boring to be sure, but better than the alternative. The ninety of us were herded into a small room and told to sit on the floor. We were urged to smoke if we so desired. For the next two hours, we were indoors and relieved of work, a seeming paradise. A pleasant enough master sergeant gave the lecture. His warm demeanor got me to drop my guard. He was without doubt an old-timer striving to be fair and benevolent. Ending his presentation, he offered, "If any of you have any complaints, gripes, or bitches about me, Lackland, the Air Force, *whatever* — you don't have to voice them or identify yourself. Just write them down on those pieces of paper scattered around the room. Don't sign them and pass them forward."

Most of the group didn't budge but a few of us, safe behind anonymity, scribbled down a few words and passed our papers ahead. I left, thinking what a fine gentleman the master sergeant was. Were this civilian life, I'd go up to shake his hand and chat some.

The next day was a Sunday, the day we could legally meander off to church and connect with the non-military world before returning to a regular schedule. Monday, however, was a different story. Wiggans did not dismiss us following our return from breakfast. Rather, he told us to stand at attention and listen to a very important message. He was moving slowly as he picked up his mini-platform, moved it in front of us, and leisurely climbed on top to address us. He adjusted his helmet and purposefully avoided our stares. Something was up. No one dared move; we were all frozen in our tracks. Was this news about the war? Someone dead at home? Some new tragedy? Finally, Wiggans lifted his head and glared at us. His face was red with rage, his eyes bulging from their sockets.

"Men," he seethed, "there is one among you who isn't a man. One of you too cowardly to address a person face-to-face. That person knows who he is. And I'd like that person to step forward."

No one moved. No one spoke. No one stepped forward. We all just stared straight ahead. Wiggans simply waited as sixty silent seconds went by. His anger seemed to be building. Finally, seeing that no one was going to step forward, he sneered, "Okay then, boys. I'll try again tomorrow. Fall out!"

Ken pulled me aside and whispered, "What the hell is going on?"

Frank leaned in. "Wiggans has a bug up his ass, and he's not going to give up until he finds whoever he's after."

Not much more was said. There was no point. No one seemed to know any details. Life went on as usual until breakfast ended the next morning. Again, Wiggans didn't dismiss us, ordering us to stand at attention again. He repeated the same thing. As before, no one moved, spoke, or stepped forward. The same again on day three, and again on day four, with Wiggans increasingly unable to control himself anymore. He began to scream and dance about on his little soapbox.

"If this individual doesn't present himself — coward that he is — the entire flight will be punished!"

Silence. As usual, no one stepped forward. I wondered if any of us really knew what he was talking about and who was involved.

"You college men," he barked. "You might think you are . . ."

I stopped listening at that point, suddenly realizing who he was looking for. I repeated to myself those words I had scrawled on the paper the previous Saturday — the ones supposed to be kept secret, the ones the benevolent old master sergeant said we could submit without signing: "Too many assholes teaching intelligent college men!" *God!* Wiggans wanted *me*, but didn't know it. I asked myself why I should turn myself in. Didn't the sergeant say we could speak our minds? Sure, the word 'asshole' might be strong language in most places, but *here*, among frustrated men, this kind of 'barracks talk' was everyday language. Another phrase came to mind: *Never trust the military!* Still, I decided to just let Wiggans stew.

Day five arrived and it was the same again. I stood directly in Wiggans' eyeline, no more than six feet away as he raved about intelligent college men, teaching, and cowardice. *A lot of hot air*, I thought.

Then he twisted the knife.

"This is your final chance. Come forward, or tomorrow *everyone* gets K.P. duty. Then, the following day, *everyone* will be punished with . . ."

Again I stopped listening. I knew what I had to do. And while it wasn't fair, I would never be in this position if I hadn't trusted the military, even for that brief moment. I stepped forward, taking four paces until I was looking directly into his eyes.

"Corporal Wiggans, sir, I'm the man you're looking for."

His mouth dropped and his face reddened. His lower lip quivered. He leaned forward to within two inches of my face and in a startled voice said, "Botek!" Apparently, this was what it took for him to get my name right. He looked up and yelled, "Group dismissed!"

The men were relieved that this business was done, and any curiosity they had was outweighed by the urge to get the hell away. They quickly broke ranks and disappeared into the barracks. Only when the last man had left did Wiggans turn to me.

"Botek," he said, with a trace of sorrow in his voice. "How could you?"

At this point I didn't know if he was going to grab me by the neck or start crying. In a moment, his eyes relaxed and that enraged man was gone. I looked closely at him. There was sorrow, triumph, and anger all wrapped together in his face. Then an almost-pleading, disappointed, and bewildered voice let out, "But Botek . . . Why *you*? I like you!"

It was then that I knew I might have a chance. Quickly and as soothingly as possible, I explained that I didn't mean him personally. He was a fine teacher, and I was a fool for being so careless with my words. I apologized profusely, explaining that I hadn't even thought he could have meant me until that day. He stepped back, straightened his hat, and blew his nose into a neatly-pressed handkerchief before raising his head high.

"Botek, report immediately to K.P. — mess hall number three. Tell the cook in charge I said to keep you for three days. You're dismissed."

"Yes, sir," I said. "Again . . . I'm sorry. Sir. And thank you, sir!"

I had escaped with a much lighter sentence than I might have gotten otherwise. Not to mention an education. Wiggans *liked* me? I never would have guessed.

The cook in charge happened to be another one of those older master sergeants — an easygoing guy who, on first impression, might seem benevolent, friendly, and fair, but I resolved not to be fooled again. I stood at attention, saluted, and proclaimed, "Sir, I've been assigned here to do whatever work you wish."

He led me to a small pantry overflowing with potatoes to be peeled. As I peeled away, I whispered to myself over and over: *Never trust the military.*

For three long days I peeled potatoes, sliced vegetables, and cracked countless eggs. Through it all, I reflected on Wiggans. So he likes me? What do you know? I shouldn't have hurt his feelings — it confused him and got him as mad as a hatter. If I hadn't, though, I never would have seen that human side of him. And now that I had stepped forward and explained myself, I think he still liked me and moreover, respected me. If not, the punishment could have been a lot worse. After all, I was on K.P. duty for fewer days than he spent yelling about the note.

Charlie's letter came back to me. I knew now he had been right. I'd heard Buddy's stories about dealing with Tommy Dorsey.

Charlie had hit the nail on the head. Both Wiggans and Dorsey were tough as nails on the one hand, but other times, they would be openly wearing their hearts on their sleeves.

* * *

There I was, knee-deep in potatoes, peeling away like a madman, and the chef walked in. He gave me a quick once-over, seemed pleased, and turned to leave, saying, "Best keep that handkerchief in your pocket, airman."

"Yes, sergeant," I replied, not knowing whether to 'sir' him or not. "I have a stubborn bit of that respiratory thing floating around the base. Do you think I could please have some orange juice?"

I knew there was a shelf stacked with large cans of fruit juice, and hoped I wasn't pushing my luck. Without a word, he turned and grabbed a tall can with one hand and a meat cleaver with the other. With skill and a bit of showmanship, he neatly cut two holes into the top of the can.

"Here, son. Forty-six ounces. It'll help you fight this fucking Texas weather. Whatever you can't finish, dump down the commode.

"Oh," he added as an afterthought, "and you won't find any bars of soap in the latrine. They're all under lock and key. You have to request, sign out, and return each bar — especially that strong yellow Fels Naptha shit."

So, the rumor had been true. And thanks to the prankster, not only had we been sick beyond belief, but now we had to sign out soap! And I was automatically suspect, being a disgruntled recruit on K.P. — after all, who *isn't* disgruntled on K.P.?

Later that morning I had a second visitor. A young black Pfc (Private first class) had wandered in, searching for something. He took a look at me and immediately grinned at the sight of me surrounded by potato peelings.

"Shit, man," he laughed. "You must've really fucked up!"

He had forgotten to close the door behind him, luckily for me. Reaching through the doorway were the strains of Lester Young's "Lester Leaps In".

"Someone here likes jazz," I grinned back at him.

"It's me," he nodded. "I picked up this powerful short-wave radio from the P.X. (Post Exchange — the military's all-purpose department store) at Randolph Field. It's a Canadian station. They play lots of jazz. Can't stand this Southern hillbilly crap. Do you dig jazz?"

I thought he'd never ask.

We talked at length, the door open so I could listen. There was Basie next, then Goodman. Finally he had to go, and I knew that we both could get in trouble if he was 'disturbing' me during my punishment.

"Hey," he said as he left. "We eat at 4:30, before the troops arrive. Tonight we're having steaks. I'll fix you a couple. How'd you like 'em done?"

I'd heard of turning lemons into lemonade, but never potatoes into steaks.

* * *

I returned home dog-tired after my three days on K.P., but I'd made new friends, and was well-fed and healthy. Wiggans greeted me at the door, looking calm, relaxed, and content. Nothing more was mentioned about the note and I thought that was fine — we *both* wanted to bury the matter forever.

"Botek," he pulled me aside, "I need someone with your qualifications to memorize this long list of Air Force rules and regulations. Next week we'll spruce up the entire barracks, the men will have a full G.I. party, and dress in our class-A uniforms to welcome a group of our squadron's inspecting officers. Before they inspect, you will meet them here at the door, salute them, and from memory, recite this list of rules and regulations. You *are* volunteering for this job, aren't you?"

At first it seemed like he was meting out additional punishment, but then it occurred to me that this might be the price of respect in the military. He may have just been testing me to see if I'd learned my lesson. Whichever the case, I wasn't about to refuse.

"Of course, Corporal Wiggans, sir," I promised. "It sounds important. And challenging. I'll do my very best, sir!"

Frank Britt was happy to see me. He jokingly said he missed me the last night when he'd been sleepwalking and awoke staring into my empty bed.

"Only three more weeks 'til graduation," he noted. "The Sunday before that, we all get our first twelve-hour pass to visit San Antonio. I'll treat you to your first two beers. Hey, you think any of those Texas ladies-of-the-night have reduced matinée prices?"

We laughed and joked about what there was to experience in the city. Frank handed me a cigarette, not his usual brand, and I asked where they came from.

"The Kools? I got them from Burton. You know, that small kid that's never in step and always complains? He told me he's been wetting the bed and can't sleep at night. Check it out — if you ever wake up around 3 a.m., he'll probably be sitting on the edge of his bed crying. He's told the officials, but they just ignore him."

Frank took a slow drag on his Kool and looked around to make sure no one was listening. He continued in hushed tones: "You know what? I think he's going to run away, go A.W.O.L. That's the only thing that'll get those bastards to pay attention. And that's why he's giving away all his things."

Frank was right. Burton did run away and none of us ever saw him again or were told what happened to him. The rumor was that he killed himself. I have to admit that it struck me as strange that someone running away would give away his *cigarettes*, but I never bothered to give it a second thought. Still, rumor didn't equate to fact — it was just all we had. Without newspapers or radio, most of us relied on the grapevine for news. We even ran tests of the 'system', making up rumors to see how much they had changed by the time they got back to us. Considering that, we realized that maybe others were doing the same and tried our best to be discerning.

Burton wasn't the only news item Frank had to relate. There was a blond, blue-eyed kid from Wisconsin who had joined our flight in the middle weeks — rumor had it that he had flunked out of flight school. He was handsome and quiet, neither of which worked in his favor. Rumor also had it that he was going to be thrown out of Lackland. Before that could happen, a captain had slipped into his tent while he was sleeping, then slipped his hand into the kid's underwear. The kid rebuffed the officer's advances and reported him to headquarters. The captain claimed the opposite had happened and headquarters was siding with the captain and about to give the kid a dishonorable discharge when the tent guard chimed in, swearing he saw the captain sneaking into the tent. He had peeped into the tent and saw enough to corroborate the kid's story.

Headquarters told the kid that the captain was the one who should receive a dishonorable discharge. Part of the disarray at Lackland had us recruits yet to be told a set of military rules that we were to swear to uphold — the very ones that Wiggans had recruited me to memorize and read at the inspection. I can't remember the name of these rules, but they effectively set forward the contract between the military and new recruits. Without that, we were safe from the extremes of military discipline. After they had been read, superior officers pretty much would run every aspect of our lives, but before that, they could do nothing. More than that, without having heard those rules, the kid's rights were primary — those of a civilian. That lapse may have saved the kid's career and ended the captain's. Frank remarked he was glad he wasn't that handsome so he didn't have to worry about being caught in a similar situation.

The Tuesday after Burton ran away we ate breakfast as usual, but then we were all marched over to our headquarters testing division to be given aptitude, psychological, and other investigative tests. This was standard procedure and had nothing to do with Burton, but I found myself wondering if things would have worked out better had they bothered to test him in the first place.

Zmuda had warned me about this department. Supposedly they could assign musicians to careers in the motor pool or a Colorado ski bum to work as a winter-weather specialist assigned to duty in Greenland or Iceland. I didn't need any career guidance and brought my Bolling Air Force Base official letter along to prove it, ready to flash it in the face of anyone there who thought of labeling me anything other than a bandsman.

We sat for five hours, paper and pencil in hand, drawing figures, answering hundreds of multiple-choice questions and plodding our way through various geometric figures, mathematical problems, and assorted visual puzzles. Everything we did was immediately collected and evaluated. When all the testing was done, we were given a short break, after which we were to be assigned to individual counselors. Over cigarettes, we used the break to draw a psychological profile of the testers.

"So what do you think they're trying to do with this?"

"Ah, they want to guess our skills. It's all stuff for the files they keep on us."

"No," I exhaled a puff of smoke assertively. "This is a one-day thing. They're going to decide all our future assignments *now*."

I patted the letter in my pocket as I went back. I needed to reassure myself it was still there.

The men interpreting our tests were not much older than we were, but they all had rank emblazoned on their arms, so we Basics would have nothing to say while they, by Air Force protocol, had the last word. I overheard the conversation with the Basic ahead of me.

"You can be a mechanic," the clerk told him. "You show good skill on this particular test. Or *here* — you scored very high on this one. We have a great fourteen-week tech school to train you in Mississippi."

I took the letter out and held it in my hand, ready to wield it like a weapon. I wanted no part of their career choices for me. I was quickly called forward and the young corporal — younger than I was — began his usual sales pitch. I allowed him to continue for a moment, then placed the letter in front of him.

"What's this?" he asked. "This doesn't mean anything."

He contemptuously pushed the letter aside and continued. I stopped him and said, "Corporal, I demand to speak to your superior."

I'm sure there was a gasp behind me. The corporal glanced angrily to the next counselor, as if asking who this idiot thought he was. Still, he summoned a young lieutenant. The lieutenant took a good minute or so to scan the letter, then looked up and quickly returned it to me.

"Go," he said. "Good luck."

"Thank you, sir," I answered, quickly heeling around to get the hell out of there. I could hear the corporal's teeth grinding as I left. Though I was the picture of self-confidence through all this, I was mouthing a silent prayer as I left: *Thank you, Lord, for helping me deal so well with lieutenants. I promise to improve my batting average with master sergeants and other non-commissioned personnel.*

Not even twenty-four hours had passed and again career guidance came up, if indirectly. Wiggans asked the assembled group, "Does anyone here type?" I knew better than to trust the military or volunteer, but even if I didn't, I would have smelled a rat. Three or four Basics raised their hands. They were then quickly escorted out of the barracks and given enough paperwork to type up that they were working solidly on it for weeks. The base had been backed up enough that they pulled them out of training to help catch up. They returned after that, but having missed weeks of basic training, they were then required to start Basic all over again with the next group, four weeks behind ours. Despite the hardships owing to lack of equipment and supplies, we may have had it much easier than later groups. In all our training, we did nothing more strenuous than an up-tempo march and I think I shot a gun *once*. We were like glorified Boy Scouts, most of us already used to regular marching with bands. It may have been that, as musicians, we were treated easier than most, but likely much of that was due to the disorganization of the day.

The next task was the inspection. I memorized the rules as I had learned to memorize music at the side of Sprigle — section by section in bite-sized bits, then piecing it together. Relaxed and ready, I rattled off the full list, and if I made any mistakes, no one noticed. We showed off our brand-new Air Force blues and stood poker straight as we were inspected.

Frank Britt later remarked, “Some of these kids had never looked so good. Or so clean!”

Wiggans was happy and proud of the group of us. He beamed through the inspection, graciously hosting the inspecting officers. Past a cursory glance before they arrived, he didn’t worry about a thing, trusting our flight completely to manage ourselves as proper soldiers. And though I can’t be absolutely sure, I got the impression that when he left our barracks, there was a special smile on his face for me.

Chapter 15 Don't Be That Way

1951 was a pivotal year for both DeFranco and myself. Buddy had contacted me on a few occasions after my basic training to wish me well with my new military career. I had returned the favor, hoping for the best with his new big band.

The group was a step in a new direction for Buddy. Count Basie had decided to go back to a big band of his own, and Buddy could have gone back to the alto saxophone section, but decided instead to stay on his own path. While he was forming his own big band, Duke Ellington offered Buddy a spot in his band, but he said no. In demand by both the Count and the Duke, Buddy still felt it was time for *his* dream, to head up his own band.

He settled back in New York, deciding it was the right base for his plans. His name was still up front as one of the players to watch (or keep watching, in his case), and that was despite his bending to the visions of other men as bandleaders. While he respected their goals, he felt that someone had to pursue his, and no one else was in better position to do it. He explained it in an interview with Leonard Feather in the March 9, 1951 issue of *Down Beat*:

> *Do you know what the trouble is? The band leaders are too old! Back in the days when Benny Goodman and Harry James and Gene Krupa were the great new names, they were still in their twenties. They were all young enough to have a common bond with the younger set, and they were the ones who influenced the school and college kids toward better musical ideas. But what about the kids who are nineteen or twenty today? They were four or five years old when Goodman and Basie hit. They don't remember the hysteria of those days, the wild excitement about Swing. We'd like to bring back that feeling. We'd like to . . . create the same kind of fervor that was there before. We want to give the kids something they*

> *can hang their hats on — bring young music to young people and start a modern idiom that they can grow up with, instead of trying to recreate a 1935 or 1940 product in 1951. . . .*

Buddy was twenty-seven now and, if he waited more, he'd be one of the older guys. He had to make his move while he was still young enough to be in touch with the younger kids. Sure, he would have a certain level of freedom with Basie or Ellington, but as much as he appreciated their goals, they weren't his. And his goals were centered around youth — not just the young players whose ideas and idioms did get attention from at least some of the older bandleaders, but the younger listeners. He wasn't content to be at the forefront of bebop, he wanted to move forward *wherever* the music took him.

For Buddy, it came down to people. Like his answer to his draft board psychiatrist: he couldn't shoot another man because he might well be a fellow clarinet player. Buddy's concerns might seem naïve to most. He turned his back on the aims of the modern world: money for money's sake, a fixation on fame at any cost, and a skewed sense of entitlement. Likewise, his band paid no heed to the customary concerns and, as a result, was doomed to fail.

Benny Goodman may have lacked pizzazz as a bandleader, but he shrewdly married into the music management business. Artie Shaw pushed the envelope, but he also knew how to play to the crowds — and he had a life that could be splashed across the gossip pages with his eight marriages, some to movie stars, his debonair style, and handsome looks. Charlie Barnet's playboy life was fully financed by his wealthy mother. The Dorseys were neurotically driven by poverty and a perfectionist father to do nothing but succeed. Buddy's own work was the work of a musician's musician, but it eschewed the worlds of commerce and publicity, and as such, didn't resonate with the public.

Buddy recalls:

> *"My manager Lenny Lewis really knew how to run a band.* [Lewis had previously managed Count Basie and Artie Shaw — at least until Shaw caught him cheating] . . . *Lenny convinced me that when I left Count Basie's band, he would help me organize a big band and become a big-name band leader. . . . We rehearsed in New York for about a month at Nola's Studios* [March and April, 1951]. *It looked like I was going to become the next popular clarinet player, right on the heels of Benny and Artie. He* [Lenny] *got the first record contract for me and it was a pretty good contract."*[1]

[1] Sylvie Mas and Fabrice Zammarchi, *A Life in the Golden Age of Jazz: A Biography of Buddy DeFranco* (Seattle, WA: Parkside Publications, 2002

The band visited Buddy's hometown of Philadelphia and opened the legendary art-deco Click Club on March 26th. There had been two previous 'trial' concerts in the New York area, as well as the band's first recording session. Buddy was exceptionally pleased with the recording, which featured standout arrangements of "Out of Nowhere", "Dancing on the Ceiling", "Body and Soul", and "Rumpus Room". The first big one-nighter had been scheduled for Allentown, Pennsylvania. Had I been in Lansford still, I would have been sure to go but instead had to simply send along my regrets and best wishes after the fact.

I was en route to Washington, DC. I had graduated basic training, and Corporal Wiggans had proudly presented me with a first-class train ticket from San Antonio to Washington. The irony was incredible — I'd joined the military and moved up to first class! Five of us boarded that train, the 'Texas Special', bound for bases in the north. We were all thrilled to finally be leaving Texas, which to us meant freezing-cold nights sleeping in tents, line-ups at the hospital, and deprivation of every kind.

We sat stiff as boards around the lunch table, all having been programmed by the military. We were largely afraid to speak and ridiculously deferential when we did. We were afraid to order alcohol, even though most of us were over twenty-one. When food arrived, it was like we had never before eaten in public. All our habits were now ingrained, and we acted like we were being watched at all times — and considering our posture and behavior, it wouldn't be a surprise if people *were* watching.

Even the waiters and red-caps, all black, were wary of us as we constantly addressed each of them as 'sir'. Three months earlier the train staff had been calling us 'sir', and now the tables were turned. Of course now we were in uniform, though with no stripes — the rumor was that stripes were no longer awarded on completion of basic training, owing to the brewing Korean War. The train staff finally loosened up around us when I asked about Franklin, our porter on the trip down. He was still in Texarkana, but the mere mention of his name got us star treatment for the rest of the run.

Aboard the train we were finally free of military protocols. We were able to talk at Lackland, but never really able to relax — Big Brother was always watching. Owing to that, we tended to make few friends. Before the train, I'd never really gotten the chance to talk one-on-one with Ken Holm. Ken was a bassoon player, something unusual that we didn't have in any of the other bands I had played with. I was more than curious about the instrument and, not having heard his playing, about that as well. In basic, we had had no time and no place to talk. Ken, like many others, hadn't bothered bringing his instrument because of the possibility of it being stolen.

We met on our way back to our seats and started to talk. When we got there, we found that the porter had already spread our seats out into beds. We felt like talking some more so, in a breach of protocol, we both climbed onto Ken's bunk, the lower one, and each took a corner, closing the curtain for privacy. I found out he was from Dearborn, Michigan, and that both our houses had the same number — he lived at 301 Dearborn Avenue and I lived at 301 East Bertsch Street. On through the night, we exchanged stories, breaking only when our ever-vigilant porter heard the noise and opened the curtain wide. Seeing nothing amiss, he quickly shut it.

"Shoot!" we heard him say to a fellow rail worker. "The Air Force has scared these poor kids so much, they're even afraid to sleep by themselves."

* * *

It was shortly after 6 a.m. that our train gave a final noisy sigh as it stopped deep inside Chicago's main railway station. We all had to change trains, each of us heading in a different direction and this was the end of our group. Parting was anything but sweet. Not only had we been coaxed into the habits the military wanted, but we had the expectation that the others were always just a yell away. It didn't really click until we disembarked to change trains that this was the end. Of course we promised each other we would write, but the truth — too big and scary to realize at the moment — was that at that moment, each one of us was totally on our own and, more than likely, we would never see each other again.

My train for Washington left at 9 a.m.; I was the last of the group to leave Chicago. The others had made their connections rather quickly and we said our farewells not admitting that they were goodbyes, but now I still had more than two hours to kill. I wandered into the large main waiting room, trying my best to appear inconspicuous. However, I had forgotten how to be on my own after ten weeks of basic training. As well, I wasn't used to being in uniform in a public place — considering the equipment issues, I was barely used to the idea of a uniform on the base.

It was there and then that it hit me. I was in my head, going over my appearance, being unused to looking this way in public, when I remembered the crew-cut. I'd forgotten — Colonel Howard hated them! Not only had I been warned about this by a number of people prior to my December audition, but a fellow Eastman clarinetist named Max Good who *always* had a crew-cut had auditioned shortly before I had and been rejected. Granted, it may have been for other reasons: Max was not far above average as a player and Eastman had refused to re-admit him for a second year. But what if it *was* the crew-cut? How would Howard react on seeing me with my hair cut short?

I had pleaded with the military barber, "Leave it a bit long." He had sarcastically replied, "You have three choices: short, medium short, or very, very short."

I spotted the station's barbershop. No customers yet and only one barber — a pleasant-enough looking man sitting alone and peacefully leafing through the morning paper. I went up and explained my situation sheepishly, expecting him to laugh in my face, but I had to try. He was warm, friendly, and helpful.

"Oh hell," he laughed kindly. "I had a second lieutenant during World War II even worse than your colonel in Washington. One of those ninety-day wonders. Talk about chickenshit! He was another haircut fanatic, but they fixed him, all right.

"As we were ordered to advance and attack at Dunkirk, the first bullet fired came from our rear. It struck him, but didn't kill him. It superficially grazed his scalp, from back to front, evenly parting his hair to both sides. He sure got the message. From that day on, he never — and I mean *never* — mentioned the word 'haircut' again.

"So, let's see. Your hair sticks up about two inches high. Tell you what — with the hot curling iron, I'll weave in some natural curls, just like I do for some of my local customers. You'll look a bit different, cute even, but no one will ever think you once had a crew-cut. After a couple of weeks, get it curled again. Eventually, it'll grow out and then you can comb it like you used to."

I agreed enthusiastically. Sure, I didn't want Col. Howard seeing me with the crew-cut, but I didn't like it myself in the first place.

He took a lot of time, but did one hell of a job. Maybe a good forty-five minutes, not including another twenty spent under the dryer, but he did better than I could have hoped. Luckily it was early and there were no other customers, so he could give me his undivided attention. We talked throughout, having a great time. When he was done, he handed me a large mirror and I smiled, admiring my 'new' head of hair. It wasn't how I would have chosen to look, but it was a damn sight better than a crew-cut. My mother or sisters probably would have wet themselves laughing had they seen me then, but, all things considered, I was more than happy.

I asked him his fee, and he asked only for the two-dollar charge noted on all the mirrors. I gave him a ten-dollar bill and told him to keep the change. He refused, handing me the change and telling me, "Spend it on your girlfriend. It was my pleasure."

I didn't spend the change on my girlfriend, Phoebe being too far away. Instead, I found the latest issues of *Metronome* and *Down Beat*. DeFranco was getting a lot of coverage, considering his then-new big band. I had to wonder if Charlie had been among the forty people who turned up for DeFranco's first one-nighter with the big band. Allentown was only forty miles away from Lansford. According to Buddy, it didn't go well. At the end of the night, only three or four of the crowd were left. Nothing worked for Buddy that night in Allentown.

Charlie and I had gone there in 1949 to see Gene Krupa's big band at the Central Park amusement park — Dorney Park, like Central, also hosted big bands regularly and, unlike Central, is still going today. When we went to see Krupa, his latest album, *Let Me Off Uptown,* had just been released and featured highlights of three live Hollywood shows. The band featured trumpeter Roy Eldridge, bebop soloist Frank Rosolino on trumpet, rising-young-star alto saxophonist Gene Quill, tenor saxophonist Buddy Wise, and singer Dolores Hawkins. The show lasted four hours, ending at 1 a.m., and we had stood there glued to the spot just a few feet from the stage, transfixed. It was a who's who of bebop and the improvisations were state-of-the-art.

The night had been so intense that it was only after the final selection that Charlie turned to me and whimpered, "Oh my God! We didn't talk to *any* of the musicians tonight!"

For Tucker this would be a mortal sin and he raced into action, looking to correct for this oversight. The dance was over, instruments were being put away, and all the band members seemed anxious to board their bus and move on. Still, Charlie spotted Gene Quill kneeling over his open case and swabbing out his horn.

"Gene!" Charlie jumped in for the kill. "Those solos were great!"

Quill just grunted, continuing to pack up. Charlie kept trying, and kept receiving only grunts and moans for his efforts — probably a politeness, considering what Quill was likely thinking of saying. Never one to give up, Charlie spotted a small rectangular brush neatly placed in the corner of Gene's saxophone case and asked, "What's that for?"

Quill looked up at Charlie for the first time in amazement. "What's that for?" he parroted.

With that, he picked up the brush and ran it through his hair a few times, then stood up and looked Charlie in the eye. He started to laugh.

"I'm sorry," he said. "You guys must be musicians."

From there, the shop talk was on. He had a Selmer sax, Brilhart #5 very open mouthpiece, Rico reed #4. . . . We talked for awhile, and Gene treated us like friends.

I found out some time later that no, Charlie didn't go to Allentown to see DeFranco's big band — he had joined the Navy. It would be a while before I heard from him again. Gene Quill was there, though. He was part of the band, a featured side man and soloist. My contact with Buddy at the time was sporadic, and I was finding out about his career a while after the fact, but I often wonder if he had asked Gene, would he remember the blond teenage kid who asked him what his hairbrush was for?

* * *

Upon my return to Bolling, after presenting my travel orders, I was assigned to an open-bay barracks where my 'area' — a partially-walled cubicle with no door — consisted of a small bed, a tan wall locker, one overhead 75-watt light bulb, and a medium-sized window that lacked curtains or blinds. Spartan, to be sure, but compared to some of what I experienced at Lackland, it may as well have been the Ritz.

"Welcome to Washington," one of my new neighbors greeted me. "This ain't the Hilton, but you'll soon find it cozy. That is, if you don't mind guys practicing, snoring, or playing their record players too loud."

I didn't. Snoring had become a fact of life at Lackland, and I was used to ignoring it. And hearing music more than for one hour a day would be heaven after basic.

The following morning I reported for band rehearsal. Sgt. Dietz remembered me and introduced me hurriedly to a few clarinet players before assigning me a seat next to a young man from Pittsburgh, Alex Shigo. We had met before at one of the State Band get-togethers when we were both in high school. He was about my age and height, friendly, and one hell of a good clarinet player. With the crunch for space that the draft was causing, he had taken his basic training right there on the base at Bolling. Being dedicated to music, Bolling was hardly by-the-book and, as a result, Shigo lacked the filters the rest of us had learned in *our* basic training.

Howard took the podium and all our chit-chat stopped abruptly. Ninety musicians seemed to be holding their breath as he took his time settling in before finally offering us a "Good morning." I was one of ten new musicians reporting for duty that day, but Howard acknowledged none of us, offering only a blank, icy stare.

Shigo whispered to me, "I've just been here a week. He's always like this. Wants to frighten us. Just play your part and don't worry about the S.O.B."

My practice time had been minimal at Lackland, but I was still confident and comfortable through rehearsal. My singing had remained unrehearsed, but I was assigned to take formal lessons. I had no real worries, as I knew I could prove myself valuable enough to the band that the Singing Sergeants could do without me.

A week passed and I was settling in nicely. With Lackland under my belt I simply followed orders, didn't look for trouble, and yes, kept my mouth shut, my bowels open, and avoided volunteering. Funnily, I had learned more about how to handle the military than I learned *from* them.

One day I was practicing in the latrine — the quietest place in a barracks full of musicians, and about the only place you could hear yourself — and a stranger came up behind me. It was some time before I realized he was there and turned around to an appreciative smile. This was Ronnie Odrich. Ronnie played in The Crew Chiefs, the jazz quintet attached officially to the larger dance band. Being fellow clarinetists, we immediately found common ground. That soon turned out to be more than we thought — Ronnie had also taken lessons from Buddy DeFranco! I soon discovered that he played a lot like Buddy, and we became fast friends. Ronnie had taken more regular and more standard lessons from Buddy than I had, most of mine being impromptu conversations backstage, over a meal, or over the phone. He had started the lessons after seeing Buddy play a gig at Birdland. Ronnie was too young at the time to be in the main room, so his father, a sax player in New York with a lot of Broadway experience, approached Buddy to arrange for his mentorship. Ronnie still practices regularly and performs weekly to this day, perfectly in the mold of DeFranco.

* * *

About this time, Buddy's band was due in town, scheduled to play the Howard Theatre (no connection to Colonel Howard). Washington's answer to Harlem's Apollo Theater, the Howard had a devoted all-black audience. As well, the band would play a couple of boat cruises down the Potomac. I honestly can't remember how I did it, but I found out which hotel he was in, and placed my usual call. I only had to identify myself and Buddy was on the line in a few seconds.

We made some small talk, his congratulating me on making the Air Force Band, and my congratulating him on his big band. I extended an invitation to show him the city, but he told me he hadn't been feeling well and would have to take a raincheck.

"Come to the Howard Theatre the day after tomorrow. Meet me backstage about thirty minutes before the show and I'll bring you up to date on things and introduce you to some of the guys."

As always, Buddy made my day.

Bolling was a military base but we were musicians, and it didn't take much to get out to see the band. I went to the back door of the Howard and announced with unflinching confidence, "I'm here to see Buddy DeFranco. I'm part of the band."

The stagehand was sleepy and slow-moving as he gave me a quick once-over. Inch by inch, he slowly opened the door — he was in no hurry. Buddy spotted me through the half-open door and grabbed my hand to pull me inside. He was meticulously dressed, but seemed tense, nervous, andpreoccupied. I was far from being a doctor at that point, but a humble layman's opinion was all it took: he looked sick.

A few orchestra members sat around fiddling with their horns and looking over their music. Buddy beckoned a few of them over and introduced me, "A friend of mine. He plays clarinet — Steve Botek."

Gene Quill was searching for a decent reed and without raising his head, waved a hello to me. The other saxophonists, Eddie Wasserman and Andy Cicalese, were playing their horns but nodded hellos, as did drummer Frank DeVito, checking the tuning of his snare. Pianist Teddy Corabi never even looked up, too focused on playing a passage over and over.

Buddy's facial tics and twitches were evident. He was also nervously moving his fingers from time to time, mimicking the finger action of playing clarinet. I'd seen him doing this before when he was prepping for those lengthy choruses under Tommy Dorsey. It reminded me of an anxious race horse chomping at the bit or a long-distance runner rocking back and forth at the starting line.

I wondered why Buddy didn't just sit down, take some deep breaths, and center himself. His psychotherapist Louis Pelletiere was an advocate of Reichian and other relaxation techniques, and Buddy knew them well. It was at this period of Buddy's career that his many physical conditions became highly disabling — allergies, asthma, even hemorrhoids.

I was worried about him until curtain time came. I stepped out into the auditorium, and from a choice front-and-center seat, I saw him playing at the top of his game. The band sounded crisp, energetic, and well-rehearsed. Each player had been well-chosen, and there was no dead wood. The arrangements were modern and great, and the choice of songs perfect. Swinging from start to finish on tunes like "Out of Nowhere", the band had the hip Howard matinée audience dancing in their seats.

Still, the band had only three trumpets and two trombones, and so lacked the force and depth of other big bands. While Buddy's solos were brilliantly conceived, at times he was struggling hard just to play the notes, losing the swing and lapsing into shopworn clichés. Certain jazz critics labeled Buddy's playing too mechanical, with too many notes. While the crowd was into it, I could see Buddy was struggling, and I could also tell that the other musicians knew it. There were no smiles and the group was working more than playing at times.

Years later, Buddy talked to me about Lenny Lewis, his manager who had promised to get the money, contracts, and organization together for the big band, calling him "the most impressive talker and operator I have ever met." It was at Lewis' urging that Buddy was told he should become a big-name bandleader. Lewis was given full rein and had plans and ideas for everything, including how Buddy should act on stage.

"Listen, Boss," he lectured DeFranco. "Here's the way it is. I mean the audience is out there with great expectations, right? You open up and grab them with a swinger, and you really put that clarinet up in the air — don't play down! You hit them with a swinging number, then you come down to a medium tempo, get them dancing, then you get slow and romantic with not too many notes, don't overdo it! Swing hard, get that band going! And — you know — smile! You don't smile enough! For Christ's sake, smile!"[1]

Buddy wasn't playing with his clarinet up in the air that night. He would later tell me, "The only guy that played with a clarinet straight up was Artie Shaw, only because he was built that way." Neither was he smiling. Maybe it was the stress of running the band and catering to everyone's needs. Maybe Lewis' vision was impinging on Buddy's. One way or the other, the stress was getting to him.

Returning to the base that afternoon, I couldn't stop thinking about how

---

[1] Mas and Zammarchi, *A Life in the Golden Age of Jazz*

important top-notch health is to top-notch playing. If the player is feeling ill, the music will suffer. Simple enough to understand, but quite difficult to compensate for. It reminded me of my own health issues at Lackland and how *my* playing had suffered. Much of my time there was spent without even thinking about my horn — my health and survival took priority.

A day-and-a-half didn't seem too soon to see Buddy's band again, despite the issues. Three of my musician buddies from Bolling would be tagging along this time, Ronnie Odrich included. As well, the shows that evening — two of them, at 9 and 11 p.m. — would both take place aboard a large ferry that would sail the Potomac, leaving from downtown Washington. That would be a new experience for me.

We arrived at about 8:15, paid the three-dollar admission and boarded the ship. I wanted to see both shows and tried to pay in advance for the second sailing, but was told that this was not permitted. Bolling treated us like musicians — at most bases, we could hardly expect to arrive back at 1:30 in the morning just because we wanted to see some jazz.

When we got on board, the stage was being readied with the band slowly setting up. I could see Buddy doodling away on his horn in a far corner. The instant he saw me, he called me over and greeted me warmly. My friends were impressed. John Hill was one of them — a trombone player who just that morning had arrived in DC following three months of basic training. John owned most of Buddy's recordings and was a true devotee. Immediately he engaged the maestro in a serious discussion about bebop. I was glad to see Buddy's energy had returned. Even so, talking to John, a funny expression kept cropping up on his face and I knew something was bothering him.

"Buddy," I interrupted, "are you wondering why John ends every sentence with 'sir'?"

Buddy nodded, and the other guys grinned, knowing where I was heading.

"Well, John just got in from Lackland Air Force Base this morning. There, he was so brainwashed that he said 'sir' to anything and everything. He has yet to end one sentence without it. He'll be okay with time. We'll start deprogramming him tomorrow."

John was a bit red-faced at that, and the rest of us teased him as we left Buddy to prepare for the show.

The band swung hard as the boat rocked its way down the Potomac. This was no sit-down affair; rather, it was one of those good old-fashioned, up-on-your-feet bashes with the audience either dancing or crowded around the stage hanging on every note. The place was packed and spirits were high. For our part, getting away from base and the dollar beers helped.

"Wow! That was incredible!" Hill shouted to us when the ninety-minute set ended. We all laughed — Buddy had played the 'sirs' right out of him!

We were ordered off the boat, and everyone was pumped about going to see the second show. As we left, we passed a line of passengers waiting to get on board. We rushed to the box office, and were again told that we could not purchase a ticket.

"Are you completely sold out?" I asked, disappointed.

"Man, can't you see?" the ticket-seller replied, motioning to the line-up. "This second show is only for Negroes!"

Driving back to the base, we all muttered about the situation. Good thing we went early! We raged about the Washington hypocrisy — whites on this side, negroes over there. John remembered a drinking fountain he saw in Birmingham — the water shot up from one central source, but then divided into separate pipes leading to faucets labeled 'Whites Only' and 'Negroes Only'.

"Thank God I grew up in Detroit, sir," he muttered.

Matthew, a quiet, soft-spoken young drummer, had been entranced by what he had seen and heard that evening and barely said a word, but finally spoke up at that: "John, man, you're the living end, and I agree with everything you said, but, seriously man, knock off the 'sir' shit. Basic's over, so keep the 'sir' stuff just for officers, and *even then* don't overdo it."

I woke up early the following morning, my head swimming with music. Buddy's selections included tunes I never thought could be used as jazz pieces. I wanted to phone Buddy and thank him — we'd left thinking we would be back aboard the second sailing and never really said goodbye to him. There was no public phone in the barracks, so I scribbled off a congratulatory penny postcard, fitting as much as I could on the back.

Early mornings were about the only time the barracks were quiet enough to think. There were thirty highly-trained and ambitious musicians living there, and silence was a rarity. Like Eastman's practice rooms, everyone played as loud as they could to drown out other sound — but there were no walls between us. A restful night's sleep was rare enough, but being able to practice and hear yourself was an impossibility, which is why I'd often, out of desperation, do my daily practice in the latrine.

* * *

Col. Howard was collecting as many young musicians as he could get his hands on — as long as they didn't have crew-cuts. Maybe it was because he had lost 95 percent of his personnel back in 1945 and felt the need to have extra men on-hand. Howard describes his World War II experiences in his autobiography *A Symphony in the Sky*.

Neophytes to the Air Force would wonder why Howard was so cold, standoffish, and uncivil, so ready to pounce and find fault, even by military standards. Howard loved to intimidate the new musicians, particularly the young or talented ones. Was he unconsciously re-enacting something from his past? In *A Symphony in the Sky*, odd pieces of information scattered throughout might help explain his behavior. He writes, "There were only six of us in my class and we felt very special and perhaps superior. At times, the school seemed to revolve around us and in our minds, it may have been the world."

There were rumors — again, the core of information in the military — supplied by some of the older band members that the breakup of Howard's first marriage had much to do with his approach. He and his wife, Florence, both worked for the Ernest Williams School of Music in Brooklyn, Howard as Dean, and his wife, Dean of Girls. After a few years he received a better offer from Mansfield State Teachers' College in Pennsylvania. He went, but she stayed on at Williams. He describes it in the book: "We both wanted our places in the sun, so I moved to Mansfield while she remained in Brooklyn as Dean of Girls."

Their marriage broke up and she remarried, choosing Dr. Ernest S. Williams, the founder of the Williams School. Rumor had it that Williams was a good-looking macho man who, over time, swept Florence off her feet. The conventional wisdom was that the breakup became quite ugly, and conjecture included physical violence before a final settlement was established, though I can't say if that violence was supposed to be against Williams or Florence. Howard had a high respect for Williams, former first trumpet with the Philadelphia Orchestra under Stokowski, prior to the divorce, and it shows in his autobiography: "A musical genius, a super music educator and conductor, and one of the greatest trumpeters and cornet soloists of all time...the personality of Dr. Williams was such that no one could say no to him. . . . There was never any question as to who was the master."

It may be telling that he uses the phrase "no one could say no to him".

Howard was a poor loser. He lost 95 percent of his men in World War II and his wife to a man he had admired and who had given him his first big-time job in the field of music. With all this behind him, was it really any wonder he was bitter? His rank was something he could hold up to keep distance between himself and the men.

Not that the military itself didn't underline the separations that come with position. Men in close quarters like to shoot the bull, and the trappings of position were a common subject: rank, emblems, decorations, uniforms, etc. The hat emblem alone was a mark of separation. Enlisted airmen were quickly identified by a small round emblem about the size of a silver dollar that attached to the center of their hat. As bandsmen, we wore a special emblem about three inches square, with a lyre displayed prominently on it. *Official* bandsmen, those in the major bands stationed at Bolling, were issued a separate hat emblem with wings, similar to those of a pilot, displayed alongside the lyre. As well, we received a half-inch wide, four-inch long semi-circular cloth patch sewn on the top of the right sleeve of our uniforms. In bright white letters on a dark blue background, the patch proclaimed 'The United States Air Force Band'. There were numerous bands stationed around the world, but this patch and emblem marked us as part of *The* United States Air Force Band, the big one. They not only never failed to arouse curiosity, rare as they were, but also garnered respect throughout the Air Force.

Here I was, five months into the Air Force, playing with the Air Force Band and singing with the Singing Sergeants Glee Club, but still with no rank. The uniform I wore bore no stripes whatsoever. I was a lowly buck private earning a mere $75 per month. Even so, the emblem and patch marking me as part of the band still commanded respect. It didn't hurt that we had freedom unheard of elsewhere in the military, considering our rank (or lack thereof) — as a member of the band, I had a special Class A identification card which stated I could travel anywhere I pleased without special travel papers. As long as I had no concert to play or rehearsal to attend, I could roam freely.

One day I went to New York, visiting Dr. Pelletiere (who was surprised to see me in uniform) and getting a saxophone lesson from Joe Allard. At Pennsylvania Station I stood waiting for my 6 p.m. train back to DC. Two military police officers started eyeing me from the far end of the platform. One was an Air Force A.P., the other a Navy S.P. I stood my ground, having done nothing wrong, but immediately started through a checklist in my head: my shoes were shined, my tie was in place, my hat was on and properly centered. With nothing out of sorts, I decided to stand still and leave it to them to approach me if they so desired.

Soon enough the Air Force cop inched toward me. Close up, I could see his two stripes, identifying him as an Airman second-class. He examined me with the greatest of care before finally speaking.

"Sir," he ventured, "are you a member of the Air Cadets?"

I chuckled to myself. He was so confused that he was calling me 'sir'!

"No, Corporal," I replied matter-of-factly. "I'm a bandsman. From The United States Air Force Band in Washington, DC."

"Thank you," he replied, turning and leaving.

He didn't even ask to see my pass. While I was wondering if anything was wrong with my uniform while the two cops were eyeing me, they were only trying to figure out my rank and position.

There was a similar incident a few months later. The band was performing for one full week in Toronto at the Canadian National Exhibition. We gave two or three concerts daily to packed houses, some including military dignitaries from around the world. Colonel Howard decided to make some additional changes to our uniform — we wore heavy double-breasted jackets, pleated pants, epaulets, and a special white Air Force ceremonial braid draped over our chests. The unique thing about the new uniform was that *none* of us wore stripes or bars, regardless of our rank. More than one Canadian commented that we looked more like high-class hotel doormen than military personnel.

Following one afternoon matinée we had no place or time to change clothes. So Alex Shigo and I meandered out into the afternoon crowds still dressed in full Napoleon-style attire. Out of nowhere, three older Turkish officers in full-dress uniform started directly towards us.

"Oh God," Shigo worried. "We'd better salute. But who goes first? Them or us? They certainly outrank us, so we should salute them first. But . . ."

"What?" I wondered.

"The way we're dressed, who knows anything about rank?" he grinned conspiratorially.

We both continued walking directly towards them and withholding our salutes. Finally they initiated the salute — crisp, snappy, and full of respect — and we smartly returned it.

"See?" Shigo laughed once they were out of sight. "It *is* the uniform that makes the man!"

Alex sure knew what he was doing that day. A few minutes after the salute exchange with the Turkish officers, we sighted two young Canadian girls. This time, we saluted first as we struck up the usual boy-girl introductory conversation. There was no way Shigo could have known then that the young lady he was facing would eventually become his wife.

Alex and I shared many other things besides travel stories and a music stand. We were about the same age and height, shared the same living quarters, and we both wore glasses. Older band members often got us mixed up. Howard simply ignored both of us as though we didn't exist.

There was usually a divide between the older and younger players — where we were in for a three- or four-year hitch, they had elected to remain for twenty or more. They kept their distance, staying cautious and tight-lipped around us. Nevertheless, things would leak out. One of the veteran clarinet players strongly disapproved of our take-it-or-leave-it attitude towards the military, but he was a musician as well as an airman and approved heartily of our playing. It was with the latter in mind that he warned us to watch out for Howard: "He'll re-audition you both at the least expected moment!"

I did what I always did when faced with a ridiculous situation — I began searching for DeFranco. I knew he was somewhere on the road and over his head in work with the new big band, but still I knew he was always ready to help. I got through to his New York booking agent Willard Alexander — a man Buddy called "above reproach, straight as an arrow, a man of great integrity and common sense"— and with his help, the long-distance operator was able to locate Buddy within minutes. I never even bothered to ask where Buddy was, instead just jumping right into the meat of the matter.

Charlie Tucker had reminded me, Buddy knew only too well about power-crazed, sadistic people like Howard. He referred me to one of Wilhelm Reich's books, even going so far as to note the page describing such people.

"Howard," he confidently told me, "is a frustrated obsessive-compulsive character with a strong neurotic need to embarrass you, to put you down. He's probably reliving and compensating for some embarrassing situation that *he* suffered in the past. Maybe he'll stop in the middle of a rehearsal, pick you out, and ask you to play alone. With a rehearsal, he'll have an audience for his games, but he'd never do it at a concert — there, the audience would hold him responsible.

"There, in front of eighty-five fellow bandsmen, he'll begin to tear apart your playing. Tommy does things like this, but thank God his band only has seventeen men.

"Be prepared," he warned. "Always have your best reed, best mouthpiece, etc. Be dressed super sharp, shaved and rarin' to go. Don't give him the slightest excuse to jump on. Don't let him scare you. Play your ass off, but even if it's perfect, don't expect him to say so. Tommy would, but Howard sounds sicker and meaner than Dorsey ever was.

"The other bandsmen, even the two-faced old-timers you spoke about, will probably come to your rescue if you perform perfectly well. Then, and only then, will Howard back down. But don't think it'll be over! It won't. He'll wait for another opportunity, maybe a one-on-one situation rather than a rehearsal. If you remain silent and don't threaten his authority — act respectful of it — even while he rants, raves, and picks your playing to pieces, then he'll probably figure he beat you enough, that you're no threat, and he'll back off — hopefully for good."

I was reassured. We talked a bit more and Buddy wished me well, reminding me to check out the Reich book and suggesting that Freud had some similar case histories I could look at, as well.

It was another near-ten-dollar long-distance call (and I didn't even know where to!), but it had been worth it. Beyond the advice, Buddy confirmed that I could handle Howard. I had copied everything down and referred to it in the next little while, though it took some time for me to figure out the right spelling to look up Reich. Buddy knew his psychology — beyond his own experience, he worked regularly with one of New York's best Reichian psychiatrists. Beyond the books and professionals, Buddy's gift for understanding the behavior of others had evolved slowly over the years. His countless personal associations from family to big band earned him an adroit understanding of human behavior.

Shigo, although no newcomer to strife and suffering, nevertheless found Howard's treatment of us new recruits utterly bewildering and unfair.

"When is something good going to happen?" he would moan. "Here we are, twenty-two of us, six months of service under our belts, still living on the base in a barracks with open cubicles!"

The older official Air Force Band members — by law — were granted off-base rations and quarters. Howard had overstuffed his allotments, leaving no room to house the entire band on base. He always wanted a bigger band — more, more, more, even if he was officially exceeding his quota.

Alex continued, "No rank, no recognition, no decent place to practice, plus no safe place to store our instruments!"

The instruments we used were our own. Some were valued in the thousands, and we were responsible for keeping them in perfect condition. This was despite a lack of storage space other than under beds and mattresses, in a building that was improperly heated. I had even taken to not trusting my footlocker to keep my clarinet safe and keeping the case under my pillow when I slept. It was hard on my head but it seemed better than the alternative.

We commiserated, but as long as Howard was there, the problems would remain.

* * *

Summer came, though, and with it, Howard left with fifty-five men for an eight-week tour of Europe, the Middle East, and North Africa. Those of us left behind busied ourselves with rehearsals and touring around Washington or using our freedom of travel to visit home. As hard to deal with as Howard was, I have to admit that he never overworked us — other than on concert tours. Rehearsals were Monday afternoon and Tuesday to Friday mornings, with the rest of our time fairly free. Officially we were listed as practicing privately for four hours daily, but most of us had trained intensely before our service started and needed no more than a good half-hour daily warm-up to stay in top shape.

Two of our twenty-two barracks-bound bandsmen were the Beals — Gerald and Wilfred, fraternal twins from Brooklyn. Nineteen years old, they were excellently-schooled violinists and highly experienced concert players. The previous summer they had toured Europe as a duo, earning upwards of twenty thousand dollars.

"Look at us now," Fred would lament. "We earn about eighty-five dollars a month, practice in latrines, and live in buildings better suited to migrant workers."

One balmy, if humid, hot summer morning, Mrs. Beal walked into our barracks, unannounced and unexpected. She had made the three-and-a-half-hour train trip from New York to check on her two virtuosi and to see first-hand what conditions were like. The four of us jumped into their 1949 Plymouth sedan — the Beal boys being the only ones in the group wealthy enough to own a car — and drove into the center of town to do some sight-seeing. I sat in the back while Mrs. Beal sat in the middle of the front seat with an arm around each son. She questioned them about everything, and I did my best to occupy myself otherwise and give them their privacy.

We drove around for about two hours, never leaving the car until we hit Union Station so Mrs. Beal could take the next train to New York. A few days later rumors began to fly — a New York congressman and a few state representatives, notably the one from Brooklyn — were supposedly pushing to investigate the adverse living conditions and other grievances concerning Bolling Air Force Base.

What irony! I thought. Brooklyn was where Colonel Howard had taught fifteen years earlier. Would New York's legislators now investigate him and the results of that day in Brooklyn when Florence left him?

The answer was no. The summer passed, and Howard came back to the base, a raging bull maybe made the worse for the accusations. Nothing pleased him during that first rehearsal after his return and no one was able to placate him. He accused those of us who had not toured with him of having wasted our summer. He belittled his assistant conductor, easily his most faithful crony, sure that this yes-man would swallow anything the Colonel had to feed him. Sure enough, he did — what choice did he have?

Following a fifteen-minute break, Howard finally seemed to have relaxed, but it was only the calm before the storm. Readying ourselves for our turn at humiliation, Shigo and I had used the intermission to find and prepare our best reeds. We were halfway through a lively clarinet passage in a Michel Glinka selection when it happened. Howard stopped the ensemble, pointed to Shigo, and barked, "You. Play."

Shigo did, and it sounded fine. Then Howard turned to me with the same command. I cut right through the passage, as Alex had, making no noticeable mistakes. I was more than satisfied with my performance, but not Howard.

"What do you have, a rag in your horn?" he griped, his eyes rolling upward and disgust plain across his face. A sigh of surprise made its way from the remaining members, some even tapping on their music stands as a sign of approval. Howard ignored it. In an effort to show us up, he ordered the first-chair clarinetist to pass his part — the solo — over to us. In the middle of the rehearsal we were to read parts that had never been assigned to us. The Colonel wanted us to fail — and fail miserably, publically, and in shame. It wasn't as if the other players didn't know better, but Howard only cared about his own satisfaction.

Alex took a quick glance over the solo part. Like myself, he was an excellent sight-reader, and I could read it in his body language: *Fuck the old bastard. I'll show him.*

Alex pushed through masterfully. Howard stopped him: "Enough! Give it to him."

Alex handed the pages over and I took my turn. I made only minimal mistakes, nothing noticeable to a layman, and that was to be expected when first sight-reading a piece. Having no one else to pass it along to, Howard didn't stop me, waiting for something he could pounce on. Instead I finished and the music stands sounded — the band members were impressed. Howard would have none of it, shouting over the clanking of the stands until the band members were silenced, going on about rags in our horns and "inferior playing". He continued, trying to convince someone by virtue of his authority alone, believing that it superseded what everyone had just heard. Finally he gave up, having satisfied himself at least of having made his point. It was telling that he let the rest of the rehearsal go without further interruptions, dour-faced as he was.

Later, back in the dorm, Shigo warned me, "Today he got his foot in the door. Beware tomorrow! He's going to want to come in lock, stock, and barrel.

"But," he added with a conspiratorial grin, "we'll be ready."

A few days after that, the fiddle players announced that they were all moving off the base. They had been given what we all wanted: off-base rations and quarters. The Air Force would pay each of them an extra stipend each month to cover living expenses and meals. Rumors flew. Everyone wanted to know why just the string players. Someone heard that Bolling's Inspector General had, under pressure from various New York congressmen, promised to examine and update the status of all the bandsmen from that state — and for one reason or another, the string section was largely from New York. Moving just the New Yorkers would show they had caved to political pressure, so instead they made it seem it was about the section. The rest of the group was mostly fellow Pennsylvanians and we felt cheated — though not for long.

A second announcement later that same day revealed that all twenty-two of us would soon be moving. As well, soon we would actually have rank — anyone who had not yet been promoted to Airman Third Class would be garnering their first stripe. There was a loud cheer throughout the barracks.

The cheer was followed by questions and soul-searching. Where were we going to move, and when? Washington was huge, and none of us had been preparing to move, with the sole exception of Bill Dupree. Bill was one of the few token black members of the band. He hailed from Roanoke, Virginia where he had trained his operatic tenor voice extensively. He was featured as a soloist in most of our concerts.

Bill had found a large, four-bedroom house in nearby Arlington and wanted to find five men to share expenses. The house was in the predominately black district of Shirlington, alone on a small side road, directly across the street from a large, well-maintained church — Sundays would be the only days we would see our neighbors. It was a private and peaceful setting, a perfect place for musicians, especially considering we needed to practice for professional gigs and a saxophone blown at full volume can likely be heard a full quarter-mile away.

The house had a garage and lots of parking — important as most of us had procured a second-hand car by this point. I had snagged a 1941 Studebaker Dictator four-door for $125. Studebaker, like all American car

Lackland Air Force Base, 1951
Basic training in both summer and winter uniforms

Steve and Alex Shigo
Still privates after 6 months of service. Where are the stripes?

Basic training, San Antonio, Texas
Steve properly saluting, but displaying passive-aggressive behavior with cigarette in mouth

Sgt M. mimicking the conductor

Weisbaden, 1953
Steve enjoying a good German beer

Police barracks in Izmir, Turkey
Bandsmen sleep on the floor
because of bedbugs

Germany, Summer 1953
Band members sitting on an ancient bridge near a castle

The Intrumentalists, 1953
Steve's combo featuring stellar trombonist Gene Brussaloff
showing off his one-of-a-kind instrument

The Singing Sergeants
Steve, wearing glasses *(back row, third from right)*

Cairo, Egypt, 1953
Arabs offering camel rides to tourists

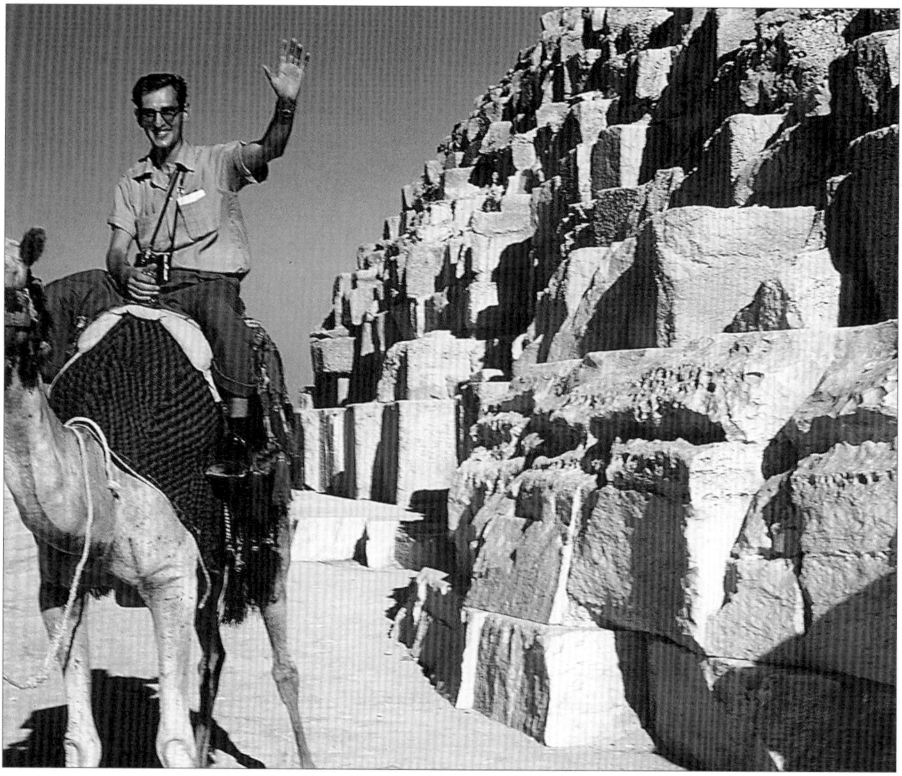

Steve bravely accepts a camel ride and happily tours the pyramids

Steve Botek playing clarinet with the Instrumentalists
Steve led the Instrumentalists for 2½ years from 1952 to mid-1955

Air Force bandsmen jam at a party, 1952
A regular occurrence in the house Steve and other musicians shared off-base

Same house party, with Alex Shigo's favorite belly dancer
(Shigo on right)

Jamming with the Icelanders (trombone and guitar), Reykjavik, Iceland, 1952
John Bainbridge on sax, John Hill on trombone,
Joseph Latinsy on trumpet, Floyd Werley on piano

Col. Howard *(inset)* and Aide, advertising concert at Berlin's Olympic Stadium

Air Force Band members ready for a European performance

Various members of the United States Air Force Band trumpet section

Frank Montosi *(left)* studied with composer Paul Hindemith and played in the Radio City Music Hall Orchestra following discharge in 1954

Steve Botek with his wife, Ruth, and long-time Pennsylvania buddy, Reuben Heller with his wife, Mildred

manufacturers, had stopped production during World War II, and probably welcomed the opportunity to halt sales of a car with that name, considering the times.

I decided in favor of the move and chose the single, smaller back room. Shigo teamed up with one of the violinists to secure another, Dupree would bunk with a young vocalist from Texas, and the other single room facing the front was reserved by our new arrival from Detroit, trombonist John Hill.

The announcement made and our plans cemented, we took stock and realized we shouldn't move too fast. The service was well-known for announcing something, then taking its sweet time making it happen, and, sure enough, this time was to be no exception.

"Hurry up and wait," Shigo griped. "Three weeks have passed and nothing has happened."

Helping to fill the time, though, was another announcement. We were going on a trip. Cleveland, Ohio may not have sounded as far-flung and exciting as Toronto, but this time we would be flying rather than packing ourselves into Freddy Beal's old Plymouth. More importantly, we would get to play at a Cleveland Red Sox baseball game. We had given plenty of outdoor concerts, even at the Capitol steps, but here we were being asked to *parade* at a baseball game. It was a unique request, something we might never get another chance to do. Col. Howard felt the band was above being halftime entertainment, and had the commitment not been made, he likely would have substituted his Drum and Bugle Corps.

The parade went well, and everyone was happy about it but Howard, who proclaimed that there would be no more such shows.

"After all," he reasoned, "this *is* a symphonic concert band, not some makeshift razzmatazz Philadelphia mummers group!"

Later that evening Howard got what he wanted. We were booked for a three-hour concert in Cleveland's symphonic hall. The building was beautiful and lavishly decorated, with a large seating capacity and one of the country's best acoustical designs — no microphones were needed, with sound carrying easily to the last row of the balcony. We were all familiar with good acoustics, even to the point of choosing to practice in a tile-walled latrine for the sake of them. We were all thrilled with the hall itself and no one really thought about the music. After all, at every performance we played basically the same selections and so, over time, the music had all become routine. We knew how to make it sound fresh, and even how to compensate for Howard and his delusions of grandeur.

We began with a typical and well-known snappy short piece to grab the crowd's attention. That would be followed by a Sousa march, then a few vocal selections by the Singing Sergeants — all a planned build-up to garner the audience's favor before we went into the more serious, complicated, and harder to perform composers like Wagner, Tchaikovsky, and Prokofiev. Howard particularly loved Wagner, and his eyes would sparkle when conducting his compositions.

We were in the middle of Wagner's "Overture to Lohengrin", Howard entranced, with twenty clarinets all playing sweet, soft, and exactingly slow in unison when the unforgivable happened. One of the clarinetists squeaked. I swear it wasn't me and it wasn't Shigo — it came from somewhere ahead of us and over to the right. Shigo nudged my foot when it happened, mouthing, "Somebody's ass is going to get chewed."

No one stopped or lost the beat, and the audience may well have forgotten the extraneous sound if they had even noticed it, if not for the death-glare on Howard's face — his skin was beet-red, his brow creased like week-old laundry, and his jaw locked in a grimace.

Wagner ended and the Colonel's visible anger subsided during a few other pieces until the intermission. No one said a word about it, but we all were waiting for the storm to begin. We knew that French-horn players crack notes all the time, as do trumpeters, and that has to be forgiven. A serious clarinet player, however, should not squeak — it would obviously be the reed, as some wooden ones have that property, but normally such a reed would be junked during rehearsal. Our understanding of the issue was not to be expected from the Colonel. Howard said nothing. Not one word.

We forgot about the squeak, not wanting to question having dodged Howard's ire, as we flew back to Washington the next day. Though I had flown before, it had always been in single-motor jobs, usually with Art Rubart showing off at the controls. This was my first experience in a large plane and I was completely enmeshed in the experience: the bucket seats, wearing a parachute, and jetting above the clouds at 200 mph. Alex and I spent the weekend recounting the experience and congratulating ourselves on our performances in Cleveland.

Monday morning, though, brought word that Shigo and I were to both put on our dress uniforms and report immediately to Colonel Howard's office. Considering the Colonel, we didn't expect praise, but we were shocked at his first words to us.

"One of you *squeaked* in Cleveland! I can't have that in my band!" he raged.

In unison, we denied culpability, and even noted how we had heard it a distance away from our seats, but Howard wasn't interested in listening.

"No," he insisted, to no one in particular, "I never had this happen before."

Our protests were ignored — his mind was made up.

"Go!" he commanded. "Start thinking of which field band you want to be sent to. I'll have you shipped there. Dismissed!"

* * *

Howard's outburst was it. There were ninety or so field bands we would have to choose from, and all because Howard wanted his scapegoat. Somebody had fucked up his "Lohengrin", and somebody had to pay for that unpardonable sin. It didn't matter to him if it was the right person, as was clear by the fact that he was sending *both* of us away for *one* squeak — obviously not produced by two clarinets. Maybe he even knew who, but didn't want to punish one of his older ass-kissing cronies. He made no effort to find out who, not even bothering to ask the guilty party to step forward. His solution was to demonstrate his authority and satisfy his paranoia about the new, young, self-assured, sons-of-bitches who needed to be taught a lesson. Again, he was probably reliving something from his past, exacting revenge for some perceived offence that had haunted him for years.

I knew this thanks to the psychology books that Buddy had recommended. With the aid of Freud, Jung, and Reich, I was better able to understand individuals like George S. Howard. Still, knowing the proper names for his behavior didn't tell me how to handle it.

Dr. Hughes in Philidelphia came to mind — not only was he a psychiatrist, he had been a commander in the Navy and understood the military as well. I planned to visit him in a week or two, once my monthly paycheck arrived — after all, the $25 fee plus the train fare would be too much for me to handle before then. I was left wondering if the time would be enough. Should I just tell ol' George to shove it? Why should I work to stay where I wasn't wanted? I could ask to be shipped to Mitchell Field on Long Island where Reuben Heller was stationed. Even if I did, though, there was no guarantee that my request would be honored. It seemed I was in a no-win situation, and the time was spent in painful soul-searching to try and figure out what I should do.

Ten days added up, then fourteen, with still no word from Howard. I had at least decided for sure that I wanted to stay. Coming up was a ten-week, nineteen-country Europe/Middle East/North Africa tour and that opportunity was too good to give up. As well, that tour was emblematic of what the band offered: travel and interesting gigs.

Various band members offered suggestions, most not worth pursuing. One of the ass-kissing old-timers offered, "If you want to stay on here with the band, you might consider shining shoes. We already have a band barber and I'm the acoustical sound man, but we've never had a shoeshine boy. And with ninety men, there sure are lots of shoes to clean."

This was coming from a man who played the E-flat clarinet, a smaller, higher-pitched version of the standard B-flat variety. Only rarely would a composition even include a part for him. He sat alone and was hardly ever noticed. Small and bespectacled, he had a sneaky air about him and reminded me of a mouse. There was potentially some merit in his suggestion, though. Howard kept on one player who he had told, "As a tuba player, I have rarely heard worse." The benefit of keeping him was that he acted as the band's 'public relations manager'. While he *did* go on ahead of the band on tours to make arrangements, rumor had it that part of those arrangements was lining up female company for the Colonel.

"No, I wouldn't even consider shining shoes — nor would Shigo," I spat out. "I'm a clarinet player and that's what I wish to remain."

The comment made it clear to me that I *did* want to stay, but on my own terms. I had no interest in serving as slave labor for Howard.

Resolved to find a way to stay, I took the train to Philadelphia. Dr. Hughes greeted me at his office with a firm handshake. He seemed quite pleased to see me and was quick to comment on my neatly-pressed uniform. I was cautious, though, having been familiarized with the habit of many psychiatrists to say one thing while thinking another.

I belched forth my story, surprised myself at how it poured out. I had no idea what type of response to expect, but things had been building up and needed to come out. Hughes was known for always having a quick answer, and this time was no exception.

"Your Colonel should be here, not you," he assured me. "His problems are much bigger than yours, but don't expect him to admit it. This type of person is not easy to live with. Have you considered leaving, since a commanding officer of this sort usually does not change his tactics?"

"Sure," I confessed. "I've thought about it a lot. I could simply split — even choose my next post."

I continued by stating what I had realized staying had to offer. Howard loved to tour: Europe, Asia, Africa, everywhere. And once on tour, according to the old-timers, he never screamed, seldom nitpicked, and always settled down. The way it was told by the older band members, he would often be seen entering his hotel with a woman on each arm — local, small-time country girls out for a good time and to make some quick money. One of the older trumpet players had summed it up as, "Howard, like any of us, feels better once he gets laid."

Hughes took this in, pensive over a few moments' silence.

"You'll hit him with a paradoxical approach," he announced suddenly. "Catch him off-guard — force his hand. You will gently and firmly stand up to him by admitting that he was absolutely right all of the time — even concerning his implication that you are not good enough to be a member of his crack outfit. Then you will quietly and respectfully ask him to do what seems like the best course of action — namely, to send you away. You will thank him for his wisdom and make it appear like he would be better off without you."

"I don't want to brown-nose him," I interjected, horrified.

"No, not brown-nosing. Diplomacy. Be diplomatic," he reassured. "By all means, do not threaten his position. This is what he fears most of all. So, be outspoken but don't push. Keep your voice friendly without arguing or accusing. Convince him that he knows best and make him believe that you are absolutely ready to give up this Washington position if he honestly believes you are not worthy of it."

Needless to say, I wasn't thrilled with the course of action, but Hughes' take made sense. On the trip back to Washington, I became more and more convinced he was right and scribbled notes the entire way.

Back at Bolling, I approached Alex and asked him if he wanted to join me.

"We'll request an audience with 'his highness'," I explained. "We will thoroughly rehearse our spiel and then, we'll see what happens.

Shigo hesitated before asking, "Suppose it backfires? Suppose he does decide to send us out? He could do it immediately if he wants."

"Then," I said calmly, having asked myself the question repeatedly on the train back, "you'll be writing me from some small base near Pittsburgh and I'll send you postcards from lovely Long Island. Which is exactly what will happen if we do nothing."

The next afternoon we got fresh haircuts and clean shaves, got our shoes shined and our uniforms pressed. Looking as perfect as we could, standing ramrod straight in front of the Colonel, we put on our best poker faces and proceeded to match wits. I can't remember the exact words, or even all the specifics we covered, but I remember being certain as we spoke that each word was the right one, with Howard's eyes opening wider, unable to hide the surprised and dazed look on his face.

"Why," he finally offered when we had spoken our piece, "you men are some of the best I have. This morning I heard the Navy Band rehearse. Why, you guys run rings around them!"

Shigo and I stood in calculated silence, leaving the next move up to him. We had said all we could and manipulated him well, judging from his response. Neither of us was going to say a word that could potentially throw our hard-earned gains out the window at this point. Howard was unnerved, flustered, and forced to think — he now had no clear path to expressing his authority, and was uncertain how to proceed.

"You're dismissed for now. I will look into this," he finally announced, forced to fill the silence himself, and obviously feeling uncomfortable with the shift in positions.

Alex and I left, with perfect military posture, the picture of the perfect soldiers all the way back to our dorm — excepting the occasional grins that broke through when we looked at each other. Still, we were on our own now. Another trip to Pennsylvania was out of the question, in case the Colonel came a-calling.

The week following was tense, with the uncertainty overcoming the triumph Alex and I had felt in the Colonel's office. Most of our fellow bandsmen were well aware of our plight, but avoided the subject altogether.

Finally, on Monday morning, a messenger arrived from the main office with the order: "Botek, Shigo, and Whelan are to report in full-dress uniform to Colonel Howard's office at 1 p.m. And bring your clarinets!"

Whelan was newly-arrived, an excellent young clarinetist who had recently played with the Washington National Symphony. I can't recall what Whelan's offence was, but we knew the three of us were in this together. Considering it was Howard, I never even bothered asking. The Colonel may have simply forgotten who he was mad at and included Whelan as he was also a young player. He might have forgotten that he hadn't come up with an excuse yet to harass Whelan. We didn't know him well, and weren't sure if it was worthwhile letting him in on the plan, so we didn't mention it, hoping that he could follow our lead if necessary. Having played with the National Symphony, he was likely able to deal with authority.

"So," Shigo sighed, "the bastard wants to hear us play? Let's show him what playing is!"

Out came the horns and we ran off to the latrines to warm up uninterrupted. I took with me a reed that Langenus sent me, one that wouldn't squeak in a hundred years. We made sure our shoes were shined, trousers pressed, and we were freshly showered. We skipped lunch, as playing on a full stomach is more difficult.

We marched into his office at precisely 1 p.m., saluted, and stood at attention. He grudgingly returned our salutes but remained seated and ordered us to take out our instruments. His office was small and cramped, so we assembled our clarinets on the floor. As we did, Howard stood, reaching into a corner to produce three large black music stands. It was a ludicrous sight — with the three of us and the three stands crammed between his mahogany desk and the door, there was barely room to move. Howard sat himself back into his overstuffed chair, a perfect little Napoleon. I stood to his left, Shigo in the middle, and Whelan to the right.

Howard gruffly handed me some music and barked, "Play!"

The first thing I noticed was how black the piece was. There was no name, no title, no composer on it — just a thousand and one notes printed in fast, intricate patterns of sixteenth and thirty-second notes. I wondered if it was Stravinsky, Shostakovich, Schoenberg — but quickly shook off the thought. I didn't know who it was, I just needed to sight-read it.

I sliced through the part as if I knew it. Sure, I missed a few notes here and there, but on the whole I was doing a splendid job for a first reading. About ninety seconds in, I was feeling confident and secure.

"Stop!" Howard snapped, grabbing the music from my stand. "You call that playing? Do you have a rag in your horn?"

Luckily I didn't, or I might have shoved it down his throat. I couldn't believe that, beyond putting us through this for no good reason, he was using the same lines as he had previously, probably having completely forgotten tossing that line at me before.

"You. Play!" he pointed at Shigo with the sheets.

Shigo grabbed the music and flew into it like a champion downhill skier. Alex had studied under the first-chair of the Pittsburgh Symphony and it showed.

Again, Howard snapped, "What kind of playing is that?"

He grabbed the music from Alex's stand and nearly threw it at Whelan. Whelan had heard enough to know the game. He had been part of the National Symphony and put all his concentration into the piece, cutting through it as well as anyone could have on a first reading. But once again, Howard cut him off.

"What kind of clarinet players do I have here?" he ranted.

He turned back to me with a brand-new sheet of music, black as coal. I caught a quick glimpse of the fire in Alex's eyes. The unspoken message was *Okay, if this S.O.B. wants more, we'll give it to him. We'll play so well he'll choke on the music.* I was agreed. If he was going to pretend our playing wasn't up to par, I was going to make sure *he* knew it was a lie.

One glance and I could tell the piece was practically unplayable. *Fuck you*, I thought. I'd played with masters like Langenus, DeFranco, and Allard and none of them would ever have subjected me to shit like this. *Fuck you*, I thought, *Let's go.*

I cut through it like a scythe through wheat. Small bits flew off here and there, but the thing held together, as impossible as the piece was. I didn't lose either my place or the tempo, and the musicality was evident through my performance. But once again, Howard bellowed in rage. This time, I took satisfaction in it. I knew his anger was in not having the excuse he wanted — that he was only going to be able to get rid of us *knowing* he had no good reason. Shigo and Whelan took their turns, with Howard getting angrier as they each gave spectacular performances.

"Enough!" he finally yelled.

He seemed speechless and none of us felt like venturing a word. We disassembled and packed our clarinets away, preparing to leave. When we were ready to, Howard growled from behind clenched teeth, "Sit down."

He produced three small chairs from behind his desk, then launched into a twenty-minute speech about *his* virtues as a musician. He rambled about his five degrees, rattled off the names of his clarinet teachers, named bands he'd been in — Ohio Wesleyan, Moosehart, the Conway Band, Goldman, Ernest Williams — and fraternities, honorary societies, this honor, that award, and on and on. I kept my mind focused on Dr. Hughes' advice, even as I knew that some of his degrees were honorary. Deep inside, I knew this lonely, bitter man would have given anything to play as well as any of the three of us. I recognized how he resented our height while tapping his elevator shoes on the floor. I saw that he still carried the loss of his wife to a better player inside him.

Finally, seeming satisfied, he stopped. Through all his put-downs, all his bragging, he had received nothing but complete support.

"I want each of you to take a lesson a week with Sergeant Dietz. He'll charge a few dollars. And you will pay for it out of your own pockets."

Silence hung in the air for a moment as the realization hit.

"Sir," I ventured. "Does that mean we're staying?"

"Yes," he offered as if this were a personal favor. "Study with Dietz and we'll see what happens down the road. Dismissed!"

Shigo and I headed out to the nearest restaurant, both to celebrate and to make up for skipping lunch. Whelan headed back to the dorm.

"You know, I think we finally convinced that old bastard," Shigo toasted. "I think from now on, he'll leave us alone."

We decided to phone Sgt. Dietz from the restaurant to arrange for our lessons.

"Haven't you guys studied enough? Langenus, the Pittsburgh Symphony, and the National Symphony?" he laughed. "I know, I know. I'll see you Wednesday at 1 p.m. in the band room."

* * *

We had a rehearsal the following day at 9 a.m. Everyone seemed calm, satisfied, and settled, with smiles all around. Word had gotten around that Botek, Shigo, and Whelan had weathered the storm. Even Howard was unusually cheerful. The music he chose for us said it all — Sousa's "Hail to the Chief" to open, followed by Wagner's "Riensi" and "Tannhäuser". He was obviously feeling secure in his power, and as such, picked heavily nationalistic selections that spoke of nothing *but* power.

We were midway through one of these triple-forte sagas when one of the older clarinet players stood up, carefully placed his horn on his chair, and quietly left the room.

Grinning, Shigo whispered, "Wagner moves both spirit and bowels."

I grinned back. Things were back to normal.

When the piece ended, Howard spotted the empty chair. He picked up the clarinet, sat down, and cued us to begin the next piece. He then put the clarinet to his mouth and joined in. There were nineteen other clarinets in the section, so I couldn't say what he sounded like. At least he didn't squeak or there was no way I'd have been able to hold it in.

Sergeant M, the band prankster, was known for constantly making fun of the Colonel behind his back. As the number ended, he pitched a small handful of pennies at Howard's feet, which landed at the back and side of his chair. We were all biting our lips — Shigo and I found this especially funny, considering our recent episode, but we also had the most to lose. We avoided eye contact with each other, lest it be too much to take and still hold the mirth in.

Howard took a moment when he heard the clinking, then turned to his side. Scooping up the pennies, he muttered, "Oh! I must be losing my change!"

That no one laughed is perhaps the best indicator of superior military discipline I have ever seen.

Leonard Feather

Born in the London suburb of Hampstead, England in 1914, Leonard Feather self-trained as a jazz pianist and clarinetist. He began writing about jazz and film while still in his teens. He also became a record producer, traveling back and forth between the U.K. and the U.S., and eventually moving to New York in 1939.

Feather's compositions have been recorded by artists as diverse as Mel Tormé and B.B. King, and he produced countless major jazz performers including Charlie Parker, Lester Young, and Dinah Washington, who had multiple hits with his compositions. At one time he even acted as publicist for Duke Ellington. Still, Feather's greatest mark in the world of jazz was as a writer.

The author of eleven books on jazz, from his first book *Inside Bebop* to The *Encyclopedia of Jazz*, Feather also wrote the liner notes for countless albums. He wrote for *Metronome, Esquire, Down Beat*, and *Jazz Times*. His writing became his primary claim to fame, with jazz aficionados following his work religiously. Easily the most influential writer on the form for most, if not all, of his career, Feather credited John Hammond with being the most important jazz critic. Hammond was definitely an inspiration to Feather, not only as a jazz writer, but as a civil-rights activist — a natural outreach for someone immersed in the world of jazz.

Feather's 'blindfold test' exposed as fallacy the idea that the race or gender of players was audible. As well as his civil-rights work, he championed the cause of women in jazz, introducing Dinah Washington and Sarah Vaughan to audiences.

Feather died in 1994, nine days after his 80th birthday.

Gene Quill

Born in Atlantic City, New Jersey in 1927, Gene Quill started playing alto saxophone as a child. By the time he was 13 he was playing professionally under Alex Bartha. He was also reported to have been a local Golden Gloves champion during this time, and fancied himself a fighter throughout his life.

Quill quickly became known for playing loud and clear, while still managing an aggressive and creative spark in his music. Through the late 1940s and 1950s he worked with dance bands led by Claude Thornhill, Miguelito Valdés, Shadow Wilson, Elliott Lawrence, Buddy DeFranco, Gene Krupa, and Bill Potts, among others. He alternated this with smaller groups, such as those of Mundell Lowe and Jimmy Knepper.

During the 1950s Quill garnered a reputation for playing at the forefront of bebop. Following in the footsteps of Charlie Parker, he was sometimes labelled an imitator, but only as one of the best.

In 1957 Quill started a New York-based combo with Phil Woods, the two having met at a jam at Teddy Charles' apartment. The unique format of two leading altos was popular and the duo became known for their 'battles' on alto sax, each driving the other to new heights. Working as 'Phil and Quill', the two were lauded for their hard bop stylings, and their recording sessions together reunited Quill with drummer Shadow Wilson. Quill and Woods also worked with Sahib Shihab and Hal Stein to create the seminal *Four Altos* album. Woods notes in his autobiography, *A Life in E-Flat*, that "Gene was the first lead alto to minimize the use of vibrato, hitting the note sans scoop, and only adding vibrato towards the end of the note." Woods would later compose a piece entitled "Quill", dedicated to Gene.

Quill's avant-garde approach to music led to his being tapped as the guest soloist on the 1958 television program *The Subject Is Jazz*, for an episode entitled "The Future of Jazz". In the early '60s he joined Gerry Mulligan's concert band, where Mulligan and Bob Brookmeyer were the primary soloists, limiting Quill's profile. In 1962 he moved on to tour with Benny Goodman, a relationship that didn't last long. The sixties saw Quill moving away from hard bop stylings to mellower tones and less complex rhythms. As his playing mellowed, though, he became more self-destructive, even punching out bandleader Johnny Richards during an opening-night concert. Through the late '60s Quill mostly freelanced, playing a lot of session work, though he also led a combo in New York on an on-again off-again basis.

Over the years he worked with numerous artists, including Jackie McLean, Jerry Wald, Art Mooney, Manny Albam, Tito Puente, Zoot Sims, Al Cohn, Quincy Jones, Chet Baker, and Buddy Rich.

In the 1970s, health issues cut his career short as a mugging left him with brain damage and a resulting partial paralysis of his right side. Quill died in his hometown of Atlantic City in 1988 a week before his 61st birthday, from complications following installation of a pacemaker.

Chapter 16 Straighten Up and Fly Right

December 28, 1951 — just after my 22nd birthday — marked my first anniversary with the Air Force. I had proven myself good enough to be a full-fledged member of the United States Air Force Band, and Howard had stopped 'testing' me as a new kid, along with Shigo and Whelan.

Tolerating Howard was far from my idea of fun, and I often considered the idea of moving to a field band at another base, but every time I would remember why I had fought to stay in Washington. The field bands worked longer hours, marched in parades, often had to wake and greet dignitaries in the middle of the night, and got stuck with more 'shit details', as military jargon would have it. In contrast, staying meant a chance at the annual tours to Europe, the Near East, and North Africa. Howard would have traveled to Hell if promised a large enough audience. Rumor had it he had accepted a week-long engagement in Reykjavik in February, and while things like winter in Iceland were daunting, they were still experiences worth having.

The overseas tours were resented by most of the married bandsmen, as they would have to leave their wives and families for the duration if they were selected to go. I was single, so hoping and praying to be selected. While closer quarters with the Colonel wasn't my idea of fun, I knew from our experience in Toronto that George was in seventh Heaven when conducting before foreign crowds — his face would beam, his eyes would sparkle, and as the crowd provided him with applause, he would become easier and easier to please, less demanding, and more considerate.

Howard was single and always on the lookout for women. We younger, unmarried bandsmen could find available girls virtually everywhere, with both our status in the military and as musicians acting as a draw. No such luck for George with his high rank and leadership position forcing him to rely on haphazard formal introductions. Prior to each trip, Sgt. M acted as our advance man, arranging everything, theoretically including Howard's female companionship.

C.I.A. intelligence briefed us, as they did before each tour — that Russian planes constantly refuel in Iceland. The group of us wondered if Howard had even heard of the Cold War, and why he would choose such a locale. Then again, understanding his motives was never something to be thought about for long — everything was simply assumed to be for his own greater glory. Howard recalls the trip being the result of a request by the U.S. State Department and an American military group known as the Iceland Defense Force.

We sat sideways and upright for thirteen hours in a large military cargo plane. Minutes away from the island, the pilot was told *not* to land because of thick fog, to remain in the air, circling. The rest of us, as was usually the case, were told nothing. It being a cargo plane, there was no intercom system and keeping us informed was not a consideration. A favorite expression in the military was 'Don't sweat the small stuff', which was applied to near everything. The 'small stuff' we didn't know at the time was that our fuel supply was running low. The next-closest place to land would be in Scotland, a few hundred miles due East, but circling used up enough fuel that we lost that option. We were between a rock and a hard place. After about twenty-five minutes of flying back and forth under the Northern Lights, the pilot was told that the fog had partially lifted and to land the plane *now*. None of us knew any of this at the time, and we just waited patiently in the cargo hold, wondering what was taking so long. I only learned the details years later in Howard's autobiography, *A Symphony in the Sky*.

We were all relieved to have Mother Earth beneath our feet again, without even knowing the details. There was no hot food on the plane and none of the sixty of us had eaten in hours. There was not going to be any quick resolution to that, however. Keflavik, the airport and its large adjoining military base were in the middle of a major flu epidemic, and had been declared off-limits to new arrivals like us. Food and rest would have to wait until after we were bused thirty miles to Reykjavik, over roads that resembled craters on the moon. As bad as the roads were, that's how beautiful the people of Iceland were. With blondes everywhere, sixty affection-starved men had our heads turning constantly.

DeFranco once described Tommy Dorsey as the 'Master of Show Biz'. I'd likewise grant Colonel Howard the title of '*Military* Master of Show Biz'.

Our tours included two ten-week runs through Europe, the Middle East, and North Africa, more than thirty one-nighters throughout five Western states, a concert in Worchester, Massachusetts with Tony Bennett (he looked pretty beat backstage, but he 'killed' during the show), another at Carnegie Hall, a few shows in Long Island which Langenus attended, presidential functions which Eisenhower attended, regular summer Sunday-night concerts on the Capitol steps, and Thursday-night concerts by the Watergate complex (pre-Nixon, of course). We were quite busy. The pay was good and girls were everywhere, with DC offering a five-to-one ratio of women to men. My contact with Phoebe had faded away bit by bit, and I was ready to play the field.

Most importantly, Howard was off our backs. Shigo and I — Whelan too — had all shaped up, without having to resort to shining shoes. It wasn't just in Howard's opinion, either. We had adjusted to being soldiers, even if in a rather unique role, and began to bear the image and weight that came with our position. We had also adjusted to dealing with Howard. We knew how to get by, even if not fully understanding his behavior. I recall once asking Dr. Hughes what it would take to fully understand Howard. The good doctor glibly replied, "I'd assume a four-year college degree, a four-year medical degree, and a three-year psychiatric residency would be a minimum requirement." Smiling, he told me not to even try. It was too complicated, he stated, and repeated that it should be Howard sitting in his office rather than me.

During this time I was living off-base in Arlington, Virginia, thirty minutes away. The benefits were numerous. As well as being out of sight, and therefore out of mind of the brass, it meant I only had to wear my uniform for daily rehearsals and public concerts, leading Shigo to call being part of the band "a civilian job in uniform". Weekends were completely free, from the end of Friday-morning rehearsal to Monday's 1 p.m. meeting. Alex could fly home to Pittsburgh and I could easily take a leisurely drive back to Pennsylvania, 195 miles away.

My 1941 Studebaker Dictator was a long, black, four-door metal monster. Its original engine had been replaced with a more powerful 1947 model, which you could hear coming a mile away. Arriving home one Friday evening I showed it to Dad, proudly telling him about the great deal I had got on it. From his body language, I could tell he was ashamed to even have it parked in front of his house.

"All right," he sighed. "Let me try it out. Let's see what it does on the mountain roads."

Off he went, white smoke belching from the exhaust pipe. Big clunkers always burn oil, after all. I started thinking I should have warned him about the brakes and hoped the master cylinder wouldn't give out. The previous week, while driving alongside the Capitol, my brakes had failed completely. I pushed my foot right to the floor, but nothing happened. Thank God for the emergency brake! Thankfully the repair job kept the brakes working for Dad. I don't know what he would have said had he known I'd had problems with them, but it wouldn't have been good He did have plenty of other things to criticize, with a number of expletives thrown in. I couldn't have cared less. This was *my* car paid for with *my* money and, regardless of what he said or thought, that was enough to be proud of.

To recover from the ride, not that he needed the excuse, he opened a bottle of Yuengling and poured himself a shot of his favorite brandy, Christian Brothers. We would joke at home that Dad, as a good Catholic, felt obliged to drink that brand by virtue of the name. The shot went down in a gulp, with the beer not lasting much longer.

"Come look in the garage," he beckoned. "Jo, who trades in *her* car every two years, just bought a brand-new 1952 Buick coupe."

I balked, immediately feeling defensive. He'd seen fit to note that Jo not only had a new car, but that she kept her cars new by trading up. I thought the point of showing me her car was simply to rub in the deficiencies of mine.

"Come on," he pleaded. "She's a beauty."

She was. Showroom clean and with barely fifteen miles on the odometer, Jo's new find put mine to shame. I was uncomfortable and, thinking this would be the starting point of a lecture on choosing a good car, I went in with a good offence.

"Nothing was wrong with her 1950 Super," I protested. "Didn't it have less than 20,000 miles on it? Why did she trade it in?"

"She didn't," my father grinned conspiratorially. "Instead, she stored it in the basement of Cal's garage, thinking maybe you'd be interested."

He gave that a moment to sink in before adding, "She's asking $1800."

"Pop," I sighed, "I earn $75 a month and —"

"I'll lend you the money," he interrupted. "You can pay me back, little by little, over time."

I rolled back to Washington and Bolling Field on Monday morning in the green-and-black Buick Super two-door coupe, looking smart in my uniform, but it isn't only the clothes that make the man. The A.P. (Air Police, equivalent to the Army's Military Police) on duty quickly scanned the car and, seeing no military sticker to identify me as an officer or enlisted man, he played it safe. Considering the car, he must have presumed me an officer, and saluted me first. I returned the salute, and his jaw dropped as my arm and its lone stripe came into view.

"Airman," he sputtered, "what in the hell did you do to end up with a swanky car like this? Is the shift three-in-the-tree? What's the horsepower? Can I take a look under the hood? Military inspection."

He grinned at the last, and I lifted the hood so he could check out the engine. I had been enjoying the car, but only at this point did it really occur to me that the car was owed to Dad teaching us to settle for nothing but the best. Maybe he wasn't such a bad guy after all.

With the Iceland trip behind me, a home off-base, and my ultra-smart Buick at my disposal, the rest of my hitch seemed like it would be a breeze. There were still two ten-week European tours yet to come as well as a thirty-day Western tour, but that would be it. In-between, I would have time to play and to plan for my life after the Air Force.

* * *

In April of 1952 Howard began to hint about our summer tour abroad, with sixty of us to go. Reactions were mixed. It was a given that anyone in the Singing Sergeants would be included but, past that, nothing was certain. I was single and couldn't wait for the opportunity, but many of the old-timers, married or not, wanted to stay home. As in any large group of men, a few of the married lifers, or career men, would cheat on their wives once on the road. On one of our bus trips between two German cities, Sgt. X (his name remains a secret, even to me) didn't want to leave his paramour behind, and so brought her aboard. No one said a word. Howard was on the bus in front of ours, but, considering his activities, I didn't know if even he would comment. I wondered if this was really happening. Sgt. X was getting laid and no one was commenting.

We were driving through a vast, uninhabited wasteland when a voice rang out, "Piss call, piss call, time to piss!"

European men don't need a private bathroom. They'll urinate at any time and place. Just turn your back, yank 'it' out, and go. After all, when in Rome . . . This might not have been an issue on a bus full of men, but I wondered how this pack of male chauvinists would handle our stowaway fräulein's need to relieve herself. All the men got off the bus and re-boarded, mission accomplished. She stood up, slung her long hair back over her shoulder, and slowly headed out into the adjoining barren field — no trees to hide behind, no bushes, no cover whatsoever. Finally, with no other alternative, she turned her back, lowered her panties, and squatted. A loud chorus of catcalls, whistles, and comments better left unmentioned burbled forth from the bus. One of the younger members, sitting beside me, smiled, "Boys will be boys." He reminded me that rank had its privileges, and Sgt. X's five stripes (he was a Technical Sergeant) coupled with the fact that he played an instrument harder to replace than a clarinet gave him the leeway to bring his *fräulein* aboard, and no such privilege extended to either of us. He also sang in the Singing Sergeants. It couldn't hurt that Sgt. X could repair anything you gave him, and likely fixed things around Howard's home.

There was a bond between the younger members of the band. We knew not to trust any of the older, career-minded guys who could lift themselves up by dragging you down. If you said the wrong thing, it was as likely as not that they would tattle to Big Brother. We knew not to room with them when we were staying in hotels. One kid, while playing a show in Thule, Greenland, shared a room with one of the careerists. Semi-asleep, he fell victim to a barrage of questions, agreeing that the Air Force sucked, the food was bad, and that Howard couldn't conduct worth a shit. About two weeks later, Howard informed him he was being shipped back to Greenland, telling him we needed fine musicians like him there. Obviously, we all knew better — Howard never let go of anyone who he considered a fine musician unless he felt they weren't respectful of his power and privilege. He went on about the virtues of Greenland, noting the P.X. was big and well-stocked, talking about the beautiful Danish girls. He recalled that he had begun his own military musical career there, before they had a band, so he had ordered forty plastic tonettes (small flutes) and organized a small rag-tag orchestra. The kid saluted and returned to the barracks where he let loose.

"That fuckin' S.O.B.!" he shouted. "I'd like to shove his tonette you-know-where! *He* should go back to Thule — I'm sure they hate him there too!"

The Colonel also abruptly dismissed another member, this time a seven-year veteran, married with a child. At the intermission of our Monday-afternoon rehearsal, Howard sternly scanned the assembly. Shigo whispered to me, "Here we go again!" Howard picked out a French-horn player in the back row with his eyes, but didn't address him directly.

"As you all know, Warrant Officer Z [the name escapes me] took my place on the podium a few weeks back when I had business out of town. He is an excellent officer and a fine conductor. Rumor has it that a few of you dislike his handling of certain pieces, Bach in particular."

It was true. Warrant Officer Z had chimed out, "more metronomic, metronomic, keep Bach strict, in the style of Bach," throughout rehearsal. Almost as one, our eyes had rolled and our teeth had gritted.

Howard continued, "His strictness was nothing to laugh at and the cat-calls and guffaws from one of you was strictly unprofessional. He deserves an apology.

"However, something more serious has been going on. Each night for the last few weeks, about 4 a.m., someone phones him at home, waking him up. The caller then quickly hangs up without saying a word. I secured the services of the F.B.I. and I now know for sure who exactly the culprit is."

With that, he pointed a long finger at the first-chair French-horn player, who I'll call Sgt. A.

"You, Sgt. A, have been doing this. I'm giving you two weeks to gather your things. You're being permanently sent to the band at Lowrey Air Force Base in Colorado."

The Sergeant's face reddened and his eyes welled up. He protested, "But sir, I just purchased a house for my family, my wife and child. Sir, I . . ."

Howard stopped him, barking, "It's Colorado for you and that's *it!* Goodbye!"

The rest of intermission was a much-needed respite. No one wanted to be facing Howard. Shigo offered that maybe Dr. Hughes could give Sgt. Z advice on handling Howard like he'd given me, but we both knew Howard wouldn't go back on his decision after announcing it in front of the band. We also talked about the upcoming European tour — I would be going, but Shigo wouldn't. He warned me to be careful as he'd heard rumors about band members reselling P.X. cigarettes and getting black market prices for them. I had to be careful about who I trusted.

* * *

Sgt. Ed Grace, who was in charge of all paperwork, was looking for men to volunteer to leave for Europe a few days early. Apparently there wasn't room for all of us on the plane assigned to fly the band. A few of us would have to leave early on the 'Blue Plate Special', a four-engine Constellation usually used to fly Washington dignitaries and military officers. Those who volunteered would have a couple of days free to sightsee in Wiesbaden, our first German stop. My hand rose immediately, ignoring the voice in the back of my head reminding me never to volunteer. This was a deal I just couldn't pass up — Europe without the maddening mob of neurotic, tattle-tale prima donnas. *Wunderbar!*

The older guys stayed out of it, having wives and families they would have to inform first, and four friends were selected alongside me to take the early flight. A few nights later, the five of us early birds boarded. It was great! Full-size reclining seats were an unimaginable luxury we hadn't expected. We were used to being strapped sideways against the wall of the plane into cramped bucket seats, with our parachutes offering the only back support. Often we would fly at low altitudes with the huge back bay doors left wide open.

I never had to jump, but one stormy Sunday night we were over Paris heading for a landing at Orley Field. Suddenly lightning struck the plane's left wing, which I was sitting directly over. A thin ball of fire danced brazenly from one edge of the wing to the other. No alarm sounded, and captain, co-pilot, and others said nothing from behind the closed cockpit door. My friend Zmuda, sitting beside me shouted out, "Jesus Christ!" I began praying *not* to hear the signal alarm that meant we had to bail out. If it went off, I would have crapped in my pants. Ten minutes later, we landed safely.

When the pilot left the cockpit, I asked about the lightning.

"Oh, we see that all the time," he said calmly. "Best not to sweat the small stuff."

Zmuda pulled me aside to say, "That slap-happy flyboy! That's okay for him to say. He doesn't need a change of underwear."

The seats on a Constellation all face the rear of the plane, to minimize impact in case of a crash. I had an aisle seat about fourteen rows from the rear. Seated next to me was a young second lieutenant, and I realized that I wouldn't have the company of my four buddies through the flight. I talked a bit with the lieutenant, we ate a hot dinner (no cold box lunch!), smoked some cigarettes, and I went to sleep, waking frequently. Flying overseas was not yet a comfortable experience for me and I began to immerse myself in my Jacobson techniques, maintaining a trance-like state for hours. The lieutenant probably thought I was avoiding him, and maybe at some level, I was. I was used to not trusting anyone with rank, after all.

The flight wasn't direct, and we landed in the Azores, a Portuguese protectorate located in the Atlantic Ocean 900 miles west of that country. We spent the night, shopped at their duty-free store, refueled, and took off again for Germany. The barracks at Wiesbaden were large stone buildings with high ceilings and wide, sturdy staircases. They looked familiar and I wondered where I had seen something similar. The next morning I was talking to the German maid as she mopped our latrine. She told me that we were in the same barracks that Nazi soldiers had used some years back. She started reminiscing, talking about cleaning for Herr someone or other. I stopped her, having gotten the point.

Three of my buddies walked in and invited me to go out and sample some of the world-famous German beer. I was more than ready to go, beer or not. We hailed a cab, and with a map and English/German dictionary, made our way to one of Wiesbaden's most popular watering holes. The beer on tap came in the percentage of your choice: four, five, up past ten. I decided to try the 6%.

From there we went to the P.X., and what I saw floored me. It was like Macy's, Sears and Roebuck, Gimbels, Wanamaker's, and Tiffany's all under one roof. They had everything you could imagine — German cameras, Swiss watches, French perfumes, Hummel figurines, Rosenthal china, jellies, jams — all at rock-bottom prices and tax-free. Every brand of American cigarette was available, as well as British ones, for $1 a carton, though we were rationed to one carton a week. They sold easily on the black market for $3-4 each. We were allowed forty-ounce bottles of Canadian whiskey once a week for $2.50 each — these would sell on the black market for $15. Neither U.S. dollars nor German Deutschmarks were accepted at the P.X., only military scrip. We all referred to these undersized bills as 'Monopoly money'. Obviously, the purpose was to prevent civilians from buying up what was meant for armed forces personnel — other than on the black market, civilians would be unable to obtain scrip. I never sold my scrip, though I always sold my cigarettes, with the profit margin a good incentive to quit smoking. I would also exchange my greenbacks for a local currency.

Every base had a post office. Gifts could be easily packaged and delivered free as far as New York City, even large wooden crates — mailing costs to anywhere in the States would be the same as the cost of mailing from Manhattan. Each package was accompanied by a customs card listing the parcel's contents, which had to be signed by an officer. Any rank would do, from warrant officer on up. My mother, three sisters, an aunt, and a few girlfriends, as well as some male relatives and friends, all deserved gifts and I quickly wrote home asking my mother to send $100 and noting possible gifts like binoculars or fishing equipment for my father and brother Francis. I asked for my sisters to name their favorite French perfumes.

Our stay in Wiesbaden was the longest stop on our tour, and the reason was simple — Howard loved the place. The band would be staying there six days and, as the early group, we had an extra two days on top of that. When the rest of the band arrived, the five of us, having served as advance scouts, filled them in on all the amenities. We had one week in Wiesbaden, and whenever Howard was out of sight we treated it like a vacation. Howard was busy himself, making his rounds. He would brag about the box seat they would reserve for him at the Wiesbaden Opera — the same one that Hitler had used. I had enough time to get gifts for everyone and send them off home.

Having grown up in a household with a retail store attached, I could spot a bargain a mile away. Further, I knew how to shop — not only what to look for in merchandise, but how to get wholesale pricing. Thus I became the official shopper for a number of bandsmen, those who were too lazy or unskilled to shop for themselves, adding a 'shopper's fee' of ten percent, sometimes fifteen depending on the item, to the actual price.

Wiesbaden's P.X. had an unbelievable selection of beautiful Swiss watches. On what must have been my fourth or fifth day of examining watches, I made a date with Gerta, the attractive saleslady. She was single, around my age, and Czech. Since her German was fluent, she could make up for my failings in that area and show me around the city. Sometime after our second date, over some excellent Wiener schnitzel and strong local beer, she confessed that she had something to reveal. I was wondering what it could be — was she married? Was I in trouble? Was she?

"Your Colonel," she confided, "is dating my best girlfriend."

"What?" I sputtered. "Say that again."

"I said your Colonel Howard is dating my best girlfriend."

"Please," I begged, "forget you told me that. Forget you said it. I don't want to know it. And please — don't mention my name to her! Or to anyone else, in fact. Please, keep our relationship secret. You must promise me you won't mention a thing."

Looking back, I must have seemed crazy or just rude beyond belief. Who tells a woman to keep their relationship secret on their second date? But Gerta must have heard stories about Howard, and immediately understood, if she hadn't already.

"I've told no one about us," she assured me, taking my hand. "You will remain my cherished secret. Please do not worry.

"I wouldn't worry so much about that Colonel of yours, anyway. He's no man. My friend told me that he can hardly get it up."

"Please stop!" I cried out.

We agreed never to discuss the subject again. Later I was in the men's room cleaning off the beer I had spilled on my tie. As I did I warned my reflection, "Be careful, young man, or your first week in Germany could be your last."

After that week we were on the road. When we weren't traveling shorter distances in a private bus, we had three large C119 planes assigned to us, cargo planes of the type I had avoided coming in on. Two would transport sixty men while the third carried our cargo, including instruments. We were each allowed one big B4 bag, which could weigh up to forty-four pounds. On the road we lacked the time to mail gifts, so the bags were getting bigger and bulging with booty. Forty-ounce bottles of V.O., perfume bottles, and such were beginning to weigh me down and I was at my limit, as were many others. That meant no more gifts — *if* you followed the rules.

One afternoon, the aircraft were lined up. Each took off in close order, the large back doors wide open. I was sitting strapped in securely in the last seat, my camera at the ready. As our plane began roaring down the field, the plane leaving before us was lifting up its wheels, just having achieved flight. A good-sized cardboard crate came flying through the air and rolling across the tarmac. We were close enough that we could see in large, bright-red letters, 'V.O.' Someone was certainly going to be sore about that.

The C119 was nicknamed 'The Flying Boxcar' and, flying in it, there was nothing to do but think. That crate got my gears in motion. Joe, a heavyset older trumpet player, and Red, the bass drummer, would both always volunteer to set up and tear down our equipment. As both sang with the Singing Sergeants, neither needed the extra job, so why would they volunteer for it? I began to think there was something more going on. My suspicions were confirmed when, a bit later in the tour, I noticed Joe moving some band equipment and adding a set of golf clubs to it. After that, I noticed him sneaking a very large wooden crate out of a P.X. in Hamburg. Printed clearly on the side was 'Rosenthal China'. I knew I needed to talk to Joe.

Sgt. Dietz had left not long before our tour and his replacement as first-chair clarinetist was anything but friendly. Sgt. M was also anything but professional — he would turn to me with a minute to go before a solo and only then cue me that I was to play it, turning to me and mumbling, "You take it." While this would happen more often than not, the uncertainty was always there. A true professional always assigns solos and gives a full rundown *before* the show. I was left at the last minute, literally, to improvise twenty-four bars. Sgt. M was an anal passive-aggressive personality who couldn't let go of anything until the very last moment — it kept everyone in the clarinet section focused on him, waiting to know what we were doing. Joe pulled me aside one day to commiserate and let me know in no uncertain terms that he knew I played jazz better than Sgt. M. He asked me to play in his jazz combo, which played whenever there was a call for some nightclub-style jazz. Joe was a technical sergeant with a perfect trumpeter's build — short and stocky with a wide chest. A New Yorker, he was street-wise and, having been in the band for six years, he knew how to play not only his horn but both ends against the middle. We had bonded as players, and I knew I could trust him.

I got the front desk clerk at our hotel to give me Joe's room number and

I found him alone there, his roommate having gone out to do some sight-seeing. A bit fat and lazy, Joe moved slowly with only two exceptions: where money and music were concerned. I knew this well, having seen him play both trumpet and poker. I told Joe that I needed to buy a lot of gifts, including a Besson trumpet for my buddy Reuben. I asked if Joe would go with me to the factory in Paris when we played there and help me pick one out. I told him Reuben would pay $25 for his time and trouble. I started asking how I could get the horn and my other purchases back home and he stopped me.

"Relax, I get it," he smiled. "You want some storage space aboard the cargo C119."

I didn't have to mention that I knew about all sorts of extras Joe and Red were taking back — golf clubs, cases of booze, etc. He told me he'd get me a tall wooden crate with a padlock and keys, about five feet high and eighteen inches square. He told me that I could pack the gifts as well as the piles of cigarettes I'd been saving up with some other guys. He neatly clued me in that he was as aware of my scam as I was of his, even noting the prices I bought and sold at. He assured me he didn't want a cut, only $15 for the crate. My name wouldn't be on the crate; it would be labeled 'SPARE AIRPLANE PARTS — PROPERTY OF THE U.S.A.F.'. I would be able to add or remove contents before or after any concert.

After he went through the entire scenario, he asked me if I understood: "*Capische?*"

I asked, "Well, all but one thing. What happens in DC when the Customs man examines all our booty?"

"Listen, Botek," he explained, "we're traveling with about sixty G.I.s. Most of them don't buy nothin' for the ol' lady. Maybe they get a few trinkets for the kids. What you buy in excess, they make up for in their frugality. Some of us buy lots, but others never shop. It all evens out."

We talked about music for a while, exchanging praise for recent solos and I left, happy. Later, though, I began to worry what would happen if Col. Howard found out. Maybe he already knew and just didn't care. Finally, I decided not to worry — it wasn't as if I was smuggling gold or guns. After I'd thought it through for a while, I was reassured things would be fine. Enough that my thoughts began going in the other direction. I slipped Joe the $15 at breakfast. He just said "Thanks," acting like it was nothing special. I had one new question for him.

"Next summer, we'll be doing the same tour," I ventured. "And I heard that cigarettes can sell in Beirut for double what we sell them for in Europe. Would you rent me *two* crates if I need it?"

"No sweat," he assured me. "But now *I* need a favor. On Tuesday we'll be in Paris and a few of us need French francs in exchange for our dollars. There's a certain bistro in the center of the city . . ."

When we got to Paris, I made my way to the bistro on the Metro with

$300 from Joe and five others, following the instructions Joe had given to the letter. There was a man selling neckties in front of the bistro, the ties spread out on a large black umbrella. I greeted him with the French phrase I was told to, then bought a tie. As Joe instructed, only after that did I invite him into the bistro for a drink. He closed up the umbrella and walked in with me. I sat down and one of the bartenders came over and sat down beside me. I asked today's rate. Joe had told me that he would start low and I had to start much higher, and in the end, settle for fifteen percent more than the legal military bank rate. After we exchanged the money, exactly as Joe said, he offered me a second drink. I refused it, also exactly as Joe told me.

Joe had warned me to do everything to the letter, as the Paris *gendarmes*, or police, were quite on the mark. Such black market money exchanges were quite standard among military personnel. A friend of Joe's, knowing that the rate was twenty percent higher in Tangiers, was part of a number of troops who gathered together $15,000 for exchange. They selected a lieutenant to take the train there from Northern France and make the exchange — he never returned, going A.W.O.L. with the money and leaving about 250 soldiers bitchy, broke, and ready to kill.

Leaving the bistro, I felt like I'd been in a spy movie. I took a cab and spent about ten minutes looking at tourist attractions, which was also part of the instructions. I guess I needed to look normal instead of rushing home from the bistro. Still, the time in the cab felt more normal and I relaxed. Finally I got the cabbie to let me out at a Metro station and returned to base. With francs in hand, we had five days in Paris. I got the trumpet for Reuben and snagged a second clarinet for myself for $100 at the Buffet factory in Paris.

At last our tour was over, and I was beat. There had only been three full days off in the whole ten weeks, and every spare second was spent shopping and amassing gifts. When we landed in DC, my B4 bag was bulging; the Customs man stopped rooting through it only when finding some dirty socks and underwear — usually the men washed their shorts nightly, by leaving them on when they took a shower! The Customs guy was friendly and seemed to treat the inspection as a formality, even allowing me two forty-ounce bottles of Canadian whiskey.

"Welcome home, son," he told me when he was done. "I understand you've been gone ten weeks!"

Still, I was left wondering where the cargo had gone. I found out that rumor had it that the cargo had been assigned to another plane for the trans-Atlantic leg of the trip and would only arrive around 5 a.m., so I went home and went to bed.

I waited until 3:30 the following afternoon to call Joe. Joe told me I could pick up my crate the next day. It would be a Sunday and, since no one would be in the rehearsal room, he would leave it there for me.

Joe told me they arrived at quarter past five that morning and had to wait for the Customs man to wake up and come over. He'd come aboard and looked over the manifest, which had all our booty itemized but spread out among the sixty men who were on the tour. After a few minutes the Customs man said, "The next time you get me out of bed for a routine bunch of stuff like this, I'll kill you."

Chapter 17
I've Got the World On A String

December 1953 meant just one more year to serve of my four-year hitch. However, all that was needed to get out was a formal request. With the Korean War over, too many men were left in uniform. My friends Jimmy and Ronnie Odrich decided to take the 'early out'. Both would return to Queens to continue their study of dentistry. Ronnie now has a Park Avenue periodontics practice and is a professor of dentistry at Columbia University. Since 1968 he's faithfully watched over my teeth and completely eradicated the almost daily toothaches of my small-town childhood.

Me, I had attained the rank of staff sergeant and the accompanying four stripes, I was being paid to live off-base, and I was the leader of a five-piece jazz group with two paying gigs per week. With all that, plus the upcoming European tour for the year, I thought it would be silly to give it up all up, so I decided to stay on. Most of the other bandsmen felt the same way, though we did lose a few.

After one rehearsal B.R., one of the career-minded clarinetists, invited me over to his house for supper, noting his wife would be out of town. After an excellent supper, he launched into a series of questions. Did I fish? Was I familiar with Alcock fish hooks? I'd never heard of them, so he pulled out a fishing magazine to show me a picture. He told me they were made in an English town where our band would be giving a concert that summer. The wholesale factory price there was about 1¢ each. In the U.S., the retail price was 23¢ each and wholesale was 15¢. We could order 1,500, hide them in a shoebox through the tour, then sell them when we returned. A quick check by phone found buyers in Lansford, and I agreed. We 'founded' the B and S Sporting Shop, laughing as we did, seeing that it was all B.S. The next day he had personalized stationery and business cards printed and sent out a letter to the English company.

I was making my own preparations. I borrowed $600 from Dad to supplement the few hundred I'd managed to save. My mother had a seamstress friend make me a money belt with three zippered compartments. Both parents understood the opportunity awaiting in the nineteen countries I would be visiting. I readied a wide assortment of bills: lots of ones, many fives and tens, some twenties, and a few fifties and hundreds. Ones were the most useful, with taxi drivers often taking a single U.S. dollar in lieu of a fare worth much more. Likewise, items like underwear, shirts, and socks could be bought much cheaper with American dollars, and sometimes cigarettes.

Finally in June we left for the tour of Europe. I hate to shop in general, but seeing the unbelievable bargains, having a U.S. post office on every base and cheap mailing costs home, and knowing I had a large wooden crate to store whatever I wanted — well, this was enough to keep me in the stores every spare moment I had. Band members who were too lazy to shop themselves or just didn't know how to barter were giving me lists of items to buy for them, and I did, adding a percentage for my trouble. They'd be happy and I ended up with even more money to spend.

My money belt fit fairly tight around my waist and was kept out of sight, under my clothes. I even slept with it on, taking it off only to shower but watching it like a hawk even then.

We performed every night as well as the occasional matinée. One day would be London, the next Paris. We'd be in Bordeaux, then find ourselves in Copenhagen. The selections however were *always* the same. We knew them so well that we could probably have played them with our eyes closed. It became so familiar, it didn't feel like work.

About halfway through the tour my wooden crate was half-full. There were at least ten bottles of expensive French perfume, a few forty-ounce bottles of Canadian whiskey, a bottle of fifty-year-old cognac, men's and ladies' wristwatches, Zeiss binoculars and Hummel figurines from Germany, lambskin sweaters from England, woolen socks from Austria, hand-carved wooden statues from Copenhagen, and countless other small items.

There were, however, no fish hooks. My conscience got the best of me, or maybe it was more my sense of self-preservation. The other items didn't contravene any military regulations, but 1,500 fish hooks looked, well, fishy. I phoned the Alcock company and told them it was impossible for me to visit England at this time and that I would maybe come by next summer. A lie, of course — we gave a concert just a stone's throw away from the factory the next day.

* * *

What sticks out most in my mind was the concert in Berlin. We spent the day visiting the Berlin Wall and seeing East Berlin with Stalin's tin soldiers posturing and parading — and I ran an errand I'll recount separately. When we got to the Third Reich's prize Olympic Stadium, just before 8 p.m., there was no sign of Howard. We readied ourselves to go on without him, all knowing that it would not hamper us in any way. The playlist was set, and all we had to do was play what had already become as familiar as a comfy couch. As we were about to begin, a helicopter appeared overhead, gleaming in the last light of dusk. We held off to let it pass, but instead it moved towards us, landing directly in front of us. Out jumped Colonel Howard in full dress uniform and even a large cape — definitely not military issue. His baton a-waving, he cued us to launch into Sousa's "Stars and Stripes Forever". The crowd, well over 125,000 strong, went wild. They were yelling, screaming, whistling, stamping their feet, and holding up thousands of little candles shimmering in the darkness. Howard's spectacle had a few band members struggling to play through their laughter.

Previously, on arrival in Berlin, I'd had a specific errand in mind. We went directly from Tempelhof airfield to our hotel, where I threw my gear across the bed and ran immediately outside to find a taxi. I had the name and address of a man who made excellent clarinet reeds. He had befriended an American reed-maker I knew in Washington, who advised me to seek him out the instant I got to Berlin. I was told that I would probably get a few samples, but the big attraction was that the man had invented a machine, about the size of a carton of cigarettes, which would produce reeds. With the help of a phrasebook, I gave the address to the cab driver and fifteen minutes later I was there.

The gentleman, whose name I forget, invited me in and introduced me to his wife and daughter. They served me coffee, tea, and strudel. I gave them a few packs of Winstons, usable as currency even if none of them smoked. He took me in to show me his small factory and after a quick tour, presented me with one of his machines. I reached for my wallet but he stopped me, telling me that it was a gift. I was shocked. I offered him a few packs of Marlboros which he *did* accept, but countered with a large bag of reeds.

"Try these ready-made ones when you get home," he urged. "But, can I ask, do you have any large sticks of cane to begin your own production?"

I didn't, and on hearing that, he handed me a full box of blanks, weighing about twenty-five pounds. Again, it was a gift! He packaged everything together neatly for me, then offered me more strudel and some Schnapps. Overwhelmed by his generosity, I unzipped my cloth bag and forced loose a cigar box-sized container full of Hershey chocolates, explaining that it was from my home state, Pennsylvania, and insisting he take it. I said my farewells and they called for a taxi.

My booty sitting in the back seat, I climbed into the front and, still beaming, said, "Take me to my hotel!"

"*Ja*," he answered. "Which one?"

I was stunned! I had checked in and run out so quickly that I forgot to take down the name of the hotel! The driver was cool about it, graciously driving me to five or six different hotels before stopping. He quizzed me for any specifics I could remember. I remembered long hallways like bowling alleys, a red-brick colonial style, and that it was very close to the railroad tracks. He spun his Volkswagen around in the opposite direction and within minutes we were at the Bahnhof Hotel.

I happily paid the fare on the meter and added a large tip but he refused any gratuity, protesting that he had had fun so it was unnecessary. I reached into my bag and pulled out four packs of Chesterfields and his eyes lit up. He couldn't thank me enough. Insisting on helping me, he even carried my box right to my room.

Immediately I sat down and phoned Joe. I told him to come over to my room and to come alone. He did and I explained about the box.

"Wow!" he said, impressed. He joked, "Find one for me full of trumpet mouthpieces."

He agreed to transport it, but we needed a new crate. The box it was in had German printed all over it and was sure to alert Customs. I handed him $5 and it was a done deal. I just had to repack it and have it ready to go by 8 a.m. when the cargo would be packed away.

It was 7 p.m. and I boarded the Air Force bus which was waiting to take us to the 8 p.m. concert. The driver, an airman second-class named Holt, was quite friendly. We chatted and I found out he was from Batavia, NY, near Rochester, which immediately became a bonding point between us. I decided I trusted him enough to explain the situation.

"Holt," I asked, "I need a crate and need it tonight — do you know where I could get one?"

"Hmm," he pondered. "Crates are pretty scarce on this base. The library and the post office need them. Why don't you use a duffel bag? It's American and about the right size."

"Where do I buy one?" I asked.

"You can't," he replied. "They're issued to us. But I'll sell you mine if you like."

We agreed on $7 for the bag and that he would deliver it to me following the concert. About an hour after the concert with Howard's entrance stunt Holt knocked on my hotel room door, duffel bag in one hand and a can of white paint and stencils in the other.

"We can blot out my name on the bag," he explained. "Then we'll stencil yours onto it."

I told him that wasn't necessary, that he could simply print 'PROPERTY OF THE U.S.A.F.' on it. He did a great job and the bag was looking quite official and ready for the cargo plane inside a half-hour. I offered him another $10 for his time, but he refused, saying it was free for the sake of good ol' Rochester. Smiling, I pulled out a forty-ounce bottle of Canadian Club and said, "Fine, but take this. And it's my turn to refuse, and I refuse to allow you to say no, or even to sample it with you. You're a hell of a nice guy, but we fly out in the morning, after all."

* * *

We touched down in Garmisch in Bavaria, right by the Austrian border, about a half-hour past noon. Our hotel was the Green Arrow, managed by the U.S. military as an R&R stop for all European service personnel. It was huge, spotless, and elegant. Rumor had it that Adolf Hitler wrote part of *Mein Kampf* there. Despite it being our R&R stop, we were to play a matinée show for the sake of the R&R of *other* military personnel there. That left us just thirty minutes to eat and fifteen minutes to prepare, so there was no time to select or request a roommate. I ended up sharing a room with three older career men, the worst mismatch to date. The room was big and beautiful with five beds and two full bathrooms, but I was crestfallen that I would have to share it with these nit-picking brown-nosing sons of bitches. Luckily my worries were soon over. The other roommates filed into the room, dropped their luggage in a corner and one told me, "Right after this concert, we're all leaving for Munich. We'll be gone for three days, so Botek, it's all yours. Enjoy yourself."

The concert was held within walking distance of the hotel, at the base of a ski-jump area. It was July, so there was just bare cement and lots of green grass. Locals were invited to come to the show and they attended in droves, as did the service personnel staying at the hotel. Seeing the exceptionally large and unexpected crowd that turned out for an afternoon show, Col. Howard decided to reward them with an extra-long performance. The more they clapped and stamped their feet, the more we played.

Garmisch was more of a town than a city. I'd guess the population at the time was maybe 15,000, and it reminded me of quaint Pennsylvania Dutch farm towns. It was sleepy, slow-moving, and somewhat short of sophisticated. The locals were unpretentious, everyday, common folk dressed in lederhosen, soft cloth hats with long feathers, and huge clodhopper shoes. It was definitely a fine place for R&R, a respite from the larger cities I'd been running all over for weeks. Likewise for them, we were a respite from the quiet life and they showed their appreciation.

After about ninety minutes, though, the summer heat was getting to all of us and Howard announced our final long selection, "At the Gremlins' Ball", a fast, catchy piece of American jazz. Halfway through, I got the signal to play the clarinet solo. I had to leave my seat, walk to the front of the stage, and improvise for twenty-four measures. As I played, I noticed a young German boy in some khaki Boy Scout-type uniform creeping up towards me, finally stopping directly underneath me. He started taking pictures of me with a Kodak Retina camera with a German Schneider lens —

the exact same one I owned. The audience applauded wildly as I wrapped up. We finished with "Stars and Stripes Forever" and the German national anthem. Our band was one of the first to play the German anthem — it had been verboten following World War II, but times had changed and it was okay again.

People were beginning to leave and I was putting my clarinet away when the young boy approached me again.

"Son, do you speak English? *Sprechen sie Englisch*?" I asked.

He told me he spoke a little English. His name was Dieter. I told him I had the same camera, and he sheepishly offered that he hoped I didn't mind his taking my photo, but he had really enjoyed my jazz. I thanked him, telling him that I didn't mind in the least. I only wished he could have taken some pictures with *my* Retina, since I had never gotten to see how I look at the microphone. I offered him a few Deutschmarks to send me some photos when they were developed and printed. He took my name and address, but refused any money.

The day was still young, so I took a taxi into the city center where I found a store that made men's suede jackets. I went in and inquired about prices and turnaround. They would be able to deliver in two to three days, plenty of time for me to take one home with me. I bartered for a good price in American cigarettes, settling on twelve cartons. We also agreed that I would return the next day for second measurements and with payment.

Leaving the store, I saw a small German marching band parading down the street. I stopped to listen and met three very attractive girls who had been cycling down the street, but pulled their bikes over to listen. They stood out from the crowd and I suspected they were American, not German. I was right — they were from Indiana on a bike trip through Southern Germany. They were staying in a run-down pension and hadn't had a decent bath or a good night's sleep in days. I suggested they come back to the hotel with me and shower, then they could be my guests for supper. They talked it over quickly and agreed. We started talking about how to get the four of us and three bicycles back to the hotel. A German taxi driver overheard and offered to drive us to the hotel with the bicycles on the roof, and we took him up on the offer.

I left the girls alone to shower, as I had promised. I only peeked in around supper time and the girls were sparkling clean and spread out through the room, enjoying the space and the amenities. I announced it was chow time and they followed me downstairs. In the dining room, I flagged two of the band members to join us.

Halfway through the meal, though, the maître d' appeared behind my chair.

"Are you Staff Sergeant Botek?" he inquired.

I told him I was.

"There is someone at the front door to see you," he told me.

I had no idea who it could be, but thought it must be bad news and the end of the party. The maître d' took me to the door, and to my surprise, there in the darkness was Dieter, the young German kid with the camera, and two of his friends. He had taken the trouble to rush his film to some fast developer so that he could present the photos to me mere hours later. I was touched.

"Please," I urged, "come in and sit down."

The maître d' stepped forward, emphatically announcing, "Sergeant, no Germans are allowed inside."

I felt deflated. These young kids were such wholesome individuals and it seemed unfair, but I knew better than to disobey military regulations so I stepped outside instead. I offered to pay Dieter in Deutschmarks, but he refused. I asked where he was staying and got the address so I could send him a gift. I apologized for the hotel's rigid rules and we chatted a bit before he and his friends disappeared into the night. It was one of the nicest moments of the entire tour.

Not that I would let that stop me from getting back to the table and the girls from Indiana. I returned to find a round of good German beer had been ordered, and we sat and talked for some time. Suddenly one of the girls got a thoughtful look on her face and inquired about the time. One of the bandsmen told her it was almost nine o'clock.

"Oh no!" she cried, her face falling.

One of the other girls explained, "We can't enter our pension after nine. We're locked out!"

"Have no fear, ladies!" I announced. "You can all stay in my room. There are five beds for the four of us. And you have nothing to worry about. Who am I to be messing with three women as powerful as you?"

They laughed and agreed. We drank and talked some more, then continued upstairs without so much as a thought to the maître d'. We said goodnight to the other bandsmen in the hall. Nothing happened that night. No one jumped under my covers, and I didn't try anything. I felt stupid and ineffectual — three girls in my room and no action. I knew I wasn't the type to send two out into the street, and the girl closest to me had made a point of telling me she was a preacher's daughter. I couldn't sleep for a while wondering why I hadn't done this or that, trying to figure out if there was anything I *could* do. Finally, I gave up and fell asleep.

We had breakfast together before they got on their bikes and rode off, never to be seen again. Months later, back in Washington, I received a letter from the preacher's daughter. It came in a pink envelope with colorful stamps and had a pronounced odor of perfume. She thanked me profusely and praised me to no end, saying she had never met a nicer gentleman. I rushed to share the letter with one of the other bandsmen from dinner that night.

"Oh, I remember her," he said. "She came back the next evening and spent the night with one of the sergeants."

"Are you sure?" I asked, shocked.

"Absolutely," he assured me. "I saw them together. I saw them go upstairs."

"But you must mean Sergeant G!" I protested. "He's older and he's married!"

"Steve, I think this conversation should end," he sighed. "But before it does, I'll remind you of the Sousa march 'Semper Fidelis'. We've all played it to death, and it became the motto of the Marine Corps. It's applicable to all things dealing with our country, but whoever said it had anything to do with marriage? Now, please pass the ketchup."

The morning after that dinner, I went for my second fitting for my suede coat. En route, I stopped at the pension where Dieter was staying only to find he had gone home to Hamburg. I managed to get an address for him there, then bought a box of chocolates from the P.X. and sent it off to him. Six weeks later when we returned to Washington his thank-you note was waiting. We became pen pals and stayed in touch for years. In 1992, I found one of his old letters and took a chance that his original Hamburg address hadn't changed. He was still there, and since then he and his wife have visited me and mine in NYC, and his grown son, also named Dieter, has become a fan of Buddy DeFranco.

* * *

That Saturday morning was sunny and warm without a cloud in the sky. We were flying to Italy in the C119s. Our pilot told us to be sure we remained strapped in with our parachutes secure, as he would be flying at a relatively low altitude, following the eastern coastline of Italy. He purposely left the huge back bay doors open, joking, "No, nobody's going to be bailing out today, but the scenery will be so beautiful that I thought you might want to take some photographs."

Sure enough, it was beautiful. We were flying low enough that we could see the bathers clustered along the Adriatic coast. Many would look up in surprise, some waving.

"Gee," one of my fellow bandsmen remarked. "We haven't even landed yet and they're welcoming us with open arms."

Our first Italian stop was Naples. It was noisy, crowded, hot, humid, and busy as hell with cars, trucks, motor scooters, and even goats hustling everywhere. Our military guide, Sgt. Cooks, warned us to beware of the 'three 'P's': pickpockets, purse snatchers, and prostitutes. No mention was made of the beggar children, the adult men urinating in public, and the sleazy waterfront Mafioso types who seemed to notice everything while doing nothing.

We left the very next morning for Livorno, known as Leghorn in English. This was Northern Italy on the Western coast, and it was completely different — much more cultured, urbane, and certainly influenced by its proximity to France. It was also the home of the Leaning Tower of Pisa. I was exhausted from Naples and missed seeing it, using the opportunity to get some rest. While the most of the band was out sightseeing, I stayed alone in my private little room.

Two days into Italy something captured my attention. Early that morning, as our bus neared the hotel, I noticed a group of people gathered around some sort of display. Noting these people in this extremely Catholic country weren't in church on a Sunday morning, I figured something was up and worth a look. They were gathered around a store window which featured a large sign reading 'Vespa'. As I inched my way to the front of the crowd, I could see three or four brand-new Vespa motor scooters on display. I was immediately hooked. Amazed to see the store was open on the Sunday, I walked in.

Immediately I was greeted by a well-dressed elderly gentleman. He greeted me in Italian, and I tried the few phrases I know until we eventually settled on a pastiche of Italian and English. The scooters were brand-new models, which is why the crowd outside was gawking. There was one in particular which was the same light green as my 1950 Buick Super. The salesman explained that it could reach speeds of up to 55 mph, it burned a blend of gasoline mixed directly with oil, it had three forward gears, it could be fitted with a plastic windshield . . .

"*Basta!*" I grinned, telling him he'd said enough.

I asked the price and he quoted me some astoundingly extravagant price in Italian lira.

"What about a price in American dollars?" I asked.

"You have dollar?" His eyes lit up.

We both began scribbling to figure out the exchange, and he put forward $327. I told him I could only pay around $300 because I had to pay to ship it home. We haggled for a while, settling on $307. I was ecstatic, though I didn't let it show. That ended when he told me that it couldn't be shipped until tomorrow as the docks were all closed on Sunday and I would have to return the next morning. I told him that I was leaving for Athens in the morning and had to buy it now or leave without it. I thought a bit, then told him I would return to my hotel, find my friend, and return. He looked disappointed and I'm sure he thought he would never see me again.

I raced to the hotel and found Joe. Luckily, he hadn't gone to see Pisa and was in his room. We worked out the details of shipping it and I promised him $27 for the deed. He was also willing to help figure out how we could get it from showroom to plane.

"Let's go see this Italian monster," he said, lacing up his shoes.

The salesman at the Vespa store was happy to see me back. Joe was impressed with the scooter, and I was just convinced — it was beautiful and

I wanted it. Fifteen minutes later we were both pushing it down the street. It took us about ten minutes to get it to the hotel and we parked it outside, where it promptly drew stares. Not that the two Americans pushing it didn't. It would have been nice to ride it, but we couldn't have any gas in it if we wanted to ship it.

Unfortunately, we left the most important part until last. Joe had told me that I needed to find a carpenter to build me a large wooden crate, secured well with strong wires inside. The hotel clerk confirmed they had a carpenter, but he never worked on Sundays. I found out he lived with his family in a first-floor room and knocked on the door. A young boy answered.

"*Papa, papa,*" I pleaded, and he called his father.

The father however had no interest, repeatedly telling me that it was Sunday. I pulled out my stash of American dollars and began counting them out — it made no difference. He began to close the door and so, desperately, I thrust a pack of Pall Malls in front of him. He stopped, and I knew we could work something out.

"*Momento,*" I told him.

I needed to find cartons of cigarettes and fast. My partner-in-crime, Jay, was transporting all of our cache from the last few days. I knew he had fourteen cartons, and I had plenty to replace them with. I went to his hotel room but no one answered. I flagged down the maid, who hesitated initially when I asked her to unlock his door, but cooperated when I pulled out a dollar for her. Routing through Jay's luggage, I found the cartons and pulled out seven before quickly racing back to see the carpenter. He came to the door himself this time, dinner napkin still dangling from his neck. I began counting off cartons: one, two, three — when I got to seven, his napkin came off and he was off to work.

Our bus to that evening's concert was scheduled for 7 p.m. I arrived early to check out the carpenter's work and saw the scooter tightly packed and looking secure inside a large sturdy wooden crate. The problem was I *saw* it. He hadn't put complete sides on the crate and anyone looking could see through the slats and easily identify the Vespa. I rushed back to his room and was insistent that he had to come out and finish the job. It took one more carton of Marlboros.

The bus was loading and preparing to leave while he and his ten-year-old bambino, hammers in hand, banged away noisily. The driver had parked directly beside where they were working, but the band members boarding never even stopped to look — it was simply some local custom as far as they knew. From the bus, I breathed a sigh of relief as I saw the final piece of plywood applied, completely covering the scooter. Joe was supposed to get a truck and fetch it, but I saw no sign of him. As the bus pulled away, I watched the scooter, now completely enclosed, sitting there unguarded. I just had to trust that Joe would handle it.

The concert used the usual songlist, and even while playing I was thinking about what might have gone wrong. At intermission I cornered Joe.

"Did you get it?" I wondered nervously.

"Quiet," he cautioned, looking around. "I said I would, didn't I? Your Italian girlfriend is safely aboard."

I thanked him and he moved on. Joe was something else. He was the only career bandsman I could trust. He'd sold his services to the Air Force but never his soul. He always played fair and square, and was always true to his word. Though quiet, shy, and unpretentious on the surface, deep down was this streetwise Brooklyn boy who got his revenge for any indignities Howard laid on us by always pulling the wool over the big man's eyes.

A few days later, with the entire touring band assembled on the tarmac, we stood and watched our cargo plane racing down the field and lifting up gently into the sky. It was a beautiful sight to see. We were still watching as it suddenly banked strongly to one side, turned around, and returned to the field. The pilot climbed down from the cockpit and walked over to Howard.

"Col. Howard," he said, "we won't be able to use this plane. Whoever filled it with fuel forgot to replace the gas cap. As a result, the fuel leaked out."

There was another plane in the hangar, and Howard told the rest of us to go on ahead so we wouldn't be late for the next concert. He would stay behind to "pull rank on these airport workers" and get them to unload the plane and reload the cargo onto the other. We went on to Beirut, but my mind wasn't on the show or the city.

"Steve, are you airsick?" Jay asked me. "You look pale as a ghost."

My mind was occupied worrying about Howard finding our illegal cargo — and doing the math on how much I stood to lose.

"Don't sweat it," Jay assured me. "We're carrying more than forty cartons with the going price $4 each. We'll room together and find a buyer. It'll help cover the losses if they find anything."

"Good," I answered. "Use the money to bail me out of jail if you hear I'm in trouble."

The concert started promptly at 8 p.m., with Howard showing up in time to conduct. Joe and Red were also there, which meant the cargo plane had made it, but I knew none of the specifics. It was no time to find out, however, and I had to shake it off and pay attention to my playing.

Intermission came and I cornered Joe. The hour had stretched into what seemed like a year and I was desperate for an answer.

"Well?" I asked frantically. "Do we or don't we?"

He smiled and told me what had happened. The Colonel had watched as everything was unloaded from the one plane into the other. Eventually, the only thing left was the big crate.

"Okay, that's not ours," Howard barked. "We're done. Let's hurry up and go!"

Joe jumped in, "Sir, those are extra airplane parts. We *have* to take them."

"Fine," Howard answered after a painfully long moment. "Get that crate on board! Hurry up or we'll be late!"

"Jesus, Joe," I sighed in relief. "Do you know how worried I was?"

"I can tell," he smirked. "But you'd better loosen up, man, or your solo will sound like shit."

Knowing what I knew then, my solo sounded *great.*

* * *

From there we moved on to Athens, where the temperature hit almost 100°F. The Air Force Information Services guide book to Greece warned us not to venture outdoors without light clothing and adequate sunglasses. I put on my new and stylish Italian specs and went out to grab a cab which, to my surprise, ended up being a full-size, late-model, sparkling-clean white Cadillac. When I expressed surprise that a Caddy would be used as a cab, the driver remarked that it was nothing unusual, fuel being much cheaper than it was in the U.S.

I spent the morning visiting the Acropolis and marvelling at the Parthenon and other sites, while my bandmates and other tourists were still sleeping. Greek salespeople, however, swarmed everywhere noisily hawking small alabaster statues, pins, postcards, flags, banners, and numerous trinkets. They spotted me and descended in hordes. Most of the wares seemed like junk, so I bought nothing. *This ain't no P.X.*, I mused.

Suddenly a man appeared from out of nowhere. Short-statured and middle-aged, he wore a long thin raincoat, looking overdressed for the intense heat. He opened his coat, pointing to the inner lining where guns were strapped tightly in rows.

"Want to buy a Beretta?" he asked. "Italian. Good. Cheap."

It took me a few seconds to say no. I wanted nothing to do with guns, but I was shocked by the offer. Beyond my own disinterest, I knew that such a purchase was too risky, even more so than the Vespa. If Colonel Howard found out, that would be the end of me, I knew instinctively. Still, the salesman was not to be deterred easily.

"Gold," he tried again. "Pure or 18 karat. Whatever you like. Coins, necklaces, bracelets, and cubes."

The cubes were one ounce each. I had no problem with exchanging money on the black market, or with selling cartons of cigarettes, or with buying gifts for myself and my loved ones, but gold and guns was big-league smuggling and nothing I wanted any part of. The things I bought were there for military personnel to buy and all legal — excepting my Vespa, of course. The Frankfurt P.X. even had Peugeots — French cars — for sale. You would buy it there and two months later it would arrive by boat in Hoboken, New Jersey. Uncle Sam made sure that its soldiers had access to pretty much anything we could get back home. While a lot of it was sold for use while overseas, it was always expected that servicemen could take their purchases back home.

Guns and gold, though, were not legal by any stretch of the imagination. Ken Zmuda still gave in to temptation and bought a German luger while we were on tour. Of course, he kept it secret and brought it back home concealed. Ken was a collector with a fondness for things tinged with darkness. He once, much later in his life, showed me a large silver spade he had acquired on a later trip to Germany, noting the German inscription marking it as the shovel Adolf Hitler used to open the Autobahn. He pointed this out to me when I was a guest at his house and about to retire for the night — sleeping in the room where the spade resided. *That S.O.B.*, I thought. *What a way to treat a houseguest!* I didn't sleep well with *der Führer*'s shovel sharing the room. I thought it macabre that he would even own it. I would have burned it or donated it to the Hebrew Museum (and hoped *they* burned it). Ken, like Colonel Howard, enjoyed those items tied to Germany's past.

I was reminded of Ken's purchase from our European trip one sad day in February 1989. His wife phoned me, still in shock, to tell me, "Ken put the luger in his mouth and blew away his beautiful head."

Chapter 18
Caravan

Jay and I woke up early the first morning of our next stop, Beirut. We found the maid and announced that we had American cigarettes to sell. She acted dumb but, as we figured, she spread the word fast.

We had a delicious American-style breakfast in the swanky seaside hotel before setting out on foot to explore the neighborhood. The air was clean and warm and the view of the sea spectacular, so with the main road stretching lazily in front of the hotel, we took our time. It was bright enough that sunglasses were a must, but we both had garnered expensive pairs while in Europe. We decided to split up and explore in different directions as we'd be meeting up that afternoon anyway.

It was about fifteen minutes before I even ran into another person. A local merchant was standing by a long display of Lebanese items, so I stopped to chat, browse, and barter. I wasn't really expecting to shop, but the beautiful handmade items and the prices that got lower each time I tried to walk away won me over. In the end, I spent about $75, and gave up two packs of Pall Malls — considering everything I bought was for a quarter of his original price, I felt more than comfortable letting the money go. After all, there were only two more countries and buying now meant I would have less shopping to do for the rest of the tour.

We shook hands and lit up a smoke each. While we were enjoying our cigarettes, I spotted something familiar out of the corner of my eye. It was a shiny Vespa — not the same model I had purchased, but very similar. I told him the story of the one I had purchased but never driven. Even worse, I didn't know how.

"We'll fix that!" he proclaimed.

He closed up shop, cranked up the Vespa, and off we went. Five minutes down the road, he stopped at an open field and gave me my first lesson.

"If you can balance a bicycle, you'll do okay with this scooter."

He was right. I took a short spin alone — he was smart enough not to trust my driving with him as a passenger. Only after I had made a few successful solo 'flights' did he position himself behind me and direct me back to his store. Once there, he refused any money for his generosity.

"One last favor," I asked. "Can you tell me which way to the American embassy?"

Our group had been invited there to swim that afternoon. He began drawing a map, but soon stopped.

"It'll be easier if my son takes you. That way you won't get lost."

His son came out, all of ten years old — too young and too tiny to properly handle the Vespa, so we walked. After a few hills and turns in the road — and several off-beat shortcuts — we were there. I pulled together a reward for this helpful, pleasant kid — a few chocolate bars and dollar bills — but he adamantly refused, even blocking me from shoving them into his pocket. He didn't have his father's command of English, but his explanation was clear enough: "Friend."

Later that afternoon Jay and I both sat at the hotel bar enjoying a glass of beer, relaxing after a long swim and a free lunch. A well-dressed Arab gentleman sat next to me and offered to buy us a drink. He seemed a bit effeminate, so at first I thought he was looking for sex, but five minutes into our second drink, he quietly whispered, "When you have something to sell, it's usually best not to trust the maids."

We quickly found out he was the hotel manager. For a moment we thought we were in some kind of trouble, but soon enough we were doing business. He was willing to buy our entire supply, giving us $200 for the lot. We had only one problem — the cigarettes were aboard the airplane. We wouldn't be able to get them until after the concert. He offered that he had a car and would drive us there now. We told him it was impossible, the plane would be guarded. He said not to worry, we could drive out and see. We agreed. What did we have to lose by taking a look?

He had his car brought around the front — a sleek black Mercedes sedan. On reaching the airport he said something to the guards. Almost immediately some of the airfield personnel boarded the plane and retrieved the crate. They placed it in the trunk of his car, but it was too big. They had to find some rope and tie down the trunk lid.

Back at the hotel, he suggested that we couldn't bring the crate to our room as there were too many people in the lobby.

"Let me have it now," he said. "Later tonight, when you return from your concert, the crate will be returned to your room, minus the cigarettes."

"And the money?" I asked cautiously.

"I'll pay you later tonight if we see each other or, if not, tomorrow."

Sure enough, the crate was in our room when we returned from the concert. Only the cigarettes had been removed, and nothing else had been touched.

"Now we just need to collect our money!" Jay remarked.

For the next two days, the manager managed all right — he managed to avoid us completely. We realized we had been cheated and would have to swallow the loss. It didn't seem that bad to me after almost losing the Vespa, never mind almost getting caught because of it, but Jay was incensed. Still, there was nothing we could do.

On the last morning of our stay in Beirut, the band sat assembled in the lobby to leave, waiting for our bus to the airfield when the manager finally came into sight. I stood up and discreetly reminded him of the payment he owed us. He joked about it, implying that the Colonel would flip if he knew, but I stood my ground. I stared him directly in the eye and let him know I was serious. The Colonel stood up and motioned our group to leave — our bus had arrived. Everyone stood up and I knew there was nothing I could do. Just then, the manager grabbed my hand and shook it heartily, something crumpled passing from his hand to mine.

"You Americans, you worry so," he whispered as we released hands.

As he walked away, I turned to one side and checked my hand. Sure enough, there were two hundred-dollar bills there. My mother always said that good things happen in threes. Considering the scooter and this, I was due for one more piece of luck.

I boarded the bus with the others, on our way to Egypt, with only Libya and French Morocco left to follow.

* * *

Alexandria was certainly alluring and exotic, but I had brought along and eaten something better left behind. I spent the entire flight with stomach cramps and diarrhea, and there was no washroom on board — only a scrubbing bucket in the corner — so I held it in the entire flight. I spent the trip muttering "Damn figs!" to myself.

The bus from Beirut to our plane had stopped in Tripoli, a town in Northern Lebanon not to be confused with the Libyan capital. The Lebanese Tripoli lies two miles inland on the Syrian border. It was a sea of bars and outdoor cafés full of elderly dreamy-eyed men nonchalantly smoking water pipes — likely hashish, but we all had known not to even ask. After we left, the bus had made another brief stop on a country road not far from the city. A peasant woman had appeared at the window, calling out "Fresh figs! Fresh figs!" I knew better than to eat unwashed fruit straight from the field in a foreign country. This time, however, I had let my guard down. Maybe I was just too hungry to think, or maybe I was just feeling invincible having managed to get my Vespa over every hurdle and having gotten my money in Beirut. I wasn't the only one who had partaken and there were a few other men who could be heard, between moans, cursing Botek and those fucking figs.

In Alexandria our hotel was beautiful. Situated adjacent to the Nile, it was a proud tribute to this archaic metropolis founded by Alexander the Great in 332 B.C. The main restaurant was large, elegant, and inviting, opening at noon for lunch. However, I had no appetite, was in pain, had hourly bowel movements, and felt dehydrated. I held back when the others went for lunch but common sense soon prevailed and I joined them — if I was sick, I couldn't play. If I couldn't play, Howard would send me home and find a replacement. While I could deal with missing the last few shows, my returning home wouldn't mean that the same applied to my cargo. I had to be able to make sure everything went fine on that front, something I wouldn't be able to do from back in Washington. It wouldn't be fair to saddle Joe with that.

I dragged myself to the door of the restaurant, faced the maître d', and realized I didn't know what to say. After a moment's silence I just blurted out my problem. He understood immediately and he escorted me to a small private table, off in a corner and quite close to the men's room.

"You need some mild Egyptian cheese, plain toast, and a pot of English tea," he said with a prominent English accent. "Later, I'll get you a banana or two and a bowl of moist white rice. If I were you, I'd stick to this diet for twenty-four hours. Within a day or so, you'll be as fit as a fiddle."

For the next three or four meals, I followed his advice to the letter. With each meal, I was regaining my strength, spending less time in the bathroom, and experiencing less and less pain. My diarrhea was gone by the time we were ready to move on to Cairo. The maître d' refused any money for his kindness and advice. I tried again, offering him a small sack with ten assorted cartons of cigarettes. He was ready to say no again until he spotted the one carton I placed dead center. Herbert Tareyton's, an English brand, was a favorite with smokers in this part of the world — the English had left their mark on Egypt, after all. He flipped that carton out of the sack and took it gladly, leaving me the rest, and wished me well on the rest of my tour, adding, "And please stay away from those bloody fresh figs!"

* * *

Cairo had its own distinct and easily recognizable odor, but considering its age, that was to be expected. We arrived at our downtown hotel and Master Sergeant Grace stood at the front desk, papers in hand. Twenty of us were to stay in this hotel while the rest of the band stayed down the street.

"Pick a roommate — two to a room — and do it quickly," Grace ordered. "It's late and the buses will pick us up at 0900 hours tomorrow."

Not one of my close friends was in this group and I hesitated in choosing. Soon, only a few of our vocalists were left — guys I usually just said 'hello' to and usually avoided for one reason or another. Grace wasn't in the mood to wait for us.

"Steve," he barked. "Donald here looks terrible. He may even have a fever. You know the temperature today was around a hundred degrees? Did he also eat those figs? If the Colonel finds out . . .

"You got better back in Alexandria. Please play doctor for Donald for the next couple of days. I'll get you some A.P.C. tablets and liquid paregorics. You'll share room 206."

Donald was four or five years younger than me, had three stripes to my four, and hailed from the New York City area. He played no instrument, but sang with the Singing Sergeants. Most of us, for the sake of job security if not money, held down two jobs and wondered how people like Donald got by with just one. Our chorus conductor had a civilian church choir in which individuals like Donald sang voluntarily. No doubt singing each Sunday helped assure his place in the Singing Sergeants — one hand washes the other, after all. The rumor mill had interesting things to say about Donald. The story was that his father arranged for his son to have the cushy job in Washington in exchange for some media coverage for Howard at the T.V. station he worked at in New York.

Donald was so tired and weak that he didn't even unpack. The room was extremely warm, had no air conditioning, and the noisy ceiling fan did very little to properly cool the place. He looked terrible: pale, weak, and exhausted. I ordered him to strip down to his underwear, swallow two A.P.C.s, and follow them with a teaspoon of paregorics. I had him lie down with a cold washcloth on his forehead which was hot enough to fry an egg on. I called room service and asked them to hurry and bring bananas, two orders of dry toast, two large bottles of mineral water, two servings of moist white rice, a large piece of parmesan cheese, and a large pot of English tea.

The food arrived in minutes. Initially Donald refused to eat, but my patient soon began to drink and then followed my lead and started to eat. Little by little, he began to regain his strength, but he still needed a day or two of rest.

"Stay here tomorrow and rest," I told him. "I'll explain to Sgt. Grace."

"What will Colonel Howard do to me?" he whimpered.

"Screw him," I said. "He won't even miss you for a day or two. Grace won't tell him. No one will."

Inside of an hour he was looking better. His color had improved and his head was not as warm. He also said the stomach cramps had gone. This was about 1:30 in the morning and I had to get him to sleep. He was too excited and worried to sleep, though, and nothing we spoke of seemed to calm him down until finally the topic of shopping came up. He was embarrassed and worried about gifts. Being a first-timer on tour, he had bought nothing to date for his friends and family. Having missed out on all the great P.X.s in Europe, he had no idea what he could buy on the remainder of the trip, let alone whether he would be in shape to go out and get anything.

"Don't worry," I told him. "In Tripoli, Casablanca, and Rabat, I'll be taking orders from many of the band members. I'll show you a list and you can tell me what you want. I'll be buying it in bulk and haggling so you can get everything at about 75 percent of the usual prices. I'll just charge you ten or fifteen percent of the final cost. So your shopping is done — just sleep."

Relieved, he fell asleep. I lowered the light and crawled into bed, promising myself that, come daylight, I'd look further into the subject of hypnosis. I thought, *Maybe you should become a doctor, Steve — you already have a patient!* I laughed to myself, then concentrated on getting myself to sleep. This was Egypt in August and the room was unbearably hot. I used Jacobson techniques and got to sleep fairly quickly.

Donald had improved considerably by the time we left Egypt for Libya, almost his old self again.

* * *

Libya itself promised an exotic adventure like nothing I had experienced before. Flying over the Sahara, I pictured Rommel chasing Patton — or the other way around. It was all serene, scenic, and sad — just a short decade earlier, this low-flying C119 would probably have been blown out of the sky. There was the U.S. military cemetery in Tunisia, vastly overcrowded by my fellow Pennsylvanians as well as those from other states. I couldn't forget the sacrifices that had been made here, where my plans were simply to play music and go shopping.

Donald had a strong memory himself. He sought out the barracks area — no swanky hotel here — where I had been assigned and almost broke down and cried on seeing me. It was best that he didn't. 'Big Brother' was all around and watching. As well, if he had hugged me, some of the older guys might have misinterpreted it.

"Sit down here," I motioned. "You look like a million bucks! North Africa must be agreeing with you."

Something in my tone must have conveyed the danger inherent in speaking freely in an open-bay billet, and he shifted his posture and tone.

"Steve, I brought you something," he told me. "I found a book. I think it's right up your alley."

A book? I thought. *Shit. More weight to worry about.* Still, I wasn't going to be impolite and I was curious what he had found. I unwrapped it and was puzzled at the sight of *The Merck Manual.*

"What's this?" I asked.

"You're a born healer," he sputtered. "I just know that someday you'll tire of music and take up medicine. Leaf through and you'll find that practically everything you prescribed for me is spelled out to the letter there.

"Yeah, Steve, I feel like a million bucks — thanks to you!"

I thanked him and he thanked me again. He also had a list of gifts for me to pick up, reminding me to take my French phrasebook along.

Tripoli turned out to be a trial more than a treat. Fighting intense summer heat while I waited for the local shops to re-open following the afternoon siesta wore me down. I should have known better, of course, not being an Englishman *or* a mad dog. When they were open, I found the stores quite elegant, well-stocked, and sophisticated. However, unlike our other stops, they mostly had fixed prices and refused to barter.

One afternoon while shopping I kept passing a street merchant. Each time we passed, he tried desperately to sell me one of his large colorful tapestries. Each time I said no. And each time we passed, he seemed to have less and less to sell — *somebody* was buying them. At our last encounter, he pleaded with me emphatically, "I can't go home until I sell this last one."

The last tapestry was bright and beautiful, a representation of summer scenes in this lazy, beguiling, and romantic city. I offered him a cigarette and we began to haggle. His starting price was $60 but we ended up settling on $8. By then our cigarettes were almost completely burnt down and he agreed only on condition I throw in the rest of the pack. If only he knew how many cigarettes I had! I still have the tapestry in my Pennsylvania home.

Back on base there was nothing to do but wait for the evening concert. I became aware that the majority of the band seemed to be worn out, spent, depressed, and lacking energy. Simply, everyone was ready to go home, though we still had a week left in French Morocco. For my part, this made me realize I was feeling a bit of depression and I *was* tired from all the running around to date. I was feeling more *oppressed* than depressed though, with the heat hanging off us like an anchor. Basic training had provided me the solution for depression and unbearable weather — there, it had been liquid codeine and A.P.C. tablets. I scoured my medical cache, finding only the tablets.

I had once asked my Philadelphia dentist how many one person could safely take. He told me he had a female patient who would take as many as *thirteen*. I decided to start lower and took six. Right after, I felt more adventurous and went up to eight. Another half-hour of thinking about it got me to move up to eleven.

As I walked, I felt like I was walking on air. My depression had lifted and I became less inhibited. There was even a shift in my overall attitude that both surprised and tickled me. The concert was a mere two hours after I took the pills and I was happy and high through it. Being called up to solo sobered me up for a moment, but I was floating on Cloud Nine again by the time I reached the front of the stage. I played with complete abandonment, my solo filled with fresh ideas and I-don't-give-a-fuck fearlessness.

The crowd went wild and I strutted back to my seat. As I skirted by him, our baritone sax player whispered urgently, "*Botek, what in the hell are you doing?*"

He was one of the older players who rarely even acknowledged me. Rumor had him hating touring and even hating using any bathroom other than the one at home. He was used to being comfortable and complacent. No doubt he saw my behavior as offensive and my playing too avant-garde for this hurdy-gurdy group. *Fuck you*, I thought. After that, I forgot completely about him until his name came up a few years later when he reportedly committed suicide. No one else said a single negative word about my solo.

* * *

Casablanca was our next stop. This beautiful seaport city in French Morocco (to become *just* Morocco in 1955 when it gained its independence from France) was steeped in international intrigue and sparkled with activity. It was also a shopper's paradise, offering everything produced in nearby Europe as well as countless handmade domestic items, all exquisite, exotic, and not to be found elsewhere. Our tour was soon to be over, so now was the time to buy and at the rock-bottom prices to be found in the city, no adroit businessman would remain idle.

The men were exhausted, wanting nothing more than to return home to their wives and girlfriends. So that left me to do most of the shopping. I gathered orders and went into town while they napped. My pockets bulged with money, too much to fit it all into my money belt — U.S. greenbacks, French francs, military scrip, plus U.S.-dollar traveler's checks and regular bank checks from my account at home. I also had a few packs of American cigarettes, a wide assortment of U.S. postage stamps, and about ten half-dollar U.S. coins, all to be given as gifts. As the sale prices got lower and lower, these trinkets were distributed more readily.

There was a free bus from the base into town and the driver let me off in front of a large bazaar, warning me to be careful.

"This is the old city," he cautioned. "G.I.s have entered alone and never been heard from since. Act like a tourist, not a soldier. And whatever you do, *don't* talk politics."

I thanked him and headed off into the old city. My mind was made up. I was going to find a large locally-run store and tell them I didn't want to haggle — I just wanted wholesale prices, usually 80 percent less than retail, and I was ready to spend anywhere from $200 to $250.

It didn't take long to find the right place. Within minutes I stumbled upon a large, nicely decorated, clean building covered with displays and photos of handcrafted Moroccan merchandise. A well-dressed, middle-aged, heavyset gentleman stood in the doorway smoking an aromatic tobacco.

"May I help you?" he inquired in perfect BBC English.

We chatted and I offered him an American cigarette. He accepted and offered me one of his, noting they were made in Turkey. I politely accepted but refrained from lighting up, having smelled his. His family, three brothers and him, had emigrated from India a few years back, his accent being the result of British-run schooling there. He claimed to be fascinated with American history — Lincoln, Roosevelt, our "enterprising spirit", etc., noting that the last made us good businessmen.

"Yes," I agreed. "And that's exactly why I'm here."

He understood me immediately and led me inside. I sat on a large sofa while he paraded item after item before me: tapestries, rugs, hassocks, jewelry, beautiful brass bracelets, rings, leather wallets and belts, sheep-skins, etc. Each item was priced at wholesale, 80 percent less than what was advertised outdoors — I didn't even have to ask. We'd break from the process here and there for coffee, beer, cigarettes, or a toast to America. Even a small lunch was served with apricots for dessert (no figs, thank God!). Jokes and anecdotes were exchanged. Altogether, it lasted almost three hours. When we were done, everything was wrapped neatly in big bundles and he ordered a taxi for me, even offering to pay for it, but I refused. The bundles filled the entire back seat, so I jumped in front, bidding him adieu.

I delivered no less than fifteen gifts to our men, and the guys were delighted, knowing their wives would be. My ten to fifteen percent cut might sound meager, but the fun I had and the stuff I learned while being treated like a maharajah will be treasured forever.

A week later we were all safe and sound in Washington, including our cargo. There was one problem, though. In transit, someone had pushed or kicked through a piece of the plywood cover of the crate that carried my Vespa. It wasn't damaged, but the fender and front wheel were in full view. I had barely gotten home when the phone rang and Joe explained the situation with an urgency I'd never heard from him.

"The Colonel saw the crate and saw what was in it!" he exclaimed. "He said if it wasn't removed from where it was now — in front of our rehearsal hall — within two hours, heads would roll!"

Joe managed to arrange a U.S.A.F. truck and got the Vespa shipped to my home in Arlington. Howard never said another word about it. Joe and Red stayed cool, but we were all waiting for the hammer to drop. It never did. I rode the scooter everywhere after that — everywhere but the base, of course. To this day I still have it, and every time I look at it I wonder if we pulled the wool over Howard's eyes or if he knew all along but just preferred not to say anything.

I do have to give credit to Colonel Howard where it's due. He was more than generous with vacation time once a job was done and we had plenty of rest coming our way. It was due to him that many of us managed to see so many esoteric and exotic places around the world — his well-crafted wanderlust led us to experiences we wouldn't have had otherwise. We also met people we'll remember always. In Toronto, we met those two young Canadian sisters, Marilyn and Ruth Paul. Alex Shigo married Marilyn two years after that. It took me another twenty years, but I followed in his footsteps and married Ruth. The happiness that I still receive from that is owing in part to Howard giving us the opportunity to meet.

What Howard lacked when he was brought up with social mores and interpersonal skills could probably be traced back to his childhood association with a sense of entitlement. That would be coupled with the overly structured environment of Pennsylvania Dutch country. Perhaps finding out that this entitlement didn't meet reality changed things when his wife left him. Having one's worldview shaken so thoroughly could well leave one so bitter. George would change though, becoming magnanimous and even supportive when he was receiving regular praise, like we did on tour.

This tour ended with the feedback all positive, and so we got most of September to 'rest, relax, and recreate' (jokingly known as the military's three R's). I got to visit my family in Lansford, feeling like Santa with all my gifts. It was more than repaid with family warmth, baked goods, and sumptuous meals.

I gave my father a powerful pair of field glasses, a hand-painted Italian silk necktie, and $600. For Mother, I had some Lanvin perfume, a pure gold lapel pin and matching bracelet from Morocco, three handmade and hand-painted vases, each from a different country, and a large glass-enclosed 400-day German clock yet to arrive by post. For my sisters, I spread out a huge assortment and set them loose, telling them to choose three items each. Silver bracelets got grabbed immediately, followed by the cuckoo clock and clever little wooden desk clocks that had no hands — instead, two eyeballs rotated, one for minutes, the other for hours. Bottles of perfume found new homes. Betty took a Moroccan tapestry and matching hassock for her husband, Ernie, noting that he had served in North Africa.

Eventually I retreated to my old bedroom, still reserved for me. I lay in bed, dead to the world for twelve hours, happy to be home and home-free. I didn't move until Mother peeped in to cue us breakfast was ready, wiggling her wrist to display her newly-acquired North African gift.

At breakfast she told me that the local postmaster had called and needed to speak to me.

"Six large packages have arrived from overseas and they all cleared Customs except one," she explained. "Could you drop in today?"

Lansford being as small as it was, the postmaster had a familiar face, though I didn't know his name. He knew who I was, though, and addressed me warmly by my first name.

"Now, Steve," he began, "I know all these packages were mailed properly from overseas bases. However, the contents of one has me puzzled. This one here."

He pointed to a well-wrapped, medium-size wooden box marked 'FRAGILE: HANDLE WITH CARE'. In turn, I pointed to its Customs declaration certificate where the contents were clearly listed.

"Oh yeah, that's my mother's clock!" I told him. "And my Swiss wristwatches."

He fixed me with an accusatory look, pointing to the certificate.

"But *eight* watches?"

He said no more — he didn't need to. The message was loud and clear, however petty I thought it was. He was ready to make trouble. I wondered how best to handle this jerk. I hadn't done anything illegal, having declared them all, but he knew that I was likely contravening military regulations. I decided not to be offensive, and my reply came to me as he lit his pipe.

"Some of us collect pipes, some of us collect wristwatches," I said, straight-faced.

I knew from working in my father's store what the habits of smokers were. Most serious devotees of pipe smoking would talk with enthusiasm about this pipe, that tobacco, and never had only one. I knew he would have to have a collection.

The answer satisfied him and soon I was on my way back home with the packages. Mom was thrilled when she saw her new clock, and I was fed like a king that day. The next morning I could hardly move after a huge and hearty breakfast, but made my way back to Washington.

I had three months left in my hitch. Sgt. Grace kept asking me if I was going to re-enlist, but I remained noncommittal, saying I hadn't decided — *yet*. If nothing else, having the superior officers work to stay in *my* good graces was the kind of about-face I could take, whether or not I decided to stay with the band.

Howard had one more tour up his sleeve, scheduled through the fall of 1954. All the travel would be by bus, covering the entire West Coast, from Seattle to San Diego. There would be thirty-five one-nighters and five matinées and 100 to 150 miles of travel daily.

We flew out West to Oregon, where we picked up three buses equipped for long-distance travel and immediately set out visiting high schools and small-town auditoriums in the state. This was a recruitment tour, encouraging kids to sign up and serve — that, not long after the military was trying to get people to *leave*. Go figure. This left us with no opportunities like we had on our summer tour — there were no P.X.s to shop at, nothing unusual to buy, no time to sightsee, and not one day off. The only perk was an extra ten to fifteen dollars per day — money I would save for our final stop, Las Vegas.

There was some excitement in that I hadn't seen any of these places before. As well, Charlie Tucker was now stationed in Seattle, having joined the Navy not long after I enlisted. We planned to spend time together when the band arrived in town. Charlie looked well, but it was strange to see him in a Navy uniform. The last contact we had had, he was stationed on Kodiak

Island in Alaska and was suffering daily. Things hadn't worked out well at his old school base in DC. He had been expecting to remain there for his entire hitch but, after just a few months, the Navy had decided they needed a good drummer aboard a certain ship. Never trust the military. After a year on the high seas they shipped him north to the ice-cold, desolate, and remote base at Kodiak — again, a request for a good drummer had come in. I still have Charlie's angry letters condemning the Navy and its shady practices, but also coming down jealously on me and my Washington-based entourage and our female companions.

Charlie was waiting in full-dress uniform when the band arrived at our hotel in Seattle. He shook my hand — neither of us saluted — and then it was Tucker Time again. He spun around and cornered Sgt. Grace, securing permission to 'come aboard' our tour for the next couple of days. Grace was easily swept up in Charlie's charm and Tucker sat next to me for two days as our bus rambled through upper Washington State.

"Charlie," I advised him, "get rid of that fucking uniform. Wear your civvies. You don't need to be so formal. Look around you. Look at *me:* boots, button-down shirt, civilian socks — I'm half in uniform, half out!"

He relaxed a bit and I asked him if he was okay. He seemed sad and I wondered what had happened to him.

"You don't know Kodiak," he sighed. "The band was horrible and there were only twenty of us. Because of flight times, we'd have to get up and meet dignitaries at 3 a.m. It was freezing cold, night and day. It would get so cold that trumpet valves wouldn't function. There were no girls and the only social life I had was church . . ."

"Whoa!" I interrupted. "*You* went to church?"

"Yeah," he shrugged. "I made friends with the priest and went to mass every day. You don't know how lucky you had it in Washington with all those wild parties and all that time away from base."

I grinned and left my response at that, figuring it was a bad time to brag.

"Hey!" he suddenly yelped. "I almost forgot to tell you! Mr. Lauer came to Alaska about the time I did. He searched me out and visited."

"Really?" I asked. "Mr. Lauer from school?"

"Yeah," he smiled. "That might have been the one good thing that happened when I was up there."

"How did you get out of there, anyway? I thought it was a two-year deal?"

"It was," he smiled. "But I couldn't take it. One day I was in the day-room alone and I happened to read a memo saying that the Seattle band needed a drummer. My leader would *never* formally transfer me, so I worked out a plan."

Ha! I thought. *Tucker Time in Alaska!*

"The mail plane flew in once a week," he explained. "That's another thing — we only got mail once a week! Anyway, the plane flew to Seattle when it was done and I decided to hitch a ride and transfer myself. I packed up a big bag of my stuff and hopped on board.

"In Seattle, I auditioned for the job and pleaded with the bandmaster in Seattle to *order* me not to return to Alaska. That way, I had no choice legally but to stay."

As was usually the case with Tucker Time, Charlie got what he wanted. Instead of two years, he managed to cut things short after eleven months. Seattle would be home for his final year in uniform.

"God, Charlie," I stammered, not having realized before how much Alaska had weighed on him. "I'm sure glad you got out of there. Now what?"

"I get out like you do," he grinned. "That'll be December. I'll buy one of those new bugs and drive it across the country."

"Bugs?" I asked.

"Those new 'Beetles' from Volkswagen," he explained. I'd seen them before in Germany, but they were new to the States and I hadn't heard the nickname for them.

"I haven't decided yet," I told him in a low whisper. "I might re-enlist."

He didn't want to have that conversation on the bus, I could tell. Still, he slowly shook his head with an urgency in his eyes.

"Also, I've saved about four or five thousand dollars," he confided. "Do you know of any good investments?"

I did, but I knew he wasn't going to like what I had to say.

"Charlie, invest it in *yourself*. DeFranco introduced me to his therapist, Dr. Pelletiere. Pay for some visits. I'll give you his address. Oh, and Dr. Hughes, too."

* * *

The rest of the Western tour went well and we made our final stop in Las Vegas. I'd always wanted to experience Vegas for myself, having *almost* done so during my senior year of high school. John L. Lewis, the outspoken and renowned leader of the American Union of Coal Miners, had hired the Coaldale Victory Band from the neighboring town to perform for one week at a miners' convention, all expenses paid. My local fame was at its peak then and the band, wanting to impress, hired me to join them for the run of the engagement. I was excused from school, a miners' convention being highly prestigious in Pennsylvania coal country — of course, it would be a while yet until I was at Eastman and realized how much those missed days cost me. We rehearsed for weeks and were note-perfect. Unfortunately, I took violently ill the night before, beginning with a severe headache.

For the next few days, I was confined to bed with the local doctor visiting daily. He diagnosed me as having a cerebral inflammation, etiology unknown. His prescription was two large sulphur tablets every six hours. My mother was forced to be my full-time nurse, and she dedicated herself entirely to the task. She wasn't about to lose a second son to a viral infection. Years before, my older brother Robert, born ten years to the day before me, had succumbed to influenza. She worked feverishly as I lay fevered. I didn't tell anyone, but I had made my first medical assessment — I knew what lay behind my illness.

The night it started, I had visited Art at his dad's pharmacy. I had been feeling blue for a few days and asked Art if he knew what was good for depression. I noticed phenobarbitol and without waiting for Art to answer, I took two tablets. From there, we headed on to a bar in nearby Tamaqua that was known to serve underage drinkers. We drank and talked for about two hours before the headache hit and I pushed Art to head back home.

Obviously I pulled through, but my hasty actions that day had haunted me, having kept me from taking what would have been the furthest trip of my life at that point. The idea of Las Vegas had been with me ever since, and it seemed like the perfect way to end our tour. Moreover, it was nearing the end of my time in the service. Soon after we returned, I would have to decide whether to re-enlist or move on. If I *did* leave, Vegas would be a great place for my last concert with the Air Force.

Now I was 24 and finally in Vegas. I was surprised at what I found. I had expected the glitz and glamor the city was known for, and had never expected to see anything else. With that in mind, I was amazed to find everyday life happened in Vegas. We performed at two high schools in one long afternoon and when we were done, drove by the university there.

That left the evening free, but my buddies seemed too tired to go anywhere. This was fairly common on our tours and, this being our last stop, the toll of the travel was weighing on them. I, however, had my youthful missed opportunity to make up for. So I went out alone, shopping and seeing what I could. Of course a casino was a must, so I headed down to the Golden Nugget, prompted by a brochure in our hotel. The place was huge and completely carpeted with an inch or so of sawdust. Two piano players banged away in opposite corners, neither of them audible from the center.

"Welcome to the Wild West," said a friendly gentleman guarding the entrance. "Check all guns at the door, please."

Inside, I ordered a beer and changed three ten-dollar bills into nickels, dimes, and quarters. I sat down to match wits with the ominous one-armed bandits. Over the next two hours, I won, lost, won, lost, won, then lost almost everything, then won again. Finally, I realized I had exactly $30 and decided to quit, having broken even.

* * *

We headed back to Washington. Time was running low. Those of us who had come in with the first wave of kids escaping the draft would all be either re-enlisting or leaving. If I stayed, it would be a different band. Sure, some kids had left when the military gave us the choice to do so voluntarily, but enough of us had stayed on. The band would definitely change, with one important exception — Howard would still be leading it.

On the plus side for re-enlistment, the war was over. I had proven myself to Howard and had considerably fewer problems with him as a result. Others would be the new kids to be picked on. I had friends in the band — though I needed to check if they would be staying on. I would see more of the world and have relatively little work to do. And of course, I had learned to profit quite well from my little sidelines during our tours.

On the down side, I would still have to deal with Howard. The new kids were an unknown. As much as I got to solo, I never got to perform the way I wanted to — unless I was hopped up on A.P.C.s like I was in Libya, that is. Most importantly, there were the friends that had left, like the Odrich brothers, and the friends I *knew* were leaving — Alex Shigo would be going back to school to major in botany and Ken Zmuda would be going back to school too, in Florida, working towards a degree in teaching.

I wondered how these fine musicians could be so interested in another career. Wasn't music their lives, as it was mine? Of course I understood the idea of having job security and earning enough money to pay the bills. There was Leonard who was going to audition for the Philadelphia Orchestra, but then he was a viola player, and that's what they do — you don't see them riffing through jazz standards in a six-piece combo. Thinking about that made me realize that I didn't want to stay where I was playing music that *wasn't* the music I wanted to play, no matter how close it was. For me, there would be no symphony, no teaching degree — not even the one at Eastman, and no more military bands with megalomaniacal conductors.

I'd stay put in Washington for the time being and take some time to think. The rent was cheap, the house and roommates were cool, the women were plentiful, and I still had a few steady gigs with my small jazz combo.

Christmas was coming up, Washington houses were being decorated, and its citizens were busy shopping, but for me the important date coming up was my discharge. It felt like my twenty-fifth birthday present.

Airmen of Note

The Army Air Force Band, running under the legacy of Glenn Miller, was disbanded in the 1950s. The will for a band in the same mold was still there, however, and the Airmen of Note, formed in 1950, took its place. The Airmen of Note took over more directly from The United States Air Force Band, stationed at Bolling Field in Washington.

The band was formed under the command of Brigadier General Sydney D. Grubbs, with Colonel George S. Howard in charge of the band. Howard tapped Chief Warrant Officer Fred Kepner to assemble and lead the band.

It was the Kepner-led band that was chosen to play the Glenn Miller Orchestra in the film *The Glenn Miller Story,* though they were not allowed to perform on the soundtrack owing to the studio's union contract. While the Miller connection was always there, even as far as Glenn's widow Helen lending her support in the band's early days, Kepner drew from the stylings and arrangements of other bandleaders. Considering that band members had been drawn from the ranks of the alumni of a number of name bands, it quickly developed its own sound.

The Airmen of Note have performed around the world, from remote bases to the White House, as well as public concerts on radio and television. However, in its earlier years the band performed almost exclusively for military engagements. Soon enough, though, they were performing broadcast concerts with the likes of Eddie Fisher, Eydie Gormé, Tony Bennett, Mel Tormé, and Helen O'Connell.

Alumni of the band include Tommy Newsom, saxophonist and occasional bandleader for *The Tonight Show with Johnny Carson.*

Chapter 19
Moonlight Serenade

I had some money saved up and was in no rush to find new income. As a G.I., I could collect unemployment benefits, and did. Money was tight and I found myself donning the uniform a few times to get the discounted rail tickets home and back — something I now see as very foolish.

At least I had plenty of time to practice and to manage my combo. We never had a steady piano player, and it was getting harder to keep one. Good jazz pianists were in high demand. It could take thirty phone calls before I'd find someone for a gig. All the practice and gigs had my playing improving steadily — remember, with the Air Force, I hadn't been playing bebop — but it was no fun being poor.

I would travel north to Pennsylvania every few weeks, driving most times. Charlie was back there after his hitch ended, Jo was there with her small combo, and there were one or two old girlfriends from high school still around and still single. Most of the Pennsylvania G.I.s, Charlie included, were talking about ways to use their G.I. Bill benefits. They could begin, or return to, college. They could attend technical school. They could apprentice in a new trade. Charlie thought it would be a shame not to use this money, especially considering how much he suffered to get it.

"Maybe I'll go to Stroudsburg State Teachers College and get a teaching degree," he mused. "That's less than fifty miles away. I could live at home and save money."

Charlie *always* talked about home. A home in the country, a nice big place somewhere in the woods by a lake — it was always about what *could* be. Charlie was a perennial dreamer who, left to his own devices, often chose incorrectly — and left to his own devices was usually the case, being the contrarian he was. He wanted to do things his own way and, if he hadn't made up his mind which way that was, he would settle for *not* the way the other guy was going. That often led to disaster for him — he had shirked my advice about joining the Air Force Band and still sulked if you mentioned his time in Alaska that resulted.

Jo was performing one night, Charlie and I watching in the audience. I realized then what a natural she truly was. You could put her in front of any group at all and it would sell. The wheels started turning. I quickly became convinced that if she and I formed a combo, it would be a success. I figured that we could add bass and maybe a guitar to her accordion, my clarinet, and Tucker's drums.

Charlie was in. He didn't have any regular gigs of his own and he knew and appreciated our playing. Jo finished and I filled her in on the concept. She immediately thought of a perfect bass man she had worked with in the U.S.O. We sat up talking late into the night, making plans. Jo and I would both disband our present groups and form a new one with her as leader. We'd hire an arranger and photographer, make some recordings for auditions, and then advertise somewhere big, like in the Sunday *New York Times*, and reach all the summer resorts like the Catskills and the White Mountains. The summer resorts were our target, we decided — one audition could land you three solid months of work.

Jo's potential bass player wasn't able to join us, but we agreed we could find another bassist between the three of us. I raced back to Washington, let my roommates know I might be moving out and would definitely return to Pennsylvania for the time being, packed up my things, let my jazz combo know I would be leaving it before the summer, and said my farewells. Jo likewise wrapped up her band, and we were set to go.

We prepared an ad for the *Times* and the three of us drove to New York the following Thursday. Jo and I both had arranged lessons in the city, so Charlie took the ad and the money to pay for it. We were to meet at 5 p.m., have a dinner and exchange notes, then return home. When Charlie met us at a restaurant later, Jo was anxious for word, grabbing him by the sleeve and demanding, "Did you do it? Did you put the ad in?"

Charlie paused before answering, then blurted out, "No, I *didn't* put it in, but wait —"

Jo wasn't in the mood to wait. She was preparing to drive her steak knife through Charlie's heart.

"The man — his name is Munson Campbell — told me *not* to do it. He didn't want us to waste money. He said we should send an exploratory letter and photos to all of the resorts and wait for replies. Then we can bring him the replies and he'll advise us as to which resort is best, how much they pay, everything. Here."

Charlie pointed to a folded-up newspaper page showing at least twenty different resorts. Both Jo and I were bewildered. Who was this Campbell guy and did he really know what he was talking about? Did Charlie screw up or did he really find us a Big Apple benefactor? We both thought about phoning Campbell and validating Charlie's story, and about going to see him in person, finally deciding against either. We both knew Tucker's promise and charm and decided we could put our faith in that and trust the advice Charlie got. After all, he was *great* at getting good advice, even if not so good at following it.

Summer was about three months away and we rushed enough to get everything mailed out within three days. Within two weeks we had fourteen replies. A few of them sounded terrific — popular resorts in New Hampshire, Massachusetts, Vermont, New York State, and Pennsylvania. Even, to our surprise, one in Aruba! We couldn't wait to run back to the *Times* and talk to Munson Campbell.

He received us quite graciously. The mention of his name to others in the building on our way up to see him had commanded instant respect, putting everyone who heard it into overdrive. Within minutes he was scanning our replies and carefully reviewing them. Suddenly he stopped, his eyes falling on one in particular. He pushed the others aside.

"Ah," he smiled. "*This* is the one! The Lake Tarleton Club in Pike, New Hampshire."

He proceeded to explain why he chose it, a subtle stammer in his speech suddenly evident. All fourteen places advertised with the *Times* and he knew them all — which ones could pay top dollar and which ones would be trouble.

"I would focus all my efforts on Lake Tarleton," he pronounced. "They have 5,500 acres, five lakes, and another hotel in Miami Beach. They will demand that you work seven days a week, take less money than you initially request, and drill you and drill you during your initial auditions. Don't let them scare you or bully you. Don't back down on salary and don't be surprised if their initial contract is temporary, maybe one or two weeks maximum. They'll want to be 100-percent sure before they hire you for the entire summer — that might seem like more work for you, but you should take it as a sign that they're serious about the musicians they hire.

"Again, stick to your guns and don't let them push you around. That's about it. Go get the job. And let me know when you do. Oh, and please — make *no* mention of me or the *Times* when you do talk to them."

We raced down the street and called Lake Tarleton immediately from a public phone, setting up an audition the following week. Munson Campbell had saved us time, money, and numerous headaches. With a little luck and effort, one can find angels anywhere — even in the Big Apple.

* * *

Jo had always been able to organize multiple things at once without losing track of anything. Thanks to superior music teaching she had excellent concentration, dexterity, and rhythm, and was able to apply them to everyday life as well as music. From working with Dad in the store she had learned not only to present, promote, and sell products of all types but, more importantly, to assess the buyer — their desires, psychology, and vicissitudes. She had a sixth sense, able to piece together a full picture of someone not long after meeting them.

DeFranco certainly had a similar ability. Play a few notes or a short passage and Buddy could hear everything about you, each idiosyncrasy. What I hadn't learned in that department from Jo I learned from him, but Jo's skills were still well ahead of mine in that regard.

Our Tarleton interview took place on the ground floor of one of the major mid-Manhattan hotels. Jo and I went in, each carrying a large case. Two gentleman — one middle-aged, the other older — greeted us as we entered a small meeting room. We were shown to a large rectangular table and told to set up there. We had not only Jo's accordion with us but a wire tape recorder — these were hard to find, so we felt obliged to bring our own, though it was bigger than a milk crate and about thirty-five pounds. Jo did most of the talking, and most of the playing as well. She had an answer ready for every one of their questions. The younger man, Jack Golbert, asked the questions while the older man, Walter Jacobs, sat in a corner, away from the table. Jack was a teacher at Manhattan's prestigious Stuyvesant High School during the year, but spent his summers as General Manager and Program Director at Lake Tarleton. He seemed to quiz us on every possible eventuality, every problem that could happen on the job, wanting to know how we would handle each. Jo answered most, with me weighing in occasionally — every answer was quickly given, resulting in a back-and-forth like a well-matched heavyweight fight.

Jack even tried a negative-sell approach, noting, "It's seven days a week, this isn't one of your Christian resorts in the Poconos. The run is ten weeks, with no days off. The men will have to wear tuxedos and Josephine will have to wear gowns. There will be extra daytime performances daily at the pool and lakeside — indoors when it rains."

None of it made any of us think twice. Maybe he was testing our resolve, trying to see any sense of fear or doubt in our eyes. If so, he saw none. Then, just as Munson Campbell had predicted, "And the contract. Initially, it will be for just *one* week at a time. If your group turns out to be as good as you say, then after two weeks we'll sign you up for longer."

That reminded us of Munson's advice about salary, and we readied ourselves for that battle.

"You're asking quite a lot," Jo ventured, reiterating Jack's list of requirements. "You'll get a tight — but *swinging* — little quartet. As well, I can function as a soloist, say, on those rainy afternoons or on those dreary days when your high-paying guests threaten to leave or your nightclub comedians and floor show acts had to cancel, I will stroll and play table to table, or on stage, offering one solo after another.

"So the price — the *fair* price — has to be $425 per week."

"That's too much," Jack replied, leaving a poignant silence.

Munson had been right on target. We had decided before entering the room that we weren't there to argue price. Jo would decide a price, quote it to them, and that would be it. We kept our composure as we wrapped up the wire recorder and Jo packed her accordion into its case. Then and only then did Jacobs step forward to the table.

"Josephine," he asked, "or you prefer Jo, correct? Yes, 'Jo and Her Beaux' — it's a nice name for your group. Can you play 'Hungarian Dance #5'?"

Jo said nothing, just hoisted her accordion up and secured it into position, then launched into this well-loved classic with faultless technique. Jacobs was shocked at her playing and on the verge of tears.

"And maybe as an encore, 'Lady of Spain'?" he suggested. "And then I'll buy dinner for you both."

Jo once again flew through the tune with a virtuoso flair. She knew all those wonderful old chestnuts and from her playing, Jacobs could tell. We were hired and we knew it, even if we had to suffer Jack trying to work us over price-wise.

At dinner I cautiously inquired what Jacobs did at the hotel.

He chuckled, "I stand at the door and greet people."

I asked no more. He was starting to really like us and was having a great time. I wasn't going to misstep and ruin things. He offered us a package of hotel literature, and there it was: 'Owners: The Jacobs family'. The literature also noted that they owned the Eden Roc Hotel in Miami, and invited guests to enjoy their winters there.

Back to Pennsylvania we went, praising each other for a job well done.

"Goddamn money," Jo suddenly blurted out. "It's always about money! We'll just have to wait. I know they want us. We'll keep the door open, but the price will remain $425 unless maybe we don't agree inside the next few weeks. Then we *might* drop it a bit. You phone Charlie when we get in. Tell him the good news."

Charlie was pleased about everything but one requirement.

"Four suits!" he cried. "Suppose the job falls through after a week? What'll I do with all those clothes?"

Hearing me trying to calm Charlie down, Jo grabbed the phone.

"Charles," she said, in a voice like a mother trying to soothe a panicky child, "we'll buy them cheap. In South Philly. A couple hundred bucks for everything."

I knew that she was concerned by the fact that she called him 'Charles'. She paused and I could tell that her suggestion wasn't enough to calm Charlie down.

"Okay," she began again. "If the job folds, Steve and I will buy back the clothes."

We will? I thought. *Oh, shit.*

"Charles, are you still there?" she ventured. "Come up tomorrow about noon. We need to start rehearsing. And we'll send out ads to both 802 [The NYC Musicians' Union] and *The International Musician*. We need a good bass player, and fast."

Charlie showed up at noon the next day, empty-handed — no drums and not even his miniature practice pad, which Jo would repeatedly tell him to stop banging on, inappropriately, in public. He looked scared, as though something tragic had happened to him.

"I'm *not* going," he told us. "The job . . . I'm not going to take a chance on losing all that money on clothes."

Jo was flabbergasted. Neither of us had ever seen Tucker so negative about anything — well, other than Alaska, that is. Jo pleaded with him to take some time and think it over for a day or so.

"Come back tomorrow," she urged, "and we'll discuss it again."

But it was no use. Charlie had made up his mind. He wouldn't go and that was it. He left, and Jo and I stood in silence for a while, disbelieving.

"Well, Jo," I finally accepted, "our trio is now a duo."

* * *

We rewrote our ad: 'Wanted, immediately, two top-notch jazz musicians (bass and drums) to join Jo and Her Beaux — a quintessential quartet.'

Jo, always fair, decided we should wait twenty-four hours, thinking maybe Charlie would change his mind. But he didn't. Jo then swore that she would never again work with him. In the years that followed, she led many different groups — some exceptionally well-paid — and Charlie would moan, "I sure missed out on some incredibly good gigs!"

Jo stayed in Lansford. I returned to Arlington, keeping in contact with Jack by phone. He wanted our group and we wanted his job, but we couldn't settle on a final price. He waited and we waited. We had one advantage, though. Only we knew that we had no comparable gig waiting. But we *all* knew that his swank 5,500-acre New Hampshire resort was still short a band for the summer.

Sure, I had plenty of irons still in the fire, but I was beginning to burn out. I needed something more secure for my future. I couldn't spend all my days haggling with the likes of Jack, didn't want to kowtow to conductors like Col. Howard, and full-time jobs in big-time name bands were getting scarcer and scarcer. I was certain Jo and I would get some summer work — if not Tarleton, then someplace else — but where would I live after that? I'd definitely have to give up my room in Arlington, so what would I do in September?

I decided to head back to Philadelphia and see Dr. Hughes. He would be able to shed some light on my dilemma. Hughes practiced what present-day psychiatry knows as 'Command Therapy'. For about thirty minutes, he listened attentively and then began.

"You need to go back to college, find some new field of study. Your music kept you going, but following another discipline won't stop you from playing. You can still compose a few things, play here and there, please a few crowds, but I ask you: how contributory is that? Find a field that will better serve mankind. Now, go. Leave. Return in three weeks and tell me definitely what you're going to study in September and where. You have the G.I. Bill money, don't waste it. Use it."

I stood up, almost saluting, and returned to Washington. Three weeks to the day, I returned.

"Psychology is all I know," I told the doctor. "How people interact and things like that. So, I'll be a Psych major."

"Fine," he agreed. "And where?"

"I have no idea," I started thinking aloud. "Definitely a city. Not Washington, though, it's too hot. And Philly, well, I've been in and out so often and my aunt and grandmother are here . . ."

I stopped. I was avoiding saying that *he* was in Philadelphia too.

"Okay," he offered. "Columbia University in New York."

It didn't take more than the suggestion to know it felt right.

I raced back to Washington and immediately called the school. They were definitely interested in ex-G.I.s and would accept G.I. Bill funding. However, I would have to get a passing grade in the College Entrance Exams. They would be given the next Saturday at 9 a.m.

I arrived fifteen minutes before the exam. I hadn't slept much, having had a dance job the night before, and having gotten up quite early to catch the first train to New York. The test lasted about four hours. I did the best I could, not having studied for it. It wasn't good enough. Two weeks later I found out I missed the passing grade by one-and-a-half points! Nevertheless I would be allowed to enter, but conditionally. I would only be able to take three courses the first semester for nine credits. If and only if I earned all A's and B's, my credits would be matriculated and I would be given transfer credits for some of my courses at the Eastman School of Music.

A few days passed and I was now sure I would be leaving Washington, probably for good. I had visited New York countless times, but had no idea what living there would be like. I had resisted the idea of living in NYC for some time, but now only time would tell if it suited me or not.

* * *

Jo phoned me, sounding excited, ready to catch me up on her progress while I'd been in Washington.

"I have good news," she sang into the phone. "Lots of it! Jack called and he was very friendly. He pleaded with me to accept his terms. He sounded like a colicky baby. Eventually we made a deal. I said we'd take the job for less money — $385 a week — but only for one or two weeks. If they want to renew the contract after that for the summer, we'll sign an eight-week contract at $425 a week. He agreed. He's a nice man at times, but is he ever a cheap S.O.B.!

"Our ad for musicians got us two Trenton school teachers. Art is our new drummer — he's a bubbly, upbeat, Mr. Personality kind of a guy. Oh, and he also plays vibes. He sounded so right on the phone that I made a special trip to New Jersey to meet him. He's perfect — a natural!

"His friend Skip is just a run-of-the-mill bass player, though he also does vocals. I wasn't impressed and didn't want to hire him. However, Art wouldn't go without his buddy, so I signed up both of them.

"And listen to this: Trenton is close to Philly. And we have to buy all those clothes, anyway. So I figured we could all get together and begin rehearsing there, in Aunt Jessie's house in Germantown. Jessie said the cellar would be ideal and we wouldn't have to worry about the noise and the neighbors. And Aunt Jessie will feed us, of course."

We had maybe one month to get this show on the road — new clothes, new arrangements, a new band to rehearse, and even new hand-painted wooden music stands. We prepared a highly-polished repertoire that included only the best of modern music, the kind one could expect to hear in a smart, sophisticated cocktail lounge. This was to be a swinging but subtle, smooth little jazz group. Danceable, sure, but our music would be more for listening. Rehearsals went smoothly, though Aunt Jessie's cellar with its trap-door and ladder entrance was dingy and unpaved.

Jack had also hired another band — a so-called 'society band' with six members. They would play a slower, quieter type of dance music for twenty minutes, after which we would swing away and liven up the joint for another twenty. Look out, New Hampshire — Jo and Her Beaux are coming your way!

Jo and I had been packing for days and the weather for the first Sunday in June was ideal. This was the day we were heading up to Lake Tarleton and my mother fixed us an early breakfast. Our route twisted through Pennsylvania's Poconos, along New York State's Catskills, continued through Western Massachusetts' Berkshires, bisected Vermont's Green Mountains, then finally crossed into New Hampshire. Jo's brand-new 1956 eight-cylinder Buick Super took the roads like candy from a baby. I had been to the Poconos before for one of my earliest Saturday nightclub dates when I was sixteen, at Split Rock Lodge, a mere forty miles from home. All the other resorts we had wound our way past were ones we knew only from having written them regarding gigs — and passing them over in favor of Lake Tarleton. We wondered if we had made the right decision as the day stretched out and most of the names we passed over were left behind us.

It was about 8 p.m. when we crossed the serene Connecticut River and left sleepy Bradford, Vermont behind us. Half-buried in the bushes was an old wooden sign pointing west and indicating 'Pike', our goal. The single narrow macadam road left us no choice but to move forward. There were no buildings, billboards, or signs of life. We were in the boondocks. We followed the road as it twisted and turned and crept up, up, up. Suddenly we found ourselves at a fork in the road and screeched to a stop.

"Now what do we do?" Jo asked. "There's not a soul around to ask for directions."

A little exploration found the sign pointing to Lake Tarleton on the left fork — it had been covered by a drooping branch. We were just four miles away. That gave us reason to reset the trip odometer and we realized how far we had traveled. At the three-and-a-half mile mark, we began to climb a steep hill. Up, up, up again but much more noticeably now. Just before the odometer clicked over to four miles, we were there.

Perched on top of the vast plateau, Tarleton stretched to the horizon in all directions: large lakes, beautiful tall trees, well-manicured shrubs and flowers, a huge golf course, horses grazing in the distance, green lawns, tennis courts — all placed and spaced perfectly. Jo stopped the car and we admired it all in awe. It was breathtaking — neither of us could believe our eyes.

"Don't tell them," Jo said, staring into the distance. "But I'd work for nothing if we had to."

Minute by minute, the realization mounted that this would be the job to end all jobs. We had found paradise. Thank you, Munson Campbell!

We checked in, our names having been left at the front desk. Immediately upon hearing 'Botek', the staff gave us the royal treatment. We retired to our rooms and slept.

* * *

Breakfast was served from 7:15 a.m., and we were the first ones there. The food was great. Jack came out and met us, then introduced us to some of the staff — all healthy-looking men and women from New England and New York. Jack would emphasize which college each attended as he introduced them. He was a natural matchmaker and made sure I knew Rebecca could "clue me in about Columbia". Jo got introduced to the staff doctor. Everything was ideal — except the weather. It was pouring rain and with more than 500 anxious guests, it wasn't hard to see trouble ahead.

Art and Skip showed up at 9 a.m. and the four of us headed downstairs to the nightclub. It was empty except for the cleaning staff. There was a gorgeous view of the lake, even through the thick rain that had started to come down. This was the nearestand largest of five lakes, about five miles long and the landing site for seaplanes bringing in new guests. We needed little rehearsing, with the week in Aunt Jessie's cellar being more than enough for our combo to gel. We took the opportunity to test the acoustics and began trying out new arrangements. Our song library had more than a thousand tunes, most of which either Jo or I knew from memory — and as all four of us were accomplished sight-readers, filling in the gaps would be easy.

"God, it sounds great!" Jack exclaimed from the stairwell.

He approached us with a wary look in his eye.

"But," he continued, "the guests have gathered in the upstairs parlor because of the rain. They have nothing to do, and on days like this, even their food tastes bad to them. How about moving everything upstairs and playing for them? Settle them down some. I'd be so grateful."

Jo smiled. She'd seen similar situations many times before and knew how to handle restless crowds.

"I'll go now and start immediately," she announced. "I'll stroll, strut, sing, and show off some. But I'll start as a single. While I do, you guys move everything upstairs and set up in the far left corner by the grand piano."

Jo's first selection was enough to calm the crowd and have them clamoring for more. We had rehearsed enough together to know where to go from there. One of our most impressive arrangements was Glenn Miller's "Moonlight Serenade". I would play the melody on clarinet and Jo would supply no less than ten notes underneath. The accordion is a unique instrument. It has both bass and treble areas, similar to a piano but is constructed to sound 120 notes rather than eighty-eight. Similar to an organ, one note can be sustained while many others are added. The overall result is that we could produce a big-band sound. People sat mesmerized. When we finished amidst the cheers, someone shouted out, "Wow! How do you get so much music from just four people?"

Art turned to his vibraphone. Like Jo, he was a born leader. He quieted the room with a particularly slow and soulful rendition of the minor key masterpiece, "Angel Eyes". The inclement weather was soon forgotten by all. Even the food tasted better — to compensate for the rain, the kitchen served lobster.

Jo asked the crowd to clear the floor for dancing. We launched into "Night Train", a loud, fast, and raucous number with a hot alto solo. The band was swingin' and the joint was jumpin'. Art was sounding like Art Blakey. I was amazed at what we had managed to put together in such a short time.

Jo announced one final tune before we'd take a break.

"This one took Miami by storm," she proclaimed.

It was a fast samba standard and I joined the percussion section, playing maracas, claves, the gourd, and a small tambourine. "Tico-Tico" never sounded better.

We bowed to raucous applause and cheers from a crowd that had been depressed and bored just a short while before. Jack wasted no time in approaching the band. He had heard everything, standing nearby with the leader of the other band, Hal Graham, and his newly-acquired piano player — a first-year, nineteen-year-old student from Juilliard, one Neil Sedaka.

Steve Botek poses with clarinet during an Instrumentalists gig

Service Club at Bolling Air Force Base
The Instrumentalists led by Steve Botek, with Alex Shigo on alto sax and featuring drummer Gene Estes (formerly with Harry James)

umentalists

Lake Tarleton Club postcard
Lake Tarleton is on a plateau with five lakes and 5500 acres

Front cover of Lake Tarleton brochure

Jo and Her Beaux playing Lake Tarleton Club

Jo and Her Beaux taking a break

Jo and Her Beaux, Lake Tarleton, 1956
Guests sitting in

Jo and Her Beaux, Lake Tarleton, 1956
Guests dancing to the quartet

Jo and Her Beaux, Lake Tarleton, 1957
Posing while playing

Lake Tarleton Saturday Night Special — 1957
Jo and Her Beaux join Hal Graham and his Six Men with Neil Sedaka on piano

Buddy DeFranco with wife Joyce, their son Chad, and Ruth Botek

Victoria, B.C., 1983
Steve *(in checkered sweater)* with Francis Botek *(left)*, Ken Zmuda, and Francine Zmuda

Jack grabbed Jo, gently pulling her off to the side. What was said was out of earshot but when I saw a couple of large sheets of paper being produced and Jo pulling out her fountain pen, I knew. Jo soon returned, paper in hand.

As we walked downstairs to get some coffee, she whispered, "Looks like you all have a job *all* summer, right up to September. And how does $425 a week sound? Oh look, I think the rain is beginning to let up."

Later, Jack showed me to my room, telling me he had saved it especially for me.

"You'll be alone, except for when the various house doctors visit. These are all M.D.s, young and bright. They come to work for a day or two. Most of them love music, so you can teach them a thing or two. I'd pick their brains as well — you never know where it might lead!"

* * *

My first roommate was a young doctor who stayed only a weekend and never got a chance to rest. Still, in the brief moments he had to spare, he confided in me. The chief cook, known for his cantankerous attitude, had come to the doctor's office and once there, his demeanor changed completely. He asked that the door be closed, then whispered that his five-year-old daughter was quite ill and needed to be taken to hospital. She had the measles, which her older sister had just recovered from. The cook was afraid that the guests would panic and the Jacobs family would fire him if they found out. The doctor had to make arrangements on the Q.T., evacuating her to a hospital in the dead of night and not getting to bed until 3 a.m. I found myself wondering what kept him going at such a pace.

The next Friday a new M.D. arrived, Dr. Jenkins, a little older than the first and hailing from Boston. Our Bostonian had an easier time of things, even getting the time to go dancing. He waved to me on the stage as he proudly waltzed by with a couple of women wrapped so closely and comfortably that it was hard to tell where any of them started and the others ended. Jo elbowed me between songs and jokingly asked, "Where are *you* sleeping tonight?"

I always joked Jo had psychic powers. We were busy enough on stage that I forgot about Jenkins until about 12:45 when a bartender called me over to take a phone call. Sure enough, it was the good doctor, wanting to know my quitting time. I told him we finished at one, and he sheepishly asked if I could come home late. I interrupted to tell him it was okay, that I needed to eat anyway and the golf shop coffee house would be open until two. Later, making our way across the golf course, I found out that Jo had overheard my part of the conversation.

"I've asked around and found out that almost all of the doctors that volunteer here are single males," Jo informed me. "They don't come here for the money — they get that at the hospitals they work at. They're looking for women, for sex. And the women guests *love* doctors. It's a match made in

Heaven — one that means you'll be sharing your room with more people than you think!"

We paused to take in the Northern Lights and I mulled this over as we did.

"But doesn't Tarleton forbid the doctors from sleeping with their patients?" I asked.

"Forbid?" Jo laughed. "Why, here in Heaven, *nothing* is verboten! That's Hell you're thinking of. Shakespeare said it, 'Nothing is good or bad, only thinking makes it so.'"

Jo's mind had been on Shakespeare since an afternoon lecture on the front lawn. An English literature expert from Dartmouth College spoke extensively on the Bard, and Jo had taken it all in like a sponge. I had missed the lecture, foregoing it for the sake of going to the Dartmouth campus itself, wanting to avail myself of their fabulous library. Hanover, New Hampshire was a mere forty-five miles south, a beautiful hour-long car trip over narrow secondary roads that snaked snugly alongside the Connecticut River. The librarian was a woman in her fifties, warm and personable. I explained about my summer job and told her that, come September, I would be at Columbia University. She took down my name, phone number, and address at Tarleton and, with no further ado, signed out the three books I had found. She told me that if I needed to renew, I could save myself the trip and do so by phone. She was obliging enough that I decided to take a chance. Buddy had mentioned certain controversial books by renegade psychiatrist Wilhelm Reich which had only recently been resurfacing. Hitler had ordered them burned and, more recently, the F.B.I. had had them under investigation.

Her jaw dropped when I asked. She asked my age again, then mumbled something about being a Psychology major at Columbia. She regained her composure then her librarian's whisper took on a more conspiratorial tone.

"Yes, we have a *few*," she confided. "They're hidden back in the stacks — safely tucked away. Would you like to go back and fetch them?"

I was steadily running out of time, with only ninety minutes before I was due on stage.

"Could you help me find them?" I urged. "I might get lost back there."

Once there, I told her that two would be enough. She pulled out two shopworn hardbound volumes. Unlike the other books, once she signed these two out, she placed them carefully in a large manila envelope.

As I left, she smiled and wished me, "Good reading!"

* * *

Health was becoming a fascination of mine. Working seven days a week required not only maintaining a strict schedule but developing stamina. Jo and I met for breakfast daily, Art and Skip preferring to sleep in. It started our days off right — not only having a good meal, but being waited on and treated like royalty. One morning I felt particularly pleased with myself.

Despite my later hours, the good Dr. Jenkins was still half-dressed and hanging over the side of his bed as I returned from breakfast.

"I'm waiting for a call from the hospital in Hanover, so I'm just going to hang out here for a while," he explained, turning down my invitation to join Jo and me for breakfast.

"Is this about the young boy who fell over in front of the hotel last night?" I asked.

"Yes," he asked, uncertain if he was being gossiped about. "Were you there?"

"Yes," I told him. "I saw you place a rolled-up handkerchief into the side of his mouth. So he didn't bite his tongue, right? It was an epileptic seizure, wasn't it?"

He was impressed. I recounted watching him take charge of the situation, getting the bellhop, a college quarterback, to lift the kid up and place him in a car the doc had ordered. Jenkins had previously jumped into the back seat and was carefully adjusting the kid as he was laid down with his head on the doc's lap.

"I don't want to sound corny," I added, "but I remember thinking that that's the kind of doctor I want if I get sick."

He thanked me, saying it was all part of the job.

"Physicians always impress me," I told him. "They always seem to know what to do."

We talked for a little while and he told me I had been lucky to only have had good doctors. He seemed to have other things on his mind as I talked and what that was became clear when the phone rang. After a brief exchange, he sighed with relief and smiled up at me.

"Good," he said, putting down the phone. "I can pick up the boy later today. Thank God that hospital is only forty-five minutes away."

He was more relaxed now and we continued to talk. He told me that sure, doctors work hard *sometimes*, but not always.

"Much like you musicians," he suggested. "They tried to teach me trombone when I was a kid, but they just ended up telling my parents I have a tin ear. I love music, but I don't understand it in any depth. My girlfriend can point out if something is in a major or minor key, and I find myself wondering how she knows. I pretend I know too, but I don't and I'm too embarrassed to tell her."

"Doc," I asked, "do you have ten or fifteen minutes to spare? There's a record player in Art's room. Come on. I'll show you how to recognize the difference between major and minor in no time."

I remember that as we walked across the meadow to Art's room, I asked him the difference between a cerebrum and a cerebellum. For the rest of the weekend, we traded information, my teaching him about music and him teaching me about medicine.

At one point he asked about the book I was carrying, suspect as it was in its manila envelope like a blue magazine. He knew of Reich, having studied him in college Psych courses, and we began a long conversation about the man and his history. Jenkins had had a Jewish professor of German origin who loved to lecture on Reich, who had left Germany when Hitler came to power. The doc had learned Reich's personal history and told me of his expulsion from Nazi Germany and a few other European countries after that before he finally settled on Long Island. Later, he began a research institute in rural upper Maine.

We talked about how old Wilhelm's support of women's rights, prisoners' rights, and unhampered sexuality were a threat to Hitler's views. Here in the States, the F.B.I. had spied on Reich's Maine research laboratories and seized some of his property. We talked about his concept of orgone, a universal life energy that existed everywhere. The Food and Drug people and the F.B.I. leapt into action when they heard these claims, even stopping one of Reich's physician-students from transporting an orgone accumulator across the border. The institute was shut down and Reich himself was arrested. He died a few months later in a Pennsylvania penitentiary. A pre-existing heart condition was cited as the cause. According to rumor, he refused proper cardiac medication.

America at the time was threatened by Wilhelm's ideas, which are still controversial today. The air here still is tinged with traces of McCarthyism and other fault-finding, self-righteous, and rigid doctrines. Given time, though, the day will come — the seeds have been sown for a revolution in our thinking with the sexual revolution, women's rights, gay rights, minority rights, and the rise of adolescents taking control of their own culture.

When Jenkins left, the weekend over, I set to reading the Reich books I had gotten from the library. It wasn't easy — big words and profound concepts made absorbing Reich slow going. I took to keeping a dictionary by my side as I read. I had already been aware of many of the concepts from Buddy, from Dr. Pelletiere, and from the readings they had both inspired me to take on. Buddy credits Reichian therapy with helping him move from thinking technical skill was all-important to being the free, wild bebopper he became. He points out "the clarinet, being constructed the way it is, can develop compulsive traits in the clarinetist. This in turn makes one mechanistic."[1] Further, he notes that prior to his exposure to Reichian therapy, "The critics called me the 'mechanical man of jazz'."[1]

At first I had been feeling the effects of Reich's theories vicariously, through Buddy. Following each lesson, life felt doable. My teenage vicissitudes faded away and the clarinet opened itself up to me. Now I was

---

[1] *A Life in the Golden Age of Jazz: A Biography of Buddy DeFranco*, Parkside Publications, Seattle

delving into Reich headfirst, on my own. It required renewing the books at the library a couple of times, but I was feeling it in my days at Tarleton and showing it in my playing. Even Jo remarked on my playing, how it became freer and more powerful as the summer went on.

I remained in touch with Jenkins after he left Tarleton and returned to Boston. He became yet another mentor to me, eventually convincing me not to just pursue psychology, telling me I was too bright not to become a full-fledged physician. He let me know that Jack Golbert felt the same. It made sense to me — connecting body and mind for the perfect gestalt.

* * *

June and July hurried by and August came in, full, ripe, and beautiful. The season would officially end with Labor Day and we would all leave. Still, some students couldn't wait that long and, tired of slaving away daily, quit early. We all knew that quitting meant we wouldn't be hired the next summer, and those who had worked previous years assured us that sticking it out meant a bonus as well as an invitation to return. Our little combo was more than comfortable and had no intention of leaving. We had won Tarleton's respect and trust and were sure to be asked back the following year.

We were so liked that when one of the kitchen staff quit, Jack asked Jo if she had anyone she could recommend for the job.

"Yes," she answered without a second thought. "My kid brother, Francis. He's relatively free for the summer. He's sixteen, honest, reliable, and multifaceted. He can take on practically anything."

I quickly seconded the idea. Francis *did* have work in front of him, of course — in the family store. However, we both knew he could use the change of scenery, and I was sure that the time away from Dad would open his eyes some to the world beyond Lansford. Jack agreed to hire him, sight unseen, and it only took a few phone calls to arrange things.

Two days later I met Francis in Bradford. He got off the train, bags in hand, and was full of questions on the drive back up to Tarleton. Once there he never asked anything else, adapting quickly to the resort and enjoying himself thoroughly. He was assigned to share a room with the resident tailor. The tailor had been at Tarleton for a few summers and knew the lay of the land. Consequently their room was much better equipped than mine. While I almost froze on certain nights, Francis would brag about sleeping half-nude without a blanket thanks to the two space heaters the tailor had procured for them.

The Botek family was now firmly part of the Tarleton family. It didn't hurt that Jack Golbert was a devoted family man and, as such, saw those of us who worked at the resort as part of his extended family. Jack's wife and teenage son Andy spent the summer with him — she kept to herself, rarely being seen in public, while Andy, on the other hand, seemed to show up everywhere. Some saw him as a spy or a snitch, gathering information to pass along to his father, so they treated him with kid gloves and were on their best behavior around him. For my part, I didn't change my approach in the least.

I felt comfortably part of the *other* family Jack had assembled from all walks of life. I was proud to be part of the Tarleton family. Bright young doctors, lawyers, students, teachers, musicians, artists, actors, and others — Jack brought us all together and seemed to have a knack for finding the right fit. We had dance instructors, a portrait artist, the tailor — every possible desire of the guests was catered to. Everyone got along well with everyone else and took their jobs seriously. Once any new staffer had begun work, Jack reveled in his matchmaking, taking special care to pair up this staff member with that one. There may have been some vested interest there, as it helped to keep us from fraternizing with the guests, but he seemed to enjoy it for its own sake, following the progress of his matches with great interest.

Every Friday I would have a guaranteed meeting with Jack. Usually around 6 p.m. he would phone me to tell me that the new doctor had arrived. As the doctors would room with me, Jack would come over to my room to personally introduce us. They were all personable men, relaxed and open, looking at their time at Tarleton as a vacation as much as a job. As with Jenkins, I would find myself in conversation with them, pumping them for information and ideas and, for the most part, they seemed equally interested in talking to me about music. Over the summer I built up a store of knowledge to take with me to Columbia University in the fall, finding myself increasingly fascinated with medicine and increasingly sure I had made the right choice. Even so, my incidental study of medicine was only a small part of my summer at Tarleton and, beyond it and my time playing music, I availed myself of the many amenities the resort had to offer.

* * *

Tarleton itself was like a small city, self-contained and with all the amenities one could possibly expect, from the cigar shop to the seaplane landing site. We even had a slot machine, completely illegal in New Hampshire at the time, but no one ever complained about it. I never asked about it and never played it. It stood six feet tall in glistening stainless steel, making no attempt to hide itself, instead perching unmissably a few feet away from the checkout at the cigar store. Once when I went in to purchase the evening newspaper I found myself waiting behind a guest bent over the various cigar boxes, picking through the wares. I was in no rush, and this well-dressed heavyset man was a guest, after all. After a short while he stood to his full height, taller than me, and to my great surprise, I noticed his uniform. This was a New Hampshire state cop! He was practically standing on top of the prohibited slot machine but seemed to look right through it. I was impressed. I'd known that Tarleton had clout, but this was a clear display of it that I hadn't expected.

For all it did have, Tarleton *did* lack one significant thing — a barber. As a public performer, I was expected to always look my best. My time in the Air Force had already built the habit of regular haircuts, especially considering Colonel Howard's pickiness on the issue — I had seen more than one of my buddies transferred because their haircuts didn't suit his standards. As my brother-in-law Ernie often remarked, "There's the right way, the wrong way, and the Army way." That had also applied in the Air Force.

There was no 'Tarleton way', no standard I had to follow, but I did have certain standards to uphold. Not only was I representing the resort, but also Jo and the band. Being removed as the resort was, it took a twenty-minute car ride to Bradford in Vermont to find a barber. This was a town with about ten thousand residents, small enough that the state highway served as the main street. Still, it was large enough to have a number of small stores lining both sides of the road, including a barber shop. It reminded me of the small Pennsylvania towns I was used to — Lansford and the others around it. I revisited the familiar comfort of a soda fountain counter at the local drug store and, ordering a vanilla milkshake, inquired about a good barber. After all, a small-town drug store owner knows everything about everybody.

The owner assured me that Anthony's, directly across the street, was the place to go. He told me to be sure to wait for Anthony himself, who was the owner and the best barber in town. He then told me to wait at the counter and my milkshake would be ready shortly.

It was. And before it arrived, I had forgotten completely about it. The waitress was tall and lithe, with a headful of billowing reddish-blonde hair. Her light green eyes sparkled as she spoke. This was Barbara. I had watched her making the shake from my seat and my dish of choice had changed by the time she brought it over to me. I was not just turned on, I was turned inside-out. I immediately made some comment about being from out of town to strike up a conversation.

"Are you from New York?" she asked me.

"Try Philadelphia," I boasted. New York was much maligned and seen almost as the enemy in small towns. "The Poconos. I'm here for the summer, though. Up at the Lake Tarleton Club. I'm a musician."

I said the last with utter assuredness. I was comfortable enough flirting and dating, but I was short on time and pulled out the most effective weapon in my arsenal. Still, she had work to do and this wasn't Washington or Rochester. In a small town, some foreknowledge is expected — after all, everybody knows everybody. I didn't know if she was married, engaged, or going steady. I could assume the first wasn't an issue — if she *was* married, she wouldn't likely be working. This was, after all, small-town Vermont in the 1950s. I knew I couldn't ask directly without making a fool of myself, and I wanted to be cautious. I might not have been from New York, but the conventional wisdom was that the locals didn't think so highly of the

Tarleton crowd, looking at us as rich, New York *types* even if that wasn't our home. I had only the brief moments when she returned to the counter to ask if everything was alright and I struggled to think of something to talk to her about. *Anything.*

"So, Anthony's is the best," I blurted out. "Do you know how much he charges?"

"My dad goes there," she smiled casually. "It's $1.50, but best to give him at least a fifty-cent tip.

"Anthony's an expert in shaping the way the hair hugs the neck. I can always tell from the back if a man's hair was cut by Anthony. It's his signature."

I was assured about the barbershop but had also committed to going there, so, having drained the last of my milkshake, I left a fifty-cent tip and promised to return soon.

It was a one-hour wait to see Anthony, but it was everything that had been promised. We got along famously, his being Italian and my having picked up the odd word during my time in Rochester and in Italy. He also loved music and we talked about jazz. When he was done, I was so pleased with the results that I gave him a full dollar as a tip.

"Come back soon," he urged. "Come again anytime, Stefano!"

There's something about a fresh new haircut. I felt energized, empowered. I decided to revisit the drug store. Barbara was still there, though much busier. Still, she noticed me the instant I came in the door.

"Turn around," she called out. "Let me see the back."

I could see her nodding in the mirror on the far wall.

"Oh, yeah, he did a great job!" she assured me, before explaining to the woman beside her, "He just went to see Anthony."

I walked over and sat at the counter, smiling, feeling brazen and daring.

"Another vanilla milkshake?" she called out.

"Definitely," I answered. "Last time was so good, I had to come right back!"

She remembered my order! That charged me even more, though it kept her from coming over to find out what I wanted. Even so, by the time she brought over my shake, I had scrawled on a napkin:

Dear Barbara,
Thanks for your help!
Will you please go out with me?
I'm not married and not going steady.
Huh? Please?
Stephen

She saw the napkin the instant she came over and quickly read it. She hesitated and then gave me a long slow once-over before looking me directly in the eyes. She walked away without a word and I sighed. *At least I made the effort*, I thought. I was barely into my second sip of the milkshake when she walked past again, slipping another napkin in front of me.

> *Dear Stephen,*
> *I'll be short and sweet: OK. Tell me when.*
> *Barbara*

My schedule at Tarleton didn't allow much in the way of dating, at least not in Bradford. We went out for a few afternoon drives when we could arrange it and the attraction between us was magnetic. It wasn't long before a series of phone calls led to plans for her to visit me at the resort. I could hardly wait as I drove down to Bradford to pick her up. We laughed and joked on the drive back up, but she was tired by the time we arrived so I brought her to my room to rest. It was mid-week so I wasn't sharing the room and didn't have to worry about the larger and more demanding weekend crowds. I told her to catch up on her rest and I would be back for a late date after my gig, promising her favorite drink, a screwdriver, on my return.

After the show, I flew back to my room to find her sprawled over my bed, leafing through a magazine. I lifted her into my arms and planted a long passionate kiss on her lips. Still, I wasn't a visiting doctor, I was salaried staff, so this wasn't the proper place for anything hot and heavy. I grabbed bottles of vodka and orange juice I had brought and led her back to the car. We drove happily into the star-filled New Hampshire night. The back roads were narrow, winding, and only seldom traveled during the day, but now they were completely clear. I found a convenient place to park deep in the woods. We cuddled there, drinks in hand, radio playing, windows open, kissing feverishly between sips.

This was some time back, and no one ever thought of such precautions as a designated driver. Being young and white, even if we came across a policeman, all we would have to do is chew some gum and claim to be lost and we would simply be led home. Still, the roads were clear and we made it back without a hitch, smiling as we made our way to bed.

I saw Barbara when I could over the rest of the summer, but cooler weather arrived and that meant an end to afternoon swims in the lake. Sweaters were donned and we all knew the summer was coming to an end. Jack invited the band back for the following year and we tentatively accepted, my schooling being one of the factors that might keep me away. Barbara threatened to hide inside my saxophone and accompany me back to New York. I hated to leave but I had to. College awaited, as did my future in medicine.

* * *

Playing music that summer was glorious and the crowds ate it up. Finally,

I'd had a real, steady, full-time job playing the music I wanted to be playing alongside musicians I respected as both players and friends. Columbia University and my medical career were around the corner, and the house doctors had shared their secrets with me, showing me more of that world I had only started to explore. It was a perfect way to blend the two career paths I had chosen, and to celebrate them both. I knew that I had chosen well.

Medicine was to be my primary career from then on, but I would never forget my first love. Jazz still resounds in my days and in my memories. Songs recall events and friends I cherish. And I like to think that as I moved into medicine, I brought some jazz into that sometimes stuffy world.

Even my father recognized that, as I found out when I eventually returned home as a fully-licensed M.D. He sat drinking brandy in the kitchen as I told him I was ready to begin repaying him. He looked up at me, furrowed his brow, and then, in a deadly serious voice, simply said, "Forget it!" before getting up and going to the grocery store.

I asked my mother, sewing beside his now-empty chair, "Is he serious? No debt?"

"Yes," she told me. "Your father always means exactly what he says." A moment later, she added with a wink, "However, half that money was mine!"

My parents both understood that Eastman, and music in general, was an important and integral part of my journey.

There are probably some who would think I wasted my time playing music when I could have started studying medicine that much earlier. They simply don't understand — it was jazz that led me to my dreams, my triumphs, and myself. I learned to improvise, a skill that applies as well to life as it does to music.

Most of all, I learned to face every challenge with a song in my heart, whether or not there was one on my lips.

Epilogue I

About fifteen years after my discharge from the Air Force, I was steeped in my study of psychiatry. Dressing for work one day, I was listening to WQXR radio in New York and heard that the Airmen of Note would be giving a free concert at Lincoln Center. I hadn't thought of my Washington days in quite some time and wondered if I should go. I didn't know what seeing the band would stir up in me — fond memories of old friends or mental anguish at remembering the unnecessary challenges set upon us. What made up my mind was hearing that one Colonel Gabriel would be conducting.

Barney Mallon and other Eastmanite friends had rushed to enlist not long after I did, to avoid being drafted. Gabriel had been the conductor at Samson Air Force Base in Geneva, NY and Barney had served under him for his hitch. Had I stayed on at Eastman, I likely would have scurried to Samson myself, the competition for the Washington band becoming too much to count on as an escape from the front lines.

I decided that seeing the band alone would not be enough, so I channeled Charlie Tucker and dashed backstage a half-hour before the opening curtain. Without even asking for identification, a sleepy security guard directed me to the conductor and I found his dressing room door wide open.

Gabriel stood there looking into the mirror, adjusting his tie. White shirttails hung outside his trousers and his suspenders looped down over his backside. His pants weren't quite down and he wasn't shaving, but I figured my mother's advice applied just the same. It was the perfect time. I walked in, apologized for interrupting, and introduced myself.

"I'm Steve Botek," I said. "I'm a good friend of Barney Mallon. We went to school together."

"Steve *Botek*?" he asked, stroking his chin before breaking into a wide smile. "Wait! You were in the band under Colonel Howard, correct?"

I was amazed. That my name could be known to him at all, these many years after my hitch, had not even crossed my mind. We talked about Barney and the band as he dressed, adjusting his trousers and donning his elaborate military jacket.

"How does it look, Steve?" he asked, demonstrating his dress uniform.

"Sir," I answered, feeling he'd earned the honor, "You look fantastic. You'll knock 'em dead."

We left together, Gabriel leading me backstage behind the still-closed curtain. He asked where I was sitting, and I explained that I had gone directly backstage and not yet found a seat. He motioned to an opening in a door through which we could see the seating.

"Do you see those vacant seats dead center in the front row?" he asked. "They're reserved for friends and family of the band. Go through this door and please use one. They're the best seats in the house."

The band, seventy members strong, completely covered the stage. I was so close I could have stood up and almost touched those in the clarinet section. And in that clarinet section was an old acquaintance, Al Bader, who I knew from our time at Bolling — he had stayed with the band all those years. Our eyes met, and he offered a crooked smile. He pointed to the percussion section and John Richardson, a loyal, cooperative sweetheart of a drummer who had played in my old jazz combo back in Washington as well as the Air Force band stationed at nearby Andrews Field. He'd always been a pleasure to play with and I smiled widely on seeing him, sticks in hand again. The next time our eyes met, Al pointed out John Mioca, yet another old friend, trumpet at the ready.

Gabriel came onstage and mounted the podium, readying to give the down beat. I readied myself for something familiarly military, expecting to hear Sousa — having gone backstage first, I hadn't had the chance to get a program. Instead, the band flew into a highly technical, vivace tempo, state-of-the-art composition I had never heard before. I was glad I hadn't brought my horn and tried to sit in — I was no longer in shape to keep up with this without weeks of practice.

I was excited by this exciting band and their challenging repertoire, so different from what I had known in Washington. Re-enlistment even crossed my mind! Had we been playing music like this, I might never have left.

When the concert ended, I jumped on stage and gave Bader a big hug. Richardson and Mioca joined us and tears welled up for each of us. I rode back with the group to their midtown hotel and shared a few drinks and laughs in the hotel bar. I teased Al when I found out he had achieved the rank of Master Sergeant, making him effectively Master Bader. As we talked, I found out that everyone was *happy*, in an unconditional manner that never would have been possible under Colonel Howard.

We hugged and said our goodbyes, but not before a toast to old times. And another to jazz.

Epilogue II

Buddy and I have stayed friends over the years. While the days of playing classical all day in school and reserving jazz for off-campus nightspots are gone, Buddy bemoans what has been lost.

"These jazz majors today are missing the hole-in-the-wall jazz joints where, years ago, jam sessions were held virtually seven days a week. They get their jazz in school, and consequently, these new jazz-major cats, sure they know their horns, but eventually they all sound alike. As though they cloned themselves! Where's the newness? Where are the innovators?"

The spotlight has shifted from those innovators to their imitators. Yes, these new kids are cats — copycats for the most part.

Buddy still practices daily. When I asked him if he wouldn't still be able to play at his standard even if he laid off for a while, his answer was uncompromising.

"That's what's wrong with the older guys — they still play, but they don't practice. If I lay off, sure I'll still be able to play, but my chops, my embouchure, will suffer and my intonation seems to have trouble. Take Pablo Casals. He preached in his later years about thinking like a young person, even as a child. He would still practice every day — even the piano, which was hard for him, not being his instrument. Each morning he would sit at the piano, pull out some Bach, and train his fingers."

I asked, "Buddy, at what age does an old cat stop practicing?"

"Never," he immediately shot back. "Do it until you drop."

Buddy still has health issues, most notably a salivary gland infection, possibly from all the years of overuse of his salivary glands to play his instrument. Even knowing that doesn't stop him from practicing and playing. He also suffers from tinnitus, a constant mild ringing in his ears — but he claims it doesn't seem to bother him when he's playing. The complaints continue: leg pain, back pain, issues with his vision made worse after a recent cataract removal. Now that I'm an M.D., I'm in position to give *him* advice, but I still learn from him constantly about music and about life.

In December 2006, I saw Buddy with his group The Statesmen of Jazz at New York's Tribeca Performing Arts Center. He was eighty-three years old at the time, and performing as part of Jack Kleinsinger's concert series, then in its 37th year. The show was effectively an old-fashioned jam session with a pick-up group consisting of Derek Smith on piano, Rufus Reid on bass, Ed Mertz Jr on drums, Randy Sandke on trumpet, and Howard Alden and Joe Cohen both on guitar. These were consummate professionals, though, so from start to finish it sounded like everything had been rehearsed for years.

The third song was "Autumn Leaves" and each player took their turn soloing, each with excellent timing and spectacular tone. DeFranco's turn arrived and his intricate improvisations demonstrated confidence, creativity, and agility that brought tears to my eyes. Here was an 83-year-old master who plays better today than he did yesterday.

This is why he practices as much as he does. Buddy couldn't be content resting on his laurels like most of us would do. He does what he loves and loves what he does. Since I first met him, he's been the same. He wraps his hands gently around the horn, his fingers hardly move, and he stoops over just a bit as if he were hugging someone. Breathing in and out in long excursions, he then totally engulfs the clarinet — he becomes one with it. It's a sensual embrace and an intimate thing to watch. Or hear. While he looks serene to the observer, his brain is moving a mile a minute feverishly improvising, each time in new directions.

No sooner had he finished when he announced, still out of breath, "Now we'll try something *really* fast."

Vintage Buddy. Just when you think he's taken things to the limits, he shows you there aren't any. The band shifted into overdrive, playing the Charlie Parker classic "Anthropology". Each player stepped up and pushed the others on further, faster, freer, and finer. The audience was electrified.

That, though, was simply a dress rehearsal for the next day when the group assembled at the Nola Recording Studios on 57th Street across from Carnegie Hall. Sitting in on that session, I heard the same boundless energy and creativity, but this time so close that it was a spiritual experience.

It was, to put it simply, *jazz*.

And I love it still.

Appendix

Lansford High School Report Card

Pupil Stephen T. Botek

Grade Twelve Year 1946 1947

Teacher Mr. Michael Oriel H. R. No. 38

Please Return Report Card Promptly

SUBJECTS	First Period	Second Period	Third Period	Fourth Period	Fifth Period	Sixth Period		Final Grade	Numerical Grade
Days Absent	6	2	5	8.5	12	16½			50
Times Tardy	0	1	0	0	0	0			
Rank	29	28	59	54	37			B+	49
Average	2.80	2.8	2.2	2.4	2.6			C+	2.40
English IV	B	B	B	A	A			B+	3.40
Algebra II	B	B	C	C	D			C+	2.20
Geometry	C	C	D	D	D			C−	1.80
Physics	B	B	B	B	C			B−	2.80
Type I	B	B	C	C	B			B−	2.60
Ins. Music									
Phy. Ed.	B	B	B	—					

SYSTEM OF GRADING

A—Superior Work
B—Good, Above Average
C—Average
D—Below Average Passing
F—Below Passing
FF—Failure

Values Assigned
A—4
B—3
C—2
D—1
F—0
FF—(-1)

No. in class 119

Steve Botek's report card from Lansford High School
Note the number of days absent and grades suffering owing to time spent in New York for music lessons

BOTEK'S MARKET
301 E. Bertsch St.
LANSFORD
"Quality Meats & Produce" PH. 645 – 5933

EASTER KIELBASSY!

— Time to place your order —

Botek's famous homemade (ready to eat). Naturally we're proud of the many compliments we get on our homemade kielbassy. We use only the finest Gov't inspected meats, add the proper touch of spices from a century old famous European recipe. The result is a delightfully delicious smoked sausage that makes your holiday meal complete with or without garlic.

NO PRESERVATIVES ADDED .... $2.79 LB.

COMPLETE LINE OF BAKING NEEDS:
• POPPY SEED • LOOSE LEKVAR • WALNUT MEATS
• YEAST • PRESSED COTTAGE CHEESE

• SPECIAL LAMB & VEAL ROASTS FOR BLESSING
• EASTER HAMS: BLACKHAWK, A&B, KUNZLER
• FRESH FISH & OYSTERS — LOOSE BUCKET HERRING

Ad for Botek's Market, circa 1982
Francis Botek was running the store at the time

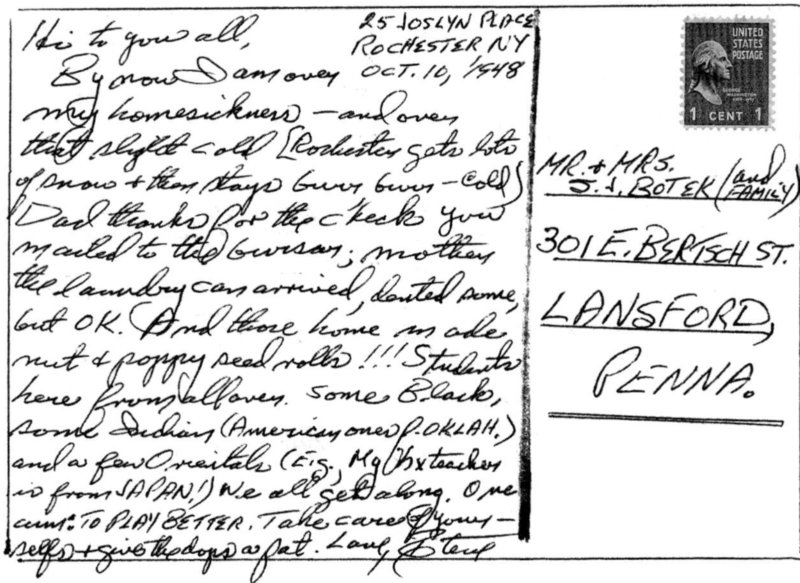
25 JOSLYN PLACE
ROCHESTER NY
OCT. 10, 1948

Hi to you all,
By now I am over my homesickness — and over that slight cold [Rochester gets lots of snow + then stays brrr brrr — cold] Dad thanks for the check you mailed to the bursar; mother the laundry can arrived, dented some, but OK. And those home made nut + poppy seed rolls!!! Students here from all over. Some Black, some Indian (American ones from OKLAH.) and a few Orientals (E.g. My Hx teacher is from JAPAN!) We all get along. One aim: TO PLAY BETTER. Take care of yourselfs + give the dogs a pat. Love, Steve

MR. + MRS. J. J. BOTEK (and FAMILY)
301 E. BERTSCH ST.
LANSFORD,
PENNA.

Postcard to family

25 JOSLYN PL.
ROCHESTER NY
OCT. 10, 1948

DEAR PROF. LANGENUS,
ROCHESTER HAS OFFERED EVERYTHING YOU SAID IT WOULD. MY TEACHERS ARE TOP NOTCH (RUFUS AREY, A MAINE ORIGINALLY IS MY CLAR. TEACHER) HE USES AN OBREN GLASS MOUTHPIECE - HE CERTAINLY KNOWS WHO YOU ARE — THEY ALL DO. THE MANY ALTERNATE FINGERINGS YOU SHARED WITH ME SURE COME IN HANDY. (I'D BE LOST W/O THEM) AND REEDS! YOU'VE ALWAYS GOTTEN ME SOME SELECT ONES & MR. LUTHER HINES in MISSISSIPPI. PLEASE ASK HIM TO MAIL ME SAY, 10. (I'll REMIT $$ QUICKLY) TAKE CARE of YOUR HEALTH. BEST to YOU BOTH. SINCERELY, Stephen

MR. GUSTAVE LANGENUS
DRAW K
E. NORTHPORT,
NEW YORK

Steve's postcard of thanks to Professor Gustave Langenus
For his invaluable teachings and encouragement to attend the Eastman School of Music

25 JOSLYN PLACE
ROCHESTER NY
OCT. 10, 1948

Dear Sgt. Dietz,
Just a note [illegible] you that I really did come to Eastman (Your generous offer to join the USAF Band in Wash. was warmly appreciated but it seems school won out.)
Recently, on radio I heard one of your band's broadcasts. A Colonel Howard I believe conducted. Sounded so fine. If your band ever comes to Rochester please look me up. Eastman wld. be glad to host you. THANKS AGAIN, Steve Bolek

SGT. GEO. DIETZ
FIRST CHAIR CLARINET
"THE" U.S. AIR FORCE BAND
BOLLING A.F. BASE
WASHINGTON,
DC

Steve's postcard of regret to Sgt. George Dietz
Graciously declining an early offer to join the United States Air Force Band

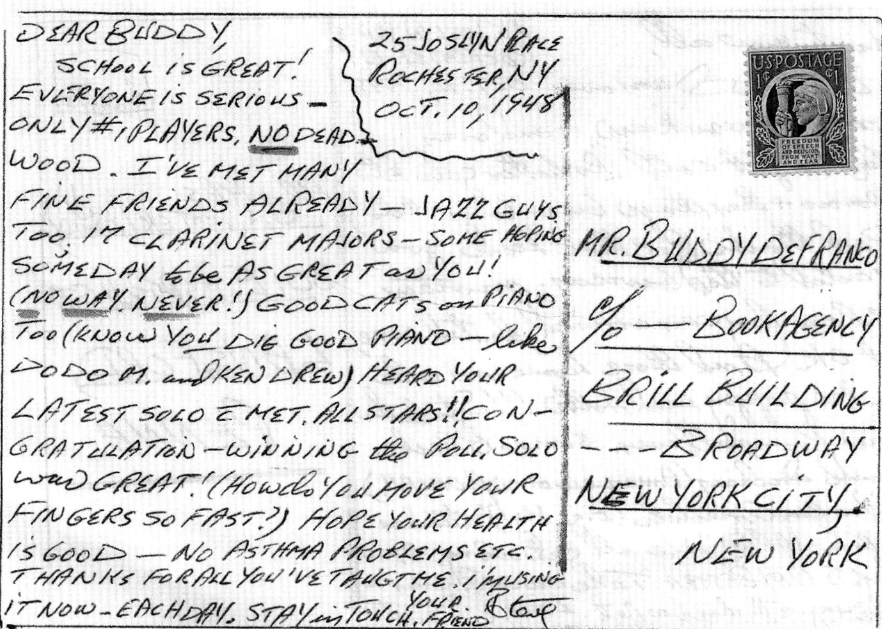
25 JOSLYN PLACE
ROCHESTER, NY
OCT. 10, 1948

DEAR BUDDY,
SCHOOL IS GREAT!
EVERYONE IS SERIOUS —
ONLY #1 PLAYERS, NO DEAD
WOOD. I'VE MET MANY
FINE FRIENDS ALREADY — JAZZ GUYS
TOO. 17 CLARINET MAJORS — SOME HOPING
SOMEDAY to be AS GREAT as YOU!
(NO WAY. NEVER!) GOOD CATS on PIANO
TOO (KNOW YOU DIG GOOD PIANO — like
DODO M. and KEN DREW) HEARD YOUR
LATEST SOLO c̄ MET. ALL STARS!! CON-
GRATULATION — WINNING the POLL. SOLO
was GREAT! (How do YOU MOVE YOUR
FINGERS SO FAST?) HOPE YOUR HEALTH
IS GOOD — NO ASTHMA PROBLEMS ETC.
THANKS FOR ALL YOU'VE TAUGHT ME. I'M USING
IT NOW — EACH DAY. STAY in TOUCH. YOUR FRIEND, Steve

US POSTAGE 1¢ 1¢
FREEDOM OF SPEECH AND RELIGION FROM WANT AND FEAR

MR. BUDDY DEFRANCO
c/o — BOOK AGENCY
BRILL BUILDING
——— BROADWAY
NEW YORK CITY,
NEW YORK

Steve's enthusiastic postcard to Buddy DeFranco from Eastman

Dr. Howard Hanson On Owning A STEINWAY ...

The Steinway is the official piano of the Rochester Philharmonic and Erich Leinsdorf, its conductor.

"It is a pleasure for me to add my praise to that of my many musical colleagues in behalf of the Steinway piano. I have always had a very great admiration for the instrument and for the painstaking care and artistry which has gone into its construction. My own Steinway is a constant joy to me,—a whole orchestra in itself."

WHEN YOUR WANTS ARE MUSICAL COME TO

Levis Music Stores Ad
Steve frequented this store while attending Eastman — note endorsement by Eastman school director Howard Hanson

ШТАБ ВОЗДУШНЫХ СИЛ СОЕДИНЕННЫХ ШТАТОЗ В ЕВРОПЕ
HEADQUARTERS UNITED STATES AIR FORCES IN EUROPE

(APO) 633 US Air Force
ПОЛЕВАЯ ПОЧТА №
6 July 1954

/Число /
(Date)

КАСАЕТСЯ : Приказ на поездку в Берлин/Германия/,и обратно.
SUBJECT: Orders for Travel to Berlin, Germany and return

АДРЕСАТ: S SGT STEPHEN T BOTEK AF13368052
(Rank, name, serial number and branch of service)

Вышеуказанное лицо , AMERICAN CITIZEN
The person named above
(Nationality)

национальности уполномочено отправиться в Берлин/Германия /
is authorised to proceed to Berlin, Germany and return

и обратно 8 JULY 1954 -- 13 JULY 1954
(Inclusive dates)

По ПРИКАЗУ LIEUTENANT GENERAL TUNNER:

HEADQUARTERS OFFICIAL USAFE

Edith R. Anderson
EDITH R. ANDERSON
1st Lt USAF
Asst. Adjutant

USAFE FORM 11 SEP 50 149 REPLACES USAFE FORM 149, 15 MAY 50 - WHICH IS OBSOLETE

Air Force—USAFE, Wsbn, Ger-123-5666

Travel Permit to East Berlin, 1954
Official permission paper allowing Steve entry into Soviet-controlled East Berlin

The Invitation
Letter of May 1955 from Jack Golbert of the Lake Tarleton Club

Sky-High IN THE WHITE MOUNTAINS

Lake Tarleton Club

PIKE, NEW HAMPSHIRE

Dear Miss Botek –

Your unit does sound interesting – but presents many problems – foremost of which is space. I cannot hire a unit without hearing it – that is your problem.

I already have a 6 pc. unit – and do need a 3-4 pc. strolling unit – which must speciali[ze] in Latin American.

The job is 7 days a week – music eve[ry] evening – plus 1 afternoon hour 5 days a week and cocktail session 5 days a week.

You can take it from there.

Cordially,
Jack Golbert

5/11/55

Tel. MA 20972

Home of the White Mountains Festival of the 7 Arts

Contract Blank

AMERICAN FEDERATION OF MUSICIANS
OF THE UNITED STATES AND CANADA
(HEREIN CALLED "FEDERATION")

LOCAL NUMBER 374

THIS CONTRACT for the personal services of musicians, made this 29 day of July, 1955, between the undersigned employer (hereinafter called the employer) and 4 (Including Leader) musicians (hereinafter called employees) represented by the undersigned representative.

WITNESSETH, That the employer employs the personal services of the employees, as musicians severally, and the employees severally, through their representative, agree to render collectively to the employer services as musicians in the orchestra under the leadership of Jo Botek, according to the following terms and conditions:

Name and Address of Place of Engagement: Lake Tarleton Club

Date(s) of employment: July 29, 1955 to ~~Labor Day~~ (Sept 4) inclusive

Hours of employment: Policy of house

Type of engagement (specify whether dance, stage show, banquet, etc.)

The employer is hereby given an option to extend this agreement for a period of ______ weeks beyond the original term thereof. Said option can be made effective only by written notice from the employer to the employees not later than ______ days prior to the expiration of said original term that he claims and exercises said option.

PRICE AGREED UPON $ 850 per week plus room & board (Terms and Amount)

This price includes expenses agreed to be reimbursed by the employer in accordance with the attached schedule, or a schedule to be furnished the employer on or before the date of engagement.

To be paid weekly (Specify When Payments Are to Be Made)

ADDITIONAL TERMS AND CONDITIONS

[illegible]

Name of Employer: Mr. Jack Golbert
Street Address: Lake Tarleton Club
City: Pike State: N.H.
Phone:

Accepted by Employer: Jack Golbert for L.T.C.
Accepted: Jo Botek (Orchestra Leader)
Address: 340 E [illegible] St.
By: Lansford Pa (Representative of Employees)

The Contract
Contract for Jo and Her Beaux to play at Lake Tarleton for the summer of 1955

Bibliography

Anonymous. "New King". *Time Magazine*, March 2, 2007. www.time.com/time/magazine/article/0,9171,762896,00.html

Anonymous. "World War Two: The Stars Wore Stripes". *Fort George G. Meade Museum*, January 6, 2007. www.ftmeade.army.mil/museum/Archive_Stars_Master.html

Artie Shaw – Quest For Perfection. Film. Directed by Russell Davies. UK: BBC, 2003.

Artie Shaw: Time Is All You've Got. Film. Directed by Brigitte Berman. Canada: Bridge Film Productions, 1985.

Bazzana, Kevin. *Glenn Gould: The Performer in the Work*. Oxford, UK: Clarendon Press, 1997.

Bazzana, Kevin. *Wondrous Strange: The Life and Art of Glenn Gould*. Oxford, UK: Oxford University Press, 2003.

Bernstein, Adam. "Swing Bandleader, Clarinetist Artie Shaw Dies". *Washington Post*, December 31, 2004. www.washingtonpost.com/wp-dyn/articles/A37911-2004Dec30.html

Bly, Robert. *Iron John*. New York, NY: Addison-Wesley Publishing Co., 1990.

Bogdanov, Vladimir, Michael Erlewine, Chris Woodstra, and Scott Yanow, eds. *All Music Guide to Jazz: The Experts Guide to the Best Jazz Recordings*, Third Edition. San Francisco, CA: Miller Freeman Books, [1988] 1998.

Burnett-James, David. *Sibelius*. London, UK: Omnibus Press, 1989.

Carnegie, Dale. *How to Win Friends and Influence People*. New York, NY: Simon & Schuster, 1936.

Carr, Ian, Digby Fairweather, and Brian Priestly. *Jazz: The Rough Guide*, Second Edition. London, UK: Rough Guides, 2000.

Carroll, Jock. *Glenn Gould: Some Portraits of the Artist as a Young Man*. Toronto, ON: Stoddart, 1995.

Caswell, Ellen and David Rife. "Jazz Fiction: An Annotated Bibliography." *Annual Review of Jazz Sales* (2000-2001).

Collier, James Lincoln. *Benny Goodman and the Swing Era*. Oxford, UK: Oxford University Press, 1989.

Cook, Brian and Richard Morton. *The Penguin Guide to Jazz*, New Edition. London, UK: Penguin Books, 1994.

Cook, Brian and Richard Morton. *The Penguin Guide to Jazz on CD*, Sixth Edition. London, UK: Penguin Books, 2002.

Feather, Leonard. *The Encyclopedia of Jazz*. New York, NY: Da Capo Press, 1984.

Firestone, Ross. *Swing, Swing, Swing: The Life and Times of Benny Goodman*. New York, NY: Norton, 1993.

Freedman, Alfred M., Harold I. Kaplan, and Benjamin J. Sadock. *Comprehensive Textbook of Psychiatry*. Baltimore, MD: Williams & Wilkins, 1975.

Friedrich, Otto. *Glenn Gould: A Life and Variations*. New York, NY: Vintage Books, 1989.

Gelly, Dave. *The Giants of Jazz*. New York, NY: Schirmer Books, 1986.

Giddins, Gary. *Celebrating Bird: The Triumph of Charlie Parker*. New York, NY: Beech Tree Books, 1987.

Gillespie, Dizzy and Al Fraser. *To Be or Not to Bop: Memoirs of Dizzy Gillespie*. Garden City, NY: Doubleday, 1979.

Gitler, Ira. *Swing to Bop: An Oral History of the Tradition of Jazz in the 1940s*. New York, NY: Oxford University Press, 1985.

Glenn Gould: A Life in Pictures. Toronto, ON: Doubleday Canada, 2002.

Griffiths, Steven. *A Critical Study of the Music of Rimsky-Korsakov, 1844-1890*. New York, NY: Garland, 1989.

Gunn, C. Chann. *Treatment of Chronic Pain*. New York, NY: Churchill Livingston, 1989.

Haine, Malou, ed. *Adolphe Sax: 1814-1894: Sa vie, son euvre et ses instruments de musique*. Bruxelles, BE: Bruxelles University Press, 1980.

Holiday, Billie and William Dufty. *Lady Sings the Blues*. London, UK: Barrie and Jenkins, 1973.

Jacobsen, Edmund. *Modern Treatment of Tense Patients: Including the Neurotic and Depressed with Case Illustrations, Follow-Ups and EMG Measurements*. Springfield, IL: Charles C. Thomas Publisher, 1970.

Jacobsen, Edmund. *You Must Relax: Practical Methods for Reducing the Tensions of Modern Living*. New York, NY: Whittlesey House and McGraw-Hill Book Company, 1934.

Jazz: A Film by Ken Burns. TV. Directed by Ken Burns. US: PBS, 2001.

Kernfeld, Barry, ed. *The New Grove Dictionary of Jazz*. New York, NY: St. Martin's Press, 1994.

Kernfeld, Barry, ed. *The New Grove Dictionary of Jazz*, Second Edition. London, UK: Macmillan, 2002.

Kinkle, Roger D. *The Complete Encyclopedia of Popular Music and Jazz, 1900-1950.* New Rochelle, NY: Arlington House Publishers, 1974.

Koch, Lawrence. *Yardbird Suite: A Compendium of the Music and Life of Charlie Parker.* Boston, MA: Northeastern University Press, 1999.

Layton, Robert. *Sibelius.* New York, NY: Schirmer Books, 1993.

Levinson, Peter J. *Tommy Dorsey: Livin' in a Great Big Way: a Biography.* Cambridge, MA: Da Capo Press, 2005.

Marsh, James H. *The Canadian Encyclopedia.* Toronto, ON: McClelland & Stewart, 1999.

Mas, Sylvie and Fabrice Zammarchi. *A Life in the Golden Age of Jazz: A Biography of Buddy DeFranco.* Seattle, WA: Parkside Publications, 2002.

McAuliffe, Kevin, ed. *Sayings of Generalissimo Giuliani*, First Edition. New York, NY: Welcome Rain Publishing, 2000.

McRae, Barry. *Dizzy Gillespie: His Life and Times.* London, UK: Omnibus Press, 1988.

Murphy, Molly, producer. "Buddy DeFranco", *Jazz Profiles* from National Public Radio, www.npr.org/programs/jazzprofiles/archive/defranco.html

Ostwald, Peter. *Glenn Gould: The Ecstasy and Tragedy of Genius.* New York, NY: Norton, 1997.

Page, Tim, ed. *The Glenn Gould Reader.* London, UK: Faber and Faber, 1987.

Peyser, Joan. *Bernstein, A Bibliography.* New York, NY: Beech Tree Books, 1987.

Pike, Lionel. *Beethoven, Sibelius and 'the Profound Logic': Studies in Symphonic Analysis.* London, UK: The Athlone Press, 1978.

Public Broadcasting Service. "Selected Artist Biographies: Benny Goodman". *Jazz: A Film by Ken Burns*, January 8, 2001. www.pbs.org/jazz/biography/artist_id_goodman_benny.htm

Rand, Ayn. *The Fountainhead.* New York, NY: The Bobbs-Merrill Co., 1943.

Reich, Wilhelm. *The Invasion of Compulsory Sex-Morality.* New York, NY: Farrar, Straus & Giroux, 1971.

Reich, Wilhelm. *People in Trouble.* New York, NY: Farrar, Straus & Giroux, 1976.

Reich, Wilhelm. *The Sexual Revolution.* New York, NY: Farrar, Straus & Giroux, 1974.

Reisner, George. *Bird: The Legend of Charlie Parker.* New York, NY: Bonanza Books, 1962.

Russell, Ross. *Bird Lives! The High Life & Hard Times of Charlie (Yardbird) Parker*. New York, NY: Charterhouse, 1973.

Selye, Hans. *Stress Without Distress*. Philadelphia, PA: J.B. Lippincott, 1974.

Shaw, Artie. *The Trouble with Cinderella: An Outline of Identity*. New York, NY: Farrar, Straus & Young, 1952.

Simon, George. *Glenn Miller and His Orchestra*. New York, NY: Da Capo Press, 1980.

Spiegel, David and Herbert Spiegel. *Trance and Treatment: Clinical Use of Hypnosis*. New York, NY: Basic Books Inc., 1968.

Spink, George. "Music in the Miller Mood". *Tuxedo Junction*, December 27, 2006. Originally published in *The Chicago Sun-Times*, December 1984. www.tuxjunction.net/glennmiller.htm

Spotlight Magazine, February 1988.

Stockdale, Robert L. *Tommy Dorsey: On The Side*. Metuchen, NJ: The Scarecrow Press, 1995.

Talbot, Michael. *The Holographic Universe*. New York, NY: Harper-Perennial, 1992.

Terkel, Studs. *Giants of Jazz*. New York, NY: New Press, 2002.

Thiollet, Jean-Pierre. *Sax, Mule & Co.* Paris, FR: H & D, 2004.

Travell, J. and D. Simon. *Myofascial Pain and Dysfunction*. Baltimore, MD: Williams & Wilkins, 1983.

Von Drehle, David. "Maynard Ferguson's Horn Screamed With Vulgar Passion". *Washington Post*, August 26, 2006. www.washingtonpost.com/wp-dyn/content/article/2006/08/25/AR2006082501440.html

Woideck, Carl. *Charlie Parker: His Music and Life*. Ann Arbor, MI: University of Michigan Press, 1998.

Woideck, Carl, ed. *The Charlie Parker Companion: Six Decades of Commentary*. New York, NY: Schirmer Books, 1998.

Wong, Herb. "IAJE Jazz Perspectives: No Cooling Down of CD Streams." *Jazz Education Journal* (May-June 2004).

Woods, Phil. *A Life in E-Flat*. Serial E-Publication. Delaware, PA: Phil Woods Enterprises, 2007.

Yanow, Scott. *BeBop*. San Francisco, CA: Miller Freeman Books, 2000.

Yastrebtsev, Vasily Vasilievich. *Reminiscences of Rimsky-Korsakov*. Edited and translated by Florence Jonas. New York, NY: Columbia University Press, 1985.

Websites Consulted

The Ainola Foundation. Ainola: Home of Aino & Jean Sibelius, www.ainola.fi

All About Jazz. All About Jazz Website, www.allaboutjazz.com

AMG Data Solutions. Allmusic, www.allmusic.com

The Artie Shaw Foundation. The Official Artie Shaw Website, www.artieshaw.com

Clarke, Donald. Encyclopedia of Popular Music, www.donaldclarkemusicbox.com

Comité Dinant Sur Internet. Le site officiel de Dinant, www.dinant.be

Estate of Benny Goodman. The Official Site of Benny Goodman: King of Swing, www.bennygoodman.com

Feather, Lorraine and Tony Morales, producers. The Leonard Feather Scrapbooks, www.leonardfeather.com

Gershwin Enterprises. George & Ira Gershwin: The Official Website, www.gershwin.com

I-Net Entertainment. Buddy DeFranco, www.buddydefranco.com

Keller, Matt. The Official Website of Maynard Ferguson, www.maynardferguson.com

Martin, Shawn C. America's Ace Drummer Man: Gene Krupa, www.drummerman.net

Michlin, Adam. The Joe Allard Project, www.joeallard.org

National Endowment for the Arts. NEA: A Great Nation Deserves Great Art, www.nea.gov

Pagano, Joseph. The Gene Krupa Reference Page, www.gkrp.net

Public Broadcasting Service and WNET New York. American Masters, www.pbs.org/wnet/americanmasters/

The Real Red Rodney, www.myspace.com/therealredrodney

Sony BMG Music Entertainment. Glenn Gould, www.glenngould.com

The Unofficial Website of the Airmen of Note, www.airmenofnote.com

Wikimedia. Wikipedia, www.wikipedia.org

Index

Note: A page number followed by a letter, for example, under Air Force Band 274a,b,f,g,h, *directs you to the eight page photo section following page 274. Bolded page numbers indicate a standalone biographical feature.*

About the Author

Photo by Kate Moore 2007

Stephen Botek was born at a unique time in American history. His childhood years were overshadowed by the Second World War, his teens saw the rise of the Cold War, and the start of his professional career was aborted by the Korean War and the ensuing draft. Through all this, the struggle of poor blacks to overcome adversity and have their rights recognized was gestating a powerful voice: jazz. It resonated through the heartland of the country, with other disadvantaged youth hearing it as a call to arms.

Growing up in a musical family, Botek heard the music and fell in love. Recognized at a young age for his skill on clarinet, he became the toast of his Pennsylvania mining town. Concerts featuring touring bands became opportunities to solicit instruction. Wanting more, the train became his ticket to a world out of reach of his hometown. In New York, he finds his master teachers in bebop pioneer Buddy DeFranco and renowned clarinet educator Gustave Langenus. Taking on the saxophone, he secured another mentor in swing great Joe Allard.

An education at the Eastman School of Music in Rochester, NY is followed by the beginning of his career as a professional musician, quickly cut short by the Korean War and the impending draft. Joining the United States Air Force Band, he tours the globe and hones his craft. Returning to civilian life, a new band leads to an interest in medicine and a second career. Through it all, Botek rubs shoulders with the greats, soliciting advice from the legends of jazz.

Now a professional psychiatrist, he lives in New York. Even as a practicing doctor, he continues to play and jazz still resounds as a significant force in his life.